This Wild Spirit

Women in the Rocky Mountains of Canada

Women in the Rocky Mountains of Canada

This Wild Spirit

EDITED BY COLLEEN SKIDMORE

 The University of Alberta Press

Published by

The University of Alberta Press
Ring House 2
Edmonton, Alberta, Canada   T6G 2E1

MOUNTAIN CAIRNS ▲ *A series on the history and culture of the Canadian Rocky Mountains*

LIBRARY AND ARCHIVES CANADA CATALOGUING IN PUBLICATION DATA

   This wild spirit : women in the Rocky Mountains of Canada / edited by Colleen Skidmore.

(Mountain cairns)
Includes bibliographical references and index.
ISBN–13: 978–0–88864–466–4
ISBN–10: 0–88864–466–3

   1. Women—Rocky Mountains, Canadian (B.C. and Alta.)—History—19th century.
2. Women—Rocky Mountains, Canadian (B.C. and Alta.)—History—20th century. I. Skidmore, Colleen
Marie, 1957– II. Series.

FC219.T458 2006   971.1082'09034   C2006–901359–4

The University of Alberta Press is committed to protecting our natural environment. As part of our
efforts, this book is printed on stock produced by New Leaf Paper: it contains 100% post-consumer
recycled fibres and is acid- and chlorine-free.

The University of Alberta Press gratefully acknowledges the support received for its publishing program
from The Canada Council for the Arts. The University of Alberta Press also gratefully acknowledges the
financial support of the Government of Canada through the Book Publishing Industry Development
Program (BPIDP) and from the Alberta Foundation for the Arts for our publishing activities.

Canada Council   Conseil des Arts
for the Arts   du Canada

Canadä

For my parents Leona and "Skid"
and
Joanne, Bill, John, and James

Contents

XII *Abbreviations*

XIII *Acknowledgements*

XVII *Introduction*

　　　This Wild Spirit: Women in the Rocky Mountains of Canada

1 **ONE** Taking a Deep Interest

　　　Métis and Aboriginal Women

21 "Hosts of Mountain Oasis" (1929)

　　　JANET MUNRO

31 "Laggan to Maligne Lake and Tête Jaune Cache and Return" (1908)

　　　Excerpts

　　　MOLLIE ADAMS

41 "The Jasper Story" (1955)

　　　Act Two

　　　ELSIE PARK GOWAN

61 "Doubletake" (1992)
The Diary of a Relationship with an Image from Partial Recall
LUCY R. LIPPARD

77 **TWO** Being a Woman, I Wanted to Tell About Them
Literary Travellers

97 "By Car and by Cowcatcher" (1887)
Excerpts
AGNES MACDONALD

105 "Our Wild Westland" (1889)
MRS. ARTHUR SPRAGGE

111 "The Rocky Mountains" (1893)
from Through Canada with a Kodak
THE COUNTESS OF ABERDEEN

117 *A Woman Tenderfoot* (1900)
Excerpts
GRACE GALLATIN SETON-THOMPSON

133 *A Social Departure* (1893)
Excerpts
SARA JEANNETTE DUNCAN

143 "The Rocky Mountains and British Columbia" (1910)
from A Woman in Canada
MRS. GEORGE CRAN

153 *Lady Merton, Colonist* (1910)
Excerpts
MRS. HUMPHRY WARD

161 **THREE** Free Among the Everlasting Hills
Botanists and Brides

179 "Glacier House Scrapbook" (1897–1910)
Excerpts

191 "Our Dear Mrs. Young" (1934)
MARY SCHÄFFER WARREN

195   "Camping in the Canadian Rockies" (1907)
MARY M. VAUX

201   "A Maiden Voyage on the 'New' Lake" (1911)
from Old Indian Trails
MARY T.S. SCHÄFFER

203   "Letters to Dr. Walcott" (1912)
MARY M. VAUX

227   "Untrodden Ways" (1908)
MARY T.S. SCHÄFFER

235   "Flowers of the Canadian Rockies" (1945)
MARY VAUX WALCOTT

239   "Flora of the Saskatchewan and Athabasca River Tributaries"
(1908)
MARY T.S. SCHÄFFER

243   "Haunts of the Wild Flowers of the Canadian Rockies" (1911)
(Within Reach of the Canadian Pacific Railroad)
MARY T.S. SCHÄFFER

249   "The Mountain Wildflowers of Western Canada" (1907)
JULIA W. HENSHAW

257   "Dearest Mother" (1930–1933)
CATHARINE ROBB WHYTE

267   *Colour Plates*

277   **FOUR**   At Civilization's Limits
Exploring Women

293   "Why and Wherefore" (1911)
from Old Indian Trails
MARY T.S. SCHÄFFER

295   "An Explanation" (1911)
from Old Indian Trails
MARY T.S. SCHÄFFER

303   "Old Indian Trails of the Canadian Rockies" (1911)
PORTLAND TELEGRAM

309   "Laggan to Maligne Lake and Tête Jaune Cache and Return" (1908)
Excerpts
MOLLIE ADAMS

317   "Trip to Jasper Park, Rocky Mountains, Canada" (1911)
Excerpts
CAROLINE SHARPLESS

329   "A Recently Explored Lake in the Rocky Range of Canada" (1909)
MARY T.S. SCHÄFFER

343   *Hunter of Peace* (1993)
Prologue and Act One, Scene One
SHARON STEARNS

349   **FIVE**   On the Rockies Stark
Mountaineers

361   "The Alpine Club of Canada" (1907)
ELIZABETH PARKER

367   "Mountain Climbing for Women" (1909)
MARY E. CRAWFORD

375   "Breaking the Way" (1904)
MARY M. SCHÄFFER

379   "A Graduating Climb" (1910)
ETHEL JOHNS

387   "Graduation" (1918)
RHODA W. EDWARDS

391   "Portrait of a Giant" (1946)
GEORGIA ENGELHARD

401   "The North-West—Canada" (1909)
MOIRA O'NEILL

403   "Canada's Mountains" (1954)
       LYNDA R. WOODS

405   "Mountaineer and Mountains" (1957)
       LYNDA R. WOODS

409   "Sonnet" (1963)
       ELIZEBETH FERGUSON

413   **SIX** Wild and Solitary and Beautiful
       Mountain Culture/Mountain Wilderness

429   "Jasper National Park" (1924)
       Canada's Vast New Mountain Playground
       IRENE TODD

435   *The Kicking Horse Trail* (1927)
       Excerpts
       M.B. WILLIAMS

441   "Honor Memory of Edith Cavell" (1926)
       CANADIAN NATIONAL RAILWAYS MAGAZINE

445   "Marilyn Monroe vs. Scenery at Roxy" (1954)
       BOSLEY CROWTHER

447   *Colour Plates*
455   *Selected Bibliography*
465   *Permissions*
467   *Index*

Abbreviations

CPRA	Canadian Pacific Railway Archives
GAA	Glenbow Alberta Archives
JYMA	Jasper-Yellowhead Museum and Archives
SAAM	Smithsonian American Art Museum
SIA	Smithsonian Institution Archives
UAA	University of Alberta Archives
WMCR	Whyte Museum of the Canadian Rockies

Acknowledgements

THIS WILD SPIRIT is a collaborative enterprise and I am grateful to those who have contributed to its emergence.

The Humanities and Social Sciences Council of Canada (SSHRC) and the Faculty of Arts at the University of Alberta generously supported the research and reproduction of works gathered here.

Many materials, particularly photographs, diaries, letters, watercolours, and graphics have been compiled from the Archives of the Whyte Museum of the Canadian Rockies, the Jasper-Yellowhead Museum and Archives, the Canadian Pacific Railway Archives, the Smithsonian Institution Archives, the Smithsonian American Art Museum, and the Glenbow Alberta Archives. Staff at these institutions have been unfailingly obliging, delving deep into their collections and persevering with good humour as traces of the lives of the women who visited or lived in the Rocky Mountains of Canada were sought and pieced together. I thank Elizabeth Kundert-Cameron, Lena Goon, Don Bourdon, Joanne Gruenberg, Meghan Power, Bob Kennell, Ellen Alers, and Leslie Green.

The British, Canadian, and American women's fiction and non-fiction books about the Rocky and Selkirk mountains which are sampled, as well as works from the *Canadian Alpine Journal*, were found in the outstanding collections of Rutherford Library and the Bruce Peel Special Collections Library at the University of Alberta. I thank Michael May and Jeannine Green for many years of fruitful searches.

The research assistance of two dedicated graduate students was essential to gathering and organizing myriad details. I thank Fiona McDonald and Katherine Milliken for their tenacity and collegiality during long hours of research and conversation exploring matters as diverse as glaciology and copyright law. I am grateful also to Sarah Eccleston who deftly compiled the index, Melanie Niemi and Don Cooper who shared research sources, and to the reviewers of the original manuscript whose incisive comments guided the anthology's final form.

The University of Alberta Press is as fine a partner as an academic writer could hope for. From concept to design and editorial polish, the collaborative and creative spirit of UAP has infused this work. I thank Mary Mahoney-Robson, Alan Brownoff, Amber Marechal, Michael Luski, Cathie Crooks, Yoko Sekiya, and Linda Cameron.

My greatest debt rests with the women whose works are gathered here. Their dignity, strength, curiosity, ambition, and purpose established a legacy of creative, intellectual, and physical accomplishment by women that enriches Rocky Mountain culture and infuses its history with complexity, diversity, and passion.

Finally, to my companions along Rocky Mountain trails, Joe Owens and Elizabeth Owens Skidmore, my gratitude for sharing and indulging *This Wild Spirit*.

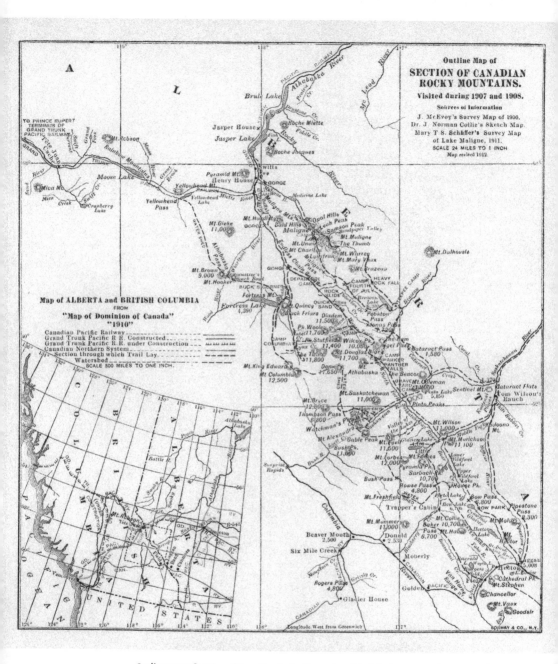

Outline map of section of Canadian Rocky Mountains visited during 1907 and 1908. Map by Mary T.S. Schäffer in Old Indian Trails, 1911.

Introduction

This Wild Spirit
Women in the Rocky Mountains of Canada

But I really think we are spoiled for travel elsewhere, after the beauty and interest

of the Rockies for no where else is there such a wealth of beauty and interest, and

I conclude that the haunts so attractive to the world have no attraction for me.

Of course golf is a fine game, but can it compare with a day on the trail, or a

scramble over the glacier, or even with a quiet day in camp to get things in order

for the morrow's conquests? Some how when once this wild spirit enters the

blood, golf courses and hotel piazzas, be they ever so brilliant, have no charm,

and I can hardly wait to be off again.

—MARY M. VAUX
Letter to Dr. Charles Walcott, 1912

On July 15, 1887, Mary Vaux, a twenty-seven year old woman from Philadelphia, arrived for the first time in the Rocky Mountains of Canada. She travelled by rail and stopped first at Glacier House near Roger's Pass in the Selkirk Mountain range. There, accompanied by her father and two brothers, she walked a mile and a half from the Canadian Pacific Railway line to touch and photograph the magnificent Illecillewaet Glacier. Captivated by the mountains and infused by "this wild spirit," Mary Vaux returned for the next forty summers to explore the wilderness, ponder the glaciers, photograph the vistas, and paint the wildflowers.

Vaux's compulsion was one shared by many women whose intellects, imaginations, and spirits rose to the challenge of the mountains between the late nineteenth and mid-twentieth centuries. These women's names and voices are common, legendary, and, if not heard as frequently as men's, certainly are as recognized and celebrated by those who live, work, and tour at length in the Rocky Mountain parks of Canada. Aboriginal women of the Stoney-Nakoda nation, such as Leah Beaver, travelled and lived along the mountain trails blazed by their bands for generations. Métis women, too, such as Suzette Swift, made their homes in the Canadian Rockies after fur traders and explorers reached the prairies and eastern mountain regions in the eighteenth century. After 1885, Canadian, American, and British women followed, arriving aboard the trains of the Canadian Pacific Railway. These women brought with them their professional and personal skills and interests. Among them were botanists, painters, essayists, novelists, travel writers, and photographers; a glaciologist, a geologist, and a prime minister's wife; teachers, physicians, and actors; hikers, climbers, and horseback riders; chambermaids, cooks, and lodge managers. Some were travellers seeking challenge and diversity in an otherwise socially circum-scribed life; others were tourists seeking the comforts of home in a wilderness playground. Many of these women engaged in interchange and exchange with Stoney-Nakoda women. They bought and wore widely admired silk embroidery and beadwork-decorated clothing, finding the buckskin jackets, gloves, and moccasins not only practical while travelling in mountain terrain and climate but also understanding that these goods represented a tangible connection to Rocky Mountain societies and cultures. In turn, Aboriginal and Métis women employed their own creative skills to secure a place, however tenuous, in the emerging Rocky Mountain tourist economy.

Inspired by the lives and legacies of women in the Rocky Mountains of Canada, *This Wild Spirit* explores their responses to that vast and magnificent land and culture. Gathered in this book are samples of the literary and pictorial work of the many and diverse women whose creative capital was the Rocky Mountain wilderness—as much an idea as a place—from the late nineteenth to mid-twentieth centuries. Only a fraction of those who wrote, painted, and photographed works that capture the imagination and linger in the mind's eye are included in this sampling. Because women's presence, pictures, and stories have never disappeared from local history and lore, *This Wild Spirit* is neither a work of recovery nor one of discovery of women's history. Rather, it is a gathering of women's images and voices, Aboriginal and non-Aboriginal alike, as a critical mass for comparison and consideration. Those included and those not share much in common as educated and erudite women with creative ambition and energetic engagement in lives of exploration, education, philanthropy, and physical, intellectual, or creative challenge.

Reading these women's own words, viewing their own pictures, and examining their own handwork allows the reader to experience the intellectual and aesthetic stimulation, pleasure, and insight evoked by the work. In turn, the historical tenor of the time and place in which they lived is invoked. Encountering and considering the original works alongside each other reveals the differences, difficulties, and details of these women's experiences and the means by which they both created and contributed to mountain history and culture. While a gathering such as this cannot reproduce the design and social context that played a role in the impact they had on their original audience, it can invigorate the historical record and reposition our understanding of women's places, presence, and impact on Canadian Rocky Mountain history and culture. When assembled, these women's books and handwork, letters and photographs, poetry and paintings, are revealed to be as abundant and diverse, lively and engaging, as those of any mountain region in the world. The creative work of the women who shared historical and geographic spaces in the mountains shows them as talented, passionate, engaged, competitive, bewildered, charming, ironic, sardonic, witty, and wicked. Through a gathering of their work, we discover a culture of women whose indelible presence enriches Rocky Mountain history.

Three principles guide the choice of works for inclusion. First, the collection offers a fair representation of the diversity of women living in or visiting the Rocky Mountains. Thus, works by and about Aboriginal and Métis women and Euro-North American and British women are included, although the former are heavily outweighed by the latter. Second, the scope and diversity of work made by and about women are apparent in the collection. To that end, photographs and paintings, novels and letters, plays and poetry, private travel diaries and published articles are gathered. Finally, the collection vividly portrays the sensibility, manner, and frequency of the intersections and interactions of women and their work.

As a result, the selected works are organized in six sections, each with an introduction to set the historical and social contexts for the materials that are included. The images and texts are arranged in an integrative manner that mixes the diverse positions from which the women engaged the Rocky Mountains with the variety of genres in which they worked. And so, there are photographs and a play about Aboriginal and Métis women in the Jasper area; novels and travel books written by literary travellers; precise paintings by botanists; diaries of exploring women; photographs and poetry of mountaineers; and the books, celebrity snapshots, and advertising graphics of women promoting tourism in the Rockies. What becomes clear through this collection are the historical, social, intellectual, and creative links among the women and their works. In the most celebrated interaction between women, Métis homesteader Suzette Swift meets Mary Schäffer and Mollie Adams, the first white women to visit the Jasper area. A young Catharine Robb Whyte meets an elderly Mrs. Charles Walcott (who, to Whyte's astonishment, was the first woman to climb Mount Stephen—when she was known as Miss Mary Vaux) and entertains at tea another young woman much like herself, climber-photographer Georgia Engelhard from New York. Vancouver author Julia Henshaw races Philadelphia photographer and writer Mary Schäffer to press with a book on mountain wildflowers after Schäffer shares her photography techniques. Glacier photographer and wildflower painter Mary Vaux is honoured when her compatriot Schäffer names a mountain after her upon reaching Maligne Lake. Popular British novelist Mary Ward infuses her heroine with shades of explorer Schäffer after meeting Schäffer at Field and includes Schäffer photographs in her 1910 novel *Lady Merton, Colonist*. In a thinly veiled promotional brochure published by the CPR's Minneapolis Soo Line, Schäffer refers readers to Grace Seton-Thompson's *A Woman Tenderfoot* for advice about clothing for mountain travel. It is clear that all these women both inspired and admired one another's accomplishments. An anecdote told by the elderly Mary Schäffer in 1937 shows this well:

> There was a Miss Gest here this summer and her birthday gift from her father had been "Trails." She tore in to ask me to autograph it. I believe she is a wonderful climber and plenty of money for all that sort of fun she wants. She seemed very nice but her excitement holding "Trails," really gave me the kindly creeps.
> (Warren, 26 November 1937)

In 1937, Lillian Gest, of Philadelphia, who became one of the most celebrated climbers in the Canadian Rockies during the mid-twentieth century, carried Schäffer's long out of print but still very popular book of 1911, *Old Indian Trails.*

. . .

ONE OF THE MORE IMPORTANT outcomes of gathering and examining women's literary and visual work together is that it allows us to see, a century and more later, how women who lived in or experienced the geographic and social challenges of the Rocky Mountains engaged with significant ideas of the day, especially those about racial difference and women's social rights and roles. These two issues weave their way throughout the materials in the chapters that follow.

Taking up the work of Métis and Aboriginal women and their exchanges with visiting women, the first section, "Taking a Deep Interest," demonstrates most clearly the problem of race and the idea of racial difference. Far more elusive than Euro-North American women's cultural endeavours are those of Métis and Aboriginal women who made their homes in the eastern Rocky Mountains. Aboriginal histories are oral gatherings in contrast to this book, a material and written gathering in the European tradition. The photographic and written artifacts included here, then, are at least one step removed from Métis and Aboriginal women's own stories and histories. Their presence and work, however, are crucial on two counts: one, these women were well-known in their communities in their day, but their presence and contributions are at risk of disappearing from the common knowledge or idea of Rocky Mountain culture; and two, their handwork was a much valued and sought after cultural product that, while admired for its aesthetic merits, was one means by which some women earned a living. As such, the tourist economy helped Métis and Aboriginal women to keep traditional practices alive during dire times. Such work in contemporary form is still made and available for purchase in the Rocky Mountain parks.

Métis and Aboriginal women's work has also been the most challenging to reproduce in a compendium of this nature. Buckskin jackets, gloves, and moccasins decorated with embroidery and beadwork were avidly purchased and worn by visiting women. Stoney-Nakoda women's own sashes and moccasins in particular were finely crafted textile works. Some of these items are preserved in museum collections where they are documented in photographic inventories. If seen first hand, however, these items, and the women who made them, are better appreciated and understood. Even then, viewers in museums today run the risk of comprehending such garments as little more than effigies of a past culture. What better conveys the sense of women's dynamic historical presence, place, and interactions are photographic snapshots and portraits of Métis and Aboriginal women and the garments that they made being worn by Aboriginal, Métis, and non-Aboriginal women alike in the days in which they were made, sold, or traded. Such images are the ones chosen for inclusion here. Visiting women's written and visual artifacts, such as these photos, reveal ideas and interactions with women of other races and heritage. What remains elusive, nevertheless, are Métis and Aboriginal women's viewpoints on the women who visited their lands and purchased their goods as well as their personal responses to Rocky Mountain wilderness and culture.

While Métis and Aboriginal women took advantage of the economic opportunities that Euro-North American women's arrival allowed after 1885, British, American, and Canadian women of European origins took advantage of the new opportunities that travel to the Rocky Mountains brought their way. Consequently, the work of literary travellers is comparatively bountiful. In the second section, "Being a Woman, I Wanted to Tell About Them," excerpts from illustrated novels and travel books published in London, Edinburgh, Toronto, and New York offer first-hand accounts by adventuresome women. Some were written under the auspices of the Dominion government and the CPR to persuade a young female audience in Britain to emigrate to Canada, especially the West. At the same time, articles and books about Rocky Mountain wilderness, tourism, railroads, and adventure were read by North American women and men whose interest sustained a vibrant travel-writing industry.

Some literary travellers were women of independent means; many were not. Most often their work was done for a fee or in exchange for passage on the CPR. These women were neither dilettantes nor amateurs. Their professional and personal reputations were made by their work, claiming for them authority, legitimacy, credibility, and expertise, while supplying intellectual, creative, and personal challenge. Given the social moment in which they travelled and wrote, such reputations were negotiated with care by the women and their audiences. Opening of the Rocky Mountains to middle-class travellers in Canada in the late nineteenth century coincided historically with "the Woman Question," the British and North American debate about woman's nature and appropriate social roles. The Woman Question is evident in every one of these works, as each author addresses the prickly problem of femininity in a changing world and the ways in which her own travel conformed to or challenged its conventions. As result, much of the conversation about women's travel revolved around two matters: its physical challenges, especially for those who sought greater adventure and fewer comforts beyond the tracks and hostelries of the CPR, and the concurrent issue of proper and safe dress.

Stepping out of the domestic sphere into the new and comparatively unregulated social activity of travel not only tested women's independence and resilience, it offered them the opportunity to mobilize latent abilities—whether physical, intellectual, or creative—and whetted the appetite for greater personal freedom. The natural sciences, particularly botany with its opportunities and demand for classification and documentation through drawing, painting, and photography, benefited tremendously from women's travel and study in the Rocky Mountains. Women often began their scientific study alongside brothers and husbands whose presence proffered both opportunity and credibility. Traditionally, women's participation and contributions to scientific study received little recognition as such acknowledgement contradicted social notions of feminine modesty and privacy. Times have changed, however, and women's contributions earn the credit due in posterity, as the articles and images of the botanists and brides in section three, "Free Among the Everlasting Hills," amply demonstrate.

"At Civilization's Limits," the fourth section, takes up the legendary Mary Schäffer who explored the Rocky Mountain wilderness in search of Maligne Lake with her travelling companions, geologist Mollie Adams and Caroline Sharpless, her sister-in-law. Schäffer's photographs and stories epitomize "this wild spirit" that infused so many women in the Rockies. The popularity of her work, her vast network of acquaintances, and the extensive archive of her photographs and manuscripts that remains intact have combined to make her work the most widely studied and distributed of women who visited the Rockies. The quality and impact of her work in 1911 and her deep commitment to the mountain wilderness makes such recognition not only well-deserved but essential to understanding the significance of women in Rocky Mountain history and culture.

The mountaineers featured in section five, "On the Rockies Stark," undertook the greatest physical challenges offered by the mountain geography. Many women climbed and hiked, and a few of them photographed and wrote about their experiences in an evocative way. Their articles and photographs appeared in magazines and journals across North America, reaching audiences as diverse as those readers of *National Geographic*, *Saturday Night*, and *American Photography*. A modicum of poetry, too, expressing something of the national pride and spiritual impact of the mountains was written and published by women mountaineers. The Alpine Club of Canada, to which most of these women belonged, was distinguished on its founding in 1906 by Elizabeth Parker and Arthur Wheeler for being open to membership by both women and men. The Alpine Club's publication, *The Canadian Alpine Journal*, is a significant source for mountaineering women's published work. Since its first issue in 1907, the journal has regularly, if sparsely, published articles, photographs, and poetry by women about their own experiences of climbing in the Rockies, as well as Rocky Mountain histories and biographies.

This Wild Spirit concludes with "Wild and Solitary and Beautiful," a gathering of images and texts that show how women and images of women became synonymous with Rocky Mountain tourism between the World Wars. Through their writing, painting, and photography, women had become well-known for their mountain travel and adventures in the early twentieth century. This phenomenon was implicitly acknowledged by the CPR, which featured women against mountain backdrops in its print advertisements from as early as 1909. The images, which were directed at women but also appealed to men, represent the centrality of women to the tourist environments that had evolved with the railway and highways that were built through the region. When the CPR took up women's images to promote its rail travel opportunities, hotels, and amenities in the 1930s, the figure of the modern, young, middle-class travelling woman was well-established, and her glamorous reputation was one that enhanced the company's reputation, as well as the aura, spirit, and idea of the woman seeking travel experiences. By this time, too, real Aboriginal women had been displaced from images of the Rocky Mountains in favour of the stereotype of the young Indian Princess. An idea of her presence as part of a Rocky Mountain adventure was well-entrenched and mobilized as well in these graphics, drawing on ideas of race and femininity. The new exotic woman in the Rockies was the movie star; notable visitors included Mary Astor and Marilyn Monroe.

The CPR's use of women's images to promote its services was neither original nor vanguard, of course, but very much part of the growing consumer environment. In the early twentieth century, at about the same time that the CPR published its first major promotional brochure to feature a woman mountaineer on the cover, the Kodak snapshot camera was also being marketed by means of a series of print graphics of stylish young women on vacation and at leisure with family, Kodak in hand. Both campaigns directed their resources to women as consumers and travellers, and they relied upon lively graphics that could be reproduced in colour in magazines and other advertising venues.

· · ·

THE VERY EXISTENCE of a rich archival resource where much of this work is gathered is the legacy of one of these women, Catharine Robb Whyte (1906–1979). Catharine Whyte, born in Concord, Massachusetts, was a graduate of the School of the Museum of Fine Arts in Boston. In 1930, she arrived in Banff as the bride of a local man, Peter Whyte. Catharine Robb had been born and raised in a well-to-do and well-connected family that prized education, art, travel, and philanthropy. She debuted to Boston society at age sixteen and was a friend of John D. Rockefeller III. Her own "wild spirit" found a compatible home when she married an aspiring artist from Banff and moved with him to his family home in the Rockies. From that moment, she was a lively and dedicated citizen, a painter, photographer, and letter writer (samples of her work along with a brief biography follow in section three) as well as a record keeper and collector, deeply interested in Rocky Mountain history and culture. Over the next five decades, Whyte and her husband amassed and organized a vast collection of Rocky Mountain materials, including Aboriginal beadwork, letters, tape recordings of Stoney-Nakoda drumming, their own paintings and photographs as well as those of others, clothing, postcards, and more. Herein lies Catharine Whyte's legacy, as in the mid-1950s the Whytes imagined and established a foundation to collect, preserve, display, and make available for study the art, artifacts, and stories of the Rocky Mountains. The foundation first emerged in 1958, named Wa-Che-Yo-Cha-Pa by Chief Walking Buffalo (George McLean), a Stoney phrase translated by Catharine Whyte as "where the good, the wise and the beautiful come together in harmony." In 1967, the foundation opened a building housing Banff's first library, as well as an art gallery that is now known as the Whyte Museum of the Canadian Rockies, and an archive preserving Catharine Whyte's own collection of heritage materials but richly supplemented by contributions from others. Whyte also contributed directly to Stoney-Nakado cultural initiatives, including financial support for the Stoney Administration Building at Morley and the Catharine Whyte Multicultural Centre in Cold Lake, Alberta. In turn, her contributions to Rocky Mountain culture were recognized when she was named an honourary Stoney chief in 1973 and awarded the Order of Canada in 1978.

Despite the generosity and deep, long-term interest of a benefactor like Catharine Whyte, an archive is not, nor can it be, a simple repository of history's most significant artifacts. The interests of its patrons, donors, and archivists (who deem what is of value for posterity and study), the emphasis and composition of its holdings, the viewpoints and ambitions of its staff, and the focus of researchers determine and drive the canon of a historical time or place. This collection of the Archives of the Whyte Museum of the Canadian Rockies has served as the primary research source for *This Wild Spirit*. Women's heritage in the Rocky Mountains is as respected, accessible, and well-known as it is in part because of Catharine Whyte's own deep engagement with life in the Rocky Mountains.

Yet not every woman who has contributed cultural artifacts of the Rocky Mountains is included in this volume. Later twentieth century and contemporary women—those from the late 1950s onwards—living, working, and exploring in the Rockies and Selkirks are not accounted for in this compilation. Their absence is as much a lament as it is a testament to the volume, scope, and value of women's mountain culture and work. Many such women have garnered local, national, and international reputations in their fields of endeavour, including climbing, guiding, writing, photography, film-making, painting, weaving, and beadwork. Most of their work has yet to be archived, and it is hoped that it will not be overlooked in future cultural histories of the region. It is also hoped that many of these women are maintaining private journals and writing letters—whether paper or electronic—that will one day be deposited in a Rocky Mountain repository.

• • •

MARY VAUX was not alone in her passion for the Rocky Mountains of Canada. The wild spirit that captured her captured other women of her time and has continued to do so through the generations that have followed. As Mary Schäffer wrote, "over an infinitesimally few those mountains had thrown a glamour and a spell so persistent and so strong, that with the first spring days, no matter where they be, warm breezes brought the call,—'Come back, come back to the blue hills of the Rockies!'" (Schäffer 1911, 2) What was "this wild spirit"? Reading and viewing women's creative and cultural legacy suggests that it was a complex physical, intellectual, and creative reaction to a majestic environment that challenged women to explore a wider world, both outside and within themselves: "No, believe me," wrote Schäffer, "there are some secrets you will never learn, there are some joys you will never feel, there are heart thrills you can never experience, till, with your horse you leave the world, your recognised world, and plunge into the vast unknown" (Schäffer 1911, 15–16). Ultimately, "this wild spirit" was liberating, invigorating, and soothing. Those like Vaux, Schäffer, and Whyte who were consumed by it lived lives rich with discovery and adventure.

ONE

Taking a Deep Interest

Métis and Aboriginal Women

...20 years ago the people of Jasper asked me to write a pageant based on their

history, I talked to old timers and new-comers, looking for the spirit of the place.

Every conversational trail led to one point—Mrs. Swift. "Mrs. Swift did beau-

tiful embroidery on buckskin." "Mrs. Swift had second sight." "When a gold

watch was lost, Mrs. Swift told where to find it." "When the famous guide,

Curly Phillips, disappeared in an avalanche, his body could not be found until

Mrs. Swift told where to dig in the snow." As the picture came into focus, I began

to see this quiet woman as the link between Indian trails of the past and the

Jasper valley of today.

—Elsie Park Gowan
"Jasper's First Lady," 1977

—

Suzette Chalifoux Swift is the central character in women's stories and photographs of the Jasper area of the Rocky Mountains of Canada in the early twentieth century. Later generations of women have also been captivated by stories and photographs of Mrs. Swift and her life in the Jasper Valley. Among these was Elsie Park Gowan, an Edmonton playwright well-known for her stage plays and pageants, as well as several drama series on CBC Radio, from the 1930s through the 1950s. Gowan's articles and pageant about Jasper Park revived and linked to the later generations the early twentieth-century tradition of women telling stories of women's lives of adventure and their crossing paths in the Rocky Mountains.

Women's encounters with each other in the course of their lives or travels in the Rocky Mountains in the early twentieth century are recorded and recounted in clothing, photographs, and literature, all made by the women themselves. It is through these materials that Métis and Aboriginal women's presence and participation in the history (or more accurately,

Suzette Chalifoux prior to her marriage to Lewis Swift, c. 1896. (JYMA PA46–24)

histories) of the Rocky Mountains, along with that of British and North American women of European descent, is most widely known. Oral tradition, maintained through storytelling, is the central means of collecting and constructing Métis and Aboriginal historical memory while European history, also collected and constructed through storytelling, is preserved through writing and imagery. It is samples of these latter historical artifacts that engage with Métis and Aboriginal women that are available in this anthology, itself a history collection in the European tradition.

The most celebrated encounter between women in the Rocky Mountains was that of homesteader Suzette Chalifoux Swift with traveller Mary Schäffer in the summer of 1908. Suzette Chalifoux was born in St. Albert, Alberta, a Roman Catholic mission and Métis farming community north of Edmonton. While divers articles and archival materials cite Chalifoux's birth variously between 1861 and 1867, the Certificate of Claim as Métis filed by Chalifoux in 1885 with the Department of the Interior records

Declaration by _Suzanne Chalifoux_

Concerning _her_ Claim

to participate in any grant to Half-Breeds living in the North-West Territories, as child.

1. What is your name and P. O. Address? _St Albert_
2. Where and when were you born? _St Albert 1866_
3. What was the name of your father? _Paul Chalifoux_
4. What was the name of your mother? _Genevieve Caumfour_
5. Was your father a Half-breed or Indian or either? _Halfbreed_
6. Was your mother a Half-breed or Indian or either? _Halfbreed_
7. Where were you living each year since you were born? _always with my friends in this district_
8. What has been your occupation?
9. If married when, where and to whom? _not married_

Declaration of Suzette Chalifoux.

No. 97
Registered
by W Anderson
Indian Agent

To all whom it may Concern

Take Notice

This is to Certify that Susette Chalifoux a halfbreed formerly taking Treaty as No 27 of Edmonton Stragglers, having this day Complied with the terms of Section 4 Act 47 Victoria Chap. 27 has Ceased to be a Treaty Indian as defined in said Treaty

St Albert
16th June 1885

W Anderson
Indian Agent

Letter of Cessation as Treaty Indian/Edmonton Straggler No. 27, 1883.

1866 as her year of birth. Chalifoux is said to have described her origins as Cree, Sioux, and French. Her parents, both born at Lesser Slave Lake, were themselves of mixed French-Canadian and Aboriginal ancestry. Chalifoux had been registered as No. 27 of the Edmonton Stragglers, an identifying term applied to Aboriginal or mixed-ancestry people who were not members of a particular Aboriginal band, including Aboriginal women who were married to non-treaty men (whether Aboriginal or white). In 1885, however, Chalifoux exercised her option to claim Métis identity and right to a land allowance or financial equivalent of $240. Like many, she took the financial settlement in the form of paper scrip, a transferable certificate from the federal government's Department of the Interior.

Records in the Jasper-Yellowhead Museum and Archives show that after being raised as Roman Catholic in the Grey Nuns convent in St. Albert, Chalifoux was employed as a maid by Mr. and Mrs. John Norris in Edmonton. In 1895, she gave birth to her first child, Albert Norris, who had been fathered by her employers' son Adolophus. Following Mrs. Norris's death, Chalifoux moved to the Wylie family home in Edmonton from where she was married to Lewis Swift in 1897. Janet Munro recounts what has since become the legend of the Swifts' lives together in her article of 1929, "Hosts of Mountain Oasis," written for the women's section of the *Canadian National Railways Magazine*. Suzette Swift's life was far more dramatic in the early years of her marriage than Munro reveals, however. Lewis Swift, who originated in Ohio, had arrived in the Jasper area in 1892 as a trapper and prospector. He built a cabin first on the site of the original Jasper House trading fort and then, after his marriage to Suzette Chalifoux, moved his homestead east of the present-day Jasper townsite in the area now known as the Palisades. Chalifoux lived there until her death in November 1946. Daughters Lottie and Ida were born in 1899 and 1901, and son Dean in 1902. The Swift's fourth child, James, born in 1904, was killed with a gun by the eleven year old Albert while the family was visiting in Edmonton in 1906. Albert was sent to live with Chalifoux's sister, Angelique Brewster, in

Above: Certificate 521 North West Half-Breed Commission, 16 June 1886.

Right: Certificate 284 North West Half-Breed Commission, 12 July 1886.

Mrs. Swift and her children, Jasper National Park. Photograph by Mary Schäffer, 1908. (JYMA PA46–7)

Fort Assiniboine and did not return to the Swift family home until 1930. A third Swift son, known as Jimmy, was born in 1907.

While central to women's experiences and accounts of Jasper, Suzette and Lewis Swift are legendary also in the annals of exploration and settlement compiled by the men of the era who spoke with admiration of Swift's homestead, his water wheel, and his family. Geologist Arthur P. Coleman, for example, who travelled in the Rockies between 1884 and 1908, wrote in 1911:

> Swift is a most interesting character, a white man of some energy and resource who married a woman of the country, an Iroquois half-breed, many years ago, and had now a brood of wholesome looking children playing about his log cabin...We had a long interesting talk with Swift, admired the children, and the bread and the

potatoes from his garden, and had praised deservedly the artistic buckskin suits embroidered with rich coloured silks by Mrs. Swift—true works of art made from her own designs.... (Coleman 1911, 276)

Suzette Swift's fine embroidery work is the centre of attention as well in Mollie Adams's diary account of the encounter she and Mary Schäffer had with Swift during their travels in the Jasper area in the summer of 1908. Clothing, textiles, and a deep appreciation for the quality of the handwork created a material link and, occasionally, a personal bond among women of different cultures or heritage whose paths intersected on Rocky Mountain trails. Mary Schäffer recounts her initial meeting with Suzette Swift in such terms:

Then Mrs. Swift (oh, we women are all alike!) unearthed a box from beneath her bed and showed us a half a dozen gowns made by herself, most of them her bridal finery, and as we looked on the carefully treasured garments, I realized—be it mansion or shack—there is sure to be stowed away just such a precious horde around which a woman's heart must always cling. Then came her fancywork which she did in the short winter days and the long evenings by candle-light, and we began taking a deep interest. She had quantities of silk embroidery on the softest buckskin I have yet seen. Her silks she dyed herself, and her patterns were her own designing. There was a most delicious odour to the skins which she said was through their being tanned by poplar smoke. Gloves, moccasins, and beautiful coats, we took everything and wished she had more; it was a grand afternoon's shopping for us all, for the lonely Athabaska woman and the two white women who had seen none of their kind for many a long day. (Schäffer 1911, 325)

The warmth of Schäffer's memories suggest that despite differences of race, education, life experiences, wealth, talents, or skills, she and Mrs.

Mary Schäffer and Mollie Adams pumping air mattresses, c. 1907. (WMCR V527/NA–102)

Swift shared a common bond based on gender and expressed through women's shared concern with and appreciation for clothing.

Mollie Adams, too, owned a buckskin jacket, which she is seen wearing while setting up camp, but her diary does not account for its origins. The buckskin jacket was popular with those women who travelled on exploratory journeys into the backcountry of the Selkirk and Rocky mountains, and a jacket of such vintage is preserved in the heritage collection of the Whyte Museum of the Canadian Rockies. Illustrated here is one worn by Mary J. Vaux, the sister-in-law of the glacier photographer and botanical painter Mary M. Vaux. Buckskin gloves and moccasins were also acquired and worn by these women travellers. Diaries, letters, articles, and books from the late nineteenth and early twentieth centuries reveal that adequate and appropriate clothing was a central concern for

*Mary J. Vaux in buckskin
jacket, Spray Lake.
Photograph by George
Vaux Jr., 1907.*
(WMCR V653/NA80–557)

women travellers from urban centres in the eastern United States and
Britain to travel in the backcountry of the Rocky Mountains. Those challenges and the solutions employed by women writers who visited the
Rocky Mountains are recounted in the next section on literary travellers.
For explorers like Adams and Schäffer, however, buckskin clothing was
appealing both for its practicality in cool mountain weather and under
hardworking physical conditions, as well as for the quality and beauty of
a garment's construction and decoration.

Women like Mollie Adams, Mary Schäffer, and Mary J. Vaux were well-
qualified to judge and appreciate the quality of the work produced by
Suzette Swift and other indigenous women who worked in the traditional
medium of buckskin clothing and decoration. During their lifetimes,
needlework was an essential skill acquired by lower- and middle-class
Euro-North American girls who, like their Métis and Aboriginal counter-
parts, were responsible for their family's clothing and linens. The quality
of one's needlecraft was a measure of accomplishment, as well, and those
with superior skills were both recognized and admired.

Photos of Schäffer and Adams on their two summer journeys seeking Maligne Lake show them in buckskin jackets and gloves. Adams's photograph of Schäffer (titled by Schäffer as *She Who Colors Slides*—a self-reference that, instead of crediting Swift, emphasizes the woman in the photograph and her own handiwork as she later hand-tinted the monochromatic slides for public lectures) displays to advantage an embroidered buckskin coat that is probably the one made by Swift for Schäffer during their camping stay near the Swift homestead (see page 30). Adams mentions in her diary excerpt that follows the many fittings required while Mrs. Swift worked on the coat and notes that a pair of moccasins made by Mrs. Swift were acquired by Schäffer and worn at a special dinner gathering with other campers encountered during their time in the Jasper area. While the whereabouts of Schäffer's Swift jacket, if still in existence, is unknown, some of Suzette Swift's paper embroidery patterns are preserved in the Jasper-Yellowhead Museum and Archives.

Other photographs made by Schäffer and her companions of Aboriginal women encountered on their journeys display the accomplishments and traditions of beadwork and embroidery design and decoration of women of the Stoney-Nakoda tribe whose traditional lands and 1877 Treaty Seven reserves lay along the foothills of the Rocky Mountains. Those whom Adams and Schäffer met on the Kootenay Plains between Banff and Jasper were families of the Wesley band, a group that had left the Morley reserve in the Bow River Valley (traditionally a favoured winter camping area because of the thick groves of trees and chinook winds) in 1892 to return to the Kootenay Plains. This area was more suitable for the Stoney-Nakoda way of life, travelling in small groups of a few families that could be supported with harvests of moose, deer, wapiti (elk), and bighorn sheep, berries, greens, and roots as the seasons dictated. Women were responsible for the moose-hide teepees, which would accommodate eight people, preservation of meat, as well as the manufacture and decoration of clothing. Traditional Stoney-Nakoda ceremonial clothing for men and women was richly decorated with porcupine quill work on buckskin shirts, pants, and moccasins, eagle feather headdresses, bear

Sampson Beaver Family.
Photograph by Mary Schäffer,
1906. (WMCR V527/NG–125)

claw and elk tooth necklaces, shell and bead ornamentation, and fur fringes on shirts and leggings. The clothing worn in photographs made in camp on the Kootenay Plains in 1906 and 1907, however, is that worn day-to-day. Just as non-Aboriginal women and men acquired and wore some buckskin clothing along with their own traditional woollen and cotton clothing, so Aboriginal women and men wore a mixture of styles and fabrics. This is easily seen in the dress of the Beaver Family as they sat for Mary Schäffer (see page 60). Sampson Beaver wears a cotton shirt, wool vest, buckskin and wool leggings decorated with ribbon appliqué, beaded buckskin moccasins, a plaid wool breechcloth, leather belt, bead necklace, as well as fur and bead hair ornaments. Leah Beaver and her daughter Frances Louise wear calico dresses and shawls and beaded necklaces. The child also wears shell earrings and beaded buckskin moccasins. Leah Beaver wears a beaded belt, a practical item commonly worn by women and girls but which also can be elaborately and complexly decorated, while a fringed plaid wool blanket that rests on the ground behind her in the seated photograph and was commonly worn as a shawl by Stoney women is used to cover Frances Louise's horse.

Catharine Whyte being honoured as Princess White Shield, with Mary Kootney, 1970. (WMCR V683)

Demand for Stoney-Nakoda women's beadwork remained strong among tourists in the Rocky Mountain parks throughout the twentieth century, sustained in part by the popular Banff Indian Days, which ran from 1889 until the late 1970s. Aboriginal women continue to make traditionally inspired clothing, ornaments, and jewellery for the tourist trade in the mountain parks as well as daily and ceremonial wear. In 1970, Mary McLean Kootney, the daughter of Chief Walking Buffalo (George McLean), presented a decorated buckskin dress that she had made to Catharine Robb Whyte to wear when invested as Princess White Shield in honour of four decades of friendship and support to the Stoney-Nakoda tribe. Nineteenth-century white and blue Hudson's Bay Company trading beads strung along fringes connects this garment and its maker with ancestral women and their practices.

The difficulty that rises for us today is how to account for or analyze the impact, value, or quality of the meetings and exchanges of these women in the early decades of the twentieth century. Aboriginal and Métis women's encounters with Europeans and Euro-North Americans are arguably the most fraught of all colonial interactions as power relations of both gender and race informed expectations, actions, attitudes, and outcomes. As Margaret Strobel argues for instance, women of European origin participated paradoxically in the politics of colonialism "as members of a sex considered to be inferior within a race that considered itself superior." As such, women who travelled in the British Empire "played a central role in shaping the social relations of imperialism" (Strobel 1987, 375). Especially puzzling is the apparent contrast of photographs made and stories told by and of women that resonate with a warm, intimate encounter of individuals at ease with each other that is foreign to the distant, "observant" ethnographic studies most common from this era as well as the racist and degrading or patronizing language used to describe Aboriginal women. Schäffer claims a personal connection based on gender, for example—her photographs of Suzette Swift, as well as Leah and Frances Louise Beaver, embrace the viewer suggesting mutual pleasure in the moment of exchange—and the language used in her book suggests the same:

> When I hear those "who know," speak of the sullen, stupid Indian, I wish they could have been on hand the afternoon the white squaws visited the red ones with their cameras. There were no men to disturb the peace, the women quickly caught our ideas, entered the spirit of the game, and with musical laughter and little giggles, allowed themselves to be hauled about and pushed and posed in a fashion to turn an artist green with envy...Yahe-Weha might photograph to her heart's content. She had promised pictures the year before, she had kept the promise, and she might have as many photographs now as she wanted. (Schäffer 1911, 176–78)

Some historians question Schäffer's claim that barriers between herself and Aboriginal and Métis women dropped, despite racial or cultural differences, because of shared interests as women. It is suggested that such a claim merely veils the imperial power discrepancies at play. Lucy Lippard takes up this problem, and in the course of her analysis offers a more nuanced assessment, reading Schäffer's text and photos as a crossing of the divide.

In "Doubletake: The Diary of a Relationship with an Image" (1992), included in this section, Lippard argues that Schäffer's written text "betrays a colonial lens." She finds that Schäffer is "condescendingly 'fond,' but not very respectful" of her Aboriginal acquaintances. In light of such writing, Lippard is surprised and puzzled by what she calls "the crisp 'present-ness'" of what is perhaps Schäffer's most famous photograph, the portrait of the Beaver Family. Lippard observes a collapsing of distance between the sitters and viewers and a lack of ethnographical overtones in favour of individuality of the sitters. She explains:

> The Beavers' portrait seems a classic visualization of what anthropologists call 'intersubjective time.' It commemorates a reciprocal moment (rather than a cannibalistic one), where the emphasis is on interaction and communication; a moment in which subject and object are caught in exchange within shared time, rather than shouting across history from their respective peaks.... (37)

Lippard argues that Schäffer's work "suggests empathy as a factor in the relationship between race and gender lurking in this subject," much like photographs made by Gertrude Käsebier and Laura Gilpin of Navaho women in the United States. These photos are cited in contrast to those made by men of Natives as "wary, pained, resigned, belligerent, and occasionally pathetic." But ultimately, Lippard concedes that Schäffer's work could be only sympathetic, and not empathetic, because despite her gender, Schäffer was, in Lippard's words, "at least indirectly allied with the oppressors"—that is, she was white.

While Lippard evocatively articulates a late twentieth-century non-Aboriginal woman viewer's response to an intangible essence in the portrait of the Beaver Family, Patricia Albers and William James's different

The Indian Madonna.
*Photograph attributed to
Mary Schäffer, 1907.*
(*WMCR V527/PS–51*)

approach casts Lippard's conclusions in doubt. These historians of Native women in photography rely on the context of practices of the specific historical moment, rather than trans-historical generalizations that mark work such as Lippard's. They have found early twentieth-century photos— the period in which Schäffer was active—to be the most accurate and intimate, portraying, as they put it, "life as it was being lived by Indian people." They attribute this to the fact that those who made such photographs lived near or travelled regularly to Native communities and developed long-term relationships within them, as Mary Schäffer did. As a result, the photos are striking in their "ordinariness," they write (Albers and James 1987, 39), not unlike the Beaver Family portrait.

Furthermore, such intimacy was also achieved on occasion by men photographers. A warm and intimate photograph of an unnamed Stoney woman and child that was published in Schäffer's *Old Indian Trails* and hand-tinted for use in lantern-slide lectures may have been made by hunter, guide, and photographer Elliot Barnes who had acquired a ranch on the Kootenay Plains in 1905 and spent much time with Stoney families in the area making a number of photographs. Schäffer talks about spending an evening at the cabin of Elliot Barnes with her travelling companions as well as two local Stoney men, Silas Abraham and Sampson Beaver—a gathering at which, Adams reports in her diary, Schäffer wore moccasins made by Mrs. Swift. Prints of this image are found in the collections of Schäffer and Barnes as well as that of Byron Harmon, another photographer who lived in the Rockies and worked with Barnes briefly in 1907 and 1908.

Portraits of Aboriginal people that exude the warmth and ease of the Beaver Family and the Stoney woman and child are rare in Canadian photographic archives. As Albers and James stress, after 1925 the only portraits marketed of Aboriginal women in North America were stereotypes with tourist appeal (Albers and James 1987, 43). Ironically, Schäffer's Beaver Family portrait is well-known today in part because it is widely distributed by the Whyte Museum of the Canadian Rockies as a poster and a postcard, tourist tokens. In fact, it was by receiving the postcard that Lippard first encountered Schäffer's work and the Beaver Family photograph.

In 1911, in its original context in *Old Indian Trails* among the panoramas and campsite views, the Beaver Family portrait represented the indigenous inhabitants of the Rocky Mountains as civilized, peaceful, and cooperative. (In the text, Schäffer tells how Sampson Beaver had drawn a map to guide her to Maligne Lake.) Aboriginal women are portrayed as mothers and wives. The children appear healthy, well-dressed and cared for. Most importantly, perhaps, the women are portrayed as equal members of a nuclear family—look at the balanced presence of Sampson and Leah Beaver—in a patrilineal society. In late nineteenth and early twentieth-century North America, a patrilineal social order in which family lineage was traced through the males was, as Wendy Wall writes, "clearly associated with civilization and citizenship; matrilineal families were a sign of savagery" (Wall 1997, 207). The photographs in *Old Indian Trails* made peaceful, domestic Aboriginal women recognizable and safe for Schäffer's audience. Readers were encouraged to see what they had in common rather than fear them as any kind of physical, social, or moral threat.

The stories and photographs of women in the Rockies remain those of non-Aboriginal women. Despite the richness and complexity of the cultures and creative works of Métis and Aboriginal women, their local prominence, and their impact on the social and political histories of the Canadian Rockies at the turn of the last century, Euro-North American women's viewpoints dominate the material remnants of encounters and exchanges. Métis and Aboriginal women's historical points of view and contemporary analyses of their exchanges with non-Aboriginal women visitors therefore remain absent, and yet they are the most crucial elements needed to inform, and reform, our knowledge and understanding of women's histories in the Rocky Mountains of Canada.

EDITOR'S NOTE

The title of this section, "Taking a Deep Interest," is taken from Mary T.S. Schäffer's *Old Indian Trails* (New York: G.P. Putnam's Sons, 1911/London: The Knickerbocker Press, 1911), 325. See quotation on page 8.

"Where travellers through the mountains are never refused: Lewis Swift, pioneer of Jasper, and his wife in front of their home which has harbored many a weary trader in the days before the railway came." Suzette and Lewis Swift at their homestead, Jasper, Alberta, c. 1928.

(JYMA 997.07.314.05)

JANET MUNRO

"Hosts of Mountain Oasis" (1929)

Story of Lewis Swift and Wife Is Real Pioneer Romance of Days
When Jasper Was Outpost of Traders

"NEVER A BEDRAGGLED TRAPPER or prospector, red or white," says Washburn, "was ever turned away from Swift's with an empty stomach. If an unfortunate lost his outfit in the river it was always, 'If we can get to Swift's place he'll fix us out.'"

And, for 30 years Swift was the only homesteader at Jasper. Between Edmonton and Kamloops there was no other place where the traveller might obtain potatoes, butter, fresh cream, and there were few travellers in that period—not a score a year—otherwise the supplies might have failed. That does not count the Indians, for up and down the passes, from Yellowhead to Athabaska, still roam the descendants of the old Iroquois voyageurs, brought in by the Hudson's Bay Company a century ago.

Today, Lewis Swift, pioneer, and Suzette Chalifour, his wife, are old people in their seventies. Not between the Atlantic and Pacific is there a finer old pair. Swift's eyes are blue as the sky spreading over the top of old Pyramid Mountain at his back; and kindly, if keen, is that "blue-eyed desert stare."

Fifty-five years ago, the call of the wild came to him while selling lightning rods in Buffalo. For a while he drove the Deadwood stage coach in Dakota. The '80's found him in British Columbia. Then he rode the Banff country before ever a tourist, Alpine climber or trail rider heard of it. He fraternized with Donald Manson at Kamloops and, still riding, came into old Fort Edmonton to shop. There he ran across some of the men who had been with Walter Moberly on the trial survey of the Canadian Pacific Railway by the Yellowhead Pass in 1872.

Moberly was an engineer, brother of H.J. Moberly, Hudson's Bay Company chief factor, author and centenarian. The Canadian Pacific abandoned the line by Yellowhead for the Kicking Horse Pass route. Not until 1911 did the Grand Trunk utilize Moberly's observations and build a railway through Jasper.

Swift listened to the stories of Moberly's men, and straightway made up his mind to settle in their beautiful Jasper Valley. Leading his pack ponies, he trekked in from Fort St. Anne to the Athabaska, and along its banks to the half-ruined and abandoned trading post of Jasper House, some 23 miles down the river from the Jasper Lodge of today.

Lewis Swift unloaded his packhorses on historic ground. David Thompson passed that way in 1810 with this assistant, William Henry, who built Henry House near the site of the present town of Jasper. The first great brigade passed through in 1814, John Jacob Astor's clerks returning east from the mouth of the Columbia by that circuitous way after the Northwest Company had acquired their post Astoria. With Gabriel Franchere in charge, were 76 men, exclusive of their families; a motley crowd of Scotch traders; Indians of half a dozen tribes; French Canadian voyageurs; Sandwich Islanders; squaws and children.

Then followed Alexander Ross in 1825, David Douglas, the botanist after whom the Douglas fir was named, and Edward Ermatinger in 1827.

Father Pierre De Smet drove gayly into Jasper House in 1846 with a cariole drawn by four dogs. In three weeks he had married or baptized every soul in the valley. That fall, Paul Kane, the Toronto artist, visited Jasper House twice. Eighteen hundred and sixty-two saw the first emigrants, a party of gold seekers from Montreal, Toronto and other eastern points, going through to the Cariboo country.

There came Lord Milton and Doctor Cheadle, who found that the "Northwest passage by land" passed right by Jasper House; Doctor Hector with the Palliser Expedition, and Principal Grant of Queens with Sandford Fleming in 1871.

Swift, following these great men, camped by the ruined fort. One end of the trading store had been burned off. He shortened the building by 20 feet, reducing the length to 30 feet, and repaired it with logs from the ruined "Okemow," or master's house at the back of the clearing. There were three open fireplaces originally. He found a heavy iron stove with the ends knocked out, used to lengthen the chimney of one of them. This stove, which must be at least a century old, now reposes in a shed on his homestead. The main building he used for his dwelling, and the fur warehouse nearby, for a trading store. Warm indeed was his welcome from the Indians, Shuswaps and Iroquois, for it had been 15 years since the Hudson's Bay Company abandoned the post.

Still, it was lonely for Lewis Swift. Taking the long trail, fording the turbulent Athabaska many times, winding through the mountains and over brule laced with blackened tree trunks, he reached Edmonton again. There he married Suzette Chalifour whose people had served the Great Company for generations. With her French blood she had both Cree and Saulteaux, and was proud of it.

Well she might be! There is no truer gentlewoman within the borders of Canada than Suzette Chalifour Swift. Returning over the long road that her people had known so well, she induced her husband to abandon the old fort for the homestead seven miles from what later became the station of Jasper on the Canadian National Railway line.

There are few spots in the mountains as beautiful as this homestead of Swift's on a tableland west of the Athabaska. Across from it are the hard, gray slopes of the Colin Range, the heartbreak of many an early traveller. Behind, apparently only a few hundred yards, but in reality, miles, stands, Pyramid Mountain. His rust-red sides, gory at dawn and sunset, contrast with the gray Colins across the river. From his glacier-capped head a stream flows down past Swift's cabin, and thereby came inspiration.

The lone homesteader of the Jasper Valley was a genius. Damming the thin cascade of water he carried the overflow in troughs made from hollowed tree trunks to the homemade mill a hundred yards behind the house. Here a wheel, its paddle, spokes and rim hewn from another giant of the forest, transmitted the power that ground the grain between two large boulders.

Thus, nearly 40 years ago, Swift had the first grist mill in the mountains within a radius of 500 miles. Today white birch trees have insinuated twining arms around the timbers of the wheel. Towering fifty feet over it they murmur sweet words of content to the brave old worker whose sides, bathed in the sparkling glacier-fed fountain, grow more moss-grown every year. When visitors from afar come, Swift and Suzette take them down the winding path, bordered with turretted tufts of fiery Prince's Plume, to the green-gold gloom that shelters the old mill.

"If our boy had lived the mill wheel would be turning today," they say.

That was the youngest boy, the standby of their old age who, after Curley Philips, was the best guide in Jasper Park. Three years ago he went on to join Lewis Swift's aristocratic old Dutch mother and Suzette's even as proud Indian forebears who were lords of a thousand miles of mountain, river and plain.

The little stream that drove the mill wheel now runs on and down over the hill to irrigate the fields where the old pioneer and a hired man work from dawn to dark in summer on a field that supplies Jasper with some of its vegetables.

No better picture of Swift's, in those early days, has been painted than that in "Old Indian Trails of the Canadian Rockies" by those intrepid mountain travellers, Mrs. Charles Schaffer and Mary Adams. That summer of 1908 they had travelled, without seeing a soul but their guides, from the Sunwapta to Jasper, aiming for Swift's place, whose location they knew from the accounts of every traveller who had written on the valley for 20 years. After numerous tribulations, chief of which were encountered at the Maligne River, northward from what is now Jasper Lodge, they record:

About 1.30 we came out on a knoll, and there lay Swift's. I wonder if three or four log buildings, a little fencing and a few acres of cultivated land ever caused much more excitement. A crude notice on a tree on the river's brink read, 'Here's the crossing.' Perhaps it was a crossing for anything that could swim three hundred yards to those canoes reposing so tantalizingly across the river...A grating thumping noise came from over the water and we beheld a man loosening the queer-looking craft. It was Swift. Chief went to welcome him. 'Women in your party? Prospecting or timber cruising? They're the first women I've seen around these parts!' He was courtesy itself.

Finally the painful and vociferous, not to say profane, operation of getting the horses and outfit over was accomplished. Swift's two little girls came down to the bank. Not a word or a smile could be extracted from either of them. They were lost in wonder at the first white women they had ever seen. They gave their father a message to hurry home as a surveyor wanted to buy some potatoes.

Their father's rejoinder was that "Two ladies had come and he was going to get all the news, potatoes or no potatoes."

Soon after, a hospitable procession made its way through the poplars. Swift carried a pitcher of new milk, the only milk in 500 miles, and, leading his youngest son, "Dean Swift," little Lottie with a pail of new potatoes all cleaned and ready for the pot, tiny Ida with a basket of fresh eggs from the only hens between the prairies and the Thompson river. Last came a noble face above a noble figure, Suzette Chalifour coming to call on the first women except Indians that she had seen since she married and settled down in the Jasper Valley.

Swift had brought in his cows, horses and chickens from Edmonton with labour impossible to calculate. He had wheat fields and oat fields, a potato patch and a vegetable garden.

The chronicler goes on to describe the cabin, then only one large room:

> How comfortable can a family of six be in such a small space! Two slept in a good-sized bed, two in a sort of box, the baby in a home-made hammock and the sixth under a table. Everything was as neat as a pin. The chairs were of home manufacture covered with skins and it was all a lovely study of what may be done with next to nothing in the land of nowhere. Then Mrs. Swift unearthed a box from beneath her bed and showed us half a dozen gowns made by herself, most of them her bridal finery. As we looked on the carefully treasured garments we realized—be it mansion or shack—there is sure to be stowed away a precious hoard around which a woman's heart must always cling.

The most delightful days of my Jasper trip in 1928, twenty years after the episode of the early women travellers, were spent in Suzette Chalifour's cabin. It now has three large, low-ceilinged rooms of log, immaculately clean, comfortable and picturesque. Suzette spoke French and Cree fluently, and English with a Scotch accent. It was not her bridal gown that she showed me, but the pictures of her boy, Dan [sic], the flowers from his grave pressed in her prayer book, his saddle and his favourite horse.

Though one of the rooms of the cabin still boasted only an earthen floor, she gave me meals from a snow white cloth, a table napkin beside my plate. Swift's wife had broken her arm not long before and it reposed in a sling. Still she worked with silk embroidery on soft buckskin, doing her own designing and dyeing the silks herself. Having been familiar in my childhood with the old Hudson's Bay store at Prince Albert, I sniffed appreciatively at the fascinating odour of the skins tanned in poplar smoke. She had gloves, moccasins and magnificent buckskin coats, snow-white deerskin baby boots, tobacco pouches and beaded bags such as would have made angels smile had they wanted anything in which to stow their wings.

Then we talked of old days. From here and there she produced copper kettles and brass cauldrons of ancient Hudson's Bay Company manufacture. One big brass pot with handmade bales, used at Jasper House a century ago, black with an inch of soot (for it had been used, latterly, for a smudge pail) is now catalogued amongst the treasures of the Archives at Ottawa. Another fine copper kettle, one of a nest of such, heavy and lidded, reposes on my desk as I write. Beside it is an Indian arrow head of stone and design similar to those used by the extinct tribe of the Hurons. The wife of Swift told me that there was an old tradition of her people that once the Indians, from far away at the salt water to the east, travelled right to the mountains and fought the Shuswaps until they fled to their hidden caves.

But it was the evenings with the Swifts that I loved the best. Then we sat at the cabin door and gazed at the outline of Roche Miette in his Elizabethan ruff, towering like doughty Drake of old over the bowling green that is the valley of the Athabaska. First the peaks of Colin's Range dissolved in wreaths of rose and gold. The opal came out on Pyramid's white head, and, up the valley, the colour died from Tekarra and Signal and the Whistler's, leaving them outlines of purple on a pale eggshell-coloured sky.

Suzette Chalifour's eyes went far up the valley's head to where Mount Edith Cavell blocked the cul de sac. High into the heavens rose her gleaming crown, a thousand jewels of the sunset, topaz and emerald, ruby, turquoise, amethyst, opal and pink pearls adorning it. Low on her breast the guarding wings of the Angel Glacier spread, white as the patriotic heart of her commemorated. Every feather of the pinions stood out curled and carved in snow 40 feet deep. Snowy angel draperies and snowy feet were buried in the intervening pines.

Lewis Swift's wistful blue eyes followed his wife's, and then he rose abruptly and walked into the cabin.

We sat on, watching the last scintillation of light on Cavell's coronet, but even after that it remained a white spire pointing to heaven. As the last ray fell away from the Guardian Angel of Jasper Valley I turned to find Suzette telling her beads, lips moving in prayer.

So in the eternal mountains will the spirits of Lewis Swift, pioneer, and Suzette Chalifour, his wife, live forever in such peace past understanding as comes after lives well spent in love and service for every God's creature that passed that way.

SOURCE

Janet Munro's "Hosts of Mountain Oasis," from *Canadian National Railways Magazine* (1929), 24–26.

She Who Colors Slides.
Photograph by
Mollie Adams, 1908.
(WMCR V527/PS−1)

MOLLIE ADAMS

"Laggan to Maligne Lake and Tête Jaune Cache and Return" (1908)

Excerpts

Henry House Camp.
Monday, Aug. 10.

WE STARTED ABOUT 8 O'CLOCK not knowing at all how far we should get—to the head of Maligne gorge anyway. The trail they had worked out up along the edge of the gorge was rather an effective one. It went along the top of a high sharp ridge forming one side, sometimes climbing a precipitous bit which looked as you saw it ahead, like going up a ladder into nothing. The other side for the first mile or so was a more gentle slope. The upper part was very deep, 150 ft. in places, and very narrow, the sides almost touching sometimes, in one spot only held apart by some broken pieces which are wedged in. It was just there that U. put his leg across. The span of his bridge was 15 or 20 ft., and it was at one of the deepest parts of the canyon. The greater part of the water must be in underground channels above the gorge, for the volume of water is many times greater below than above, and at some places we could see it apparently gushing out from the sides. We crossed not more than 100 yds. above the falls where the stream tumbles into the narrow crack, and there were a few harrowing moments when Muggins ran out into the water and stood on a boulder prepared to jump in and swim. If he had, he would almost certainly have been swept over the falls, it was so swift. Fortunately he hesitated, W. yelled at him, U. came along, picked him up and carried him over. The difficulty in getting down to the Ath again on the other side was not bad timber, but a series of rock bluffs. W. went and had a look ahead while we took a few photos, and decided to risk it although it had not been explored. And we had no trouble, although somewhat steep and slippery in spots. On the flats along the Ath were trails everywhere, made by a bunch of horses running there. In fly time they travel almost all day to get away from them. But we poked along down the river, getting landed up in muskeg and sloughs a few times, until at about 1.30 P.M., we saw Swift's place across the river—several low shacks and a fence looking to us like quite a town. Our trail was half a mile from the river, however, and sloughs between, and we kept on down as no trail branched off to any probable landing. When a mile or so below Swift's, behold, another mansion and garden patch right in front of us. Then we remembered having heard rumors of some half breeds named Moberly who lived not far from Swift and also ferried people across the river, and concluded this was their place. W. went in while we waited outside the fence. He came back reporting that no one was at home, no livestock around, and things looking as if shut up for some time. A boat was tied up on the opposite shore of the river; a blaze on a tree not far from the house had written on it "This is the crossing!" We decided to camp there— then 2 P.M.—and dumped the greater part of the stuff near the blazed tree. It was not a nice place to camp at all—so dirty; lots of people have camped there, especially Indians and it was anything but attractive. U. fired two rifle shots in case anyone was within hearing distance, and one of the boys was to go up opposite Swift's and get in communication with him later in the afternoon. M. and I had just sat down to lunch while the horses were being driven outside the fence to feed, when I heard the unmistakable sounds of boat and paddles bumping around being made ready to shove off. And it was a real live, disreputable looking man. We were beginning to feel as if our 13 horses had really hoodooed us and that we were never going to get across that river, and felt sure that Swift was probably away too. At first we thought it was an Indian in the boat, but as he came nearer, decided it must be Swift. The boat is of beautifully simple construction, and perfectly safe—two big dug-out canoes lashed together catamaran fashion, and each one of the canoes could carry a thousand pounds. The general shape of the canoes was like a Maine dory. Swift seemed to come across easily, paddling in the stern. There is a sand bar in the middle of the river and he went up along the edge on his side quite a distance, crossed to the bar, coasted down to the lower end and up the other side of it, then came wobbling across to where we were. W. met him and brought him up and introduced him properly, and he conversed as politely as if we had not been dressed in breeches, and partook of a slight amount of refreshment, including a modest taste from our whiskey flask. He is rather tall but slouchy, with blue eyes and a several weeks' stubble of gray beard, and we learned from him later that he is a native of Buffalo, N.Y., came west in '74 and has prospected almost everywhere along the line from Denver, Colo., northwestward. It is 13 years since he took up this land and settled here. He thought he could put us across the river in two loads, so they piled on the first everything but the saddlery, tents and ourselves. U. helped him paddle across while W. got in the horses. They put them in to swim from a point a little lower down, where there is only one channel perhaps 125 to 150 yds. wide. We watched the act from our landing—saw the horses take to the water amid a perfect pandemonium of yells and sticks and stones thrown at them. But before they had gone far, first Dandy, and then more and more of the others turned and swam back, and they all came ashore again. The same thing happened the second time, but the third time Dandy's manoeuvres did not succeed, not one would follow his back, but all went trailing across after Fox, who had led them in the water each time, so Dandy decided he would go too. From where we were, they looked more like a string of ducks than anything else—thirteen little dark bobbing spots—just their heads above water—moving slowly across the broad, muddy river; Fox in the lead, then Nibs; Black Bess was the last, she swam slowly some distance behind the bunch. Then when our turn came in the boat, a shower which had been hanging around, came up the river, and the wind was so strong that it blew us upstream, against that heavy current, and they had to paddle down to get around the sand bar. Two of Swift's children were waiting where we landed—funny little girls dressed in long blue denim dresses. He wanted us to move on up and camp near his house, but as it was then after 5 o'clock, we thought best not. W. said he would fetch in our saddle horses and M. and I could ride up and call (Swift had told W. that he would like us to go up just to "gas with the woman." "The woman" is a half breed.) However, the horses, after their long cold swim, had gone out for exercise, and W. did not return. U. went out to help him after half an hour or so, and Mr. Swift sat on, apparently pleased with our society. It began to grow darkish and cold and was raining perceptibly when he finally said he would have to go. He said there was a man from an outfit down the river waiting for him at the house, to get some potatoes, but he guessed he would just have to wait. We heard afterwards that he had sent word to the man that he could go t———whenever he pleased—but that there were two white ladies crossing the river, and when he got them across he was going to stay and talk to them. U. came back soon after Swift left, not having found either the horses or W. It was a scrubby camp that night, but we all turned in shortly after supper.

Moberly Camp.
Tuesday, Aug. 11.

We decided to move up and camp near Swift's today, as his accounts of B.C. trails made us give up the idea of going in by way of the big bend of the Columbia to Donald, or any of the other ways in that direction, so we shall have to come back here on the way home, and can leave part of our grub in his store house. When we arrived in sight of the shack there seemed to be a great many people running around, especially small boys, but really there was only one boy, younger than the two girls we had seen yesterday. Perhaps he seemed so plenty because he was trying to express his joy at our coming. They said that when the girls, Lottie and Ida, came back last night and told him they had seen two white women, he wept and wailed and reproached them bitterly for not sending for him to come and see the strange beings too. They say that several years ago there were two white women who went up the other side of the river with Fred Stephens, but we are the first to come over on this side. We camped in a little clearing among poplar trees a short distance from the shack, and had a constant stream of visitors except when we were out visiting ourselves. Mrs. Swift came with the baby, eighteen months old, on her back, and the other three children were right there with their eyes glued to us, with only slight intermissions during the rest of the day. And if we "gassed with the woman" Mr. Swift certainly did his share of "gassing" too, with anyone he could get hold of. We were pleased, however, and found him very interesting. After lunch we returned Mrs. S's call. She had some very pretty work, silk embroidery on buckskin, in which of course we invested somewhat largely. Her house, just one room, was neat as could be, and we did not feel at all afraid to sit down on her chairs, of which there were two. They made us a present of a pot of potatoes!, a pitcher of milk!!, and a dozen fresh eggs!!! Just at supper time another outfit arrived from down the river, an Englishman going up to some newly discovered graphite somewhere toward the Yellowhead Pass. He came over to our camp after supper, evidently having just shaved for the occasion, with his two French Canadian packers. His name is Lister, a nephew of Lord Lister, and he says he is always called "Listerine" out here. Swift was also of the party, and the two little girls who tried to go home several times during the evening, but did not dare until they were escorted, because "the bull was on the trail". They stayed till 10.15, which seemed fearfully dissipated to us, 8.30 to 9 being our average bedtime lately. .

Swift Camp.
Wednesday, Aug. 12.

We packed our three little duffle bags with the three children watching every motion. They don't speak much English. Mr. Swift says the boy, Dean, speaks the most, but he could not be induced to say a word to us, even when we made him a present of an old red neckerchief, and tied it around his neck. I wondered how he came to be named so appropriately "Dean Swift," but we found it was for a pal of Mr. Swift's, "Jack Dean." The whole population saw us off, of course, and Mr. Lister rode along with us, not intending to go far, but eventually went all the way to the mouth of the Miette, 3 1/2 hrs, where we camped, and stayed "gassing" most of the afternoon. We may run across him again somewhere up near the pass or beyond. He is going as far as the Tete Jaune Cache, about 15 miles beyond the Grand Forks, which is where we go for Mt. Robson.

We met John Moberly and family of squaw and 8 kids, who live in the shack on the other side of the river where we crossed. He has been hunting up between the Miette and Whirlpool rivers, and to the Ath Pass.

Caledonia Camp.
Thursday, Aug. 13.

We were 4 hrs. on the trail and camped at a place which McEvoy says is 8 miles in a straight line from the mouth of the Miette. There are two trails, one to use at low water and one at high water. The low one is best when the river is fordable, and we meant to take it as one outfit has been over it already, but found ourselves on the high trail before we knew it. We thought we must be on it, and knew it when an outfit passed on the other side of the river. We had been told there was a Grand Trunk outfit coming on the way to Edmonton. The trail is pretty bad for one that is used so much, very rocky, and mud holes in spots. Swift told us there was one very bad place where the horses had to jump down 3 ft., and if they jump a little too far they go over a cliff. We did not think it too bad as compared to some we had seen elsewhere, but there were bones of the horses who had gone over at the foot of the cliff. A scrubby camp as usual, in burnt timber. M. got a lot of blueberries for supper. Northern lights in the evening, and I saw two quite brilliant meteors, reddish color, one following close after and in the path of the other, from n.e.

Tête Jaune Cache.
Thursday, Aug. 20.

Laid over today to give our horses and ourselves a rest after the hard road we have been travelling so long—and we have to go straight back over it again. W. does not cease to wish for an air ship, and is occasionally heard to exclaim in the most heartfelt tone "oh Lord, I wish I were ten thousand miles from here!"

Visitors dropped in during the morning, Mr. Reading and Mr. Finch. They took us for a gentle stroll to see the ruins of what may be the original Tête Jaune Cache—two heaps of stones which might once have been chimneys and a slight ridge on the ground which might have been a banked up foundation of a shack—all overgrown with brush. And a little way off in the thick woods came cribwork of very old rotting logs enclosing a space perhaps 8 ft. square, a good deal larger than any cache an Indian would build nowadays, as if it might have been a small shack. This last seems as if it might really be it. It was about a hundred years ago that the Yellowhead had his cache. We stopped on the way back where one of the prospector men was examining the set fishing lines they keep dangling in the river. The bull trout are not at all sporty and don't rise to anything, the lines were baited with pieces of fish and a chicken gizzard, but there was nothing doing today. They say it is time for the salmon to be here, and while we were loafing around Mr. R.'s shack we heard a splash which they thought might be one jumping. The salmon are said to arrive as regularly as hay fever on the 15th of Aug., but this year they did not come up to date. We were invited down there to supper tonight and the whole population of the town was invited to meet us—in other words the two Chicago prospector men. They had both had a shave for the occasion and ate supper with their hats off, not being afflicted with baldness—bugs not quite as bad as last night anyway. The dining room was about 6 x 6 ft.—a little roof projecting at one end of the shack, and a real table made of split logs, and benches around it. Eight people squeezed in with a pinch, M. and I having the seats of honor on the longest bench, with our backs to the shack, and the two prospectors, Mr. Kaecke and Mr. Sommer opposite us. M. was very much dressed up. She had on a pair of new moccasins Mrs. Swift made, and was carrying a clean handkerchief never used before, of a bright lilac color, which was anything but harmonious with the red bandanna she wears around her neck. We had fish, bacon, beans, potatoes, tea and cocoa, and peach tapioca for dessert; the viands, after the fry pans and cooking pots had been passed around, being placed upon the ground behind where someone could make a long grab for them if needed....

Swift Camp.
Monday, Aug. 31.

Laid over, and W. spent the morning taking the shoes off the horses. M. and I ambled back and forth between our house and the Swift shack, as Mrs. S. was finishing a buckskin coat embroidered with silk work for M., and it had to be tried on a good many times. The old man came over to our camp fire in the evening and edified us with lurid tales of the days in the 70's in Wyoming when the Deadwood stage was held up regularly every night, and the "bullion wagon" was robbed even in the daytime; and "Wild Bill," "Persimmon Bill," "The Lone Star" etc., ran around shooting up the towns. We sat gaping and petrified or else struggling to smother our giggles, for his language was sometimes even more lurid than the stories he was telling. We decided that Swift's yarns were quite near enough the real thing for us, and that it was just as well we had not become better acquainted with Bill Spitel of the stubby red beard (he has a red complexion according to Swift) for Swift says "Bill is a rough talker, " and what he would call a rough talker must be something rather more than we would bargain for.

Swift Camp.
Tuesday, Sept. 1.

Rain in the night. While the packing was being done, M. and I went with Swift to see the flour mill. He has made a most ingenious waterwheel, etc., and has quite a system of water works supplying his irrigation ditches from the same sluice which taps the creek for the mill. We got off about 10 and by noon the whole outfit was once more across the Athabasca ready to start on the home stretch tomorrow. John Moberly being at home, put us across this time.

SOURCE
Excerpts of Mary [Mollie] Adams's unpublished diary "Laggan to Maligne Lake and Tête Jaune Cache and Return," 1908. WMCR M79/11.

The cast of "The Jasper Story," 1956. L-R: Les MacLachlan (as Lewis Swift), Betty Everett
(as Suzette Swift), Jack McCreath (Director), Elsie Park Gowan (Author), Jim Atkinson
(Superintendent of Jasper National Park), Gordon Taylor (Minister of Railways and
Telephones), and Bob Crawley (as the Cook). (JYMA PA34–40)

"The Jasper Story" (1955)

Act Two

Twentieth Century.

Lewis Swift. *A pioneer.*

Suzette. *His wife.*

Lottie Swift, *10.*

Ida Swift, *7. Very shy.*

Dean Swift, *6.*

Surveyor's Quartet: Steve *(leader)*, Paddy, Tom, Winslow.

Mary Schaffer. *A Quaker lady, in buckskin. Dark, sturdy, attractive woman in mid-thirties.*

Billy Warren. *Good looking, dark. About 30, English.*

Sidney Unwin. *English gentleman turned woodsman. 30.*

Guide. *Surveyor in Chief.*

The young old-timers. *About 8. Costumes 1908.*

The Tourists. *About 8. Assorted sports clothes.*

Haida Chief.

MUSIC: THEME WEST SOUNDS SOFTLY.

(Lights come on full. There is now a log cabin upstage right. Suzette Swift steps out of the cabin door, a baby in her arms. She looks off (down R) and sees two children and her husband coming home. First Dean, riding a "horse" stick, then Ida and Lewis. Ida carries a small pail of berries she has picked. She shows them proudly to her mother, who kneels down so that Ida can pop one into her mouth. Lewis Swift has a mattock or spade over his shoulder. He sets it against the cabin. Suzette and Ida go indoors. Swift takes a proprietary look around the place, hitches his pants, and goes in. Dean copies everything his father does...the "King of the castle" look, the hitch, then follows him inside.)

MUSIC: WEST THEME FADES

GUIDE: *(Voice)* Fifty years ago. Mighty important time in Canada's history, when the country was tying herself to-gether, you might say, with bands of steel.

MUSIC: SLIDES INTO THE SURVEYOR'S SONG

GUIDE: 1908...the Act of Parliament setting up Jasper Park was one year old. That was the year the crews came up the valley...laying the Grand Trunk Pacific Railway.

(Four surveyors, Steve, Tom, Paddy, Winslow come in L. carrying transit and survey pole. They take sights and proceed to put in stakes direct to the cabin. This pantomime to be worked out with technical advice.)

GUIDE: The steel was going through the Yellowhead to the coast. Bridging rivers...blasting rock. We crossed the Athabasca above Jasper lake. It was easy going, here on the flat under Palisade mountain...

STEVE: *(Sings)* In nineteen hundred and oh-oh eight
The crews were out to cal-cu-late
To run a line both true and straight,
Sur-vEY-ing for the railway!

QUARTETTE: Bridge the rivers and blast the rock
Bridge the rivers and blast the rock
Bridge the rivers and blast the rock
To make track for the railway!
(Each singer steps out for his verse while the others carry on.)

TOM: Oh, we ain't seen a gal for a month and a week

And the only liquor is in the creek

It's mighty hard on a man's physique

Sur-vey-ing for the railway!

QUARTETTE: Bridge the rivers and blast the rocks.

Bridge the rivers and blast the rocks

Without a woman...to darn our socks

Sur-VEY-ing for the railway!

WINSLOW: Oh we live in a tent and it leaks in the rain

It's *beans* for dinner and *beans* again

The life we're living just ain't hu-mane...

Takes MEN to build a railway!

QUARTETTE: Bridge the rivers and blast the rocks. *(etc.)*

PADDY: But the G.T.P. is a damn fine line

With curves and trestles of good design

We'll hit salt water by nineteen nine

Sur-vey-ing for the railway!

QUARTETTE: Bridge the rivers and blast the rocks

Bridge the rivers and blast the rocks.

Bridge the rivers and blast the rocks

To make track for the railway!

(During the last verse, Dean runs out of the Cabin, sees the surveyors, and stands transfixed. Then he darts into the house, comes back with his father. Swift takes in the situation, motions to Dean who whips inside and brings out the shot gun. Swift takes it and waits grimly on the doorstep. He raises the gun and aims at the ground behind Paddy.)

GUIDE: That's how it was. The mountain survey was no picnic, but nothing was going to stop them...

(Swift fires. Paddy yells "Hey!" and leaps in the air. Steve swings round.)

STEVE: Afternoon, Mr. Swift.

SWIFT: *(Dry)* Sorry I scared you, mister. Just taking care of a gopher that's been bothering my garden.

PADDY: You want to be careful! Shooting in the National Parks...that's a criminal offence.

SWIFT: You aint in any Park now, mister. You're on my property. Git those stakes out of here.

STEVE: Mr. Swift, I explained to you yesterday...we'll take care of moving the cabin. You'll be compensated...

SWIFT: And I explained to you. This cabin aint going to move. Not for the railway. Not for anybody. *(To Dean)* Git your mamma.

(Dean goes indoors.)

STEVE: Now look, let's be reasonable...

SWIFT: I like my house where she sits now. Aint that reasonable? That's why I built it here when I come to the valley in '95. Nobody can bluff me out nor buy me out. Government of Canada tried to move me last year, when they set up here "Jasper Park" and give it back to the animals. I know my rights. I got title deeds.

(He aims another shot behind Paddy. The boys duck.)

STEVE: Title deeds won't help a charge of murder. There's a Mountie back at Ten Mile Camp...

SWIFT: I'll shoot any varmint that crosses my line. That goes for gophers, porcipines, mountain goats,...or surveyors.

(Suzette appears, with the baby. Ida behind her.)

STEVE: Good day, Mrs. Swift.

SUZETTE: How do.

SWIFT: Are you moving that contraption?

STEVE: Take it back for now, boys.

(The boys hastily and thankfully move the transit.)

SWIFT: *(To his wife)* Hold the gun.

(She pops the baby into a cradle on the doorstep and takes the gun expertly.)

DEAN: My mamma can shoot too. She shot a bear once.

(Swift steps down, jerks out the stake near the cabin and "stabs" Steve with it.)

SWIFT: Go run your line where it dont go through the middle of my home!

(Lottie runs in from C. She is very excited.)

LOTTIE: Papa...papa...there's people riding up from the river!

SWIFT: Dont bother me now. *(To Steve)* Do you want a hole in your hat, just to convince you we mean business?

STEVE: Take a break, boys. Bring the transit. I'll be back, Mr. Swift. You can't stop the Grand Trunk Pacific.

SWIFT: I'll be waiting for you.

(The surveyors go off L.)

LOTTIE: Mamma...one of the outfit's a woman...and she's got man's breeches on! *(The children laugh.)*

SWIFT: You watch your language. *(He takes the gun.)*

SUZETTE: A woman?

SWIFT: A white woman is one wild critter I never seen in these parts.

SUZETTE: What would I say to her?

SWIFT: What's she doing here?

LOTTIE: Coming to visit. She spoke to me. She's the same shape as Mamma...sort of.

SWIFT: *(Looking off)* Judas priest, here she comes!

(Mary Schaffer with Billy Warren and Sid Unwin ride in. They all swing down from their horses. She throws her lines to Warren.)

MARY: *(Smiling, pleasant, friendly)* Mr. Swift?

SWIFT: Yes, mam'

MARY: The Swift place at last...I cant believe it! A garden...a field of wheat...and children's voices. All I've heard since we left Louise were the wild birds.

SWIFT: *(Incredulous)* You come from Louise on that C.P.R. railway?

MARY: Ten weeks on the trail...a glorious summer! Excuse me...I'm Mrs. Schaffer. *(Shakes hands)*

SWIFT: Glad to know you, ma'am. This your husband?

MARY: No. No, I'm a widow, Mr. Swift.

WARREN: *(Unruffled)* An educated lady like Her Nibs wouldn't be married to a rough-neck like me. Warren is my name.

SWIFT: Billy Warren? *(They shake hands.)* I've heard tell of you from around Banff.

WARREN: Meet Sid Unwin...packing for us.

UNWIN: How do you do, sir.

WARREN: String of pack ponies down by the creek. If you dont mind us camping...

SWIFT: Help yourself. I'll send the kids down with some milk and fresh eggs.

UNWIN: Milk and fresh eggs! My word, nector and ambrosia! The grub we're carrying has been wet and dry so many times the tea tastes like coffee and the coffee tastes like...excuse me, ladies!

(Swift has crossed left with Dean at his heels, and the three men stand talking by the horses, pointing east towards Maligne now and then. Mary goes to Suzette, who turns shyly away.)

MARY: Mrs. Swift...

SUZETTE: Yes, madame...

MARY: May I see the baby? *(Suzette turns, smiling)* A boy? *(Suzette nods.)*

LOTTIE: *(Muscling in for attention)* My name is Lottie and this is my sister Ida and that's my brother Dean.

MARY: Hello. What's your dollie's name, Ida?

IDA: *(Head down)* Mary.

MARY: That's my name too. *(She undoes her colored scarf.)* Maybe your Mary would like this for a shawl. *(Puts it on doll)*

LOTTIE: Well, say thank you!

IDA: *(Head way down)* Thank you.

LOTTIE: Why do you wear trousers? Haven't you any dresses?

SUZETTE: *(Reproving)* Lottie...

MARY: Plenty of dresses, in Philadelphia. But on the trail, I like to ride free, [unhampered by] a skirt.

LOTTIE: Have you any children in Philbell...where you said?

MARY: No, my dear. No children.

SUZETTE: Excuse me...she has not good manners. Ten years old. She has seen no white lady.

MARY: Have you always lived here, Friend?

SUZETTE: Eleven years, since I am his wife. In Edmonton, I was
married...in a fine white dress...

MARY: With a veil?

SUZETTE: Oh yes, very pretty! Like a lady too, I was that day.

(They smile at each other. Mary glances at Warren.)

SUZETTE: He will be your husband, the dark man.

MARY: Why do you say that?

SUZETTE: Sometimes I see...what will happen, in time to come. Already,
your heart turns to him.

MARY: Yes.

SUZETTE: You dont tell him?

MARY: I'm older than he is. I have money. And he is proud.

SUZETTE: A woman is not too proud to hold out her hand. After the
summer comes seven times...you will take his name...

(Unwin has ridden off, leading the horses. Swift turns back to the cabin.)

SWIFT: Well, I hear you folks been exploring Maligne Lake.

MARY: Yes, we found it.

SWIFT: Uh-huh. You prospecting...cruising for timber?

(She shakes her head.) No? What brings you into the country?

MARY: The Rockies, Mr. Swift. The beauty of the mountains.

SWIFT: That's a new one. We've had fur traders in these parts...hunters
and surveyors. Last year a party was aiming to climb Mt. Robson. But
you're the first came just for the *scenery*...!

MARY: For the peace and silence of the wilderness.

SWIFT: Silence...hunh. That wont last long, with locomotives snorting
and howling up the valley. By God, here's that varmint again!

(Steve has strolled on.)

STEVE: Don't shoot...I'm alone!

SWIFT: You changed your plans?

STEVE: I sent the boys back to get the boss.

SWIFT: What boss?

STEVE: In charge of the mountain survey.

SWIFT: You git the Prime Minister of Canada, I don't care. *(To Mary)* This son-of-a-gun wants to run a line thru my cabin.

MARY: Don't let him do it! I hate railways.

STEVE: Do you now. I suppose you rode your horse all the way from Boston?

LOTTIE: From Philadelphia.

SWIFT: Mrs. Schaffer came to see the mountains. The scenery and all.

STEVE: You dont say. And who does she think the scenery belongs to? Them that can afford to hire twelve horses and two men? These mountain parks belong to the people of Canada. Farmers...book-keepers...plumbers...shop girls. The railway will bring them here.

MARY: I know what you'll bring. The hideous march of progress. Crowds of tourists. Empty bottles...tin cans. I dont want the country spoiled. I love it the way it is now...the way God made it.

STEVE: You're here for a holiday. You don't live in the mountains permanent, like Mrs. Swift.

MARY: I would live there, like Mrs. Swift...*(The women exchange a look.)* if anyone asked me to stay. Away from the noisy streets...the hurry and strain of life. I'm happy here...on the wilderness trails.

MUSIC: WILDERNESS TRAILS

MARY: *(Sings)* Wilderness trails...wilderness trails

Far from the city's roar

Wind in the pine trees calling

Sunlight on far peaks falling...

Mountain and sky

clouds passing by

Where summer's sweet music prevails

Saddle, and ride!

Love is your guide

When you travel the wilderness trails.

(Lights may dim to spot on Mary and Warren.)

Wilderness nights...wilderness nights

Stars on the floor of heaven

Golden the camp fire embers

Always my heart remembers...

call of the loon...the lake where the moon

Rides over silvery heights.

Comrades I knew

Loyal and true

In my memory of wilderness nights.

(When the song ends she is close to Warren.)

MARY: I mean it. I'd follow the wilderness trail all my days...with a good comrade.

WARREN: Your Nibs is still dreaming. You'll wake up...on the C.P.R. going east.

MARY: Please don't call me "Your Nibs." My name is Mary...

WARREN: *(Grins at her)* "Quite contrary." You hired me for a packer and guide, Mrs. Schäffer. We'll leave it that way.

(The head engineer has arrived, followed by the survey crew. He wears his golden tan costume and is unmistakably our old friend the Guide.)

STEVE: *(Confident)* Alright...here's the boss. Now we'll get this thing settled.

SWIFT: *(With gun)* I been settled thirteen years. I don't aim to get unsettled! *(To Guide)* You giving orders to these smart alecs?

GUIDE: They're my crew...

SWIFT: You tell 'em to tear my house down? Answer me that!

STEVE: The line has to go through!

SWIFT: Through my cabin?

STEVE: Through to the coast. *(To Guide)* All Swift is doing is hold up progress. The country needs the railway...it serves the people.

WARREN: So you start up this valley by riding roughshod over the settlers.

STEVE: Look...we have to be in the Tete Jaune before snow flies. We're wasting time...and time means money.

WARREN: Couldn't you back up a little...

STEVE: Couldn't you mind your own business?

WARREN: Making trail is my business...and I wouldn't ride over a wild bird's nest.

DEAN: There *is* a bird's nest... up there in the rafters. A Phoebe.

GUIDE: Making trail has always been my business too...

STEVE: We'd be past Henry House by now if it wasn't for this stubborn jack-ass...

SWIFT: *(Raises gun)* Jack-ass...who are you calling jack-ass?

DEAN: Shoot him, Papa!

SUZETTE: Lewis...no!

PADDY: Hey...

MARY: Please, friend, no violence! *(To Guide)* You must listen to him.

GUIDE: I'm ready to listen. *(He sits down. C.)* State your case, Mr. Swift. *(Everyone settles)*

SWIFT: My case is, I own this land. When I come here, there was nothing. Only the grass blowing in the wind, and the creek running down from Palisade. And I made a homestead. Dug me a ditch to irrigate my garden...built me a water wheel to grind my grain. And this house. Cut the logs on the hill yonder...hauled 'em and notched 'em and raised the walls with my two arms. Mixed the clay from the bank of the creek to chink up the cracks. And there she sits, where I planted her. My children was born in that cabin. It aint going to move.

MUSIC: AINT GOING TO MOVE

SWIFT: *(Sings)* When I come to the valley it was all my own
I left the world behind me.
For to be independent and to live all alone
Where rules and regulations can't find me.
So I plowed my land and planted my wheat
I found me a woman's who's lovin' and sweet
I built her a cabin and a cradle complete
And I raise my kids to *mind* me!

Aint going to move for a court or a king

Aint going to move for the Grand Trunk Line!

For I live where I like and I like where I live

On the little piece of earth that I call mine.

SWIFT: *(Sings)* When I come to the West I was crazy and young

My thoughts was fixed on min-ing.

There was talk about gold on the tip of my tongue

And clouds just had to have a silver lin-ing.

But I found me a farm by a mountain stream

My hens lays eggs and my cows give cream

And the prettiest gold is the lamplight gleam

In the door of my cabin shin-ing.

Aint going to move for a court or a king!

Aint going to move for the Grand Trunk Line

For I live where I like and I like where I live

On the little piece of earth that I call mine.

The little piece of earth...

The stony piece of earth...

The only piece of earth that I call mine!

DEAN: My papa is a good singer.

(Pause. All look at Guide for his verdict.)

GUIDE: Well. So that's the situation. I see. Time *has* been wasted here.

STEVE: *(Triumphant)* Wha'd I tell you, Chief! *(Turns)* Come on boys, get busy, and...

GUIDE: *(Grasps Steve by the collar spins him round.)* And *you're* the jack-ass who wasted it!

STEVE: Me? Why, I been...

GUIDE: Mr. Warren! What do you do when you run into an immovable object?

WARREN: Why, I make track around it.

GUIDE: Make track around it! If it were only a mountain, we'd tunnel through it. But a free man, defending his home...! *(To Steve)* You continental idiot. Don't you recognize a genuine, gilt-edged, dyed-in-the-wool double-barreled *immovable object...(Points at Swift)* when you see one?

STEVE: I was only...

GUIDE: Acting like one of your own mules. Now get back...a mile and a half, and change your angle to bring the line twenty yards west of where I'm standing.

STEVE: But Chief...

GUIDE: Get at it, *now!* "Time means money and you have to be at Tete Jaune before snow flies."

(The surveyors go off, L., Steve still arguing. General jubilation by the cabin. Dean runs to the door and calls up to the rafters.)

DEAN: It's all right, Phoebe...we don't have to move!

(Sings) We don't have to move for a court or a king

CHILDREN: We don't have to move not a stick or a stone

ALL: We live where we like and we like where we live

On the little piece of earth...

The stony piece of earth

The only piece of earth we call our own!

(The children may link hands and dance, drawing all the grownups into it. The victory dance ends, they all begin to stroll down stage, the women to-gether, Swift with Warren and Guide.)

SWIFT: *(To Guide)* Well, thanks, Chief. Sure a relief to have some common sense around here.

GUIDE: The steel will bring changes to the valley, Mr. Swift.

SWIFT: Yep. Doggone it. People.

WARREN: Be a town in these parts before long. Church bells ringing. A school for the children.

LOTTIE: *(Alarmed)* A school! How do you know?

WARREN: Why, there's bound to be...

LOTTIE: But why will there?

WARREN: Well, you see...you know what a railway train looks like?

LOTTIE: Yes sir. I saw pictures in a book.

WARREN: That's right. And the steam engine...that's the iron horse...he needs a drink of water, like any horse. They have to curry him down...check him over for spavins. Takes men on the job 24 hours a day, living hereabouts with the people who belong to them.

LOTTIE: I dont think I want a town...or anything to change.

LOTTIE: Do you want to be a little girl always?

LOTTIE: No...

GUIDE: Growing up is part of the adventure of living. Your town will be a fine place...ten years from now, when you're a young lady. Come. *(Takes her hand)* I'll show you your town.

LOTTIE: Where is it?

GUIDE: In the future. You're not afraid?

LOTTIE: Not now.

GUIDE: Good. Pioneers are never afraid.

MUSIC: JASPER TOWN

(The tempo is lively but not jazzy. This is the world interpreted to a child.)

GUIDE: *(Sings)* Oh there's going to be a town in Jasper Valley.

There's going to be a town in Jasper Park

There'll be laughter, there'll be sparking

There'll be skittles and sky-larking

When the young folks go out dancing after dark!

We'll have a station here

A Congregation here

Civilization here...before too long

Then every railway man

Will have a family plan

And Home Sweet Home will be a railway song!

Build the grade

Lay the tracks

Hear the trains...wooo wooooo!

For there's going to be a town in Jasper Valley

There's going to be a town in Jasper Park!

(All the group are now well down stage. When the lights come on behind them, flats resembling Jasper (in fantasy) have appeared. As the song goes on, people appear among the buildings. They are the young old-timers. Railway men and pretty girls in light colorful costumes of 1908. Perhaps a girl who resembles Lottie.)

GUIDE: Yes, there's going to be a town in Jasper Valley.

There's going to be a town in Jasper Park

There'll be chickens, there'll be roosters

There'll be bears employed by Brewsters

And birds around will sure include the stork!

A population here

Part of a nation here

And transportation here...by G.T.P.

Then every engineer

Will be a mountaineer

And drive his six white horses to the sea!

Build the grade

Lay the track...

Hear the trains...wooo wooo...

(A little train like a child's picture book chugs on.)

She'll be coming round the mountain when she comes

She'll be coming round the mountain when she comes

For there's going to be a town in Jasper Valley

There's going to be a town in Jasper Park!

(The town people meet the train waving happily. Tableaux.)

LOTTIE: I *like* my town! Dont you, papa?

SWIFT: Reckon we'll get used to the idea, Lottie.

LOTTIE: *(To Warren)* What will you do, when everything changes?

WARREN: The mountains won't change, M'dear. Always be plenty of places you cant reach on wheels. Visitors getting off every train...some want to hit the high trails...some dont. Four thousand square miles is a lot of country. Room for everybody. For me, and my horses.

LOTTIE: Your Mary too?

(Warren looks at Mary. She comes to him holding out her hand.)

WARREN: My Mary too. *(Takes her hand)*

MARY: And all the people who want to hear the wind in the pine trees.

WARREN: *(Sings)* Yes, they're going to need a town in Jasper Valley

MARY: They're going to need a town in Jasper Park

    There'll be campers, there'll be climbers

WARREN: There'll be golfers and good timers

    From Switzerland, for Frisco and New York

DUET AD LIB: A fine location here

    For a vacation here

    And relaxation here...wearing plus fours

    They'll fish for rainbow trout

    And get their cameras out

    A'taking pictures big as all outdoors

    Blaze the trails

    Start a store

    Build the Lodge...Some style!

    For there's going to be a town in Jasper Valley

    To welcome all the world to Jasper Park!

(Tourists in a variety of sports clothes, ancient and modern. Song reprise in chorus. Finale tableaux of town people and tourists. Black out of town. Swift family with Guide, Mary and Warren are in spotlight well down stage. Suzette goes slowly to the Guide and looks at him fixedly.)

SUZETTE: Who are you...who show my children what the years will bring?

GUIDE: You know who I am, Suzette.

SUZETTE: I think you have walked through this valley many times.

GUIDE: Many times.

SUZETTE: In my blood, I belong to the old people of the West. Sometimes their spirits speak to me from the earth. They tell me you were here long ago.

GUIDE: Long ago. Before the maps were made.

SUZETTE: They tell me you were here on a day when a great man came up the river in a canoe with voyageurs.

MUSIC: PIPES FAR AWAY *(All listen)*

SUZETTE: You pointed the way beyond the Athabasca...beyond the Great White Mountain of the Grande Traverse.

GUIDE: I was here with the men of the fur trade. I crossed with Simpson to the Columbia.

MUSIC: PIPES *(Fades)*

SUZETTE: I see you again, with another company, on a night when a mother cried for her lost child. But the child was alive, and with you. So hope could live again in their hearts.

VOICES: *(Softly)* Alive...alive oh-oh

Alive alive oh-oh

Here's Jamie, young Jamie. Alive alive-oh!

GUIDE: I was here. I went with the Overlanders by the Yellowhead Pass.

SUZETTE: You are always here.

GUIDE: To-day I mark the path of a railway. Yesterday I guided the pioneers.

SUZETTE: You have many names...

GUIDE: I am known to all who travel this valley. They find me here.

SUZETTE: When travellers come to-morrow, will they think of the fur brigade? Will strangers remember *who* first made the Yellowhead road? The shades of the past are here and speak to me. They ask for a sign that their memory lives, here where the Miette meets the Athabasca.

VOICES: *(Softly)* Give us a sign.

SUZETTE: You show my children a dream of the future. Now show me that the dream of the past will not be forgotten.

VOICE: Give us a sign. Give us a sign.

(A spotlight picks out two groups, the Furbrigade on one side, with Simpson and his piper from Scene 1. On the other, a group of Overlanders, with Thomas and the Schuberts.)

GUIDE: There will be a sign, of brave men who passed this way. It will
come from Pacific...a sign all people can read.

*(Roll of thunder. All lights dim. When they come on a Haida Chief stands C. On
another roll of thunder, he raises his arms and the totem pole rises beside him.)*

HAIDA: I am the great chief who lives by salt water.

I am the chief who carved the sky pole.

Haida is my tribe.

Raven is my guardian spirit.

Why does the white man set my pole by his lodges

Far from the salmon hunting and the salt water?

GUIDE: Chief, we ask your pole as a sign to the valley. For a hundred
years, white men have travelled by this gateway, into the cedar forest
beyond the mountain barrier. They have traced the rivers to your salt
water. The Pacific was always their dream and their desire. Your
Totem is the symbol of their dream. Carved of cedar, tall and proud,
painted in brave colours...a sign to the world that we have reached our
goal...we who went through these valleys to the shore of the Pacific.

HAIDA: Let the Raven Totem stand.

It came from the salt water.

Let it be a sign to the world that memory lives

And that these things are not forgotten.

MUSIC: "WEST" THEME

*(The Guide with the 1908 group move forward to join the people of the past. The
stage is now a living picture of Jasper's history. The Guide's final position may be
between Suzette, who represents the people of the plains, and the Haida.)*

GUIDE: *(Stepping foward)* Good friends, we have traced the story of the
Jasper Valley, as it is written by the lives of the pioneers, here at the
gateway between the Plains and the Pacific. But the Jasper story is not
ended. For I am the spirit of *adventure* and I am always here! Now travellers will find me for themselves, in the beauty of our mountains, the
mystery of our Totem, the challenge of high trails across the Great
Divide. Now the Jasper story is theirs for to-day...and to-morrow.....

(All move forward singing.)

CHORUS: West! The word is West, boys

Where the skies are shining and new.

West! The road is west, boys

There's a world for the taking, where our dreams come true.

Trails may be long, our hearts have a song

A song that will see us through.

West! We take the west star

Where the far far mountains stand

And our valley will be, from the prairie to the sea

The Gateway of the Great West Land!

FINALE

SOURCE

Elsie Park Gowan's "The Jasper Story," Act two, unpublished manuscript, 1955, UAA 87–123.

Minor formatting changes and silent corrections have been made from the original typescript to aid the reader.

The Beaver Family. *Photograph by Mary Schäffer, 1906.* (WMCR V527/NG–124)

LUCY R. LIPPARD

"Doubletake" (1992)

The Diary of a Relationship with an Image[1] from Partial Recall

First Take.

Sam[p]son Beaver and his Family. This lovely photograph of Stoney Indian Sam[p]son Beaver was taken by Mary Schaffer in 1906. She was a writer, naturalist, photographer and explorer who lived and worked in the Rockies for many years. Mary Schaffer is one of several notable women who visited the area early in the century and fell captive to the charm of the mountains.

—Caption on contemporary postcard from Banff, Canada.

I AM SURPRISED BY THIS PHOTOGRAPH, which seems so unlike the conventional images I've seen of Native people "taken" by white people. It is simple enough—a man and woman are smiling warmly at the

61

photographer while their little girl smirks proudly. The parents are seated comfortably on the ground, the man with his legs crossed, the woman perhaps kneeling. The child stands between them, closer to her father, holding a "bouquet" of leaves. Behind them are signs of early spring—a tree in leaf, others still bare-branched.

I'm examining my deep attraction to this quiet little picture. I have been mesmerized by these faces since the postcard was sent to me last month by a friend, a Native Canadian painter and curator who found it in a taxidermy/Indian shop (he was bemused by that conjunction). Or maybe I am mesmerized by the three cultural spaces between the Beaver family and Mary Schaffer and me.

They are not vast spaces, although we are separated at the moment by a continent, national borders, and eighty-four years. They consist of the then-present space of the subjects, the then-present, but perhaps very different, space of the photographer, and the now-present space of the writer in retrospect, as a surrogate for contemporary viewers. Or perhaps there are only two spaces: the relationship between photographer and subjects then, and between me/us and the photograph now. I wonder where these spaces converge. Maybe only on this page.

Good photography can *embody* what has been seen. As I scrutinize it, this photograph becomes the people photographed—not "flat death," as Roland Barthes would have it, but flat life. This one-way (and, admittedly, romantic) relationship is mediated by the presence/absence of Mary Schaffer, who haunts the threshold of the encounter. I am borrowing her space, that diminished space between her and the Beaver family. She has made a frontal (though not a confrontational) image, bringing her subjects visually to the foreground, into the area of potential intimacy. The effect is heightened by the photograph's remarkable contemporaneity, the crisp "presentness" which delivers this image from the blatant anthropological distancing evident in most photographs of the period. The Beavers' relaxed poses and friendly, unselfconscious expressions might be those of a contemporary snapshot, except for the high quality of the print. At the same time, they have been freed from the "ethnographic present"—that patronizing frame that freezes personal and social specifics into generalization, and is usually described from a neutral and anonymous third-person perspective. They are "present" in part because of their undeniable personal presence. A certain synchronism is suggested, the "extended present" or "eternal present" cited by N. Scott Momaday, among others.

What would happen to the West, Johannes Fabian has mused, "if its temporal fortress were suddenly invaded by the Time of its Other"?[2] I think I've been invaded. I feel as though I know these people. Sampson Beaver and his wife seem more familiar than the stiff-backed, blank-faced pictures of my own great-grandparents, the two pairs who went west in the 1870s and 1880s, among those pushing their way into others' centers from the eastern margins of the continent.[3] Five years ago, while I was despairing of ever finding the structure for a book about the cross-cultural process, I dreamed I was climbing a vast grassy hill toward a weather-beaten wooden cabin at the top; on its steps sat three Native people, silently encouraging me to keep going. Although they were elderly, the expressions on their faces were those of the young Beaver family in this photograph.

As I begin, I'm also looking at this triple portrait cut loose from all knowledge of the people involved—an aspect that normally would have informed much of my own position. With only the postcard's caption to go on, my response is not neutral, but wholly subjective. I'm aware that writing about a white woman photographing Native people is a kind of metaphor for my own position as an Anglo critic trying to write about contemporary Native North American art. I'd rather be Mary Schaffer, a courageous woman in long skirts who seems to be trusted by this attractive couple and their sweetly sassy child. How did she find her way past the barriers of turn-of-the-century colonialism to receive these serene smiles? And I want to be Sampson Beaver and his (unnamed) wife, who are so at home where they are, who appear content, at least in this spring moment.

Second Take.

I SHOWED THE PICTURE and my "diary" to a friend, who said she was convinced that the real relationship portrayed was between the photographer and the child, that the parents liked Schaffer because she had made friends with their little girl. Certainly the photograph implies a dialogue, an exchange, an I/eye (the photographer) and a you (her subjects)— and we the viewers, if the photographer would emerge from beneath her black cloth and turn to look back at us. At the same time, the invisible (unknowable) autobiographical component, the "viewpoint" provided by the invisible photographer, "writer, naturalist,...and explorer, who lived and worked in the Rockies for many years," is another factor that shaped what is visible here. I have written to the Whyte Museum of the Canadian Rockies, in Banff, for information about her.

The cultural abyss that had to exist in 1906 between the Beaver family and Mary Schaffer was (though burdened by political circumstances and colonial conditioning) at least intellectually unselfconscious. It may have been further diminished by what I perceive (or project) as the friendly relationship between them. The time and cultural space that usually distances me—self-consciously but involuntarily—from historic representations of Another is also lessened here. Schaffer's photograph lacks the rhetorical exposure of "authenticity." But the Beavers are not universalized into oblivion as "just folks," either. Their portrait is devoid of cuteness, and yet it has great charm. Despite the inevitable veneer of exoticism (a function of the passage of historical time and the interval implied by the dress of almost ninety years ago), it is only secondarily quaint. This is not, however, the Edward Curtis view of the Noble Savage, staring moodily into the misty past or facing the camera forced upon him or her with the wariness and hostility that has been co-opted by naming it "dignity."

It is now common to observe that one of the hegemonic devices of colonialism (postcolonialism is hardly free of it either) has been to isolate the Other in another time, a time that also becomes another place—The

Past—even when the chronological time is the present. Like racism, this is a habit hard to kick even when it is recognized. Schaffer's photograph is a microcosmic triumph for social equality as expressed through representation. The discontinuity and disjunctiveness that usually characterize cross-cultural experience are translated here into a certain harmony—or the illusion thereof. This is a sympathetic photograph, but it is not, nor could it be, empathetic. (Is it possible to honestly perceive such a scene as idyllic within the dystopian social context?) The three figures, despite their smiles and amicable, knowing expressions, remain the objects of our gazes. We are simply lucky that this open, intelligent gaze has passed into history as alternative evidence of the encounter between Native and European, of the maintenance of some human interaction in the aftermath of genocide.

The Beavers' portrait seems a classical visualization of what anthropologists call "intersubjective time." It commemorates a reciprocal moment (rather than a cannibalistic one), where the emphasis is on interaction and communication; a moment in which subject and object are caught in exchange within shared time, rather than shouting across history from their respective peaks. The culturated distance between photographer and photographed, between white and Native, has somehow been momentarily bridged to such an extent that the bridge extends over time to me, to us, almost a century later.

This is the kind of photograph I have often used as an example of the difference between images taken by someone from within a community and by an "outsider." I would have put it in the former category. Yet it was not taken by a Stoney, but by an adventurous white lady passing through the northern Rockies, possibly on the quest for self (or loss of self) in relation to Other and Nature that has been a major theme in North American culture.

The Beaver family (I wish I knew the woman's and child's names) is clearly among friends, but the picture might still have been very different if taken by a Native insider. Of course we have no way of knowing what that image might have been. A press release from the American Indian

Community House Gallery in New York in 1984 set out some distinctions between non-Indian and Indian photographers; among them: "These photos are not the universal images of Indians. They are not heroic, noble, stoic, or romantic. What they do show is human warmth and an intimacy with their subject..."[4] This is the feeling I get from the Beavers' portrait. Am I just kidding myself? Overidentifying with Mary Schaffer?

Another explanation for Native avoidance of photography raises old taboos—the "photos-steal-your-spirit syndrome," which is not, in fact, so far off. The more we know about representation, the more obvious it becomes that photography *is* often a spirit snatcher. I "own" a postcard which permits me to "have" the Beaver family in my house. The Oglala warrior Crazy Horse never allowed his photograph to be taken, and it was said of those Native leaders who did that "they let their spirits be captured in a box" and lost the impetus to resist. Contemporary AIM leader Russell Means has described the introduction of writing into oral traditions as a destructive "abstraction over the spoken relationship of a people." As Dennis Grady observes, the camera was another weapon in the wars of domination:

> How fitting it must have seemed to the victims of that process— the natives of North America, whose idea of "vision" is as spiritual as it is physical—when the white man produced from his baggage a box that had the power to transcribe the world onto a flat paper plane. Here was a machine that could make of this landscape a surface; of this territory, a map; of this man, this woman, this living child, a framed, hand-held, negotiable object to be looked at, traded, possessed; the perfect tool for the work of the "wasi'chu," the greedy one who takes the fat.[5]

Our communal "memory" of Native people on this continent has been projected through the above-mentioned stoic (*numb* is more like it), wary, pained, resigned, belligerent, and occasionally pathetic faces "shot" by nineteenth- and early twentieth-century photographers like Edward

Curtis, Adam Clark Vroman, and Roland W. Reed—all men. Looking through a group of portraits of Indians from that period, I found one (*Indian with Feather Bonnet*, c. 1898) in which the expression was less grim, more eye-to-eye; the photographer was Gertrude Käsebier. The photographs by Kate Cory (a "midwestern spinster" who came to Arizona at age forty-four), taken in the Hopi village where she lived for seven years, also diverge from the general pattern as do Nancy Wood's contemporary images of Taos Pueblo and some of Laura Gilpin's works. All of which suggests empathy as a factor in the relationship between race and gender lurking in this subject.

Of course Mary Schaffer, despite her gender, was at least indirectly allied with the oppressors. She may have been an "innocent" vehicle of her class, her culture, and her times. She may have been a rebel and independent of some of its crueler manifestations. Less likely, she may have known about the then-new "comparative method" of anthropological investigation, which was to permit the "equal" treatment of all human culture in all times and in all places (though, of course, it failed to overturn the edifice of Otherness on which it was built). She may have been an enthusiastic perpetrator of expansionism.

Perhaps this photograph was already tinged with propaganda even at the time it was taken. Perhaps Mary Schaffer herself had an ax to grind. She may have been concerned to show her audience (and who were *they*?) that the only good Indian was not a dead Indian. Perhaps this portrait is the kind of "advocacy image" we find in the production of leftist photographers working in El Salvador. The knowledgeable, sympathetic tourist is not always immune to cultural imperialism. I wonder if Mary Schaffer, like so many progressive photographers working in poorer neighborhoods and countries, gave her subjects a print of this photograph. Was it their first, their only image of themselves? Or the first that had not disappeared with the photographer? Is a curling copy of this picture given a place of honor in some family photo album or on the wall of some descendent's home?

I'm overpersonalizing the depicted encounter. To offset my emotional attraction to this image, let me imagine that Schaffer was a flag-waving imperialist and try to read this image, or my responses to this image, in a mirror, as though I had taken an immediate dislike to it. Can I avoid that warm gaze and see in these three figures an illustration of all the colonial perfidy that provides its historical backdrop? Do Sampson Beaver and his family look helpless and victimized? They are handsome, healthy people, perhaps chosen to demonstrate that Indians were being "treated well." The family is seated on the ground, perhaps placed there because the photographer was influenced by stereotypical representations of the "primitive's" closeness to the earth. The woman is placed at a small distance from her husband and child—like a servant? They are smiling; perhaps Schaffer has offered the child a treat, or the adults some favor. Still, it is hard to see these smiles as solely money-bought.

A virtual class system exists among the common representations of an Indian family from this period: the lost, miserable, huddled group outside a tipi, the businesslike document of a neutrally "ordinary" family, or the proud, noble holdouts in a grand landscape, highlighted by giant trees or dramatic mesas. For all the separations inherent in such images, there is no such thing as "objectivity" or neutrality in portrait photography. Personal interaction of *some* kind is necessary to create the context within the larger frame of historical events. Even the Schaffer photo is "posed." And the pose is an imposition, since Native people had no traditional way of sitting for a portrait or a photograph; self-representation in that sense was not part of the cultures. But at least the Beaver family is not sitting bolt upright in wooden chairs; Sampson Beaver is not standing patriarchally with his hand on his wife's shoulder while the child is properly subdued below. Man and wife are comfortable and equal as they smile at the black box confronting them, and the little girl's expression is familiar to anyone who has spent time with little girls.

Today I received some scraps of information about the Stoney Indians, who were Assiniboine, offshoots of the Sioux. (The name is an anglicization based on the Ojibwa word *assine*, which means stone.) They called themselves Nakodah and arrived in the foothills of the Rockies in the eighteenth century, in flight from smallpox epidemics. With the advent of settlers and the founding of Banff, the Stoneys were forced into a life of relatively peaceful interaction with the townspeople. In the late nineteenth century, Banff was already a flourishing tourist town, boasting a spa and the annual "Indian Days" powwow, begun in 1889. The Whyte Museum there has a massive archive of photographs of the Native people of the Rockies (including this one, and one of Ginger Rogers on vacation, sketching Chief Jacob Twoyoungman in a Plains headdress). Eventually forced to live off of tourism, the Stoneys were exploited but not embattled. And Mary Schaffer, for all her credentials, was a tourist herself.

Last Take.

THE BOOKS ordered from Banff have finally arrived. I dove into them and of course had to revise some of my notions.

The Beaver photograph was taken in 1907, not 1906; not in early spring, but in late September, as Schaffer was completing a four-month expedition to the sources of the Saskatchewan River. Having just crossed two turbulent rivers, she and her companions reached the "Golden Kootenai Plains," (the Katoonda, or Windy Plains) and, weaving in and out of yellowing poplars, they

> spied two tepees nestled deep among the trees....I have seen not one but many of their camps and seldom or never have they failed to be artistic in their setting, and this one was no exception. Knowing they must be Silas Abraham's and Sampson Beaver's families, acquaintances of a year's standing, I could not resist a hurried call. The children spied us first, and tumbling head over heels, ran to cover like rabbits....Above the din and excitement I called, "Frances Louise!" She had been my little favorite when last we were among the Indians, accepting my advances with a sweet baby womanli-

ness quite unlike the other children, for which I had rewarded her by presenting her with a doll I had constructed....Love blinded the little mother's eyes to any imperfections, and the gift gave me a spot of my own in the memory of the forest baby....In an instant her little face appeared at the tepee-flap, just as solemn, just as sweet, and just as dirty as ever.[6]

It was this group of Stoneys (members of the Wesley Band) who the previous year had given Schaffer her Indian name: Yahe-Weha, Mountain Woman. Banned from hunting in the National Parks, they were still able to hunt, trap, and live beyond their boundaries. In 1907 she remained with them for four days. Of this visit she wrote:

When I hear those "who know" speak of the sullen, stupid Indian, I wish they could have been on hand the afternoon the white squaws visited the red ones with their cameras. There were no men to disturb the peace, the women quickly caught our ideas, entered the spirit of the game, and with musical laughter and little giggles, allowed themselves to be hauled about and pushed and posed in a fashion to turn an artist green with envy....Yahe-Weha might photograph to her heart's content. She had promised pictures the year before, she had kept the promise, and she might have as many photographs now as she wanted.[7]

Sampson Beaver's wife Leah was no doubt among the women that afternoon. He was thirty years old at the time, and she looks about the same age. In the latently desirous language of the tourist, Schaffer described him crouching to light his pipe at a campfire:

...his swarthy face lighted up by the bright glow, his brass earrings and nail-studded belt catching the glare, with long black plaits of glossy hair and his blanket breeches...[8]

It was Sampson Beaver who then gave Schaffer one of the great gifts of her life—a map of how to reach the legendary Maligne Lake, which she had hitherto sought unsuccessfully—thereby repaying his daughter's friend many times over. He drew it from memory of a trip sixteen years earlier, in symbols—"mountains, streams, and passes all included." In 1908 Schaffer, her friend Mollie Adams, "Chief" Warren (her young guide, whom she later married), and "K" Unwin followed the accurate map and became the first white people to document the shores of Chaba Imne (Beaver Lake), ungratefully renamed Maligne for the dangerous river it feeds. In 1911 she returned to survey the lake and its environs, which lie in what is now Jasper National Park.

Mary Sharples Schaffer Warren (1861–1939) was not a Canadian but a Philadelphian, from a wealthy Quaker family. Her father was a businessman and "gentleman farmer," as well as an avid minerologist. She became an amateur naturalist as a child and studied botany as a painter. In 1894 she married Dr. Charles Schaffer, a respected, and much older, doctor whose passion was botany and with whom she worked as an illustrator and photographer until his death in 1903. After completing and publishing his *Alpine Flora of the Canadian Rocky Mountains*, she conquered her fear of horses, bears, and the wilderness, and began her lengthy exploring expeditions, going on horseback with pack train deep into the then mostly uncharted territory for months at a time.

Schaffer's interest in Indians and the West had been awakened when, as a small child, she overheard her cousin Jim, an army officer, telling her parents about the destruction of an Indian village in which women and children were massacred; afterwards he had found a live baby sheltered by the mother's dead body.[9] This story made a profound impression on Mary, and she became obsessed with Indians. In her mid-teens she took her first trip west, met Native people for the first time, and became an inveterate traveler. The Canadian Rockies were her husband's botanical turf, and for the rest of her life Schaffer spent summers on the trails, photographing, writing, and exploring. She finally moved to Banff, and died there.

When Schaffer and Mollie Adams decided to take their plunge into the wilderness, it was unprecedented, and improper, for women to encroach on this steadfastly male territory. As Schaffer recalled:

...there are times when the horizon seems restricted, and we seemed to have reached that horizon, and the limit of all endurance—to sit with folded hands and listen calmly to the stories of the hills we so longed to see, the hills which had lured and beckoned us for years before this long list of men had ever set foot in the country. Our cups splashed over. We looked into each other's eyes and said: "Why not! We can starve as well as they; the muskeg will be no softer for us than for them...the waters no deeper to swim, nor the bath colder if we fall in"—so—we planned a trip.[10]

These and many other hardships and exhilarations they did endure, loving almost every minute of it, and documenting their experiences with their (often ineptly hand-colored) photographs of giant peaks, vast rivers, glaciers, and fields of wildflowers. When they were returning from the 1907 expedition, they passed a stranger on the trail near Lake Louise who later described the incident:

As we drove along the narrow hill road a piebald pack-pony with a china-blue eye came round a bend, followed by two women, black-haired, bare-headed, wearing beadwork squaw jackets and riding straddle. A string of pack-ponies trotted through the pines behind them.

"Indians on the move?" said I. "How characteristic!"

As the women jolted by, one of them very slightly turned her eyes and they were, past any doubt, the comprehending equal eyes of the civilized white woman which moved in that berry-brown face....

The same evening, in a hotel of all the luxuries, a slight woman in a very pretty evening frock was turning over photographs, and the eyes beneath the strictly arranged hair were the eyes of the woman in the beadwork who had quirted the piebald pack-pony past our buggy.[11]

The author of this colonial encounter was, ironically, Rudyard Kipling.

As Levi-Strauss has pointed out, the notion of travel is thoroughly corrupted by power. Mary Schaffer, for all her love of the wilderness (which she constantly called her "playground") was not free from the sense of power that came with being a prosperous "modern" person at "play" in the fields of the conquered. At the same time, she also expressed a very "modern" sense of melancholy and loss as she watched the railroad (which she called a "python") and ensuing "civilization" inching its way into her beloved landscape. More than her photographs, her journals betray a colonial lens. She is condescendingly "fond," but not very respectful, of the "savages" who are often her friends, bemoaning their unpleasantly crude and hard traditional life. In 1911, for instance, her party passed "a Cree village where, when we tried to photograph the untidy spot, the inhabitants scuttled like rabbits to their holes." In 1907, on the same Kootenai Plains where she took the Beavers' portrait, her camp was visited by "old Paul Beaver," presumably a relative of her darling Frances Louise. He eyed their simmering supper "greedily," but

> our provisions were reaching that point where it was dangerous to invite any guests, especially Indians, to a meal, so we downed all hospitable inclinations and without a qualm watched him ride away on his handsome buckskin just as darkness was falling.[12]

For all its socially enforced static quality, and for all I've read into it, Mary Schaffer's photograph of Sampson, Leah, and Francis Louise Beaver is "merely" the image of an ephemeral moment. I am first and foremost touched by its peace and freshness. I can feel the ground and grass, warm and damp beneath the people sitting "here" in an Indian summer after disaster had struck, but before almost all was lost. Despite years of critical analysis, seeing is still believing to some extent—as those who control the dominant culture (and those who ban it from Native contexts) know all too well. In works like this one, some of the barriers are down, or invisible, and we have the illusion of seeing for ourselves, the way we never *would* see for ourselves, which is what communication is about.

NOTES

1. This essay was originally written for *Poetics of Space*, an anthology edited by Steve Yates, forthcoming from the University of New Mexico Press. My thanks to the late Jon Whyte of the Whyte Museum in Banff, author of *Indians in the Rockies* (Banff: Altitude Publishing Ltd., 1985).

2. Johannes Fabian, *Time and the Other*, p. 35.

3. They were Frank Worthington Isham and his wife Mary Rowland, and Rev. Roselle T. Cross and his wife Emma Bridgman. Between them, they spent years in Dakota Territory, Colorado, Wyoming, Nebraska, and Washington.

4. Press release from American Indian Community House, New York City, publicizing a traveling exhibition of Native photographers.

5. Dennis Grady, "The Devolutionary Image: Toward a Photography of Liberation," *S.F. Camerawork* (16:2–3, Summer/Fall 1989), p. 28.

6. E.J. Hart, ed., *Hunter of Peace: Mary T.S. Schaffer's Old Indian Trails of the Canadian Rockies* (Banff: Whyte Museum, 1980), p. 70.

7. Hart, *Hunter of Peace*, p. 71.

8. Hart, *Hunter of Peace*, p. 72.

9. This sounds like a description of the 1864 massacre of Cheyenne and Arapaho at Sand Creek, in Colorado. A photograph exists of a sad-looking little girl, dressed in elegant European clothes, inaccurately described as the sole survivor of the massacre, later adopted by white people.

10. Hart, *Hunter of Peace*, p. 17.

11. Hart, *Hunter of Peace*, p. 2.

12. Hart, *Hunter of Peace*, p. 69.

SOURCE

Lucy R. Lippard's "Doubletake: The Diary of a Relationship with an Image," in *Partial Recall: Photographs of Native North Americans* (New York: New Press, 1992), 34–45.

TWO

Being a Woman, I Wanted to Tell About Them

Literary Travellers

In 1900, seasoned Rocky Mountain traveller Grace Gallatin Seton-Thompson assuaged her readers' trepidation in *A Woman Tenderfoot* about travel in wilderness with this dry advice: "Always regulate your fears according to the situation, and then you will not go into the valley of the shadow of death, when you are only lost in the mountains" (Seton-Thompson 1900, 111). Seton-Thompson's admonition illuminates the politics of behaviour that underpinned British and North American women's travel at the turn of the century. Later a world traveller, with a deep and abiding interest in women's politics and women's writing, she had little patience for the delicacies of feminine comportment and infinite determination to secure larger, more adventurous lives for women. *A Woman Tenderfoot* stands as a hallmark of the literary woman traveller—real or imaginary—whose sense of adventure was challenged less by the dangers and deprivations of wilderness (or even tourist) travel than by the constraints of social expectations for feminine behaviour that circumscribed women's attempts to fully engage in and adapt to experiences outside the norms of day-to-day life.

Travel became a viable and popular pastime for middle-class women in Europe and North America as steamships, trains, and hotel accommodations opened opportunities for tourism after the mid-nineteenth century. At the same time, the question of women's rights and roles arose as the most significant political issue of the late nineteenth and early twentieth centuries in North American and European societies. Women writers who travelled through and published books about the Rocky Mountains of Canada at that time, whose education and the social position of their families made possible pursuits that pressed against the boundaries of conventional domestic life, were clearly engaged with the social politics of their environments as they consistently and consciously framed their work through the lens of the Woman Question. In turn, gender politics shaped the ways in which the work of these literary travellers was regarded by publishers, critics, and readers.

The Woman Question and the spectre of the New Woman offered travel writers the opportunity to imagine complex female characters.

Sir John and Lady Macdonald at Stave River, British Columbia, CPR Line. Photograph by Otto B. Buell, 24 July 1886. (GAA NA–4967–132)

More often than not, both fictitious and real-life women travellers emerged in the literature as ambiguous if not contradictory protagonists who defied convention while nodding to it, living and travelling independently, earning income through travel writing published in serial form in women's journals and as popular books, challenging proprieties of femininity while embracing them through self-deprecating descriptions of their own feminine foibles. Only a few of these women, like Grace Seton-Thompson, set out to demand a new world for women. Rather, for the most part, they responded to opportunities and defended their choices to those who protested.

Women travellers who wrote of their visits to or through the Rocky Mountains of Canada in the decades around the turn of the twentieth century competed in a genre of travel writing that rang with the vigour and rigour of the heroic male explorer who took pride in, and garnered a public reputation for, his exploration of the rugged, empty mountain wilderness. Clearly transgressing the genre as a means of staking a claim, women writers invariably set themselves in comical comparison to the standard male model, seen through the eyes of men as a bit ridiculous, but in the end showing themselves to be the wiser, saner, and more daring traveller. In 1886, for example, during the summer after completion of the Canadian Pacific Railway, Agnes Macdonald travelled by train across Canada with her husband, Prime Minister John A. Macdonald. Lady Macdonald's audacious demand to ride the train through the heart of the mountains seated on the "cowcatcher" at the front of the engine, narrated against a backdrop of male disbelief, sets the tone—and standards of adventure—for subsequent women's travel experiences. Riding the cowcatcher became a fad; it also came to represent women's greater sense of adventure, crossing boundaries of behaviour. And while there survive a few photographs depicting tourists seated on the cowcatcher— a tinted photo in the Glenbow Museum of the Duke of York (later George V) and his companions seated on the royal train stopped at Glacier House in September 1901 is the best example—contrary to popular historical imagination in Canada, no photograph was made of Agnes Macdonald's revolutionary ride. Fortunately, Canadian novelist Sara Jeannette Duncan did not miss her opportunity to play with this fad. Her well-illustrated book, *A Social Departure* (1893), conveys the spirit of adventure in an engraving of the heroines in full flight on the cowcatcher.

The women writers whose work is selected here did not work independently, of course. The impact of their publishers' expectations and needs on the shape and tone of their tales is evident in the ways in which all of these books strike an engaging balance between stories of high adventure and risk that is uncommon in ordinary women's ordinary lives and the manner in which adventurous women looked and were seen to behave by others while on these adventures. To attract a maximum number of readers and retain a respected reputation as a publisher, such a book had to intrigue but not offend. Critics in turn responded to this

You feel with wonder that you are not doing anything very extraordinary after all. From Sara Jeannette Duncan's A Social Departure, *1893.*

strategy, more often than not proclaiming surprise or amazement at the woman's stories, praising the quality or value of the book, and always commenting on their perception of the extent to which the writer had strayed beyond the bounds of respectable femininity.

An early example of the writer-publisher-critic interchange among Rocky Mountain travellers is Britain's Isabella Bird. Prior to Agnes Macdonald's fabled trip, Lady Bird (who in 1854 began travelling to North America), had published two editions of *A Lady's Life in the Rocky Mountains*, the story of her travels in the Colorado Rockies during the autumn and early winter of 1873 (the first edition with publisher J. Murray of London, the second with Putnam's in New York, both in late 1879). Bird's book is a classic of the literary genre of women's travel, written with lively style and generously illustrated. In content and tone, it was the model for those who followed in the Canadian Rockies. Aware that travel was not yet a widely approved activity for Victorian women in the 1870s, especially to the more exotic reaches of the Empire, Bird began with what became the standard woman writer's disclaimer of modesty: that she had no intention of writing a book about her travels but had been pressured to publish, for others' education and enjoyment, letters that she had written for the pleasure of family or friends (specifically her sister, in Lady Bird's case). Responding in the spirit of an age engaged with debate on women's appropriate behaviour, critics were invariably quick to temper any perceived threat of an equally enthusiastic response from themselves or among the general reading public by casting doubt, however circumspect, on the writer's feminine propriety. No doubt such reviews served a writer and publisher well, generating controversy and engaging the attention of a larger audience.

A commentary in the *Times* of London of 22 November 1879 in response to the British edition of Lady Bird's book represents well the usual tone. In that review, the world learned that Lady Bird had travelled in "masculine habiliments for greater convenience." Sensitive to the implications of what today would seem an innocuous statement, but in fact was understood to suggest that she had compromised her femininity by setting aside conventions of dress, Bird hastened to salvage her reputation. In the North American edition that followed later that year, Lady Bird set straight the record, making it clear that her garments had been appropriately feminine, dressed as she was in what she called the "American Lady's Mountain Dress": " a half-fitting jacket, a skirt reaching to the ankles, and full Turkish trousers gathered into frills which fall over the boots—a thoroughly serviceable and feminine costume for mountaineering and other rough travelling in any part of the world" (Bird 1879, vii–viii).

Dress was a rallying point of contention in the debate on the Woman Question, and so it played a central role in the writings of women travellers. Lady Bird's pronouncement on dress was echoed frequently over the next forty years as anticipated criticism was deflected through descriptions of the propriety of the innovative garments designed to allow for safe and healthy travel in the mountains, especially if travelling by horse, and information about the preparations needed to trim excessive accoutrements of their urban lives to make travel a simple affair. Travelling and writing more than two decades after Lady Bird's visit to the western United States, Grace Seton-Thompson (1872–1959) devoted an entire chapter, with drawn illustrations, to clothing and packing for convenience and comfort during wilderness travel. The soundness of her opinion on these matters was endorsed by subsequent women travellers including Mary Schäffer a decade later in "Untrodden Paths in the Canadian Rockies," a publicity brochure written and illustrated with photographs by Schäffer for the CPR's expanding Soo Pacific Line. In the meantime, Mary J. Vaux was a leader in the arena of women's dress. Her wilderness wardrobe that year, as documented photographically, included both skirts and trousers.

A Woman Tenderfoot, written with wry humour, was addressed to the woman tourist who favoured the comforts of European summer travel but was duty bound to follow her husband's wishes for western adventure—despite her better instincts: "Of course wives should believe their husbands," Seton-Thompson wrote. "The economy of State and Church

*Mary J. Vaux and William Vaux
at Lake O'Hara, 1907.*

(Vaux Family Fonds, WMCR
V653/ NA–546)

would collapse otherwise" (Seton-Thompson 1900, 171). That Seton-Thompson was a lively and well-known advocate for women's rights should not come as a surprise to today's reader. She first joined the suffrage movement at the age of seventeen and remained an activist throughout her life. As a young adult, she studied printing and bookmaking, skills that she later employed to assist her husband, naturalist Ernest Seton-Thompson, with his work. Seton-Thompson and her husband divided their lives between winter homes in New York City and summers in the country, including camping trips. Seton-Thompson's skills and dedication to outdoor life led her to assist with the founding of the Camp Fire Girls organization in 1912. She also became a devoted world traveller and visited the Middle East, Northern Africa, and Asia numerous times. Her books always included observations and commentaries on the lives and status of women in these areas. In addition to her commitment to travel and women's rights, Seton-Thompson was especially interested in women's writing. She served with a variety of associations of women writers and collected a library of two thousand books and one hundred pamphlets by women writers that became known as the *Biblioteca Femina*, now conserved at Northwestern University in Illinois.

The woman travel writer's greatest challenge, perhaps, was finding a middle ground between the New Woman argument for women's right to political and economic independence and the less radical idea of women as humanly equal to men but nonetheless duty bound to family. Seton-Thompson's book, like that of many women writers up to the beginning of the First World War, demonstrates less an equivocal feminism than a response to publishers' concerns that such matters be addressed as a means of ameliorating social hostility to women's greater independence— an essential element of the genre—so as to enjoy widest advantage of the considerable market for women's travel writing. (Heaps 2001, 89–90; Foster and Mills quoted in Heaps, 90).

While the greater part of Seton-Thompson's visit to the west was in the American Rockies—where she and her husband "Nimrod" became lost while crossing the Continental Divide, encountered a rattlesnake, endured cold, snowfall, and a "multi-murderous cook" (Seton-Thompson 1900, 128)—there followed a train trip from Winnipeg ("you do not want to know how we got there," she writes (293)) to Vancouver with a day's stop at Banff and two at the Illecillewaet Glacier in the Selkirks. Seton-Thompson's awareness of the issue of femininity as a regulator of women's sense of freedom, adventure, and travel was countered by her well-concealed impatience with it. The thoroughness of her attention to the matter of dress does alert readers a century later that women's clothing, especially the restrictive, health-compromising Victorian women's wear of corsets and voluminous fabrics, was an especially vexatious issue for women seeking to expand their horizons to traverse.

In Rocky Mountain literature, the complexity of the problem of femininity is revealed most vividly where racial difference is invoked. Travelling women were clearly aware of, and sensitive to, pressures to behave and look ladylike according to the social codes of the day despite their seemingly unfeminine or traditionally masculine pursuits. The risk of transgression of social codes weighed more heavily for women travellers than the risk of striking off the worn paths of tourists into back-country wilderness—the latter a risk that even colonial adventurer Rudyard Kipling declined in the Rockies. Moreover, the matter spilled beyond conventions of social class into distinctions, from non-Aboriginal viewpoints, of race. Clearly irked by Mary Schäffer's legendary presence as a wilderness adventurer, preceding and preempting any claim he could make to cast himself in that role at that far corner of Empire, Kipling's crass description of Mary Schäffer on her return from four months of exploration in the interior of the Rocky Mountains is itself legendary for its distasteful racial and gender denigration:

> As we drove along the narrow hill-road a piebald pack-pony with a china-blue eye came round a bend, followed by two women, black-haired, bare-headed, wearing beadwork squaw-jackets, and riding straddle...

> 'Indians on the move?' said I. 'How characteristic!'

> As the women jolted by, one of them very slightly turned her eyes, and they were, past any doubt, the comprehending equal eyes of the civilised white woman which moved in that berry-brown face.

> ....The same evening, at an hotel of all the luxuries, a slight woman in a very pretty evening frock was turning over photographs, and the eyes beneath the strictly-arranged hair were the eyes of the woman in the beadwork jacket.... (Kipling 1920, 188–89)

In contrast, Schäffer invoked to her literary advantage readers' interest in what it meant to look and act in a feminine manner in the age of the Woman Question when she used conventions of women's dress to illustrate the appeal of wilderness travel upon the return of her travelling companions and herself from their first four-month trip in the back-country in 1907. In doing so, Schäffer turned the tables on Kipling with her own account of their encounter, cast within the same feminine and racial conventions he had used but with the added weight of women travel writers' self-deprecatory humour. Writing in *Old Indian Trails*, Schäffer was clear about her preference for the freedom from feminine and white middle-class conventions to which she was bound and how this was manifest in clothing:

> And then we struck the highway and on it a carriage with people in it! Oh! The tragedy of the comparison! The woman's gown was blue. I think her hat contained a white wing. I only saw it all in one awful flash from the corner of my right eye, and I remember distinctly that she had *gloves on*. Then I suddenly realised that our own recently brushed-up garments were frayed and worn and our buckskin coats had a savage cast, that my three companions looked like Indians, and that the lady gazing at us belonged to another world. It was then that I wanted my wild free life back again, yet step by step I was leaving it behind. (Schäffer 1911, 199–200)

In a private letter written almost two decades later, Schäffer's gracious deflection of Kipling's patronizing commentary turns the spotlight on how his travels as a tourist compromised his credentials:

> There was no doubt he had written of the right parties, but not in his usual wonderful strain. Who could wonder? He was passing through a great country on a red plush seat and anyone knows that red plush, a dining-car, a bumpy bed at night, and a buck-board are not conducive to hailing the muses to your side. I felt sorry for the part he had been forced to miss. Had Kipling gone into the places where we had gone, the world would have been the richer for his songs. O U R tongues and brains had not been adequate to tell in

verse the joys of the nightly camp-fire, while he would have left a lasting and beautiful memory of some of the wonderful snowstorms in the hills, the roaring rivers, the sweet, calm days in the many sunny valleys. (Warren quoted in Beck 2001, 186–87)

Schäffer was one of many women whose travel in the Rocky Mountains increased in quantity immediately after the CPR began transcontinental service. In 1893, following in Lady Macdonald's intrepid steps, Ishbel Gordon, Marchioness of Aberdeen and Temair, published *Through Canada with a Kodak*, an account of her first trip across Canada in 1890. Lady Aberdeen was an advocate for women's rights—including suffrage—in Britain and Ireland. In her capacity as wife of the Governor General of Canada between 1893 and 1897, part of her work on behalf of Britain, and central to the imperial agenda, was promoting women's capabilities and extolling their potential for the settlement and development of Canada. Illustrated with her own Kodak snapshots, professional photographic views by Notman and Sons, Boorne and May, and others, as well as sketches of Aboriginal artifacts, Aberdeen's travelogue includes scenic descriptions (a convention satirized that same year by Sara Jeannette Duncan in *A Social Departure*), personal anecdotes about people met, and commentaries on the country's social, industrial, and economic development. While the book represents a model of the dutiful imperial wife, it cannot be taken at face value, for in addition to Aberdeen's advocacy for women's suffrage and economic independence, her marriage was less conventional than might be expected. Marjory Harper explains that one of the men to whom Aberdeen dedicated her private travel journals was Henry Drummond, a Scottish theologian believed to have been her lover (Harper's introduction to Aberdeen 1994, lvii). Drummond met up with Lady Aberdeen and her husband on the west coast and joined them for the return train journey east.

Women writers, such as Mrs. George (Marion Dudley) Cran of Scotland, were also employed to persuade young British women to immigrate to western Canada. Cran (1879–1942) was born in South Africa and educated in Britain. She was employed as an editor for *Connoisseur*, *Burlington*, and other magazines, and published numerous books and articles in two areas of expertise: gardening and migration in the British Empire. With these credentials, Mrs. Cran spent half a year in Canada in 1908, with her expenses covered by the Dominion government and travelling on passes with the CPR and CNR, to write *A Woman in Canada*, a book about the country and its opportunities for young women:

> For the Dominion Government is aware that England is overcrowded with women, and that her own prairie lands are crying for them by the thousand. Canada wants women of breed and endurance, educated, middle-class gentlewomen, and these are not the women to come out on the off-chance of getting married. They may be induced to come to the country if they can farm or work in some way to secure their absolute independence. (Cran 1910, 22)

Cran crafts her experience as one in which her original, unfounded idea of Canada as a dull and barren country is resoundingly disproved by her experience. Her conclusion? "If I had to earn my living I would go to Canada" (283).

One woman who did earn her living in Canada was Mrs. Arthur Spragge (1854–1932), née Ellen Elizabeth Cameron in Toronto. A journalist and painter, Mrs. Spragge travelled on the first train to cross Canada from Montreal to the West Coast in the summer of 1886. A series of articles recounting her journey was published in the Toronto *Week* while the adventure was underway. These were then gathered together as *From Ontario to the Pacific by the C.P.R.*, published in 1887. In 1889, she again published a series of stories about her adventures, this time in *The Dominion Illustrated*, of which one installment is included here. Mrs. Spragge, like many of her contemporaries, entertained her readers as much with studies of the characters she met en route as with the places visited and sights seen, often setting her own simple tourist tastes and behaviour in contrast to others who apparently travelled in high style, with all of the comforts and amenities of their homes. Settling down for a morning of watercolour sketching in Banff, for example,

> I had not long been at work when my anti-type appeared upon the scene in the person of a vigorous American, who set up an ostentatious easel, seated herself upon the well-known and advertised folding-stool, and erected the protecting umbrella. When a heavy shower drove me temporarily beneath the spreading tree where she was established, I found that she was diligently libelling nature on a vast canvas of good solid oil paint. (Spragge 1889, 183)

Quick wit and self-deprecating humour are the hallmarks of the narratives of these early footloose feminists.

Another Canadian journalist, Sara Jeannette Duncan (1862–1922), also published newspaper articles of her travels. Prior to her marriage in 1891, she wrote under the pseudonym "Garth Grafton" for the Toronto *Globe*, the Toronto *Week*, the Montreal *Star*, the Memphis *Appeal*, and the Washington *Post*. In 1889, she posted dispatches from her journey around the world with a female companion. In 1890, drawing upon her experiences, Duncan turned to fiction to deploy her considerable wit in her first novel, *A Social Departure: How Orthodocia and I Went Round the World by Ourselves*, an imaginary travel journal that took up the convention of the single travelling woman and her companion, and their adventures and mishaps in travelling around the world. As Denise A. Heaps has demonstrated, Duncan satirizes the conventions of women's travel writing, from the "hackneyed narratives and descriptive conventions" (Heaps 2001, 75) to "the genre's reputation for fabrication and embellishment" and "travel raconteurs who insist on the authenticity of their texts" (79). The Rocky Mountains of Canada do not escape her notice. Duncan's novel takes up the already well-worn tales of riding the cowcatcher and climbing the Illecillewaet Glacier at Glacier House, along with the frequently repeated claim that few women had travelled that way. The question of why a writer such as Duncan, known for her strong support of women's suffrage, would characterize women's work in this way is answered by Heaps as appearing

> to be a gambit to disarm potential critics and attract a larger audience. Her female travelling clowns cajole readers into embracing a travel tale of two single young women who do successfully voyage around the world without a chaperone....Thus, while Duncan satirizes female travellers...she nevertheless affirms a woman's right to roam the globe freely. (Heaps 2001, 90–91)

Duncan moved to India after her marriage where she continued to write, publishing a novel almost every year from 1891 to 1914.

Famous real-life women travellers and fictive travelling heroines crossed paths with some frequency in the Rocky Mountain travel novels that appeared around the turn of the century. As Duncan's main character sets out on her journey around the world, she is reading a "pirated edition of *Robert Ellsmere*," the very popular 1888 novel written by Mrs. Humphry (Mary) Ward that sold over one million copies. In the 1870s and early 1880s, Ward (1851–1920) wrote for journals such as the *Manchester Guardian*, *Saturday Review*, and the *Oxford Spectator* prior to her success as a novelist. Ward is especially intriguing for her seemingly contradictory views of the Woman Question. She was socially, politically, and economically active (as a patron of the social reform movement, leader of the anti-suffrage league, and with an active and successful career as an author of twenty-five novels and fifteen books of literary criticism and recognition as Britain's first woman war correspondent). Nevertheless, Ward believed that while women were the human equal of men, their social role emerged from their biology as caregivers and nurturers, and so their position should remain behind the scenes both at home, maintaining the integrity of the family as moral foundation of society, and in politics, making women's suffrage unnecessary and unwise.

In 1908, the popular Mrs. Ward visited the Rocky Mountains while travelling as a guest of William Van Horne on the CPR. In 1910, she published in Toronto *Lady Merton, Colonist*, the story of a young British widow who travels by train across Canada, finds love, and chooses to settle there with her new husband who was *Canadian Born* (the title by which the novel was published, with some minor variations, in Britain). Almost twenty years after Duncan's work appeared, Ward's novel employs the same strategy of fictionalizing the travel genre, but with a romantic rather than satirical cast. It did not enjoy widespread popularity and is mentioned only in passing in recent academic reconsideration of Mary Ward's place in the history of British literature. Mary Schäffer's own critical response to the novel might explain why:

Poor, dear Mrs. Ward. I know some folk liked her writings or else she would not have located publishers. She and her daughter Dorothy took herself very seriously. I believe she was considered very clever in political writing. The C.P.R. brought her out as a fine ad. for that road. We met over flowers and she was with me a few days at Field just before I went off on my search for Maligne. After locating it, I enjoyed sending her a description of our experiences as well as some photos. That is the last I thought about it till I received from her direct a copy of the book you mention. But the worst blow was when she wrote that I was her heroine. Ye gods and little fishes, I could have died under such an idea. All I could think was that no one would ever think of such a thing and I don't believe they did. I was doing the work just to keep down the terrible grief of losing my wonderful husband. It was all such peace to be in the wilderness and to be alone so much of my time.

I still have the book and dear Mrs. Ward is long gone, but it was too horrible and I never showed it. I rather think she dedicated it to me but it's on a very dark shelf and I try to think she did her best. It just was not her true form and a terrible travesty for what

she had undertaken. She could never grasp my loved country.
(Warren, 24 June 1936)

In the small world of mountain travel, both Marion Cran and Mary Ward met Mary Schäffer in Field, B.C. during their own visits by train through the Rocky Mountains. Schäffer often gave photographs to those she met, and Cran and Ward were no exception. Ward included Schäffer's photograph of the newly explored Maligne Lake, which she cast as Lake Elizabeth, in her final chapter. Cran, who also published a Schäffer photo of Maligne, described her encounter with the photographer in this way:

> I study her closely; she has fair hair that has been burned fairer by the sun, a skin once fair, now deeply tanned, slim arms that are browner still, and a smooth voice with a strong American accent. What can this little woman have in her so fearless that she is gaining the reputation of an intrepid explorer? Her manner is gentle; one derides the notion of a bias to masculinity...

> Later in the day we meet and talk, and I see the companion of her travels for the last three expeditions, Miss Adams a little dark, neat woman and a keen geologist, with a head shaped beautifully like that of an Egyptian priest. They talk amusingly, and without the least pride of the 'trip,' they show me countless photographs taken on the way.

> "...Here is our pack-train—yes, the figure on horseback is me— we both wore breeches in the wild, it's safe, skirts are a concession to civilization...."

> So they talk; telling vivaciously, without vanity, of their amazing venture; giving photographs, some of which appear in this chapter.
> (Cran 1910, 182–86)

The women whose work follows in fragments here are just a few of the professional women writers who visited and wrote about their travels through the Rocky Mountains of Canada. Literary women travellers, like women in general, were divided over the Woman Question. Some women shared the conservative view of Mrs. Ward. Others, such as Grace Seton-Thompson, challenged convention and demonstrated through their own actions that women were not only capable, but that such a life was favourable for a woman's health and life. Nevertheless, these women travellers were also pragmatic writers: to embrace as wide a readership as possible in the interests of commercial success, pain was taken to ensure that the women who travelled and wrote to popular acclaim remained publicly "feminine," that is, properly dressed and well-mannered.

As for readers, many of the books written by women travellers in the Rocky Mountains of Canada were extremely popular with their original audience and remain so with readers today. Such popularity shows that these writers "spoke powerfully" (Sutton Rampseck 1999, 218) to the women and men who read them. Their popular acclaim also raises the question of why their work was so well-received. That these women writers and their readers were living in a complex moment is clearly shown in the travel narratives. Virtually every one of them engages a combination of exhortations to break boundaries and invocations of readers' understanding that the writer throughout had retained her femininity, demonstrating at all times socially sanctioned good behaviour and appropriate modesty, especially in serviceable and safe dress choices. As such, these stories of adventure and romance in the Rocky Mountains were about more than exploration of a larger world; they were also an exploration of the debate and confusion of women's appropriate social role that was appreciated by readers who were themselves considering, arguing, and seeking their own position on the Woman Question (Thompson 1999, 8).

EDITOR'S NOTE

The title of this section, "Being a Woman, I Wanted to Tell About Them," is taken from the preface of Grace Seton-Thompson's *A Woman Tenderfoot* (New York: Doubleday, 1900). See quotation on page 117.

AGNES MACDONALD

"By Car and by Cowcatcher" (1887)

Excerpts

Part I.

...How beautiful is the country in which I find myself on awaking
a few hours after! We are among the "Foot hills," or lowest range of the
Rockies—great, mound-like, smooth, softly-tinted hills that swelled into
many a lovely curved shape, holding in their wide folds winding blue rivers
and great stretches of fine grazing land, over which, as the sweet morning
air stirred through the grass, little billows of pale green seemed to pass.
These are some of the cattle ranches of which we have "heard tell" so
often lately.

As we travel slowly onward—slowly, so as to enjoy all to the fullest
extent—these plains widen and stretch away into flat quiet distances, soft
and misty, lying below farther hills outlined against the sky. Sharper risings
and rougher ledges appear. By and by the wide valleys change into broken
ravines, and lo! through an opening in mist made rosy with early sunlight,

we see far away up in the sky, its delicate pearly tip clear against the blue, a single snow-peak of the Rocky Mountains! There is a general rush to see it;—perhaps general disappointment. Surely that fragile, almost quivering point rising so high over the pink drapery that sweeps to the valley below, can have nothing to do with the rugged heights and mountains we have come to see!

Our coarse natures cannot at first appreciate the exquisite aerial grace of that solitary peak that seems on its way to heaven; but as we look, its fading gauzy mist passes over, and it has vanished.

On again we go, now through long stretches of park-like country, now near great mountain shoulders, half-misty, half-defined, with occasional gleams of snowy peaks far away before us like kisses on the morning sky.

The Kananaskis River flows directly across the pass that leads into the mountains which here begin to close in round us. We stopped at the Kananaskis Station, and walking across a meadow, behold the wide river a mass of foam leaping over ledges of rocks into the plains below.

We reach Canmore,—sixty-eight miles from Calgary. Here the pass we are travelling through has narrowed suddenly to four miles, and as mists float upwards and away, we see great masses of scarred rock rising on each side—ranges towering one above another. Very striking and magnificent grows the prospect as we penetrate into the mountains at last, each curve of the line bringing fresh vistas of endless peaks, rolling away before and around us, all tinted rose, blush pink, and silver, as the sun lights their snowy tips. Every turn becomes a fresh mystery, for some huge mountain seems to stand right across our way, barring it for miles, with a stern face frowning down upon us; and yet a few minutes later we find the giant has been encircled and conquered, and soon lies far away in another direction.

Mount Cascade is perhaps one of the most remarkable of these peaks. Approaching its perpendicular massive precipice front, streaked with a thousand colours which glow in the sunshine, we half shrink from what seems an inevitable crash! From this precipice falls a narrow cascade making a leap of about 1800 feet. Surely it will presently burst over us! — but no; a few minutes later Mount Cascade has mysteriously moved away to the right, and its silver waterfall soon gleams in the distance.

Many of the mountains were skirted with low dark forests. Some had a vegetation of small evergreens marking out wide ledges; but beyond a certain height, fissured rock, in which tiny glaciers and snow-beds found a resting place, rose alone into the sky. Sometimes this bristling beard of rugged trees was sharply defined against great walls of white and grey above, with crags and peaks and ledges, in all sorts of fantastic forms, breaking the outline. Below, all was in deep shade, but above sunlight fell in a sharp, bright line across those mighty walls, and glistened, with beauty inconceivable, upon fairy-like points in the sky.

At Banff, six miles from Canmore, sulphur springs of great medicinal value had been only lately discovered; but already, from our car window, we can see the timbers for an hotel awaiting transportation up the winding road to the springs. One of our party informs us that the Government has reserved 20,000 acres for a public park in this beautiful place, and that arrangements are already being made to render it available for this purpose. It is an enchanting spot, encircled by mountains—said to contain many more valuable springs—the air fragrant with sweet odours from low spruce-trees clothing their sides.

Here the Bow River, which we have skirted since leaving Calgary, winds through the wide green plateau, its waters of a dull China blue. About five miles farther on Castle Mountain is before us, standing a sheer precipice 5000 feet high—a giant's "keep," with turrets, bastions, and battlements complete, reared against the sky.

As we rise toward the summit, near Stephen, about thirty-five miles farther on, the railway's grade gets steeper, tall forests gather round us, and a curious effect is produced by glimpses of snowy spurs and crests peeping through the trees, and of which, though apparently near us, we see no base. This conveyed to me an idea of our elevation, and it was delightful to think of oneself as hidden away among those solitary mountains, even for a few short hours, with all the troubles and worries of life left in noisy bustling cities far away!

At the Laggan Station, more than thirty miles from the summit, a huge engine,—in curious black contrast to a small white house near by,—stood on a siding with all steam up, waiting for our train. I then learned that this monster is necessary for the steep grades, both ascending and descending, over which we have to go.

The General Superintendent (whom I have already mentioned as having joined our party at Winnipeg—Mr. E.___) in an unlucky moment suggested I should walk forward, examine this big "mountain" engine, and see its heavy proportions and fine machinery. I say "unlucky," because from the instant my eyes rested on the broad shining surface of its buffer-beam and cowcatcher, over which a bright little flag waved from a glossy brass pole, I decided to travel there and nowhere else for the remaining 600 miles of my journey!

Part II.

From Calgary to Laggan I had travelled in the car of the engine, accompanied by a victimized official. Perched on a little feather bench, well in front, and close to the small windows, I had enjoyed an excellent opportunity of seeing everything. Besides this, I had gained a great deal of useful information about engines, boilers, signals, &c., which may come in "handy" some day. During our stoppages the engineer and firemen had not failed to explain these things, and I had even ventured to whistle "caution" at a "crossing." The signal went very well for an amateur, but the Chief's quick ear had detected a falter, and at the next halt he sent a peremptory message, desiring me "not to play tricks," which, addressed to a discreet matron, was really quite insulting. I had even questioned the engineer as to the probable effect of a bad collision while I occupied this post. He promptly suggested, "most likely killed;" and added, reflectively, as he carefully oiled an already dripping valve, "which would be a bad job"!

When I announced my desire to travel on the cowcatcher, Mr. E—— seemed to think that a very bad job indeed. To a sensible, level-headed man as he is, such an innovation on all general rules of travelling decorum was no doubt very startling. He used many ineffectual persuasions to induce me to abandon the idea, and almost said I should not run so great a risk; but at last, being a man of few words, and seeing time was nearly up, he so far relented as to ask what I proposed using as a seat. Glancing round the station platform I beheld a small empty candle-box lying near, and at once declared that was "just the thing." Before Mr. E—— could expostulate further, I had asked a brakesman to place the candle-box on the buffer-beam, and was on my way to the "Jamaica" to ask the Chief's permission. The Chief, seated on a low chair on the rear platform of the car, with a rug over his knees and a magazine in his hand, looked very comfortable and content. Hearing my request, after a moment's thought, he pronounced the idea "rather ridiculous," then remembered it was dangerous as well, and finally asked if I was sure I could hold on. Before the words were well out of his lips, and taking permission for granted by the question, I was again standing by the cowcatcher, admiring the position of the candle-box, and anxiously asking to be helped on.

Before I take my seat, let me try, briefly, to describe the "Cowcatcher." Of course every one knows that the buffer-beam is that narrow, heavy iron platform, with the sides scooped out, as it were, on the very fore-front of the engine over which the headlight glares, and in the corner of which a little flag is generally placed. In English engines, I believe, the buffers proper project from the front of this beam. In Canadian engines another sort of attachment is arranged, immediately below the beam, by which the engine can draw trains backwards as well as forwards. The beam is about eight feet across, at the widest part, and about three feet deep. The description of a cowcatcher is less easy. To begin with, it is misnamed, for it catches no cows at all. Sometimes, I understand, it throws up on the buffer-beam whatever maimed or mangled animal it has struck, but in most cases it clears the line by shoving forward, or tossing aside, any removable obstruction. It is best described as a sort of barred iron beak, about six feet long, projecting close over the track in a V shape, and attached to the buffer-beam by very strong bolts. It is sometimes sheathed with thin iron plates in winter, and acts then as a small snow-plough.

Behold me now, enthroned on the candle-box, with a soft felt hat well over my eyes, and a linen carriage-cover tucked round me from waist to foot. Mr. E— had seated himself on the other side of the headlight. He had succumbed to the inevitable, ceased further expostulation, disclaimed all responsibility, and, like the jewel of a Superintendent he was, had decided on sharing my peril! I turn to him, peeping round the headlight, with my best smile. "This is *lovely*," I triumphantly announce, seeing that a word of comfort is necessary, "*quite lovely*; I shall travel on this cowcatcher from summit to sea!"

Mr. Superintendent, in his turn, peeps round the headlight and surveys me with solemn and resigned surprise. "I—suppose—you—will," he says slowly, and I see that he is hoping, at any rate, that I shall live to do it!

With a mighty snort, a terribly big throb, and a shrieking whistle, No. 374 moves slowly forward. The very small population of Laggan have all come out to see. They stand in the hot sunshine, and shade their eyes as the stately engine moves on. "It is an awful thing to do!" I hear a voice say, as the little group lean forward; and for a moment I feel a thrill that is very like fear; but it is gone at once, and I can think of nothing but the novelty, the excitement, and the fun of this mad ride in glorious sunshine and intoxicating air, with magnificent mountains before and around me, their lofty peaks smiling down on us, and never a frown on their grand faces!

The pace quickens gradually, surely, swiftly, and then we are rushing up to the summit. We soon stand on the "Great Divide"—5300 feet above sea-level—between the two great oceans. As we pass, Mr. E— by a gesture, points out a small river (called Bath Creek, I think) which, issuing from a lake on the narrow summit-level, winds near the track. I look, and lo! the water, flowing *eastward* towards the Atlantic side, turns in a moment as the Divide is passed, and pours *westward* down the Pacific slope!

Another moment and a strange silence has fallen round us. With steam shut off and brakes down, the 60-ton engine, by its own weight and impetus alone, glides into the pass of the Kicking Horse River, and begins a descent of 2800 feet in twelve miles. We rush onward through the vast valley stretching before us, bristling with lofty forests, dark and deep, that, clinging to the mountain side, are reared up into the sky. The river, widening, grows white with dashing foam, and rushes downwards with tremendous force. Sunlight flashes on glaciers, into gorges, and athwart huge, towering masses of rock crowned with magnificent tree crests that rise all round us of every size and shape. Breathless—almost awe-stricken—but with a wild triumph in my heart, I look from farthest mountain peak, lifted high before me, to the shining pebbles at my feet! Warm wind rushes past; a thousand sunshine colours dance in the air. With a firm right hand grasping the iron stanchion, and my feet planted on the buffer beam, there was not a yard of that descent in which I faltered for a moment. If I had, then assuredly in the wild valley of the Kicking Horse River, on the western slope of the Rocky Mountains, a life had gone out that day! I did not think of danger, or remember what a giddy post I had. I could only gaze at the glaciers that the mountains held so closely, 5000 feet above us, at the trace of snow avalanches which had left a space a hundred feet wide massed with torn and prostrate trees; on the shadows that played over the distant peaks; and on a hundred rainbows made by the foaming, dashing river, which swirls with tremendous rapidity down the gorge on its way to the Columbia in the valley below.

There is glory of brightness and beauty everywhere, and I laugh aloud on the cowcatcher, just because it is all so delightful!

SOURCE

Excerpts of Agnes Macdonald's "By Car and by Cowcatcher," appearing as two parts in separate issues of *Murray's Magazine* (1887), 215–35 and 296–315.

MRS. ARTHUR SPRAGGE

"Our Wild Westland" (1889)

XII.

The Situation of the Banff Springs Hotel—Its Exterior—Valleys of the Bow and Spray River—A Sketching Expedition—The Lower Hot Spring—Inner and Outer Bathing Facilities—The Grotto and the Pool—Upper Hot Spring on Sulphur Mountain—Extent of the National Park.

ON THE MORNING OF JULY 1ST (Dominion Day), which last year fell upon a Sunday, I woke to the beauties of Banff, and, drawing aside the curtains of my window, beheld a vision of mountain peaks, off which the mists were slowly rolling. The Banff Springs Hotel faces due north, and my apartment, being in the front, commanded an extensive view across the Bow Valley to the Rockies. An unimproved foreground of ugly stumps, through which the road wound, made an unattractive approach to the building, which, in my humble opinion, should have turned its back to this barren unpromising region and its front to the valleys of the

Bow and Spray. It must be remembered, however, that in 1888 the place was yet in its infancy, being only just opened to the public, and, no doubt, the dreary waste between the town and the hotel has since undergone much improvement, as it might be most advantageously laid out in lawns and terraces. When we adjourned to the dining-room for breakfast, I discovered that my surmises had been correct, as from that side of the building the best scenery may be enjoyed. The Bow unites with the Spray immediately below the high bluff on which it is situated, the valleys of both rivers being separated by a fine mountain, called from its peculiar formation the Twin Peaks, rising abruptly at their confluence and terminating in a series of bold serrated crags, which are sharply defined against the sky.

We discussed over an excellent repast the division of our party's limited time to its best advantage among the lions of Banff. I had come on sketching intent, so that my object and destination was the most picturesque and attainable locality in the neighbourhood. Two of our number were in favour of an immediate visit to the invigorating Hot Springs, my husband desired to discover an old friend resident in the town, while the senior member of our little company (a grave and reverend signor) placed himself at my disposal as guide and counsellor. We sallied forth accordingly to contemplate the exterior of the hotel, which we had approached at midnight. It was pronounced by my escort, who is the architect of the Pacific Division of the C.P.R., and, therefore, a competent authority, to be in the Schloss style of the Rhenish Provinces, characterised by octagonal towers, with the addition of wide verandahs, having open galleries above. At the ends of two of the wings these galleries are enclosed with glass and form delightful reading and smoking rooms. The building is laid out in the form of the letter H, and the general effect of the design is both artistic and imposing.

The view from the front as we emerged, looking away over the stumps of the foreground, revealed magnificent mountains, rising in the north, where they enclose the Bow Valley, their bases so near apparently in the clear atmosphere as to be almost within reach, while their summits glittered with eternal snow in the bright sunshine. Masses of mist as we gazed swept off their rocky sides, wreathing vast expanses of rock and timber in clouds of gray gossamer, while away from the west to south-easterly the Bow River rolls in the winding channel it has cleft for itself, in ages past, between the serried ranges of the Rocky Mountains. After thoroughly investigating the landscape, we decided to descend from the elevation of the hotel to the south valley, and slid and scrambled down a precipitous path to the level of the river, near its junction with the Spray, *behind* the Banff Springs Hotel. At this point the Bow, which has changed its course a mile above the hotel and taken a southerly bend, tumbles over a pretty fall into a deep dark pool, formed by the backwater from the swiftly flowing current. I soon found a charming view of this cascade, looking northeast directly up the river, which is apparently hemmed in by two noble mountains, round whose bases it winds. I ensconced myself on a block of wood provided by my cavalier, who had rambled across the iron bridge over the Spray to spy out the land beyond.

On these sketching expeditions I feel distinctly and insignificantly an amateur. I travel with neither artist's easel, stool, nor umbrella. My outfit is of the simplest,—a sketching block portfolio, a bag containing paint box, water bottle, sponges, wipers, etc.—these, with my own stout gingham, supply my humble needs and proclaim that I am neither ambitious nor professional.

I had been not long at work when my anti-type appeared upon the scene in the person of a vigorous American, who set up an ostentatious easel, seated herself upon the well-known and advertised folding-stool, and erected the protecting umbrella. When a heavy shower drove me temporarily beneath the spreading tree where she was established, I found that she was diligently libelling nature on a vast canvas of good solid oil paint. In a short time I succeeded in securing a fair representation of the view, and my guide having returned from his explorations and warned me that it was past mid-day and another meal awaited our patronage, we duly scaled the high cliff we had descended, and rallied round the table assigned to our party. The bathers appeared with enormous appetites, the result of their dip in mineral waters, and my husband had discovered his friend, Mr. E.A. Nash, Assistant Dominion Land Agent at Banff, so the morning was pronounced fruitful in cause and effect. Mr. Nash having offered me his services for the afternoon in the substantial shape of the national buckboard and pair of Indian ponies to investigate districts not within reach of pedestrians, I prepared for my initial experience of the above mentioned western vehicle, which I found extremely comfortable. We drove first down through the southern valley of the Bow, below the hotel, which, together with the town of Banff, is located in the Canadian National Park, an immense domain containing 216 square miles. A more beautiful spot it would be difficult to conceive. The Park lies northeast by southwest, bourded by a range of snow-capped mountains. It is intersected by the Bow and Spray Rivers, and within its limits are Cascade Mountain, Sulphur Mountain, (the source of the hot springs), and the Twin Peaks. Nestled among these rugged heights lies the Devil's Lake, a fine expanse of water, from whose surface the surrounding scenery can be fully appreciated. Throughout this extensive tract the Government have made excellent macadamised roads. One of these we took, and crossing the Spray bridge, followed the course of the Bow River, through some prettily wooded land, opening into a fine bit of prairie, which we could have explored for many miles had I not desired to see the far-famed hot springs, distant one mile and a-half from the hotel and not far from the town. Thither the horses' heads were accordingly turned, and in a short time we drew up at the Lower Hot Spring, which issues from the base of the Sulphur Mountain. Its mineral waters are the property of the Dominion Government, who have erected very ornamental and commodious bath-houses, in rustic style, for the convenience of visitors. This spring issues from its source in two entirely distinct ways, offering the peculiarity of both inside and outside natural bathing facilities in hot water. Deep in the bowels of the earth is a large circular grotto enclosing a pool 90 feet in circumference, from whose bottom several springs of very high temperature rise. They are moderated, however, by a stream of cold water that falls from one of the walls and reduces them to a tepid state. This grotto was originally entered through a small opening in its roof, scarcely large enough to admit a man's body, which a ladder connected with the deep pool below. It now serves for purposes of light and ventilation. Another small outlet was subsequently discovered and converted into a tunnel 100 feet long, at present giving access to the interior. The basin of the grotto is lined with concrete, and surrounded by a wooded platform, furnished with seats. Taking one of these, I gazed first down into the dark water then up to the arched vault above, carved by the action of sulphuric forces into every conceivable stalactite and fungoid formation; inhaled brimstony vapours at a temperate of 95 degrees; and fully realised the possible horrors of the Infernal Regions. No more weird or infernal spot could be imagined. A truly Stygian resort, wherein troops of devils might come forth and disport themselves in the dead of night.

Outside, not 100 yards from the grotto and immediately at the base of a high grass cliff, is the pool, which has been enclosed and made into an ideal swimming bath. The water is regulated to any desired depth by means of a waste pipe, which can be opened and closed at will. It is of clear turquoise blue colour, and the source of the spring is distinctly visible at the bottom in deep round indigo blue spots. The temperature is quite as warm as that of an ordinary hot bath, and bathing may be enjoyed in its sparkling bosom beneath a brilliant blue sky, whose every cloud shape is reflected in the pool below. Two miles from the town and hotel is the upper and hottest spring, high on the side of Sulphur Mountain. This I visited the next morning, thanks to the useful buckboard. I found that the water, gushing out of a wall of rock at 120° Fahrenheit, was too warm to dip my hands in. From this spot it is conveyed by iron pipes to the Banff Springs Hotel below, where there is a fine bath house and every convenience to enable its visitors to benefit by the springs without leaving the building. The Dominion Government had in 1888 made no improvements at the upper spring, where, however, Dr. Brett has established excellent bathing accommodation in connection with his larger institution near the town. An impending rainstorm drove me home in two senses of the word before I had time to complete my examination of this hottest spring. The early part of the afternoon I devoted to sketching the south valley of the Bow from one of the glass galleries in the hotel, and the latter portion to fishing in the river, the senior member of our party, an accomplished disciple of the venerable Isaac, taking me under his charge. The vaunted trout in the Bow, however, declined to be tempted even by the most insinuating and natural flies. Common beef, though scouted by my companion, produced a few desultory nibbles; but the sport was not good enough for us and was soon abandoned. Trout fishing in the Bow, we learnt afterwards, is practically exhausted, being open to all comers, though first-class fishing may be had at Devil's Lake, seven miles from Banff, where large black trout abound. The following morning (Tuesday, July 3rd,) we were roused from our beds at the witching hour of four to catch the Pacific express, which bore us swiftly back to the Columbia Valley. For those requiring total change of air and scene, with rest of body and mind combined, with cool bracing mountain air, and the absence of the dressing and dancing of ordinary fashionable summer resorts, no more suitable place than Banff could be selected. The temperature at its elevation of over 4,000 feet demands warm wraps as additions to every wardrobe. The early morning air is always cool and the evenings decidedly chilly. We found no mosquitoes during the first week in July, and if these pestilential insects do appear there later in the season, their sojourn must of necessity be a short one.

SOURCE

Mrs. Arthur Spragge's "Our Wild Westland: Points on the Pacific Province," from *The Dominion Illustrated* (21 September 1889), 183.

"The Rocky Mountains" (1893)

from Through Canada with a Kodak

AND NOW WE HAVE COME to the last part of the trip through which I have endeavoured to act as your conductor. And if I have felt myself inefficient in that capacity during the earlier parts of our journey, still more do I feel the impossibility of doing justice to all the glories of the scenery through which we shall now pass. For even the prairies of the North West prove themselves to be not so limitless as they appear at first to those traversing their vast extent day after day; and one night, as we peep out of our berths behind the closed blinds of the car, we find ourselves standing still at the very foot of the Rockies. In the conflicting light of the stars and early dawn, we see ourselves guarded by three high purple peaks, known as the Three Sisters, and we feel ourselves once more safe at home in the bosom of the mountains. Soon the heavy engine which is to pant up the steep inclines in front of us comes, and hooks us on, and all day long, as we clamber the snow-covered Rockies, and steam on slowly through the heart of the Selkirks, along the Columbia River, and the wild waters which sweep down the Kicking-Horse Pass, and pass under the shade of the crags of huge "Sir Donald," we rush about from side to side, and from end to end of our car, attempting, if not to photo-graph or sketch, at least to imprint some memory of the magnificent panorama unrolling itself before our eyes. But all in vain! There is such a thing as being surfeited with fine scenery, and it is a transgression against nature to hurry, as we did through these glorious scenes. All that remains now is a remembrance of towering snow-capped peaks rearing themselves up in all their strength above us, and stretches of mountains changing in the varying light of sun and cloud, from palest blues and greys to rich tones of yellow and red and purple, as we come nearer, and as the autumn foliage shows itself blending with the deep browns and blueish-green colours of the waters foaming below. To appreciate scenery such as this frequent halts should be made, and time should be allowed for the eye and mind to drink in and realise what is before them. Solitude too, and deep, unbroken stillness, are needed, if you would be in harmony with these surroundings, if you would have nature lead you up irresistibly to nature's God, if you would be able from your heart to bow yourself down and say:—

"These are Thy glorious works, Parent of good.
Almighty, Thine this universal frame,
Thus wondrous fair! Thyself how wondrous then!
Unspeakable! who sits above these heavens
To us invisible, or dimly seen
In these Thy lowest works, yet these
Declare Thy goodness beyond thought
And power divine."

Another time we hope to be able to stop at various places on this route, for a day at any rate, and perhaps I shall thus be better fitted to be your guide on some future occasion. The only halt we did make in these regions we enjoyed immensely. It was at Banff, where the Government are forming a National Park, twenty-six miles long by ten broad, and where the C.P.R. have put up a most comfortable hotel, 4000 feet above the sea, overlooking the Bow River. The hotel is about one and a half miles from the station. Our train arrived at the station about 1 A.M., and we shall not soon forget the brisk drive in the bright, frosty air, over snow-besprinkled grounds, amidst snow-covered mountains, with stars glimmering overhead. The hotel is a prettily-designed wooden building, capable of accommodating a hundred guests, and in the large entrance-hall a huge log-fire, crackling away on an open hearth, bids welcome to weary travellers from East and West, whatever hour of the night they may arrive. Well, we had what is termed in America "a lovely time" at Banff. The sun shone brilliantly, the air was exhilarating, and we made the most of our one day. We walked, and we sketched, and we "kodaked"—we visited the hot sulphur springs, which are much resorted to by invalids, and which boil out of the ground at different degrees of temperature up to 90 or 92 degrees. Some of these look most tempting to the bather, the clear green-blue water bubbling into a large pool, enclosed by high rocks, and the rays of the sun glinting through the opening above. And in the afternoon Captain Harper, one of the Inspectors of the Mounted Police, came round with his break and four-in-hand, and took us for a drive round the Park, charioteering us most skilfully up and down the steep roads, winding round Tunnel Mountain, and showing us many beautiful views.

The time for departure came all too soon, and as we were standing near the station in the darkness, waiting for the arrival of the train, I heard a familiar Aberdeenshire voice putting the question, "Do you remember 'Titaboutie?' 'Remember Titaboutie!'" I should think we did! The voice belonged to a daughter of one of Lord Aberdeen's Tarland tenants, and we found that she and her sister had both come out to Canada. One was engaged at the Banff Sanatorium, the other was with her brother on one of Sir John Lister-Kaye's farms, and both said they liked the country. It was a touch of home where we had least expected it, but it was by no means a solitary experience. Wherever we went, it seemed as if we met "oor ain folk," and these same folk seem generally to get "the guiding o't." That reflection should do more than fill our hearts with pride of old Scotland, it should bring home to those of us who are parents the additional responsibility of being parents of children who belong to a race who seemed bound to rise to high position and influence wherever they may go, the world over. The thought that the destinies of countries far away may one day largely rest in our children's hands should fill us with a noble ambition for them, that they may be able to say with others who have gone before—

"We cross the prairie as of old
    The pilgrims crossed the sea,
To make the West, as they the East,
    The homestead of the free.

"We go to plant her common schools
    On distant prairie swells,
And give the Sabbaths of the wilds
    The music of her bells.

"Upbearing, like the ark of old,
    The Bible in our van,
We go to test the truth of God,
    Against the foes of man."

Undoubtedly Scotchmen have largely had to do with the making of Canada, and happily they have for the most part left their mark on her for good. We find their names much associated too with the making of this wonderful railway, by means of which all this marvellous scenery is witnessed. If we think of what was considered a good road in these parts before the railway came, and then when we travel by this iron road cut through, or cut out of the sides of, perpendicular cliffs, the workmen in some cases having had to be lowered by ropes from above in order to get at their work, we get some idea of the change which has been wrought. From side to side of rushing waters the train crosses on trestle bridges like that of which we give you an illustration, and finds its way along ledges of rock, twisting and turning in every direction on the brink of the precipices below. On some parts of the road great wooden erections, called snow-sheds (having something of the character of tunnels), have had to be put up to protect the line from snow in winter. By this means the road is scarcely, if ever, blocked, even during heavy falls of snow. And thus, by one device and another, and by the exercise of constant, vigilant inspection, this railway company, though their system covers such an extent of country, and has to face so many perilous places, can, up to the present time, thankfully record that they have only lost the life of one passenger, and that was in consequence of his standing on the steps of the car after being warned by the conductor not to do so.

SOURCE

Excerpt of the Countess of Aberdeen's chapter ten, "The Rocky Mountains," from *Through Canada With a Kodak*, first edition 1893, with an introduction by Marjory Harper (Toronto: University of Toronto Press, 1994), 131–41.

and finally, from five varieties of divided skirts and bloomers, the following practical and becoming habit was evolved.

I speak thus modestly, as there is now a trail of patterns of this habit from the Atlantic to the Pacific coast. Wherever it goes, it makes converts, especially among the wives of army officers at the various Western posts where we have been—for the majority of women in the West, and I nearly said all the sensible ones, now ride astride.

When off the horse, there is nothing about this habit to distinguish it from any trim golf suit, with the stitching up the left front which is now so popular. When on the horse, it looks, as some one phrased it, as though one were riding side saddle on both sides. This is accomplished by having the fronts of

COSTUME FOR CROSS SADDLE RIDING.

Designed by the Author.

Costume for cross-saddle riding, designed by the author. From Grace Gallatin Seton-Thompson's A Woman Tenderfoot, *1900.*

GRACE GALLATIN SETON-THOMPSON

A Woman Tenderfoot (1900)

Excerpts

THIS BOOK IS A TRIBUTE TO THE WEST.

I have used many Western phrases as necessary to the Western setting.

I can only add that the events related really happened in the Rocky Mountains of the United States and Canada; and this is why, being a woman, I wanted to tell about them, in the hope that some going-to-Europe-in-the-summer-woman may be tempted to go West instead.

—*G.G.S.-T.*

New York City, September 1st, 1900.

I.
The Why of It

THEORETICALLY, I have always agreed with the Quaker wife who reformed her husband—"Whither thou goest, I go also, Dicky dear. What thou doest, I do also, Dicky dear." So when, the year after our marriage, Nimrod announced that the mountain madness was again working in his blood, and that he must go West and take up the trail for his holiday, I tucked my summer-watering-place-and-Europe-flying-trip mind away (not without regret, I confess) and cautiously tried to acquire a new vocabulary and some new ideas.

Of course, plenty of women have handled guns and have gone to the Rocky Mountains on hunting trips—but they were not among my friends. However, my imagination was good, and the outfit I got together for my first trip appalled that good man, my husband, while the number of things I had to learn appalled me.

In fact, the first four months spent 'Out West' were taken up in learning how to ride, how to dress for it, how to shoot, and how to philosophise, each of which lessons is a story in itself. But briefly, in order to come to this story, I must have a side talk with the Woman-who-goes-hunting-with-her-husband. Those not interested please omit the next chapter.

II.
Outfit and Advice for the
Woman-Who-Goes-Hunting-with-Her-Husband

IS IT REALLY so that most women say no to camp life because they are afraid of being uncomfortable and looking unbeautiful? There is no reason why a woman should make a freak of herself even if she is going to rough it; as a matter of fact I do not rough it, I go for enjoyment and leave out all possible discomforts. There is no reason why a woman should be more uncomfortable out in the mountains, with the wild west wind for companion and the big blue sky for a roof, than sitting in a 10 by 12 whitewashed bedroom of the summer hotel variety, with the tin roof to keep out what air might be passing. A possible mosquito or gnat in the mountains is no more irritating than the objectionable personality that is sure to be forced upon you every hour at the summer hotel. The usual walk, the usual drive, the usual hop, the usual novel, the usual scandal,—in a word, the continual consciousness of self as related to dress, to manners, to position, which the gregarious living of a hotel enforces—are all right enough once in a while; but do you not get enough of such life in the winter to last for all the year?

Is one never to forget that it is not proper to wear gold beads with crape? Understand, I am not to be set down as having any charity for the ignoramus who would wear that combination, but I wish to record the fact that there are times, under the spell of the West, when I simply do not *care* whether there are such things as gold beads and crape; when the whole business of city life, the music, arts, drama, the pleasant friends, equally with the platitudes of things and people you care not about—civilization, in a word—when all these fade away from my thoughts as far as geographically they are, and in their place comes the joy of being at least a healthy, if not an intelligent, animal. It is a pleasure to eat when the time comes around, a good old-fashioned pleasure, and you need no dainty serving to tempt you. It is another pleasure to use your muscles, to buffet with the elements, to endure long hours of riding, to run where walking would do, to jump an obstacle instead of going around it, to return, physically at least, to your pinafore days when you played with your brother Willie. Red blood means a rose-colored world. Did you feel like that last summer at Newport or Narragansett?

So enough; come with me and learn how to be vulgarly robust.

Of course one must have clothes and personal comforts, so, while we are still in the city humor, let us order a habit suitable for riding astride. Whipcord, or a closely woven homespun, in some shade of grayish brown that harmonizes with the landscape, is best. Corduroy is pretty, if you like it, but rather clumsy. Denham will do, but it wrinkles and becomes untidy. Indeed it has been my experience that it is economy to buy the best quality of cloth you can afford, for then the garment always keeps its shape, even after hard wear, and can be cleaned and made ready for another year, and another, and another. You will need it, never fear. Once you have opened your ears, "the Red Gods" will not cease to "call for you."

In Western life you are on and off your horse again at the change of a thought. Your horse is not an animate exercise-maker that John brings around for a couple of hours each morning; he is your companion, and shares the vicissitudes of your life. You even consult him on occasion, especially on matters relating to the road. Therefore your costume must look equally well on and off the horse. In meeting this requirement, my woes were many. I struggled valiantly with everything in the market, and finally, from five varieties of divided skirts and bloomers, the following practical and becoming habit was evolved.

I speak thus modestly, as there is now a trail of patterns of this habit from the Atlantic to the Pacific coast. Wherever it goes, it makes converts, especially among the wives of army officers at the various Western posts where we have been—for the majority of women in the West, and I nearly said all the sensible ones, now ride astride.

When off the horse, there is nothing about this habit to distinguish it from any trim golf suit, with the stitching up the left front which is now so popular. When on the horse, it looks, as some one phrased it, as though one were riding side saddle on both sides. This is accomplished by having the fronts of the skirt double, free nearly to the waist, and, when off the horse, fastened by patent hooks. The back seam is also open, faced for several inches, stitched and closed by patent fasteners. Snug bloomers of the same material are worn underneath. The simplicity of this habit is its chief charm; there is no superfluous material to sit upon—oh, the torture of wrinkled cloth in the divided skirt!—and it does not fly up even in a strong wind, if one knows how to ride. The skirt is four inches from the ground—it should not bell much on the sides—and about three and a half yards at the bottom, which is finished with a five-inch stitched hem.

Any style of jacket is of course suitable. One that looks well on the horse is tight fitting, with postilion back, short on hips, sharp pointed in front, with single-breasted vest of reddish leather (the habit material of brown whipcord), fastened by brass buttons, leather collar and revers, and a narrow leather band on the close-fitting sleeves. A touch of leather on the skirt in the form of a patch pocket is harmonious, but any extensive leather trimming on the skirt makes it unnecessarily heavy.

A suit of this kind should be as irreproachable in fit and finish as a tailor can make it. This is true economy, for when you return in the autumn it is ready for use as a rainy-day costume.

Once you have your habit, the next purchase should be stout, heavy soled boots, 13 or 14 inches high, which will protect the leg in walking and from the stirrup leather while riding. One needs two felt hats (never straw), one of good quality for sun or rain, with large firm brim. This is important, for if the brim be not firm the elements will soon reduce it to raglike limpness and it will flap up and down in your face as you ride. This can be borne with composure for five or ten minutes, but not for days and weeks at a time. The other felt hat may be as small and as cheap as you like. Only see that it combines the graces of comfort and becomingness. It is for evenings, and sunless rainless days. A small brown felt, with a narrow leather band, gilt buckle, and a twist of orange veiling around the crown, is pretty for the whipcord costume.

One can do a wonderful amount of smartening up with tulle, hat pins, belts, and fancy neck ribbons, all of which comparatively take up no room and add no weight, always the first consideration. Be sure you supply yourself with a reserve of hat pins. Two devices by which they may be made to stay in the hat are here shown. The spiral can be given to any hat pin. The chain and small brooch should be used if the hat pin is of much value.

At this point, if any man, a reviewer perhaps, has delved thus far into the mysteries of feminine outfit, he will probably remark, "Why take a hat pin of much value?" to which I reply, "Why not? Can you suggest any more harmless or useful vent for woman's desire to ornament herself? And unless you want her to be that horror of horrors, a strong-minded woman, do you think you can strip her for three months of all her gewgaws and still have her filled with the proper desire to be pleasing in your eyes? No; better let her have the hat pins—and you know they really are useful—and then she will dress up to those hat pins, if it is only with a fresh neck ribbon and a daisy at her belt."

I had a man's saddle, with a narrow tree and high pommel and cantle, such as is used out West, and as I had not ridden a horse since the hazy days of my infancy, I got on the huge creature's back with everything to learn. Fear enveloped me as in a cloud during my first ride, and the possibilities of the little cow pony they put me on seemed more awe-inspiring than those of a locomotive. But I had been reading Professor William James and acquired from him the idea (I hope I do not malign him) that the accomplishment of a thing depends largely upon one's mental attitude, and this was mine all nicely taken—in New York:—

"This thing has been done before, and done well. Good; then I can do it, and *enjoy* it too."

I particularly insisted upon the latter clause—in the East. This formula is applicable in any situation. I never should have gotten through my Western experiences without it, and I advise you, my dear Woman-who-goes-hunting-with-her-husband, to take a large stock of it made up and ready for use. There is one other rule for your conduct, if you want to be a success: think what you like, but unless it is pleasant, *don't say it.*

Is it better to ride astride? I will not carry the battle ground into the East, although even here I have my opinion; but in the West, in the mountains, there can be no question that it is the *only way*. Here is an example to illustrate: Two New York women, mother and daughter, took a trip of some three hundred miles over the pathless Wind River Mountains. The mother rode astride, but the daughter preferred to exhibit her Durland Academy accomplishment, and rode side-saddle, according to the fashion set by an artful queen to hide her deformity. The advantages of health, youth and strength were all with the daughter; yet in every case on that long march it was the daughter who gave out first and compelled the pack train to halt while she and her horse rested. And the daughter was obliged to change from one horse to another, while the same horse was able to carry the mother, a slightly heavier woman, through the trip. And the back of the horse which the daughter had ridden chiefly was in such a condition from saddle galls that the animal, two months before a magnificent creature, had to be shot.

I hear you say, "But that was an extreme case." Perhaps it was, but it supports the verdict of the old mountaineers who refuse to let any horse they prize be saddled with "those gol-darned woman fripperies."

There is also another side. A woman at best is physically handicapped when roughing it with husband or brother. Then why increase that handicap by wearing trailing skirts that catch on every log and bramble, and which demand the services of at least one hand to hold up (fortunately this battle is already won), and by choosing to ride side-saddle, thus making it twice as difficult to mount and dismount by yourself, which in fact compels you to seek the assistance of a log, or stone, or a friendly hand for a lift? Western riding is not Central Park riding, nor is it Rotten Row riding. The cowboy's, or military, seat is much simpler and easier for both man and beast than the Park seat—though, of course, less stylish. That is the glory of it; you can go galloping over the prairie and uplands with never a thought that the trot is more proper, and your course, untrammelled by fenced-in roads, is straight to the setting sun or to yonder butte. And if you want a spice of danger, it is there, sometimes more than you want, in the presence of badger and gopher holes, to step into which while at high speed may mean a broken leg for your horse, perhaps a broken neck for yourself. But to return to the independence of riding astride:

One day I was following a game trail along a very steep bank which ended a hundred feet below in a granite precipice. It had been raining and snowing in a fitful fashion, and the clay ground was slippery, making a most treacherous footing. One of the pack animals just ahead of my horse slipped, fell to his knees, the heavy pack over-balanced him, and away he rolled over and over down the slope, to be stopped from the precipice only by the happy accident of a scrub tree in the way. Frightened by this sight, my animal plunged, and he, too, lost his footing. Had I been riding side-saddle, nothing could have saved me, for the downhill was on the near side; but instead I swung out of the saddle on the off side and landed in a heap on the uphill, still clutching the bridle. That act saved my horse's life, probably, as well as my own. For the sudden weight I put on the upper side as I swung off enabled him to recover his balance just in time. I do not pretend to say that I can dismount from the off side as easily as from the near, because I am not accustomed to it. But I have frequently done it in emergencies, while a side-saddle leaves one helpless in this case as in many others.

Besides being unable to mount and dismount without assistance it is very difficult to get side-saddle broken horses, and it usually means a horse so broken in health and spirits that he does not care what is being strapped on his back and dangling on one side of him only. And to be on such an animal means that you are on the worst mount of the outfit, and I am sure that it requires little imagination on any one's part to know therein lies misery. Oh! the weariness of being the weakest of the party and the worst mounted—to be always at the tail end of the line, never to be able to keep up with the saddle horses when they start off for a canter, to expend your stock of vitality, which you should husband for larger matters, in urging your beast by voice and quirt to further exertion! Never place yourself in such a position. The former you cannot help, but you can lessen it by making use of such aids to greater independence as wearing short skirts and riding astride, and having at least as good a horse as there is in the outfit. Then you will get the pleasure from your outing that you have the right to expect—that is, if you adhere to one other bit of advice, or rather two.

The first is: See that for your camping trip is provided a man cook.

I wish that I could put a charm over the next few words so that only the woman reader could understand, but as I cannot I must repeat boldly: Dear woman who goes hunting with her husband, be sure that you have it understood that you do no cooking, or dishwashing. I think that the reason women so often dislike camping out is because the only really disagreeable part of it is left to them as a matter of course. Cooking out of doors at best is trying, and certainly you cannot be care free, camp-life's greatest charm, when you have on your mind the boiling of prunes and beans, or when tears are starting from your smoke-inflamed eyes as you broil the elk steak for dinner. No, indeed! See that your guide or your horse wrangler knows how to cook, and expects to do it. He is used to it, and, anyway, is paid for it. He is earning his living, you are taking a vacation.

Now for the second advice, which is a codicil to the above: In return for not having to potter with the food and tinware, *never complain about it.* Eat everything that is set before you, shut your eyes to possible dirt, or, if you cannot, leave the particular horror in question untouched, but without comment. Perhaps in desperation you may assume the rôle of cook yourself. Oh, foolish woman, if you do, you only exchange your woes for worse ones.

If you provide yourself with the following articles and insist upon having them reserved for you, and then let the cook furnish everything else, you will be all right:—

An aluminum plate made double for hot water. This is a very little trouble to fill, and insures a comfortable meal; otherwise your meat and vegetables will be cold before you can eat them, and the gravy will have a thin coating of ice on it. It is always cold night and morning in the mountains. And if you do not need the plate heated you do not have to fill it; that's all. I am sure my hot-water plate often saved me from indigestion and made my meals things to enjoy instead of to endure.

Two cups and saucers of white enamel ware. They always look clean and do not break.

One silver-plated knife and fork and two teaspoons.

One folding camp chair.

N.B.—Provide your husband or brother or sister precisely the same; no more, no less.

Japanese napkins, enough to provide two a day for the party.

Two white enamel vegetable dishes.

One folding camp table.

One candle lamp, with enough candles.

Then leave all the rest of the cooking outfit to your cook and trust in Providence. (If you do not approve of Providence, a full aluminum cooking outfit can be bought so that one pot or pan nests in the other, the whole very complete, compact and light.)

Come what may, you have your own particular clean hot plate, cup and saucer, knife, fork, spoon and napkin, with a table to eat from and a chair to sit on and a lamp to see by, if you are eating after dark—which often happens—and nothing else matters, but food.

If you want to be canny you will have somewhere in your own pack a modest supply of condensed soups and vegetables, a box or two of meat crackers, and three or four bottles of bouillon, to be brought out on occasions of famine. Anyway it is a comfort to know that you have provided against the wolf.

So much for your part of the eating; now for the sleeping. If you do not sleep warm and comfortable at night, the joys of camping are as dust in the mouth. The most glorious morning that Nature ever produced is a weariness to the flesh of the owl-eyed. So whatever else you leave behind, be sure your sleeping arrangements are comfortable. The following is the result of three years' experience:—

A piece of waterproof brown canvas, 7 by 10 feet, bound with tape and supplied with two heavy leather straps nine feet long, with strong buckles at one end and fastened to the canvas by means of canvas loops, and one leather strap six feet long that crosses the other two at right angles.

One rubber air bed, 36 by 76 inches (don't take a narrower size or you will be uncomfortable), fitted with large size double valve at each end. This bed is six inches thick when blown full of air. Be sure that sides are inserted, thus making two seams to join together the top and bottom six inches apart. If the top and bottom are fastened directly together, your bed slopes down at the sides, which is always disagreeable.

A sleeping bag, with the canvas cover made the full 36 inches wide. This cover should hold two blanket bags of different weight, and if you are wise you will have made an eider-down bag to fit inside all of these for very cold weather. The eider bag costs about $16.00 or $18.00, but is worth it if you are going to camp out in the mountains after August. Do without one or two summer hats, but get it, for it is the keynote of camp comfort.

Then you want a lamb's wool night wrapper, a neutral grey or brown in color, a set of heavy night flannels, some heavy woollen stockings and a woollen tam o' shanter large enough to pull down over the ears. A hot-water bag, also, takes up no room and is heavenly on a freezing night when the wind is howling through the trees and snow threatens. N.B.— See that your husband or brother has a similar outfit, or he will borrow yours.

The sleeping bags should be separated and dried either by sun or fire every other day.

Always keep all your sleeping things together in your bed roll, and your husband's things together in his bed bundle. It will save you many a sigh and weary hunt in the dark and cold. The tent and such things, you can afford to leave to your guide or to luck. If one wishes to provide a tent, brown canvas is far preferable to white. It does not make a glare of light, nor does it stand out aggressively in the landscape. You have your little nightly kingdom waiting for you and can sleep cosily if nothing else is provided. Whenever possible, get your bed blown up and your sleeping bags in order on top and your sleeping things together where you can put your hands on them during the daylight, or if that is impossible, make it the first thing you do when you make camp, while the cook is getting supper. Then, as you eat supper and sit near the camp fire to keep warm, you have the sweet consciousness that over there in the blackness is a snug little nest all ready to receive your tired self. And if some morning you want to see what you have escaped, just unscrew the air valve to your bed before you rise, and when you come down on the hard, bumpy ground, in less time than it takes to tell, you will agree with me that there is nothing so rare as resting on air. Nimrod used to play this trick on me occasionally when it was time to get up—it is more efficacious than any alarm clock—but somehow he never seemed to enjoy it when I did it to him.

For riding, it is better to carry your own saddle and bridle and to buy a saddle horse upon leaving the railroad. You can look to the guides for all the rest, such as pack saddles, pack animals, etc.

My saddle is a strong but light-weight California model; that is, with pommel and cantle on a Whitman tree. It is fitted with gun-carrying case of the same leather and saddle-bag on the skirt of each side, and has a leather roll at the back strapped on to carry an extra jacket and a slicker. (A rain-coat is most important. I use a small size of the New York mounted policemen's mackintosh, made by Goodyear. It opens front and back and has a protecting cape for the hands.) The saddle has also small pommel bags in which are matches, compass, leather thongs, knife and a whistle (this last in case I get lost), and there are rings and strings in which other bundles such as lunch can be attached while on the march. A horsehair army saddle blanket saves the animal's back. Nimrod's saddle is exactly like mine, only with longer and larger stirrups.

You have now your personal things for eating, sleeping and riding. It remains but to clothe yourself and you are ready to start. Provide yourself with two or three champagne baskets covered with brown waterproof canvas, with stout handles at each end and two leather straps going round the basket to buckle the lid down, and a stronger strap going lengthwise over all. Or if you do not mind a little more expense, telescopes made of leatheroid, about 22 inches long, 11 inches wide and 9 inches deep, with the lower corners rounded so they will not stick into the horse, and fitted with straps and handles, make the ideal travelling case; for they can be shipped from place to place on the railroad and can be packed, one on each side of a horse. They are much to be preferred to the usual Klondike bag for convenience in packing and unpacking one's things and in protecting them.

It is hardly necessary to say that clothes have to be kept down to the limit of comfort. Into the telescopes or baskets should go warm flannels, extra pair of heavy boots, several flannel shirt waists, extra riding habit and bloomers, fancy neck ribbons and a belt or two—for why look worse than your best at any time?—a long warm cloak and a chamois jacket for cold weather, snow overshoes, warm gloves and mittens too, and some woollen stockings. Be sure you take flannels. This is the advice of one who never wears them at any other time. A veil or two is very useful, as the wind is often high and biting, and I was much annoyed with wisps of hair around my eyes, and also with my hair coming down while on horseback, until I hit upon the device of tying a brown liberty silk veil over the hair and partially over the ears before putting on a sombrero. This veil was not at all unbecoming, being the same color as my hair, and it served the double purpose of keeping unruly locks in order and keeping my ears warm. A hair net is also useful.

Then you must not forget a rubber bath tub, a rubber wash basin, sponge, towels, soap, and toilet articles generally, including camphor ice for chapped lips and pennyroyal vaseline salve for insect bites. A brown linen case is invaluable to hold all these toilet necessaries, so that you can find them quickly. A sewing kit should be supplied, a flask of whiskey, and a small "first-aid" outfit; a bottle of Perry Davis pain killer or Pond's extract; but no more bottles than must be, as they are almost sure to be broken. In your husband's box, ammunition takes the place of toilet articles. I shall pass over the guns with the bare mention that I use a 30.30 Winchester, smokeless.

For railroad purposes all this outfit for two goes into two trunks and a box—one trunk for all the bedding and night things: the other for all the clothing, guns, ammunition, eating things, and incidentals. The box holds the saddles, bridles, and horse things.

In a pack train, the bed-rolls, weighing about fifty pounds each, go on either side of one horse, and the telescopes on each side of another horse—in both cases not a full load, and leaving room on the top of the pack for a tent and other camp things. The saddles, of course, go on the saddle horses. The cost of such an outfit, in New York, is about two hundred dollars each; but it lasts for years and brings you in large returns in health and consequent happiness.

I am willing to wager my horsehair rope (specially designed for keeping off snakes) that a summer in the Rockies would enable you to cheat time of at least two years, and you would come home and join me in the ranks of converts from the usual summer sort of thing. Will you try it? If you do, how you will pity your unfortunate friends who have never known what it is to sleep on the south side of a sage brush, and honestly say in the morning, "It is wonderful how well I am feeling."

But to begin:—

XV.

Someone Else's Mountain Sheep

...HOWEVER, all this flower and fruit piece was but an episode; the event of that journey was the intimate acquaintance we made of the Great Glacier of the Selkirks, and the nice opportunity I had to lose my life. And the only reason this tale is not more tragic is because, given the choice, I preferred to lose the opportunity rather than the life.

I wonder if I can give any idea to one who has not seen it what a snow slide really is; how it sweeps away every vestige of trees, grass, and roots, and leaves a surface of shifting, unstable earth almost as treacherous as quicksand.

Nimrod and I had paid a superficial visit to the Glacier the day before: that is, we had gone as far as its forefoot, a hard but thoroughly safe climb, and had explored with awe the green glass ice caves with which the Great Glacier has seen fit to decorate its lower line, wonderful rooms of ice, emerald in the shadows, with glacial streams for floors.

So the next morning we started out, intending a little bit to further explore the vast, cold, heartless ice sheet (vaster than all the Swiss glaciers together), but more to hunt for the warm beating heart of a mountain sheep, whose home is here. We had been travelling for miles in the wildest kind of earth upheavals, for the Selkirks are still hard and fast in the grip of the ice king; huge boulders, uprooted trees, mighty mountains, released but recently from the glacial wet blanket, when Nimrod discovered the stale track of a mountain sheep. We followed it eagerly till it brought us across the path of a snow slide. At that point it was about five hundred feet across, at an angle of forty-five degrees; below us a thousand feet was a vicious looking glacial torrent; above, an equal distance, was the lower edge of the glacier, the mother of all this devastation.

The fearless-footed mountain sheep had crossed this sliding crumbling earth and gravel incline with apparent ease. For us it was go on or go back. There was no middle course. The row of tiny hoof marks running straight across from one safe bank to the other deceived us. It could not be so very difficult. We dismounted; Nimrod threw the bridle over his horse's head and started across, leading his beast. The animal snorted as he felt the foothold giving way beneath him, but Nimrod pulled him along. It was impossible to stand still. It would have been as easy for quicksilver to remain at the top of an incline. Amid rattling stones and sliding earth they landed on the firm bank beyond, fully three hundred feet below me.

It was a shivery sight, but I started expecting the horse would follow. He, however, jerked back snorting and trembling, which unexpected move upset my equilibrium, uncertain at best, and I fell. Nothing but the happy chance of a tight grip on the reins kept me from sliding down that dreadful bank, over the rock into the water, and so into eternity (Please pardon the Salvation Army metaphor).

I had barely time to right myself and get out of the way of my horse, which now plunged forward upon the sliding rock with me. The terrified animal lost his head completely. I could not keep away from his hoofs. He would not let me keep in front, I dare not get above for fear I should slip under his feet, or below him for fear he should slide upon me. I lost my balance again while dodging away from him as he plunged and balked, but managed to grab his mane and we both slid a horrible distance. I could hear Nimrod shouting on the bank, but did not seem to understand him. I had the stage, centre front, and it was all I could attend to.

We were now opposite to Nimrod, but only half way across. Such an ominous rolling and tumbling of stones and tons of earth sliding down over the low precipice into the water! I expected to be with it each instant. Nimrod had started out after me. Then I understood what he was shouting: "Let go that horse." Why, of course! Why had I not thought of that? I did let go and, thus freed, managed to get across, falling, slipping, but still making progress until I reached the safe ground one hundred feet lower in a decidedly dilapidated condition. My animal followed me instinctively for a short distance, and Nimrod got him the rest of the way—I do not know how. It did not interest me then.

And the saddest of all, the mountain sheep had vanished into the unknown, taking his little tracks with him, so we had to back in a round-about way, without sheep, without joy—and without a tragedy.

SOURCE

Excerpts of Grace Gallatin Seton-Thompson's *A Woman Tenderfoot* (New York: Doubleday, 1900 / Page, 1900): the preface, "This Book Is a Tribute to the West," 7; chapter one, "The Why of It," 15–16; chapter two, "Outfit and Advice for the Woman-Who-Goes-Hunting-with-Her-Husband," 19–58; and chapter fifteen, "Someone Else's Mountain Sheep," 301–11.

SARA JEANETTE DUNCAN

A Social Departure (1893)

Excerpts

V.

...WE HAD, AS WE THOUGHT, but one day to spare in order to reach
Vancouver in time to set our foot on the ship, and sail according to the
instructions on our tickets; and while yet the lamps were lit outside our
swaying curtains, and a man from Little Rock, 'Arkansaw,' snored rhyth-
mically in the upper berth across the aisle, we devoted half an hour to a
vigorous discussion as to whether we should get off at Banff or The Glacier.
When we awoke we were forty miles beyond Banff, so we concluded
between the buttoning of one boot and the discovery of the other that the
phenomena at The Glacier must naturally be much better worth a visit
than the fashionable and frivolous life at Banff, and that there would
probably be just as good a hotel there, and just as many people anyway.
But these were the consolations of the crestfallen. As a matter of fact,
nobody ought to pass Banff. If you do you lay yourself open to the charge
from everybody who has gone before of having missed the very finest bit
of scenery on the trip. You may expect it, maddening as it is, from the most

amiable of your friends—not one of them will be able to refrain. The natural attitude toward this statement, and the one we persistently assumed, is of course one of flat negation, but privately I should advise you to avoid it, and see Banff.

Orthodocia and I had our first glimpse of the Rockies from the window of the 'ladies' toilet-room' between the splashes of the very imperfect ablutions one makes in such a place. It was just before sunrise, and all we could see was a dull red burning in the sky behind the wandering jagged edge of what might have been the outer wall of some Titanic prison. Orthodocia raised her hands in admiration, and began to quote something. I didn't, one of mine being full of soap, and ransacked my mind in vain for any beautiful sentiment to correspond with Orthodocia's. I found the towel though, which was of more consequence at the time; and then we both hurried forth upon the swaying rear platform of the car to join our exclamations with those of a fellow-passenger, whom we easily recognised to be the man from Little Rock, 'Arkansaw.'

As we stood there on the end of the car and looked out at the great amphi-theatre, with the mountains sitting solemnly around it, regarding our impudent noisy toy of steam and wheels, we remembered that we should see mountains with towers and minarets—mountains like churches, like fortifications, like cities, like clouds. And we saw them all, picking out one and then another in the calm grandeur of their lines far up along the sky. Orthodocia cavilled a little at the impertinence of any comparison at all. She thought that a mountain—at all events, one of these great western mountains, down the side of which her dear little England might rattle in a landslip—could never really look like anything but a mountain. It might have a superficial suggestion of something else about its contour, but this, Orthodocia thought, ought to be wholly lost in the massive, towering, eternal presence of the mountain itself.

'Let us go into abstractions for our similes,' said Orthodocia; 'let us compare it to a thought, to a deed, that men have thrust high above the generations that follow and sharp against the ages that pass over, and made to stay for ever there, and not to some poor fabrication of stone and mortar that dures but for a century or so, and whose builder's proudest boast might well be that he had made something like a mountain!'

'That's so!' said that man from Little Rock, 'Arkansaw.'

Orthodocia shuddered, and consulted her muse further in silence, while the dull red along the frontier east burned higher, flinging a tinge of itself on the foam of the narrow pale-green river that went tearing past, and outlining purple bulks among the mountains that lay between. There was something theatrical about the masses of unharmonised colour, the broad effects of light and shadow, the silent pose of everything. It seemed a great drop-curtain that Nature would presently roll up to show us something else. And in a moment it did roll up or roll away, and was forgotten in one tall peak that lifted its snow-girt head in supremest joy for the first baptism of the sun. It was impossible to see anything but the flush of light creeping down and over that far solemn height, tracing its abutments and revealing its deep places. It seemed so very near to God that a wordless song came from it, set in chords we did not know. But all the air was sentient with the song....

'How many feet, naow, do you suppose they give that mountin?' said the man from Little Rock, 'Arkansaw.'

Orthodocia and I stood not upon the order of our going, but went at once, vowing that it would be necessary to live to be very old in order to forgive that man.

Field is a little, new place on the line, chiefly hotel, where I remember a small boy who seemed to run from the foot of one mountain to the foot of another to unlock a shanty and sell us some apples at twenty-five cents a pound. But Field is chiefly memorable to us as being the place where the engine-driver accepted our invitation to ride with him. He was an amiable engine-driver, but he required a great deal of persuasion into the belief that the inlaid box upholstered in silk plush and provided with plate-glass windows that rolled along behind, was not indisputably the best place from which to observe the scenery. 'You see, if you was on the ingin' an' anythin' 'appened you'd come to smash certain,' he observed cheerfully but implacably. 'Besides, it's ag'inst the rules.'

Whereupon we invoked the aid of a certain Superintendent of Mechanics, who was an obliging person and interceded for us. 'Lady Macdonald did it,' he said, instancing the wife of our Premier, 'and if these young ladies can hold on'—he looked at us doubtfully, and Orthodocia immediately gave him several examples of her extraordinary nerve. We coveted a trip on the pilot—in vulgar idiom the cow-catcher—a heavy iron projection in front of the engines in America, used to persuade wandering cattle of the company's right of way. My argument was that in case of danger ahead we could obviously jump. The engineer appreciated it very reluctantly, and begged us on no account to jump, obviously or any way. And we said we wouldn't, with such private reservations as we thought the situation warranted. Finally we were provided with a cushion apiece and lifted on. To be a faithful historian I must say that it was an uncomfortable moment. We fancied we felt the angry palpitations of the monster we sat on, and we couldn't help wondering whether he might not resent the liberty. It was very like a personal experiment with the horns of a dragon, and Orthodocia and I found distinct qualms in each other's faces. But there was no time for repentance; our monster gave a terrible indignant snort, and slowly, then quickly, then with furious speed, sent us forth into space.

Now, I have no doubt you expect me to tell you what it feels like to sit on a piece of black iron, holding on by the flagstaff, with your feet hanging down in front of a train descending the Rockies on a grade that drops four and a half feet in every hundred. I haven't the vocabulary—I don't believe the English language has it. There is no terror, as you might imagine, the hideous thing that inspires it is behind you. There is no heat, no dust, no cinder. The cool, delicious mountain air flows over you in torrents. You are projected swiftly into the illimitable, stupendous space ahead, but on a steady solid basis that makes you feel with some wonder that you are not doing anything very extraordinary after all, though the Chinese navvies along the road looked at Orthodocia and me as if we were. That, however, was because Orthodocia's hair had come down and I had lost my hat, which naturally would not tend to impress the Celestial mind with the propriety of our mode of progression. We were intensely exhilarated, very comfortable and happy, and felt like singing something to the rhythmic roar of the train's accompaniment. We did sing and we couldn't hear ourselves. The great armies of the pines began their march upwards at our feet. On the other side the range of the stately Selkirks rose, each sheer and snowy against the sky. A river foamed along beside us, beneath us, beyond us. We were ahead of everything, speeding on into the heart of the mountains, on into a wide sea of shining mist with white peaks rising out of it on all sides, and black firs pointing raggedly up along the nearer slopes. A small cave in a projecting spur, dark as Erebus; the track went through it, and in an instant so did we, riding furiously into the echoing blackness with a wild thought of the possible mass of fallen-in *débris* which was not there.

Orthodocia and I wondered simultaneously, as we found out afterwards, what we should do if the rightful occupant of the cow-catcher—namely, the cow—should appear to claim it. It was impossible to guess. I concluded that it would depend upon how much room the cow insisted upon taking up. If we could come to terms with her, and she didn't mind going 'heads and tails,' she would find a few inches available between us; otherwise—but it would be unpleasant in any event to be mixed up in an affair of the sort. Cows suggested bears, not from any analogy known [in] natural history, but because a bear on that road was a good deal more probable an episode than a cow. Supposing a bear suddenly hurled in to our society, would he feel fear, or amazement, or wrath? Would he connect us in displeased astonishment with the immediate cause of his disaster, or would he sympathise with us as fellow-victims trapped further back? In either case, would he make any demonstration? These considerations so worked upon my mind that I actually expected the bear. In imagination I saw him tramping through the undergrowth to meet the great surprise of his life and of mine, and my sympathy was divided between us. I dwelt with fascination upon certain words of an American author— 'And the bear was coming on,' and I thought of the foolhardiness of travelling on a cow-catcher without a gun. With an imaginary rifle I des-patched the gross receipts of the cow-catcher for a week with great glory. I wondered what would be said in our respective home circles if the bear really came on. And as we alighted at The Glacier I confided to Orthodocia my bitter regret that he did not come.

VI.

IT WAS A STRANGE THING to find there in the silent solemn heart of the Rockies, under the great brow of one mountain and among the torrent-washed feet of its fellows, an elaborate little hostelry which pretended to be a Swiss *châlet* to match the scenery. One admires the *châlet* idea exceedingly from the outside, but with an entire and thorough apprecia-tion of the inconsistencies of the inside, which include various attractions and conveniences unknown to the usual Swiss *châlet*—from electric bells and hot-water baths to *asperges glacées* and pretty American waitresses with small waists and high heels to bring it to one. The conception can-not be defended on artistic grounds perhaps, but one must be far gone in aestheticism not to approve it on general principles. I must be pardoned for introducing the hotel at this point, for there was really nothing else to introduce, except the 'Loop' and the Great Glacier itself, which is its own post-office address. The Loop occurs a mile or two further on, and is as wonderful a convolution in engineering as any successful candidate could make in politics immediately after an election. We walked down to inspect this railway marvel the evening we arrived, while yet the thought of the bear that we might have met on the cow-catcher dwelt in our imaginations. Twilight was coming down among the mountains that went straight and sheer up into the evening sky at our very feet, and the tall pines and shaggy juniper bushes behaved in an extraordinary manner. In consequence of these things, Orthodocia and I saw five bears apiece and ran all the way back with the ten in hot pursuit: which is one reason why I can't adorn this page with an exact description of the remarkable engineering feat we went to see. But the bears are worth something. There was one more, by-the-way, a baby-bear chained up in the hotel grounds, who would tear one's clothes in the cunningest way, in as many places as one would permit, for an apple. In Orthodocia's note-book he figures as the eleventh bear we experienced in the Rockies: but this being a sober chronicle I prefer to give its readers what might be called the benefit of the doubt.

Next morning we sallied forth to climb the Glacier. We took a small boy as a mere formality on account of the bears, but we found him useful before long on other accounts. For, while horses and mules are promised to convey the tourist of next year to the base of the phenomenon aforesaid, the tourists of last year had to walk; and the walk is a two-mile climb, more properly, over rocks, across (by stepping-stones) the torrent that the sun sends down from the Glacier every day, and under Douglas firs that tower seventy feet above you, with the sunlight filtering down through them upon mosses that are more vividly, vitally green than anything I ever saw out of British Columbia. The grimy small boy's grimy small hand as he skipped from rock to rock over the clear green water that swirled past them, was an invaluable member. A small dog was attached, necessarily, I suppose, to the small boy—an alarmist small dog, who persisted in making wild excursions into the forest, barking volubly in the distance, and adding potential bears to Orthodocia's note-book. This is the way she put them down:

Bear (?)

But she used a lead pencil, and I dare say the interrogation point became obliterated in the course of time.

We maintained our purpose of climbing the Glacier with the utmost steadfastness the whole way. In fact, we took it for granted that we should get to the top in the course of the morning—that everybody did—so confidently that we didn't think it necessary to mention the matter to the small boy until we were almost there. The manner in which he received our intention was not encouraging. He whistled. It was a loud long contemptuous whistle, with a great deal of boy in it: and we resented it, naturally.

'What do you mean?' said Orthodocia. 'Don't people usually go up?'

'Naw!'

'Has nobody *ever* got to the top? That's just like you Americans!'—to me—'What do you think Providence gave you mountains for, if he didn't intend you to climb them? I suppose'—scornfully—'you're waiting for somebody to put up "elevators" for you?'

'Ye-p—No-p!' answered the small boy, a trifle confused. 'Three or four English blokes went up explorin' this summer, but not this way. They went round somehow'—describing an indefinite arc with his arm—'an' it took 'em ten days. Found a bed of ice up there seven mile wide, an' mountin sheep that jest stood still an' got shot, lookin' at 'em. Ladies,' continued the small boy, with mighty sarcasm, 'generally git s'fur's this. Then they say, "How perfeckly lovely!" an' go back to th' 'tel. Ladies ain't meant for explorin'. I ain't ben up there myself yet, though.'

Thus consoled, we decided that life might be worth living even without including the conquest of the Great Glacier of the Rockies. It looked rather a big phenomenon to take liberties with when we arrived at its base, though Orthodocia ascended it to a height of at least five feet and was brought down again in safety by the small boy. Its wavelike little hollows were slippery and ankle-breaking, and great cracks yawned through it suggestively. On close inspection it was a very dirty Glacier indeed, to look so vast and white and awful a little way off, though the torrent that rushed from its feet down through the valley to the canyon of the Fraser was clear as crystal. Being athirst, we wanted to drink the glacier water, but the small boy, for whom we were beginning to acquire a prodigious respect, would not permit this. 'Snow-water,' he said, would give us fever—we must find a spring. Then we entered, and sat down in a beautiful blue ice-cave under the Glacier, fell into the usual raptures an ice-cave inspires, and took two bad colds which lasted longer.

The windows of our special corner of the *châlet* were low and broad, and the mountains that were gathered about brought night down soon. We leaned out, and looked and listened, after the last tourist soul besides ourselves had closed his door on his dusty boots and sought repose. The moonlight gleamed broadly on the still gray sea in the gap; a shining white line chased itself, murmuring, down the dark height before us; over the mighty head of 'Sir Donald' a single star hung luminous. We left our shutters wide for the song of the one and the benediction of the other.

There is a satisfaction that is difficult to parallel in getting as far as you can go. Orthodocia and I felt it when we had left the snow-capped mountains, in their stern, remote, inaccessible beauty, behind, and sped through the softer, kinder, cloudier heights of the Yale Canyon to Vancouver.

SOURCE

Excerpts of Sara Jeannette Duncan's *A Social Departure: How Orthodocia and I Went Round the World by Ourselves*, third edition (London: Chatto & Windus, 1893), 40–51.

Camp at Maligne Lake. *Photograph by Mary Schäffer, 1908. From Mrs. George Cran,*
A Woman in Canada, *1910. (WMCR V527/NA–65)*

MRS. GEORGE CRAN

"The Rocky Mountains and British Columbia" (1910)

from A Woman in Canada

FROM EDMONTON TO CALGARY. The pulses dance to think of it, for that means a journey afterwards through the Rocky Mountains, the wonderful, the world-famed! Before I leave the prairie city, however, which to me must ever be connected with pictures of the Agricultural Commission and long talks on poultry, I meet Mrs. Balmer Watt, an interesting journalist, whose little book *Town and Trail* is very well worth reading by any woman who thinks of settling in Edmonton. The Press all over Canada has been very good to me; here and now I would like to tender it my heartiest thanks. Mrs. Balmer Watt has been caught by the spirit of the West, the bias of her mind leads her to analyze and brood over it, unlike the majority who merely take it for granted and enjoy it. "Out on the prairies," she says, "face to face with their naked souls, men and women come into possession of a depth of wisdom impossible to attain surrounded by the distractions of the town. And what, after all, is the secret

143

of the spirit that animates the whole West...from the centre of the newest cities to the uttermost ends of the farthest distant homesteads...but the joy of labour, the satisfaction of knowing in each man's hands lies the possibility of his own future?" True words.

I leave Edmonton, the beautiful, prosperous capital of Alberta, built on the banks of a gold-bearing river, and storm Calgary in a mazy hurry to see Mr. Turner's ranch; he is out of town, so I miss the ranch, but am entertained delightfully by the editor of the *Calgary Herald*, with whose wife I have a long talk about the need of maternity nurses on the prairie. More of that later. And then Calgary, the capital of Ranchland, the gate to the Rocky Mountains—happy Calgary nestling in the beautiful cup that is neither prairie nor mountain, but girt with both—Calgary moves away from the train, and I watch her fade into distance; we are approaching the great gate of the mountains which stretches between the prairies and the Pacific slopes. Travellers tell of it, how it towers to heaven and leans to hell, how it is riven of valleys and gives back sound with a terrible voice, how it is ranged by the bear and shadowed by the lone eagle. Men with pens dipped in fire have told of the Rockies, I will be betrayed into no competition with them. The air that sweeps by is brilliant and rare, so rare that it makes a novice "out of breath," but it gives at the same time a tremendous exhilaration of spirits. That phrase comes old and stale, it sounds like the sort of thing everybody will say who speaks of mountains, but it means a very great deal, it means that one is happy—and happiness is the gift of the gods, sought desperately all the world over, from the loafer in a gin-palace to the King watching his horse win the Derby. I lean from the end of the car, and the silver rails slip away from our wheels. As we approach the greatest scenic track of railway in the world a fellow-traveller tells of the old days of the road when men fed on fishy pork—pork which in its lifetime had wandered by the shore eating dead salmon—the days when they shot for the pot and not for sport, when they lived for a week on a trumpeter swan and fed on white beans for a fortnight. Here is the perfected result of those days of travail for all the world to enjoy. As the train enters the Bow River Valley and the mountains close in upon us, I learn the taste of awe.

Under Mount Stephen stands a brown house built of wooden shingles, in the hall is a great open hearth where logs burn continuously. Here the sportsmen come and go—go in a flurry of earnest hope, and return excited or depressed as they have found the sport, though they never come back empty-handed. If they have not grizzly bear they have black bear, if not caribou they have deer. Standing by the dancing logs I watch the last bear-parties come in from Leanchoil, very happy and excited, with three splendid skins; a slight fair woman who has been standing near the fire too, for the first snow has fallen, goes up to them and talks about their sport. Presently one of them calls her by name, "Mrs. Schäffer"; I look at her with intense interest, there could hardly be two women of that name in this particular spot. It is known to everyone that she started from here in June intending to go over the Wilcox Pass, down the Athabasca, and up the Miette River, across the Yellowhead to the old Tête Jaune Câche. Every one has heard how she started on horseback with one other woman, two guides and a pack-train of twenty-two horses. There can hardly be two Mrs. Schäffers, I tell myself, at this place in September. I study her closely; she has fair hair that has been burned fairer by the sun, a skin once fair, now deeply tanned, slim arms that are browner still, and a smooth voice with a strong American accent. What can this little woman have in her so fearless that she is gaining the reputation of an intrepid explorer? Her manner is gentle; one derides the notion of a bias to masculinity; perhaps she is so sincerely an artist that she loves the virgin wild before its bloom is pushed aside by the white man's presence, for the red man defiles no more than the caribou or wandering bear. If this is the Mrs. Schäffer I mean, she is the woman who lectures before geographical societies, who illustrated with her brush the *Alpine Flora of the Canadian Rockies*, who has written for the *Canadian Alpine Journal* and the *Geographical Journal of Philadelphia*, and who lectured in Boston before the Appalachian Club; the woman who goes on exploring expeditions for three or four months at a time—and who is mentioned by Kipling in his *Letters*.

Later in the day we meet and talk, and I see the companion of her travels for the last three expeditions, Miss Adams, a little dark, neat woman and a keen geologist, with a head shaped beautifully like that of an Egyptian priest. They talk amusingly, and without the least pride, of their "trip," they show me countless photographs taken on the way. "First you must meet Mr. Muggins. He is the dearest. See his sad face, he got to thinking us a parcel of lunatics at times when we kept him too long on the raft. Oh! and you *must* see the raft, it was the most primitive thing, but we were so proud of it. When we found the horses could not swim the Maligne we 'unpacked' them and got across on the raft, it was the only way. Another time we had to unpack them and coax them one by one over a twenty-foot bluff with a rope. I say 'we' did, but really our two guides did; they are both Englishmen, and nobody can imagine the care and trouble those two men took! The passing of that bluff is becoming history in the country. It was always supposed to be impassable. I am afraid the photograph is rather indistinct."

It is rather, but I manage to make out the figure of a perturbed horse coming down a precipice at an acute angle, and a row of others looking nervously on from above.

"Here is our camp on the Maligne Lake. We had great trouble in finding that lake. We got there eventually from a map drawn by Sampson Beaver, one of the Stony Tribe, an Indian who had never seen a map in his life. It was the crudest pencil sketch in the world, but it served its purpose. It is twenty miles long, and has never known a sound save the moccasined foot of the Indians. Ours was the first white man's camp in that far-away hunting ground. Here is our pack-train—yes, the figure on horseback is me—we both wore breeches in the wild, it's safer, skirts are a concession to civilization. Say, isn't this child cute? Her mother is a quarter-breed and her father a white man, yet look at the Indian in that child! See the way she carries her doll. And she brought it in a moss-bag!

Here is a tiny picture of the raft going over the lake; do look at Mr. Muggins being carried over the Saskatchewan, he is very amusing when the water is at all rough. He just sits and cries till he is carried, and when he is safe in his master's arms he looks as proud and indifferent as possible. Here is our dinner-table. You see it shows five diners, and obviously another present to take the photograph. That comes about because the first month we had Mr. Brown the botanist and his guide with us. After that we were only the four. Here is Mount Robson, the highest mountain in the Rocky range, and at the most only photographed twice before."

"What made you begin?" I ask.

"Well!—I began with the botanical work, making small explorations in search of plants. In that way I learned to live on horseback, to camp out two days, four days, a week, two weeks, a month, four months, and so on; to jump muskegs, to take a loaded animal up and round rock ridges, to keep a foothold on slippery, sliding mud. After I had learned so much it was hard to sit with folded hands listening politely to the stories of Colin, Stutfield, Wooley, Outram, Fay, Thompson and Coleman of the hills I so longed to see—stories of the vast unexplored glorious country *beyond!* It bred rebellion. We looked to each other and said, 'Why not? We can starve as well as they; a muskeg will be no softer for us than for them, the ground will be no harder to sleep on, the waters no deeper to swim nor colder if we fall in.'"

So they talk; telling vivaciously, without vanity, of their amazing venture; giving photographs, some of which appear in this chapter. The "muskeg" referred to is bogland; it is the word used over here for dangerous, treacherous bogs which seem to abound both in the Rockies and Ontario. (I am liable to remember the Ontarian belt as I was caught in the Kenora washout, where a cloud-burst washed away a long stretch of track built over difficult boggy land, and my train was thirty hours late arriving at Winnipeg!) I met Miss Agnes Laut, the authoress; I go to Emerald Lake and wonder, as every traveller wonders, at the deep green waters, clear and brilliant, cradled among the mountains, with no apparent excuse for their wonderful colour. The châlet is empty, it is late in the year for travellers, but the man in charge comes out to see how we are impressed with his beautiful lake. Directly he speaks I know him for English—he is a Birmingham man. We chat a little, he is of the rover type and loves the wild mountain fastnesses. We mention New Street, the Arcade, Five Ways, Hagley Road—each name painting a different picture of the busy Midland metropolis to our English minds—the words strike crudely on the ear by the calm waterside, they echo incongruously up the steeps, though we speak softly—he takes his pipe out of his mouth and looks across the green water—looks at the jagged heights about him, looks to the sunset and grows silent. He would not go back. He could not. If he did the mountains would call till his heart broke. Returning to Mount Stephen, Otto the guide shows me how to "shy" straight. He sees a spruce-partridge on a bough and kills it with a stone. I am impressed less with his skill than with the instinct to kill which animates all his conversation, and is after all his means of livelihood. He tells me that the spruce-partridge is usually known as the fool-hen because of its silly habit of sitting still to be stoned, also that the ruffed willow-grouse is protected by law. He has lived at Leanchoil and Field for seven years, and knows all the trails for two hundred miles round. I ask if one can fish much here, and he tells tales of the trout in the Kootenays, of the silver and grey heckle, of fishing up to ice-time till my ears ache to hear the keen swish of a line cleaving the air, my eyes to see a silver fly tip the water. Next day I find the west-bound train is cancelled, so start forth to try riding astride; the indescribable mosses, the trees gnawed by porcupine, the thickets bright with scarlet bunch-berries lure one to brave the passes; I find a beast which proves a very Samson among gees; after two or three hours he makes for home just as violently as he started away from it; he has galloped and curveted up the Yoho Pass in great good humour, utterly regardless of the tremors which might possibly possess a rider unused to Rocky Mountain roads. I am wondering if there is any chance of slipping into the hotel unseen—there are no side-saddles "out West." Walking feels odd in this kit. Other women can look very smart and workman-like in the queer Mexican saddles, and out of them too, but I haven't yet "got the habit." Round the last perilous corner, past the livery barn, and over the shining railway track we dash to the hotel steps. I peer about me in the dusky light and cautiously prepare to dismount. No one who has not been in one knows how many humps there are on these Western saddles. I am swaying and struggling in great disturbance of mind when a civil voice offers help.

A lady of apparently forty or so, with one of those even voices that go with "decided" opinions, has seen my difficulties. I explain my modest apprehensions, and she tells me she has felt the same, also that she has been up the Burgess Pass alone and is only just down. I am engineered over the humps and out of the funny wooden stirrups, and I thank her with great respect. Fancy climbing the Burgess alone! The Yoho with a horse is bad enough.

We meet at breakfast next morning and I find she is a very handsome girl of twenty-seven or there-abouts, brilliant in conversation, intelligently vague in all her opinions. It is impossible to *think* and be "decided" since the discovery of radium. There are some buckwheat cakes on the menu, and we have two helpings, then tell each other we are greedy.

"But all nice things are greedy," she says, "babies, you know, and dogs and roses."

I tell her of my vain efforts to grow roses on the sand in Surrey; she tells me to try basic slag, and we wander into a highly technical discourse on rose manners, on habits and varieties, winding up with Mendelian theories.

"I am taking home some seeds of the wild prairie-roses," I tell her, "to try and breed out a garden variety that will stand hard winters."

"So am I," she cries.

We stare, then laugh. Here we are, two lone Englishwomen who have drifted together for an instant in the toil of travel, and a chance word reveals us both bent on the same quest, infinitely interested in the same problems.

She has some relatives lately settled in British Columbia, and has heard so much talk of Canada that she has come out to see for herself if she would like to live in it. She has trained as a horticulturist, and asks what chances there are for women out here.

"Endless ones for the right kind," I answer warmly. "England is glutted with female labour, Canada faints for want of it. It looks like the simplest problem in the world to solve. In reality it is bristling with difficulties."

Her clever face crinkles into lines of perplexity.

"How?" she asks.

"Because Englishwomen are used to a communal life. That's why," I answer.

She muses, and I watch her strong, fine face with interest and pleasure. She seems to me to be the embodiment of the best kind of Englishwoman, the kind so greatly needed out West. There is courage in her and endurance, gentleness and refinement too, and all these qualities are lit by the radiant intelligence that beams from every glance.

"You are sure to stay at Victoria later on," she says. "Will you ring me up and tell me if you have time and inclination to stay a few days with me out on the farm?"

We say good-bye. I see her embark on the west-bound train with regret—another of the "ships that pass in the night."

SOURCE

Excerpt of Mrs. George Cran's "The Rocky Mountains and British Columbia," chapter ten from *A Woman in Canada* (London: John Milne, 1910), 179–91.

Maligne Lake. *Photograph by Mary Schäffer, 1908. Published as* Lake Elizabeth *in Mrs. Humphrey Ward's,* Lady Merton, Colonist, *1910.* (WMCR V527/PS–69)

MRS. HUMPHRY WARD

Lady Merton, Colonist (1910)

Excerpts

A Foreword.

TOWARDS THE END of this story the readers of it will find an account of an "unknown lake" in the northern Rockies, together with a picture of its broad expanse, its glorious mountains, and of a white explorers' tent pitched beside it. Strictly speaking, "Lake Elizabeth" is a lake of dream. But it has an original on this real earth, which bears another and a real name, and was discovered two years ago by my friend Mrs. Schäffer, of Philadelphia, to whose enchanting narratives of travel and exploration in these untrodden regions I listened with delight at Field, British Columbia, in June, 1908. She has given me leave to use her own photograph of the "unknown lake," and some details from her record of it, for my own purposes; and I can only hope that in the summers to come she may unlock yet other secrets, unravel yet other mysteries, in that noble unvisited country which lies north and northeast of the Bow Valley and the Kicking Horse Pass.

—*Mary A. Ward*

Chapter VII.

OH! THE FRESHNESS OF THE MORNING on Lake Louise!

It was barely eight o'clock, yet Elizabeth Merton had already taken her coffee on the hotel verandah, and was out wandering by herself. The hotel, which is nearly six thousand feet above the sea, had only just been opened for its summer guests, and Elizabeth and her party were its first inmates. Anderson indeed had arranged their coming, and was to have brought them hither himself. But on the night of the party's return to Laggan he had been hastily summoned by telegraph to a consultation of engineers on a difficult matter of railway grading in the Kootenay district. Delaine, knocking at his door in the morning, had found him flown. A note for Lady Merton explained his flight, gave all directions for the drive to Lake Louise, and expressed his hope to be with them again as expeditiously as possible. Three days had now elapsed since he had left them. Delaine, rather to Elizabeth's astonishment, had once or twice inquired when he might be expected to return.

Elizabeth found a little path by the lake shore, and pursued it a short way; but presently the splendour and the beauty overpowered her; her feet paused of themselves. She sat down on a jutting promontory of rock, and lost herself in the forms and hues of the morning. In front of her rose a wall of glacier sheer out of the water and thousands of feet above the lake, into the clear brilliance of the sky. On either side of its dazzling whiteness, mountains of rose-coloured rock, fledged with pine, fell steeply to the water's edge, enclosing and holding up the glacier; and vast rock pinnacles of a paler rose, melting into gold, broke, here and there, the gleaming splendour of the ice. The sun, just topping the great basin, kindled the ice surfaces, and all the glistening pinks and yellows, the pale purples and blood-crimsons of the rocks, to flame and splendour; while the shadows of the coolest azure still held the hollows and caves of the glacier. Deep in the motionless lake, the shining snows repeated themselves, so also the rose-red rocks, the blue shadows, the dark buttressing crags with their pines. Height beyond height, glory beyond glory—from the reality above, the eye descended to its lovelier image below, which lay there, enchanted and insubstantial, Nature's dream of itself.

The sky was pure light; the air pure fragrance. Heavy dews dripped from the pines and the moss, and sparkled in the sun. Beside Elizabeth, under a group of pines, lay a bed of snow-lilies, their golden heads dew-drenched, waiting for the touch of the morning, waiting, too—so she thought— for that Canadian poet who will yet place them in English verse beside the daffodils of Westmoreland.

She could hardly breathe for delight. The Alps, whether in their Swiss or Italian aspects, were dear and familiar to her. She climbed nimbly and well; and her senses knew the magic of high places. But never surely had even travelled eyes beheld a nobler fantasy of Nature than that composed by these snows and forests of Lake Louise; such rocks of opal and pearl; such dark gradations of splendour in calm water; such balanced intricacy and harmony in the building of this ice-palace that reared its majesty above the lake; such a beauty of subordinate and converging outline in the supporting mountains on either hand; as though the Earth Spirit had lingered on his work, finishing and caressing it in conscious joy....

Epilogue.

ABOUT NINE MONTHS LATER than the events told in the last chapter, the August sun, as it descended upon a lake in that middle region of the northern Rockies which is known as yet only to the Indian trapper, and— on certain tracks—to a handful of white explorers, shone on a boat containing two persons—Anderson and Elizabeth. It was but twenty-four hours since they had reached the lake, in the course of a long camping expedition involving the company of two guides, a couple of half-breed *voyageurs*, and a string of sixteen horses. No white foot had ever before trodden the slender beaches of the lake; its beauty of forest and water, of peak and crag, of sun and shadow, the terror of its storms, the loveliness of its summer—only some stray Indian hunter, once or twice in a century perhaps, throughout all the aeons of human history, had ever beheld them.

But now, here were Anderson and Elizabeth!—first invaders of an inviolate nature, pioneers of a long future line of travellers and worshippers.

They had spent the day of summer sunshine in canoeing on the broad waters, exploring the green bays, and venturing a long way up a beautiful winding arm which seemed to lose itself in the bosom of superb forest-skirted mountains, whence glaciers descended, and cataracts leapt sheer into the glistening water. Now they were floating slowly towards the little promontory where their two guides had raised a couple of white tents, and the smoke of a fire was rising into the evening air.

Sunset was on the jagged and snow-clad heights that shut in the lake to the eastward. The rose of the sky had been caught by the water and interwoven with its own lustrous browns and cool blues; while fathom-deep beneath the shining web of colour gleamed the reflected snows and the forest slopes sliding downwards to infinity. A few bird-notes were in the air—the scream of an eagle, the note of a whip-poor-will, and far away across the lake a dense flight of wild duck rose above a reedy river-mouth, black against a pale band of sky.

They were close now to the shore, and to a spot where lightning and storm had ravaged the pines and left a few open spaces for the sun to work. Elizabeth, in delight, pointed to the beds of wild strawberries crimsoning the slopes, intermingled with stretches of bilberry, and streaks of blue and purple asters. But a wilder life was there. Far away the antlers of a swimming moose could be seen above the quiet lake. Anderson, sweeping the side with his field glass, pointed to the ripped tree-trunks, which showed where the brown bear or the grizzly had been, and to the tracks of lynx or fox on the firm yellow sand. And as they rounded the point of a little cove they came upon a group of deer that had come down to drink.

The gentle creatures were not alarmed at their approach; they raised their heads in the red light, seeing man perhaps for the first time, but they did not fly. Anderson stayed the boat—and he and Elizabeth watched them with enchantment—their slender bodies and proud necks, the bright sand at their feet, the brown water in front, the forest behind.

Elizabeth drew a long breath of joy—looking back again at the dying glory of the lake, and the great thunder-clouds piled above the forest.

"Where are we exactly? " she said. "Give me our bearings."

"We are about seventy miles north of the main line of the C. P. R., and about forty or fifty miles from the projected line of the Grand Trunk Pacific," said Anderson. "Make haste, dearest, and name your lake!—for where we come, others will follow."

So Elizabeth named it—Lake George—after her husband; seeing that it was his topographical divination, his tracking of the lake through the ingenious unravelling of a score of Indian clues which had led them at last to that Pisgah height whence the silver splendour of it had first been seen. But the name was so hotly repudiated by Anderson on the ground of there being already a famous and an historical Lake George on the American continent, that the probability is, when that noble sheet of water comes to be generally visited of mankind, it will be known rather as Lake Elizabeth; and so those early ambitions of Elizabeth which she had expressed to Philip in the first days of her Canadian journeying, will be fulfilled....

It seemed as though the golden light could not die from the lake, though midsummer was long past. And presently up into its midst floated the moon, and as they watched the changing of the light upon the northern snow-peaks, they talked of the vast undiscovered regions beyond, of the valleys and lakes that no survey has ever mapped, and the rivers that from the beginning of time have spread their pageant of beauty for the heavens alone; then, of that sudden stir and uproar of human life—prospectors, navvies, lumbermen—that is now beginning to be heard along that narrow strip where the new line of the Grand Trunk Pacific is soon to pierce the wilderness—yet another link in the girdling of the world.

SOURCE

Excerpts of Mrs. Humphry Ward's foreword, chapter seven, and epilogue from *Lady Merton, Colonist* (Toronto: Musson Book Co., 1910), 129–31, 329–32, and 336–37.

THREE

Free Among the Everlasting Hills

Botanists and Brides

"I AM NO MOUNTAINEER, only a very ordinary walker," wrote Mary Gibson of Glasgow, Scotland while visiting Glacier House near the Illecillewaet Glacier in the Selkirk Mountains on 11 July 1902. And while she found the walk from the hotel to both Marion Lake just to the west and the glacier to the southeast to be "comparatively easy," she realized that "Some climbing I think is necessary if one wants to understand how fascinatingly beautiful the scenery is. The true grandeur of the mountains can hardly be understood by looking at them from the hotel" (Gibson in Glacier House Scrapbook 1902).

Gibson's comments encapsulate two streams of women writers and photographers whose Rocky Mountain travel narratives struck a chord with readers around the turn of the twentieth century: both arrived by train but one group, gathered in the previous section on literary travellers, experienced a mountain holiday as a by-product of the trains and hotels built to attract tourists in comfort; the second sought something more physically demanding, intellectually challenging, and personally invigorating. Members of the latter group, whose work makes up this section and the two following, often spent three to four months a year in successive years in the area, using the CPR hotels as departure points for travels "off the beaten path" of the railways into the Rocky and Selkirk mountains. Their accommodations were tents, their transportation was by horseback, and their accomplishments were outstanding in the fields of landscape photography, botanical watercolour painting and photography, and travel writing. Their friendships were warm, their spirit of adventure mutual, their assistance to one another essential, and their respect for one another's achievements immense. Among their shared adventures in the Rockies, Mary Vaux and Mary Schäffer were the first white women to explore the Nakimu Caves discovered near Glacier House in 1905, a day on which they also found new wildflower specimens.

While the Banff Springs Hotel was the birthplace of tourism in the Rocky Mountains, Glacier House launched mountaineering in Canada, for women and men alike, and was the first area to offer the services of professional

Swiss mountaineering guides. The Glacier House Scrapbook in which Gibson wrote was maintained at the hostelry first built by the CPR in 1887 in Glacier National Park in the Selkirk Mountains. The Illecillewaet (or Great) Glacier had descended to five thousand feet in 1886 when the CPR carved its way through nearby Rogers Pass affording rail passengers a magnificent view. The steep grade of the area made it prohibitive for locomotives to pull heavy dining cars through the area, and so Glacier House was built as one of three stopping points between Calgary and Vancouver for rail travellers to have a meal (the others being Mount Stephen House at Field west of the Kicking Horse Pass over the Continental Divide and the Fraser Canyon House at North Bend).

Between 1897 and 1920, Glacier House was managed by three women in succession. The first two were Annie and Jean Mollison, Scottish immigrants who joined the staff of the CPR in 1888 as housekeepers at the Banff Springs Hotel. Both women moved among the various CPR Rocky Mountain hostelries at Field, North Bend, and Lake Louise, serving as managers, until the First World War. At Glacier House from 1897 until 1899, they were succeeded by Mrs. Julia Young from Montreal, who had trained at Mount Stephen House, and her assistant Helen McGibbon until 1920. (Mary Schäffer explains how Mrs. Young came to be in the employ of the CPR in a letter of 1934.) Glacier House closed in 1926, its popularity having declined from 1916 when track was tunnelled through the area, eliminating both the grade problem and repeated closure of the tracks because of avalanches, but bypassing Glacier House. In addition, peaks in the surrounding area had all been climbed successfully, and so mountaineers who had used Glacier House as their base moved further afield in pursuit of first ascents. The building was torn down in 1929.

The Glacier House Scrapbook was a collection of visitors' comments on the scenery, geography, and experiences in the area that convey a taste of the crowd enticed to spend some time there; from these entries one can imagine the tenor and tone of end-of-day conversations after walks to the Illecillewaet Glacier and climbs in the area. (In the 1890s, the glacier was a twenty minute walk away; between 1895 and 1995, it receded about one and a half kilometres and is now about a three-hour uphill hike from the Glacier House site.) An occasional entry by or about women in the Scrapbook accounts for a variety of experiences and viewpoints. Perhaps more importantly, these entries draw attention to some of the ways in which women climbers and explorers, such as Mary Gibson, were thinking about themselves at the time. Alpinist and author William Putnam examined the Scrapbook when it emerged among CPR historical materials in 1965. It disappeared again shortly thereafter but, to posterity's good fortune, Putnam had made a photocopy, and so reproductions are available in the archives at the Whyte Museum of the Canadian Rockies and at the National Archives of Canada while Glacier House's guest register is extant in the collection of the British Columbia Archives.

The woman most closely associated with the Illecillewaet Glacier was Mary Vaux Walcott (1860–1940) who spent forty summers working in the Banff, Glacier, and Yoho mountain parks as an amateur botanist, watercolourist, photographer, and glaciologist. Vaux first visited the Selkirk and Rocky mountains, along with her younger brothers George Jr. (a lawyer) and William (a structural engineer), in 1887, travelling on the new Canadian Pacific Railways. Stopping at Glacier House with their Kodak camera, they made photographs of the Great Glacier. When they returned in 1894, the Vauxes were startled by the recession of the glacier that had taken place and within five years had established formal studies of its movement, followed by those in the neighbouring Yoho area. They published their studies, including photographs and texts, for scientific purposes. Mary made the photographic prints while the texts were written both alone and together by the men, William until his death in 1908 and George Jr. until 1910 when he withdrew from the glacier project. Prior to 1910, Mary Vaux's publications and lantern slide lectures focused on mountain wildflowers, camping, and photography. After 1910, she occasionally published glacier work, including a brief article in the *Canadian Alpine Journal* in 1913. Her last glacier publication in 1922 was a third edition of the

Mary M. Vaux with Swiss guide crossing snow bridge, c. 1900. (Vaux Family Fonds, WMCR V653/NA–181)

Vaux family's foundational 1900 work, *The Glaciers of the Canadian Rockies and Selkirks*, a work written for the general public and distributed by the CPR as a promotional brochure.

The Vaux family's home was in Philadelphia where they were active Quakers. As such, Mary belonged to a society that valued women's rights and education as well as held a deep reverence for the natural world. Unlike her brothers, Mary Vaux was not afforded a post-secondary education after their mother Sarah died in 1879; nevertheless, her work in the mountains of Canada is valued for both its scientific and aesthetic qualities. The mapping of the recession of the Illecillewaet Glacier between 1887 and 1913, which included extensive photographic documentation, is the Vaux family's most famous and valued work. Among these grand images, embracing both panoramic vistas as seen only from peaks, such as that

Mary Vaux with ice axe at the Illecillewaet Glacier, 1899. (Vaux Family Fonds, WMCR V653/NG–596)

made in 21 July 1900 when Mary Vaux became the first woman to summit Mount Stephen and enclosing terrain along glaciers or from streambeds in valleys are photographs that the Vaux siblings made of each other and their exploring companions. Certainly the most engaging image of Mary Vaux is that made on 17 August 1899. She poses in profile at the forefoot of the Illecillewaet Glacier, the rubble and small stream over which she has scrambled in the foreground, dressed in her standard hiking garment of a long dark skirt and jacket, and brimmed hat (essential for protection from both sun and rain). Her ice axe was of a type in common use at the time, an indispensable tool for gaining a grip on ice, cutting steps for footholds, and probing the terrain ahead of their steps for hidden crevasses.

Vaux was responsible for developing the dry glass plates and printing the photographs which she did, while at Glacier House, in a basement

Takakkaw Falls
from Below, *1901*.
(Vaux Family Fonds,
WMCR V653/NG–855)

room that was set up to suit her needs. She was a skilled photographic printer who excelled in platinum prints that preserved the nuances of the glaciers' tonal range. Her photographs were printed and published to support the men's scientific publications as well as the CPR's promotional interests. They also appeared in a feature on the British Empire in *National Geographic* in 1916. The Rocky Mountain landscape subject matter and fine composition of the platinum prints distinguished these photographs when they were also exhibited in fine art photograph exhibitions first with the Photographic Society of Philadelphia and then in New York among the Photo-Secessionists who were gathered together by Alfred Stieglitz. Vaux also applied her watercolour skills to the photographs by producing hand-tinted lantern slides for her lectures on wildflowers and camping in the Rocky Mountains during winters in Philadelphia. "A camera is a very delightful adjunct," Vaux wrote in 1908:

for it is pleasant to have some tangible results to show, on your return home. A kodak, if no larger instrument can be managed, yields most satisfactory results, although the better records from a larger-sized camera are an increased delight, when one has the patience and skill to obtain them...Then, when you return to civilization, you will have many happy memories, and the "call of the wild" will so enter your blood, that you will count the days till you can again be free among the everlasting hills. (Vaux 1908, 69–70)

Vaux's memberships in numerous societies are an indication of the range of her knowledge, interests, and accomplishments. These included the Academy of Natural Sciences in the United States, the American Association for the Advancement of Science, both the American and Canadian Alpine clubs, the Photographic Society of Philadelphia, and the Photo-Secession in New York. She also served as president of the Association of Women Geographers in the United States and on the Board of Indian Commissioners in the late 1920s. Furthermore, Vaux was a respected botanical photographer and painter whose extensive and well-regarded descriptive and illustrated work *North American Wildflowers* was published by the Smithsonian Institution in 1925.

Mary Vaux's avocation as a botanical artist and photographer represents a common thread among nineteenth- and early twentieth-century women travellers in North America, especially those in the Rocky Mountains of Canada. Botany was a field of scientific endeavour well-populated by amateurs, women and men alike. Among Quakers for whom scientific study and the natural world were held in esteem, collecting and identifying botanical specimens under the Linnaean system of classification was a widespread and serious activity for both professionals and amateurs, women and men. Amateur scientific study in general was a significant activity for educated North Americans. The Vaux family's glaciology studies, for example, while taken seriously by professional scientists, were nevertheless the work of keen, well-informed amateurs. In the Victorian age,

Prairie Crocus, Pasque-Flower, or Wind-Flower (Anemone patens), *also known as* Anemone des prairies. *Photograph by Mary M. Vaux.* (WMCR V653/PS—164)

botany was considered a suitable feminine pursuit. Not only was it associated with domestic hobbies such as gardening, flower arranging, and flower painting, it engaged women in the natural world that many believed proved God's existence through its creation. Botany also offered an activity outdoors that provided healthy exercise for both body and mind. Mary Vaux explains:

> Wild Flowers were a joy and inspiration in the happy days of childhood when I was taught to observe and sketch them under the direction of a skilled artist. Years passed before a botanical friend at Glacier, British Columbia, asked me to portray a rare and perishable alpine flower so as to preserve its beauty, color, and graceful outline as a living thing. During succeeding seasons I painted other rare specimens until many of the "living flowers that skirt in the

eternal frost" in the wildflower gardens of the Canadian Rockies were transferred in color and form to the East. (Walcott 1925, Foreword)

Scientific study, from glaciology to botany also proved to be a common meeting ground for men and women, especially so along the CPR line through the Rocky and Selkirk mountains. In 1914, Vaux married Charles Walcott, a geologist and invertebrate paleontologist at the Smithsonian Institution whom she met near Field, B.C., where he was engaged in study of his most famous discovery, the fossils of the Burgess Shale. Vaux's letters to Walcott, written prior to their marriage and now in the collection of the Smithsonian Institution, demonstrate clearly shared interests in their intellectual lives. Vaux's friend and fellow Philadelphia Quaker, Mary Townsend Sharples, also met her first husband, physician and amateur botanist Charles Schäffer, when introduced by the Vaux family at Field in 1889. They too shared an interest in the natural world.

Like Vaux, Mary Sharples Schäffer's childhood education in Philadelphia included flower painting, and she first earned a name for herself in the 1890s working as a photographer and painter on her husband's project as an amateur botanist to catalogue the wildflowers of the Rocky and Selkirk mountains between Banff and Glacier House. After Dr. Schäffer's death in 1903, Mary Schäffer finished the project with the assistance of Stewardson Brown, a professional botanist at the Philadelphia Academy of Natural Sciences. Their work, published under Brown's name in 1907 as *Alpine Flora of the Canadian Rocky Mountains*, included seventy-nine colour paintings and monochromatic photographs by "Mrs. Charles Schäffer." Schäffer went on to publish a variety of articles, illustrated with her photographs, of alpine flora.

Schäffer's accomplishment in seeing her husband's work completed seemed diminished, however, at least in Schäffer's eyes, when Mrs. Julia Henshaw, whom she had taught to photograph wildflowers in the Rocky Mountains, betrayed her fellowship by publishing *Mountain Wild Flowers of America* one year earlier. Mary Vaux's photograph of Henshaw with walking stick in hand and Schäffer on horseback is a rare artifact of these women's

Julia Henshaw and Mary Schäffer. Photograph attributed to Mary M. Vaux. (WMCR V653/NG 4–908)

interwoven paths. Born and raised in Durham, England, Julia Wilmotte Henderson (1869–1937) emigrated to Canada in 1887 after marrying Charles Henshaw of Montreal. They settled in Vancouver where she worked for four years on the editorial staff of the *Vancouver Province*, writing under the pen name of Julian Durham. She also contributed articles to a variety of magazines, including *The Girls' Own Paper, Lady's Pictorial*, and *The Traveller*. She published her first book, *Hypnotized? Or the Experiment of Sir Hugh Galbraith*, in Toronto in 1898, followed by *Why Not Sweetheart?* (1901) prior to publishing three botanical books between 1906 and 1915. Julia Henshaw also served as vice-president of the Vancouver Women's Canada Club and was a member of the Canadian Society of Authors as well as the Society of Authors of England, the Alpine Club of Canada, and the Authors' Club in London, England.

Schäffer's anger was still sharp in 1937 when, following Henshaw's death, she wrote:

When Dr. S. was working among the plants at Glacier, those long gone years, I began to note Julia's interest in his work. She asked so many inane questions regarding his form of work, then she annoyed me by insisting that she watch my painting. She had no art drill and of course it was quite useless. Then she got interested in my part of photographing plants. That is an art in itself and I gladly showed her what is called vertical photography. But it never entered my head what had already gone into her own.
(Warren, 26 November 1937)

Henshaw sought a popular rather than scientific audience, as the title of her work suggests, and organized her catalogue by colour of flower, in contrast to Schäffer and Brown's organization by the scientific relationship of the various species. Furthermore, Henshaw's descriptions were more narrative than scientifically descriptive, as the excerpt to follow shows, and all illustrations were black-and-white photographs. Schäffer was acutely aware of the difference. Describing her work with Stewardson Brown to complete Dr. Schäffer's botanical study in the Rockies, Schäffer wrote:

We were at it at least three years and just about the time it was to come from the press, I learned Julia had brought out the edition of which you must have seen many copies. Knowing this, I wrote her as kindly a letter as I could, told her I was glad hers had come first for mine was only meant in memory of a great botanist and I trusted it would not interfere with her work. No reply.

Then I went to Glacier to go on with other work wh. meant thousands of slides all colored. I knew the book was good because scientific societies, etc., rushed to buy the work and I then brought out a second edition. The C.P.R. by this time, was taking no interest in scientific books and it was getting very expensive to go on issuing the work.

Reaching Glacier the following summer, I was aghast that Julia would not speak. By this time I knew in what way I could MAKE her speak for I knew she would be after the slide tricks. It came about as I knew and then she urged me to color at least 500 slides for her. This I refused to do. I was too tired of being colied and then hearing absurd statements. I suppose you know what her "war work" consisted of as well as I do. She truly HAD to earn the living but one could feel sorry at the methods she took.

(Warren, 26 November 1937)

This incident and Schäffer's perception of it reveals something of the serious nature of amateur botany and the competitive environment in which these women worked.

In 1907, opportunity for women and men to publish articles, photographs, and poetry about their mountain experiences in Canada—rather than full-length books whose popularity waned after the First World War—emerged with the launch of the *Canadian Alpine Journal* published by the newly founded Alpine Club of Canada. Vaux, Schäffer, and Henshaw all published with the journal. The majority of contributors were (and remain) hikers and climbers who are alpinists and mountaineers first, writers or photographers second. Their primary audience is Club members who share a passion for mountain exploration and who read of others' experiences for both entertainment and information, as the earliest explorers and climbers did with the travel books of the later nineteenth century. The *Journal* is especially important for women's mountain history and culture because it is one of the few venues in which their work is to be found in any quantity. Even then, women's contributions are sorely outnumbered by those of men, a phenomenon that has not abated in the early twenty-first century.

Peter and Catharine Whyte, c. 1935. (WMCR V653/I.c.2.b)

In contrast are the private letters of painter, photographer, and philan-thropist Catharine Robb Whyte (1906–1979). Whyte was the daughter of a well-to-do family in Concord, Massachusetts with a lineage in both the arts and business. She arrived in Banff in 1930, newly married to a local man, Peter Whyte (1905–1966). Catharine and "Pete" had met as student artists at the School of the Museum of Fine Arts in Boston in the late 1920s and settled in Banff after their marriage. Whyte was trained as a figure painter in the academic tradition but turned to landscape painting when she moved to Banff and spent much of the spring, summer, and fall months sketching with Pete and other artists, such as J.E.H. MacDonald, in the Rocky Mountains backcountry. In the 1930s, along with her husband, she returned to portrait painting for a period of time as they made a series of works of locally significant people from outfitters to Stoney chiefs. During that decade, she and her husband also concentrated and collaborated, like the Vaux family before them, on photographing Rocky Mountain landscapes and vistas. Whyte did not pursue a professional career and almost never sold her work. An exchange took place on one occasion, however, when Whyte traded her portrait of Mrs. Twoyoungmen for a grizzly bear skin owned by Norman Luxton. Although she produced and retained a body of landscape sketches in oils, Whyte finished very few large works and exhibited rarely. A notable exception was an exhibition of works in Concord and Ontario in 1948 and 1949.

Like many women in the Rockies before her, Whyte too became a world traveller who explored beyond the Rockies to Asia, the Pacific, Europe, and North America. She was also a prolific and engaging correspondent whose letters, written for the pleasure of her mother and family in Massachusetts, are vibrant with details of life and people encountered in the Rocky Mountains. Unlike the correspondence of women travellers of the generation who preceded her in the Rockies, however, these letters were never published as a book. Nor do they read as though Whyte ever wrote with such an intention in mind. Although she must have met and known Schäffer, no mention of the legendary resident can be found in Whyte's letters. She did meet and know Mary Vaux, however, as well as many of the other women named in this collection.

Whyte invested considerable time and talent in her letter writing, and there is a sense throughout that she was aware that the quality of her writing would be subject to scrutiny and comment—probably by her mother, Edith Morse Robb. Over one thousand letters are extant, the output of a dutiful daughter whose façade cracked one time only in a letter dated 31 August 1931, never sent to her mother, yet retained. An intensely personal expression, the letter rings with Whyte's tension and frustration at her mother's treatment of her as a child, her sense of coming second in her mother's love, the strong mutual bond with her father, and her dedication to her husband. The figure that emerges is that of a mid-twentieth century woman of means (one letter refers to her allowance of $300 a month) who attended to expectations of feminine priority and duty to family and was generous with time and attention for others—much like the women before her. What distinguishes Whyte is that she brought with her to Banff an American philanthropic tradition that she ultimately funnelled into the Whyte Foundation with its mandate to collect and disseminate the history of the Rocky Mountains of Canada. Whyte's own extensive and well-organized collection of Rocky Mountain artifacts and ephemera formed the foundation of an extraordinary repository.

Unlike Vaux and Schäffer's published and unpublished accounts of their journeys and a growing abundance of popular and academic literature on Vaux and Schäffer's lives and work, Whyte's letters are unedited and unpublished (although stringently selected in their gathering here), and her painting, collecting, and philanthropic practices have not been studied. Catharine Whyte's letters merit publication in association with a critical biographical study of her writing, painting, and philanthropy in the context and tradition of well-educated and materially comfortable eastern American women—established by Vaux, Schäffer, and their contemporaries—travelling to the Rocky Mountains of Canada.

Rocky Mountain women looked to one another across the generations for friendship, competition, inspiration, and advice. In a profound gesture of friendship and gratitude that stands today as evidence and symbol of these women's diverse and important relationships, Mary Schäffer, upon achieving her greatest ambition as an explorer, remembered and honoured Mary Vaux by naming a mountain overlooking Maligne Lake in tribute. A striking view of *Mount Mary Vaux at the Head of Maligne Lake* was subsequently published in Schäffer's book. Naming the peak, and memorializing it and its namesake in a published photograph, was a resounding claim for women's right to seek their place in Rocky Mountain wilderness, scientific study, and human history.

EDITOR'S NOTE

The title of this section, "Free Among the Everlasting Hills," is taken from Mary M. Vaux's "Camping in the Canadian Rockies," *Canadian Alpine Journal* 1 (1908), 70. See quotation on page 198.

"Glacier House Scrapbook" (1897–1910)

Excerpts

LOOKOUT MOUNTAIN. SEPTEMBER 10, 1898

A party composed of the following persons ascended to Glacier Crest. Mrs. Dr. Schäffer, Mrs. Nesbitt, Miss Reid, Mr. Nesbitt and Mr. F.M. Bell-Smith with two porters. The trail up to the timber line is steep but well defined and the summit was reached in three hours. Here the artist Mr. Bell-Smith stopped to paint while the rest of the party continued on to the crest. Several very successful photographs were made by Mrs. Schäffer notably one overlooking the Glacier, the crevasses being seen to great advantage from this point. The weather was very fine and warm the sky being almost cloudless.

[Anon]

I have spent a very pleasant week at this hotel, & nothing could exceed the kindness & attention I have received from Miss Mollison & the rest of the staff. My only climb was Eagle Peak, which, the guide being unwell, I had to do alone. I could obtain no information from anybody as to any portion of the route, so the following notes may be useful. Ascend to the top of the 2nd Cascade (a trail might with advantage be cut to this point)— follow the stream up the valley to small glacier at the head of the latter. Turn to left up rock and stone slopes; follow long straight couloir up to final rocks. Bear slightly to the right, & an easy but amusing scramble takes you to the summit. The view is superb. The ascent should take 5–6 hours, & for fairly good mountaineers is not difficult or dangerous, tho' it appears to be rarely attempted. A lantern should be always taken.

It seems a great pity that more facilities are not afforded to would-be climbers in this delightful district. If more were cut, & competent guides for rock and ice work were obtainable, Glacier House would soon be a popular centre for mountain excursions. I would also suggest that the C.P.R. authorities should provide a big telescope with stand &c., of the type familiar in Alpine hotels. Such things are always popular.

Hugh E.M. Stutfield
6 Charles St. Berkeley Square. London W.

I came here yesterday meaning to leave for the West today, but much knocking about the world has taught me the wisdom of devoting a little extra time to the enjoyment of a really charming place when I am fortunate enough to find it; so "today" has come, the train has come and gone, and I am still happy in the thought that my kind hostess, Miss Mollison, will for another day at least, make me forget that there is aught in this world but such sweet content at Glacier.

W.A. Fraser
Georgetown, Ont. Canada

THE FIRST ASCENT OF SIR DONALD BY A LADY. AUGUST 3, 1901

On Aug. 3rd 1901 my wife & self reached the summit: she thus being the first lady to accomplish the feat. Having done so much, she thinks that I should undertake the task of writing the account.

I may say that neither of us had done any mountain climbing before. My sole experience had been the ascent of Mt. Avalanche a few days before as experiment: hers had been confined to stiff though not dangerous climbs to Avalanche Crest, the slopes below Mt. Abbott, & the summit of Asulkan Pass, & fossil beds on Mt. Stephen. We therefore made our attempt with some feelings of diffidence, not being able to derive much comfort from a perusal of the very different accounts of previous trips contained in the interesting Minute Book.

I may say however that we did not expect "the mere saunter over flat ledges" which one gentleman enjoyed: perhaps the road has been broken up a little since his trip! Anyway the rocks did not remind us much of the pavement of Piccadilly. Still, practised mountaineers no doubt look at these things with a more lenient eye than do mere novices. On the other hand we hoped to escape the dreadful storm & tempest mentioned in another account and in this we were indeed fortunate, the weather being perfect.

On the whole we derived most comfort from Mr. Stutfield's calm & temperate account & certainly took to heart his advice "not to hold any mountain too cheaply."

We however held ourselves rather cheaply when we rose at the unearthly hour of 2 A.M. on the eventful morning.

We had only confided our secret to a chosen few, not being over-confident of success, but one or two others seemed to 'smell a rat': one gentleman, in particular, asked me once or twice the day before whether we were going to try. I could reply with perfect truth that I was *thinking* of it: and I certainly *did* think hard during the day & night before.

Soon dressed, we made our way toward the kitchen, guided by a savoury smell of fried bacon and found the guides ready with an excellent breakfast, Clarke being a great cook in addition to his other accomplishments. We cannot pretend to give a scientific account of our climb: words such as arête, couloir, névé, bergschrund etc. were unknown to us and for all we knew, might have been the names of ferocious animals which inhabit these mountains.

We had no barometer or thermometer, though the genial Mark Twain relates that he found the latter instrument very useful: he used to boil it! and as water boils at a lower temperature at great heights, he evolved the great theory that the higher you appear to be, the lower you really are!

We started at 3:15, my wife riding a pony kindly furnished by Mrs. Young, who did all in her power to help us. She was thus able to ride for nearly an hour, which was a great help. We started under a bright moon which about the time we passed the great glacier began to pale before the rival luminary. (N.B. I am *not* getting a penny a line). We left the pony about 4 and went steadily up the rest of the trail, or to the glacier of Sir Donald & up the snow slopes: here my wife slipped and fell, but only lost her axe, which careened gaily down for a long distance: however the ever-active Clarke soon retrieved it and caught us up in time for second breakfast at 7 o'clock on the snow, under the rocks of the great amphitheatre...It was decidedly cold and we stayed 20 minutes, then started for the real work....

We found quite a crowd on our arrival and my wife was quite embarrassed by the kind and hearty reception when she rode on to the lawn. I did not state that she was dressed for the occasion, in—er—well—certain nether garments of mine and putties, as she thought that even the shortest skirt might be inconvenient or even dangerous....

R. Berens
England

AUGUST 4, 1901. A MERE WOMAN'S ACCOUNT

It really seems very hard on me that I should be made to write an account of our climb—but being an obedient child—I always do (sometimes) as I am told. Before deciding on taking the trip I was greatly puzzled as to what I should wear. As for being a new woman, I had nothing intentionally packed away at the bottom of my trunk, and did not think it safe to attempt the climb, cliff and thrills. After talking to some kind friends, Mrs. Schaeffer suggested I should go through my husband's wardrobe. The result was I picked out a pair of something and naturally, being a woman, I picked out the best. Having been a girl all my life, it was certainly embarrassing, to say the least, suddenly blossoming into a boy. However, that trial being over we started off. I must mention one thing that generally amused me. I kept unconsciously holding a piece of cloth in my hand when we were walking on the level—I suppose being a girl so long I had got accustomed to holding up my dress....

I only want to write from a woman's point of view, but what I would like to suggest to any lady climbing is first, to wear knickers; second, puttees to prevent her legs being knocked to pieces by the rocks; third, good preparation with plenty of rest; fourth, to start as early as possible; fifth; to be sure and to have a sandwich, and an orange or lime, if thirsty on the way; sixth, a coat, which the guides will carry, to wear on the top as it is cold up there. I should not advise gloves on the rocks, as they are apt to get wet and slippery and one can get a firm hold with the figures.... As I said before that I have not that wonderful *gift* of sitting down and writing page after page—but trying to describe such grandeur as is to be seen at the top of Sir Donald is utterly beyond.

E. Evelyn Berens
St. Mary Cray
K[ent] E[ngland]

JULY 11, 1902

Arriving at Glacier Hotel on the 4th inst. with my friend, I have spent a very pleasant week. Although it rained heavily when I came and continued to do so all the following day I did not feel discouraged or let some good folks make up my mind to leave next day and see if the sun is not shining some other place further on. From the window of our delightful little sitting room I watched the wonderful mist clouds passing over the two splendid summits of Sir Donald and Eagle Peak and I would say to those disheartened travellers who arrive here in wet weather and can only give vent to their feelings in grumblings that if they look up to the mountains and watch the wonder & beauty of the clouds passing over there they will, I think find a pleasure that will make them confess that even in rain the rocky peaks heaving through the mists can look grand and even "awesome." The path up to Marion Lake I found easy and most delightful as it is under the pines all the way and shaded from the sun and the wooded surroundings are so pretty. I am no mountaineer only a very ordinary walker and I found this walk, also the one up the cascade on the hill opposite the Hotel, and also to the Great Glacier comparatively easy. The enjoyment has been great, and I am sure everyone who comes to Glacier ought to spend some days so as to properly see the beauties of it. Some climbing I think is necessary if one wants to understand how fascinatingly beautiful the scenery is. The true grandeur of the mountains can hardly be understood by looking at them from the hotel.

Mary Gibson
Glasgow, Scotland

JULY 11TH

I cordially endorse what my friend Miss Gibson has written, and merely wish to add that the view of the Great Glacier from the path up to Cascade Summit is the finest to be had by those who, like myself, do not care to climb very high. The path is very good and the time required not more than half an hour. I must also express our gratitude to Mrs. Young and Miss M. Gibbion [McGibbon] for their kind attention to us in arranging everything for our comfort and [quiet] in our part of the hotel.

Jane E. Dawson
Glasgow, Scotland

MOUNT BONNEY, ASCENT BY A LADY. SEPTEMBER 2, 1904

On Sept 1st I chanced to be seated comfortably on Mt. Afton with Christian Bohren, from where Mt. Bonney looked so superlatively beautiful that then and there we decided to "try it" next day. Wherefore by 3:15 A.M. on the 2nd Sept. Bohren and I were astride sure-footed cayuses & on these we made our way to the second bench on Mt. Abbot. The moon had paled

& the stars had fled before the first rays of the sun, when at 5:15, we parted from our steeds & their guide.

We started at a steady pace to the right passing a patch of snow which bore the foot-prints of some huge bear. Soon we had turned the shoulder of Abbot & Mt. Bonney came into view, a steady scramble over boulders brought us to the valley between Abbot & Afton, more scrambling over large boulders varied by struggles through scrub pine & rhododendron and we reached the first moraine of the Lily Glacier. The foot of the Lily was crossed, then its second moraine and by 8 o'cl we were by the foot of Bonney's huge fissured glacier.

Now we had to decide our route, for Ch. Bohren had never been on Mt. Bonney before, moreover very few ascents had ever been made; we were far to the left of the glacier, and in front of us, afar off, there was a saddle, steep snow & a small amount of rock appeared to lead to it. To the right for a great distance the rocks were perpendicular, we decided to go for the saddle. Many detours had to be made to avoid the crevasses and there was much step cutting. At length we reached the base of the mountain and work began in earnest, up a long steep ice & snow field we scrambled & reached the bad piece of rock we had seen from below; here Bohren was prospecting for some feasible way upwards when an avalanche pounded down the slope we had just left. Snow did not seem so interesting for a little while. With some difficulty we found a way over the bad bit of rock, and eventually reached the snow-wall & cornice at the top. It was 10:30, half an hour after we made our first halt and had some most welcomed breakfast. The views were magnificent; to the south stretched a vast snow-field then over the Geikie snow-field we saw Dawson, Deville & Fox with many other magnificent peaks, most of them as yet nameless & unscaled. Sir Donald & the adjacent peaks were to the eastward over the peaks on the Asulkan to the west lay the steep snow-fields which we had yet to cross to reach the summits. After half an hour we started & made the first point on which is a cairn presumably erected by Mr. Wheeler—a long descent & very steep snow-field brought us to the next summit on which we built a stone-man and we immediately started for the third point a considerable distance off but of about the same altitude. Here there was a cairn & this was the summit made by Mr. Green in '88 when he had made the first ascent of Mt. Bonney. We reached this summit at 1 o'clock. We then proceeded down an easy snow slope for 1/2 an hour & made a second short halt. By two o'cl we began the descent. We had decided not to return over the various points & considered the distance to the moraines of Ross Peak too great, though this would probably have been the best way. The slope we had chosen soon turned into wet shale devoid of footholds, & this in turn gave place to an excessively steep ice field wherein ladder-like steps were cut with much difficulty. After two extremely unpleasant hours we reached the glacier by four o'clock, were off it by five and started home across the shoulder of Afton & Abbot. This homeward scramble became somewhat severe after dark and it was ten o'clock before we reached Glacier House—We had been nineteen hours out—Christian Bohren's skill and patience were beyond praise.

Henrietta L. Tuzo
Warlingham England

SEPT. 5, 1904

Ascent of Avalanche Crest by the undersigned—a little girl of 6 years & 7 months.

Eleanor Carrole Robbins

Avalanche, 9365 ft., is a high and hard enough mountain to scale for anyone who does not claim to be an especially skillful climber. A very thirsty pony took me a little beyond the Summit Cascade, and at 8.10 A.M. Eduard Feuz Jr. and I commenced our day's work. We did the moraine slowly and comfortably, and roped upon having reached the first glacier. Soon a thrilling incident happened. Eduard lost his pipe, which came sliding towards me but was promptly stopped in its wild and mad career down the glacier. The loss of this comforter would have been a serious blow to Eduard, and might have spoiled his temper and our trip. A wide crevasse across the glacier—a part of the actual Bergschrund—presented a wonderful, awe-inspiring sight. Eduard pronounced it more like a thousand ft. deep—we could not see the bottom of it—and huge icicles had formed in it adorned its walls like so many gigantic prisms. Once across the Bergschrund, the ascent was soon accomplished and we reached the summit at 10.00 P.M [A.M.]—not a bit tired. The weather was ideal, the view of the Selkirks perfect but the Rockies hidden, owing to smoke. I tried to count the glaciers and snow peaks which were ever increasing in number as we approached the summit, but found it an impossible task; suffice it to say that the sight of that still, white world of eternal snow and sublime grandeur can never be forgotten by one who has been fortunate enough to behold it. We encountered again some difficulty in crossing the Bergschrund on our way down, but Eduard proved himself master of the situation and had no pity on me when I declared myself unable to cross the Schrund where he wanted me to. I simply had to do it and accomplished the seemingly impossible feat quite easily after all. Now followed two most exhilarating glissades, and then the walk across the glacier, or rather snowfield, to Avalanche Crest. Here we unroped and our homeward journey began in earnest. A brood of ptarmigan bade us welcome on our return into the world of the living, and the little things were so ignorant of fear and the wiles of men, we could have caught them on the spot. We reached the hotel a few minutes to seven, after a 12 hours' most enjoyable outing. The view from Avalanche amply compensates for "that tired feeling" which the excursionist will experience upon his return, and Eduard Feuz Jr. cannot be improved upon as a guide.

Lulu Grau

Honolulu, Hawaiian Islands

AUG. 19, 1905

MT. ABBOTT BY A LADY IN AN AFTERNOON.

A little stroll up to Marion Lake, made for exercise on a rainy afternoon developed quite unpremeditatively into a delightful ascent of Abbott Peak, which is here recorded to encourage any good walker with some experience on steep slopes to try the same.

Starting at 1.45, Miss P. F. Morris of Philadelphia and the writer left Glacier House in the characteristic *rainy* weather of this place, and reached Marion Lake in something less than an hour. Ignoring adverse conditions and led on by the hope of a change, we pressed on in clouds and rain over the amphitheatre at treeline (marked by numerous stone-men) and scrambled up the steep slopes to the ridge, which was reached about 4. To our delight, the weather then suddenly changed and the clouds broke away; revealing a most wonderful view on all sides. After a halt of 15 minutes, we passed along the mile or so of arete with speed, and arrived at the summit of Mt. Abbott at 5.05, Mt. Afton towering above us very near and temptingly. Lack of time prevented thoughts of its ascent, however. The view of the Sir Donald, Dawson, Bonney & Swiss groups of peaks was magnificent.

Return was made the same way, starting at 5.20, & Glacier House was reached at 7.10, the descent from Marion Lake being made in 18 minutes. The whole trip was made in quick time for a lady.

A phenomenon worth noting occurred on the ridge. After the breaking up of the worst clouds, the sun shone clearly on the western side of the arete, while for a 1/2 hour the mists continued thick on the east side. Our shadows were cast very distinctly on the mists, around these were perfect rainbow shadows in circles like halos—a most extraordinary mist effect.

J.H. Scattergood
Philadelphia

SEPT., 1906

A fable for authors. Once upon a time an American Lady came to Glacier and not only visited the Glacier itself, but also met a gentleman whom she called a Little Englander, because the area of his mind was scarcely as big even as the little island he came from. Knowing his kind, she asked him with a spirit to be envied and with due solemnity whether the C.P.R. had put the Glacier there as an advertisement. Solemnly he treasured the sample of the intelligence of ladies from the States, and when with a friend he wrote his little book he solemnly printed the story on page 222. And the American Lady has often told it all with glee to her American friends. *Moral*: When Little Englanders travel here, they should be accompanied by some one from the "States" to point out to them what is a joke, and what is not a joke.

U.S.A.

SOURCE

Excerpts of the Glacier House Scrapbook, unpublished, 1897–1910. WMCR M352.

MARY SCHÄFFER WARREN

"Our Dear Mrs. Young" (1934)

Dec. 20th.

Dear Humphrey,

Now what possessed you to remember the little tale attached to the holly? It was most kind of you but you MUST have remembered I had someone very dear who never forgot me.

I had known her from girlhood and she looked on me as someone she must shelter which she did after my first husband died. She was deeply attached to him and one of the last things he did was to have a particular stone made into a brooch for her and it arrived after she knew he had died very suddenly. It was most beautifully set and she wore it almost constantly. She belonged to an old Montreal family, very highly educated but not such that she could use it for earning a living. Her husband was ill a very long time, but a wealthy brother of his came to see him one day and told him not to worry about his wife's future as he had enough to make her most comfortable. Strange mockeries of fate will come along some-times. The brother MEANT to make a will leaving a large sum to his sister-in-law and died before the will was written and his brother died next day. This left our dear Mrs. Young entirely bereft and finally she accep-ted a position as manager with the C.P.R. in their mountain hotels. Her husband's family knew exactly what the brother had meant to do but they walked right over her and she was too stunned to fight for her bare rights.

I met her first at Field, a most perfect woman and then she took Glacier where she was adorable. She took me to her heart when I went to her and without the most perfect husband that ever lived. I was happier with her than with anyone else and spent a lot of time with her. Finally the day came when she wrote the C.P.R. that she felt her days of usefulness were done and dear knows what she had in mind to keep the wolf from the door.

They finally wrote and asked her if she would take care of the library at the Empress Hotel, she would have her own room & all her meals also a pension. That is what the Co. thought of my dear old friend. The very first year after Dr. died, she sent me a box of holly and I know she never forgot the gift as long as she lived. It always makes me choke and yet the memory is so beautiful.

Such is the story my dear boy, of the holly. This may be almost too sad to dim your ideals of Xmas. I think it's a day for children and not for some of us who have so many, many memories.

Dear Mrs. Young died in Vancouver and tho I asked the best I could about the tiny brooch, I never heard where it had wandered.

I am morally certain she knew life was growing very short for her and she repeatedly told me to choose anything she had, to keep. I simply could do nothing of the kind. Am glad I did not. To look at some of her beautiful china could bring no HAPPY glow to-day.

If you know the Longstaffs they were as much in love with her as I was. They are two such dear people. The Major could have searched the world over and found no nicer woman than the one he married. I knew pretty much all the Longstaffs and dear Mrs. L. belongs where she is. I had a card from them enclosing a photo of Peyto lake and the two standing on the summit of Bow Pass—a very well known stamping ground of mine.

I hope you have plenty of fun, dances and all good things as you deserve. Lots of love to you, dear boy,

Mary Warren

SOURCE

Mary Schäffer Warren's letter to Humphrey Toms, "Our Dear Mrs. Young," unpublished, written 20 December 1934. WMCR M429.

Takakkaw Falls
from Below, 1901.

*(Vaux Family Fonds,
WMCR V653/NG–855)*

MARY M. VAUX

"Camping in the Canadian Rockies" (1907)

WE MAY TAKE LAGGAN AS A STARTING POINT, as more good trips are available from there than from any other point in the mountains. The trip may be either long or short, varying from a day's ride to Moraine lake or Paradise valley, a three-day excursion to Lake O'Hara and McArthur lake, to a week or more as far as the Pipestone pass, returning by the Bow. On any of these trips, it is well to make an elastic arrangement, so that one can stay a day or two longer than the actual time required; for there is much delight in a quiet day in camp, when you do not have to do your twelve miles on foot, or your fifteen miles on horseback, and can sleep as long in the morning as you wish, get acquainted with the flowers and birds, and enjoy the delights of a quiet walk; where there is really time to receive deep mental impressions.

For a four-days' trip, there is no place more delightful than Lake O'Hara— a lovely clear sheet of water, filtered through the rock slide at its head. Its banks are carpeted with flowers; in front are seen, in succession, Mts. Biddle, Hungabee, Yukness, Lefroy, Victoria, Huber, and Wiwaxy peaks, while behind come Cathedral, Stephen and Oderay; so that one is almost bewildered by the number and grandeur of them all. Then, a short walk of three miles brings you to Lake McArthur, a true alpine lake, with glaciers from the slopes of Mt. Biddle breaking off in miniature icebergs; and where the grassy moss-grown slopes are a favorite feeding ground of the mountain goat. Their beds and rolling places are frequently seen; and the noise of falling rocks, as they climb to a point of vantage, aids you in discerning their retreating forms.

By following the stream that feeds Lake O'Hara, a beautiful chain of lakes is discovered, with cascades and waterfalls between, ending in Lake Oesa, whose surface is only melted for a very few weeks at mid-summer. Or, if one wishes a still higher climb, one can venture across Abbot pass (9000 feet above sea) and down the Victoria glacier to Lake Louise. But this is only safe with an experienced Swiss guide, as the pass is frequently traversed by avalanches on its northern side. Unfortunately, there are no fish in any of these waters, although it is stated that the lakes are well provided with trout-food.

From Hector station to Lake O'Hara it is about ten miles, over a good trail. The earlier miles are marred by burnt timber, but the lake and its surroundings well repay any discomfort of this part of the way. In addition, several other short excursions can be made to advantage, and a little exploring done on one's own account.

Now as to appliances and outfit: To begin with, a good tent is required, plenty of warm blankets, and a canvas sheet to spread under and over the blankets on the bough-bed, to prevent dampness from above and below; then, a small pillow is a great luxury, and takes but little room in the pack. Of course, it is pre-supposed that the women of the party wear rational clothes: knickerbockers, a flannel shirtwaist, and knotted kerchief at the neck; stout boots, with hobnails, laced to the knee, or arranged for puttees; woollen stockings, a felt hat with moderate brim, and a sweater or short coat completing the outfit. A light waterproof coat, opened well behind, to allow it to part over the horse's back, and which may be fastened to the saddle, is very necessary in a region where storms must be expected frequently. Each person should be provided with a canvas bag, which can be securely buttoned, wherein to place the necessary toilet articles. An extra pair of light shoes, a short skirt to wear in camp and a golf cape with hood, add greatly to the comfort of the camper; also a good-sized piece of mosquito netting, to keep off intruding bulldogs, if you wish to rest in the tent in the heat of the mid-day sun; while a hot water bottle and a box of mustard may be tucked in along with a few simple medicines in case of emergency. On two occasions I would have given a great deal for a mustard plaster, and on a third occasion it was of great value.

The food taken is largely a matter for personal selection. We have eliminated canned things very largely, and find the change to dried foods not at all distasteful—of course, with the proviso that they are properly cooked. Bacon, ham, tea, coffee, evaporated cream, butter, oatmeal, rice, beans, flour, canned tomatoes, canned soup, onions, potatoes, pickles, marmalade, cheese and dried fruits can be so prepared that, with hunger sauce, there is nothing left to be desired in the way of a larger bill of fare. Trout and game are always a welcome addition to the larder. Cakes of chocolate and raisins may be added to the list, when it is desirable to have something in the pocket on a day's climb, and the return to camp is uncertain. In all preparations it must be remembered that the altitude at which we camp is considerable, and that a necessary attribute towards a good time is to be warm and comfortable at night, when the thermometer may probably fall to 28°, and there will be ice along the brook-sides, in the morning. Then, do not forget the cold dip in the mountain stream, as the crowning luxury of all.

A camera is a very delightful adjunct, for it is pleasant to have some tangible results to show, on your return home. A kodak, if no larger instrument can be managed, yields most satisfactory results, although the better records from a larger-sized camera are an increased delight, when one has the patience and skill to obtain them. For changing plates in camp, an improvised tepee can be made of the blankets, and, if this is done after sundown, is quite satisfactory. We have never known plates to be fogged by the operation. Cut films are more convenient than glass plates, as they are so much lighter and not subject to breakage, although not so easily handled. The actinic properties of the light are very great and care must be used to avoid over-exposure. It is very desirable to develop the plates as soon as possible, for in this way you can more readily understand the conditions and change the exposures to suit. We have found medium plates better than the quick ones, especially with a rapid lens. Telephoto work has not been very satisfactory, as on high places the wind is so great that it is not possible to obtain a sharp picture, with the unsteady condition of the camera, when the long draw is in use. We have also found that panoramas, made with the ordinary camera, give a better idea of extended views than can be had by any other method. The panoram cameras, as a rule, distort so much that they are useless when great heights and depths are to be rendered.

Then, when you return to civilization, you will have many happy memories, and the "call of the wild" will so enter your blood, that you will count the days till you can again be free among the everlasting hills.

SOURCE

Mary M. Vaux's "Camping in the Canadian Rockies," from *Canadian Alpine Journal* 1, no. 1 (1907), 67–71.

Mount Mary Vaux at the head of Maligne Lake, 1908. From Mary T.S. Schäffer, Old Indian Trails, *1911. (WMCR V527/NA–73)*

MARY T.S. SCHÄFFER

"A Maiden Voyage on the 'New' Lake" (1911)

from Old Indian Trails

AS WE CAME UP, Chief had just chopped out a smooth surface on the side of a small tree, and there, for the first time and only in all our wanderings, so far as I can remember, we inscribed our initials and the date of our visit.

Even then I think we all apologised to ourselves, for, next to a mussy camp-ground, there is nothing much more unsightly to the *true camper* than to see the trees around a favourite camping site disfigured with personal names and personal remarks, which never fail to remind one of the old adage taught the small boy in his early youth when he receives his first knife.

And one more name we left behind, not carved upon a tree but in our memories. All day the thought of one who loved the hills as we did ourselves was in my mind, and though she could not be with us, yet did I long to share our treasures with her. On the lake's west shore rose a fine symmetrical peak, and as we stepped cautiously aboard our craft (I could never get over the idea that she would go over with a sneeze), I said: "With every one's sanction I call that peak Mount Mary Vaux." There was no dissenting voice.

SOURCE

Excerpt of Mary T.S. Schäffer's, "A Maiden Voyage on the 'New' Lake," from *Old Indian Trails: Incidents of Camp and Trail Life, Covering Two Years' Exploration through the Rocky Mountains of Canada* (New York and London: G.P. Putnam's Sons, 1911/The Knickerbocker Press, 1911), 254–56.

MARY M. VAUX

"Letters to Dr. Walcott" (1912)

1715 Arch Street
Philadelphia

Arr 3–8–12
Dear Mr Wolcott [*sic*]

Many thanks for thy kind letters which reached me this morning, and also for the photographs, which are most interesting. I am very pleased to see those of the glaciers, which as thee knows, are always especially interesting to me. I think thee is quite right in thy view that the long rolls are more satisfactory for scientific purposes, but I would like to see a good platinum print of some of them, printed under tissue paper, & then perhaps they would be as brilliant, as some we have had. They are certainly very beautiful, and most satisfactory.

I am sorry thee was not near enough to drop in night before last, and hope I may see thee here when thee is passing again through Phila.

Space is often much in the way, of accomplishing many things. I hope thee will have a good rest in the south, if it is only for a week. Father & I went to Charleston three years ago, and very much enjoyed it. This year I could not persuade him to go again, even for a week. If thee stops off there be sure & go to the gardens on the Ashley river. The azaleas are so beautiful when in full bloom next month, and the japonica and jasmine are lovely. It would be in great contrast to the day Mrs. Young & I spent in Washington when the wind was driving the snow before it in clouds. I am hoping to print for thee the first opportunity one of my own long panormas of the Victoria Glacier. I think perhaps thee may see something of interest in it, as it has Fairview, Aberdeen, the Milne, Lefroy & Victoria, all included, and the light, was all that could be desired.

Sometimes I feel that I can hardly wait till the time comes to escape from city life, to the free air of the everlasting hills. I sometimes wonder how it is that those who love the out of doors so much, seem always to have their lots cast in the man made town, while the country folk travel to the cities as fast as possible.

Thee spoke of a paper by A.D. Von Engelu [?] on Glacier Wastage & Drainage. I suppose I can obtain a copy by writing to him.

Again thanking thee for the photographs, and hoping thee will have a restful journey, I am

Very sincerely
Mary M. Vaux
2/19 1912

·1715·ARCH·STREET·:
·:PHILADELPHIA·:

Dear Mr Wolcott

Many thanks
for thy kind letter which
reached me this morning,
and also for the photographs,
which are most interesting.
I am very pleased to see
those of the glaciers, which
as thee knows, are always
especially interesting to
me. I think thee is quite
right in thy view that
the long rolls are more
satisfactory for scientific
purposes, but I would

Letter from Mary M. Vaux to Dr. Charles D. Walcott, 19 February 1912. (SIA record unit 7004, box 5, folder 2, 2005–26210–16)

like to see a good plati-
num print of some of them,
printed under tissue
paper, & then perhaps
they would be as bril-
liant, as some we have
had. They are certainly
very beautiful, and most
satisfactory.

I am sorry thee was not
night before last,
near enough to drop in,
and hope I may see thee
here when thee is passing
again through Phila;
Space is often much in
the way, of accomplishing
many things. I hope thee
will have a good rest in

the south, if it is only for a week. Father & I went to Charleston three years ago, and very much enjoyed it. This year I could not pursuade him to go again, even for a week. If thee stops off there be sure & go to the gardens on the Ashley river. The azaleas are so beautiful when in full bloom next month, and the japonica and jasmine are lovely. It would be in great contrast to the day Mrs Young & I spent in Washington when the wind was driving the snow before it in clouds.

I am hoping to print for
thee the first opportunity
one of my own long pano-
ramas of the Victoria Glacier.
I think perhaps thee may
see something of interest in
it, as it has Fairview, Aberdeen
the Mitre, Lefroy & Victoria, all
included, and the light
was all that could be desired.
Sometimes I feel that I can
hardly wait till the time
comes to escape from city
life, to the free air of the
everlasting hills. I sometimes
wonder how it is that those
who love the out of doors so
much, seem always to have
their lots cast in the man
made town, while the country folk travel to the cities

as fast as possible.

Thee spoke of a paper by
C. W. Von Eengeln on Glacier
Wastage & Drainage. I suppose
I can obtain a copy by writing
to him.

Again thanking thee for
the photographs, and hop-
ing thee will have a restful
Journey, I am

Very sincerely
Mary M. Vaux

2/19 1912

3/11 1912
1715 Arch Street
Philadelphia

Dear Dr Walcott

Thy letter of the eighth reached me this afternoon, and I hasten to write
and thank thee for it, and also for the Glacier paper, which I shall study
with interest and return to thee a little later on.

I am so sorry that the dull weather has gone so far to the south. We
did not see the sun all last week, and there is not the first suggestion of
spring except the song of a sparrow that I heard at Bryn Mawr, & wondered how he knew that spring was so near, when all was frozen & gray.
But I really think we are spoiled for travel else where, after the beauty &
interest of the Rockies for no where else is there such a wealth of beauty
and interest, and I conclude that the haunts so attractive to the world
have no attraction for me.

Of course golf is a fine game, but can it compare with a day on the
trail, or a scramble over the glacier, or even with a quiet day in camp to
get things in order for the morrow's conquests? Some how when once
this wild spirit enters the blood, golf courses & hotel piazzas, be they ever
so brilliant, have no charm, and I can hardly wait to be off again.

I had hoped to get a good day to print before this but there has been
no sun, tho I hope this will soon be remedied, & I can get a morning to
work with the negatives. What with my regular work, and the farm, and
the demands that father makes on my time, I find the days all too short
to accomplish many things that I wish could be done. I am wondering if
thee _did_ go on to Miami, or is back in Washington now. At any rate I hope
the tired feeling has gone, & that thee will come back with renewed vigor,
to the many interests that demand thy attention.

We are all looking forward to the Academy Anniversary next week. The
additions to the building are about completed, and the library & collections have a suitable home at last. Perhaps thee will be coming to the

meeting, and be sure & let us see thee here if thee comes to Phila. Father & I shall always be glad to welcome thee, and now that we are so much alone our friends mean a great deal to us.

I wonder if thee ever studied the wonderfully beautiful pools with their wealth of life near Monterey? I have never been to the tropics, where I suppose much greater beauty can be seen, but those were most interesting to me, when we were last in California, several years ago. I hope that "jassemine" will be out in bloom more before thee returns. The southern forest with its gray moss, would seem very sombre without the dainty yellow flowers to brighten it up. I suppose thee would not be likely to see the arbutus in bloom either if the weather is still so cold. But St. Patrick's day is near at hand, & after that the spring cannot be far away.

I will send this to Washington, as I am not sure of any other address from thy letter. Again thanking thee for thy kind letter, I am

Very sincerely thine
Mary M. Vaux

3/11 1912

Dear Dr Walcott

Thy letter of the eighth reached me this afternoon, and I hasten to write and thank thee for it, and also for the Glacier paper, which I shall study with interest and return to thee a little later on.

I am so sorry that the dull weather has gone so far to the south. We did not see the sun all last week, and there is

Letter from Mary M. Vaux to Dr. Charles D. Walcott, 11 March 1912. (SIA record unit 7004, box 5, folder 2, 2005–26210–13)

not the first suggestion
of spring except the
song of a sparrow that
I heard at Bryn Mawr,
+ wondered how he knew
that spring was so near,
when all was frozen + gray.
But I really think we
are spoiled for travel
else where, after the beauty
+ interest of the Rockies
for no where else is there
such a wealth of beauty
and interest, and I con-
clude that the haunts
so attractive to the world
have no attraction for me.

Of course golf is a fine game,
but can it compare with
a day on the trail, or
a scramble over the glacier,
or even with a quiet day
in camp to get things
in order for the morrow's
conquests? Some how when
once this wild spirit enters
the blood, golf courses &
hotel piazza's, be they ever
so brilliant, have no charm,
and I can hardly wait to
be off again.

I had hoped to get a good
day to print before this but
there has been no sun,

tho I hope this will soon
be remedied, & I can get
a morning to work with the
negatives. What with my
regular work, and the farm,
and the demands that father
makes on my time, I find
the days all too short to accomplish many things
that I wish could be done.
I am wondering if thee did
go on to Miami, or is back
in Washington now. At any
rate I hope the tired feeling
has gone, & that thee will come
back with renewed vigor, to
the many interests that
demand thy attention.
We are all looking forward
to the Academy Anniversary

·:1715·ARCH·STREET:·
·:PHILADELPHIA:·

next week. The additions
to the building are about
completed, and the library
&collections, have a suitable
home at last. Perhaps thee
will be coming to the meeting, and be sure &let us
see thee here if thee comes
to Phil͟a. Father &I shall
always be glad to welcome
thee, and now that we
are so much alone our
friends mean a great
deal to us.

I wonder if thee ever chided

the wonderfully beautiful pools with their wealth of life near Monterey? I have never been to the tropics, where I suppose much greater beauty can be seen, but those were most interesting to me, when we were last in California, several years ago. I hope the "jassemine" will be out in bloom more, before thee returns. The southern forest with its gray moss, would seem very sombre without the dainty yellow flowers to brighten it up! I suppose thee would not be likely to see the arbutus in bloom either

if the weather is still so
cold. But St Patrick's day
is near at hand, & after
that the spring cannot
be far away.
I will send this to
Washington, as I am
not sure of any other
address from thy letter.
Again thanking thee
for thy kind letter, I am
Very sincerely thine
Mary M. Vaux

Dear Dr Walcott

Thy kind letter reached me in good season, and I am very pleased that thee likes my panorama. I know that our method is not so good for thy work, where, as thee says, you want the sweep across the rocks, without breaks. Thee did not tell me whether there was any thing shown in the picture that was of interest geologically, and in this I am deeply interested. If we go to the mountains next summer, it is likely that father and I, with father's secretary, would go alone, and so I shall soon begin to plan my work. The glaciers must be measured, and I shall hope to use the camera seriously, and get all I can. Last summer's work was such a disappointment in photographic results.

I had some time to myself last evening, and so took up thy report on the Burgess Fossil bed. I was most interested in the wonderful fossils, and hope I may, some time, have an opportunity to see them. We have some very beautiful trilobites from Mt Stephen, that we got before the location was so much patronized, but they are only the common ones. How much we pass by, owing to our lack of knowledge in recognizing the value of what we see. Please don't forget thy promise to tell me about the Yoho Valley. Thee knows I feel a sense of ownership in it, being the first white woman that visited it, and besides I have compassed it on the high levels, going in from Sherbrook Lake, & making a complete circuit over the snow fields & glaciers as well as making the approach from Bow Lake over the Bow Glacier, by Vulture Col & Balfour Glacier, & across Yoho Glacier to the Valley. It is to me the loveliest spot to be found, and always quickens my blood when I hear and speak of it, and I can imagine no greater delight than camping there away from the tourist, and the noise of the iron horse.

I am sorry thee has such a tiring time since thy return to Washington. Don't work too hard these everlasting spring days, & please forgive this lengthy epistle, but I feel that I want to thank thee for the opportunity thee has afforded me of reading thy reports, and very much wish I knew more of this interesting subject.

I don't think the photograph of thyself in the Geographical Soc. Magazine is a very good likeness! As to the handkerchief:—father uses a different sort, and George's are all marked with his initials, so I think thy ownership is proved.

I am just going to the farm so will close.

Always sincerely thine
Mary M. Vaux
1715 Arch St.
4/1 1912

Dear Mr. Walcott,

Thy kind letter reached me in good season, and I am very pleased that thee likes my panorama. I know that our method is not so good for thy work, where, as thee says, you want the *surely* across the rocks, without breaks. Thee did not tell me whether there was anything shown in the picture that was of interest geologically, and in this I am deeply interested. If we go to the mountains next summer, it is likely that father and I, with father's secretary, would go alone, and so I shall soon begin to plan my work. The

Letter from Mary M. Vaux to Dr. Charles D. Walcott, 1 April 1912. (SIA record unit 7004, box 5, folder 2, 2005–26210–18)

glaciers must be measured, and I shall hope to use the camera seriously, and get all I can. Last summer's work was such a disappointment in photographic results.

I had some time to myself last evening, and so took up the report on the Burgess Fossil bed. I was most interested in the wonderful fossils, and hope I may, some time, have an opportunity to see them. We have some very beautiful trilobites from Mt Stephen, that we got before the location was so much patronized, but they are only the common ones. How much we pass by, owing to our lack of knowledge in recognizing the value of what we see! Please don't forget the promise to tell me about

the Yoho Valley. Thee knows I feel
a sense of ownership in it, being
the first white woman that visited
it, and besides I have compassed
it on the high levels, going in
from Sherbrook Lake, & making
a complete circuit over the
snow fields & glaciers as well
as making the approach from
Bow Lake over the Bow Glacier,
by Vulture Col, & Balfour Glacier,
& across Yoho Glacier to the Valley.
It is to me the loveliest spot to
be found, and always quickens
my blood when I hear and speak
of it, and I can imagine no greater
delight than camping there away
from the tourist, and the noise
of the iron horse.

I am sorry thee has such a tiring
time since thy return to Washington. Don't work too hard these
enervating spring days, & please
forgive this lengthy epistle, but I
feel that I want to thank thee

for the opportunity thee has afforded
me of reading thy reports, and very
much wish I knew more of this
interesting subject.

I don't think the photograph
of thyself in the Geographical Soc.
Magazine is a very good likeness!

As to the handkerchief:— father
uses a different sort, and George's
are all marked with his initials, so I think thy ownership
is proved.

I am just going to the farm so
will close.

Always sincerely thine
Mary M. Vaux

1715 Arch St.
4/1 1912

SOURCE

Mary M. Vaux's letters to Dr. Charles D. Walcott, unpublished, 19 February 1912, 11 March 1912, and 1 April 1912. SIA record unit 7004, box 5, folder 2, images 2005–26214–16, 2005–26210–13, and 2005–26217–18.

Mount Athabasca
(from Wilcox Pass).
Photograph by
Mary T.S. Schäffer, c. 1907.
(WMCR V527/PS–58)

MARY T.S. SCHÄFFER

"Untrodden Ways" (1908)

IN THE SUMMER OF 1907, on June 20th, two women and two guides left the little station of Laggan, Alberta, and started for the vast wilderness to the north. It was cold and raw, snow flew in our not over-jubilant faces, the way was one of grind over fallen timbers and through the most discouraging muskegs. For our trail lay up the Bow Valley, across the summit of the same name, down Mistaya Creek to its junction with the Saskatchewan River, and from thence on by the various branches of the Saskatchewan and Athabasca Rivers.

Not as the crow flies, but as the trail winds, we reached in our wanderings a point about 200 miles from Laggan, not far from the junction of the Whirlpool and Athabasca Rivers. In this section there are four distinct streams: the Chaba, which flows up from the south and joins the West Branch of the Athabasca about twelve miles from its own source; a branch which flows from the south-east and joins the Chaba about three miles from the latter's source; the West Branch mentioned above, and the Sun Wapta, which joins the main stream several miles below. About half way

Fortress Lake. *Photograph by Mary T.S. Schäffer, c. 1907.* (WMCR V527/PS–21)

up the Chaba, and to the west of it, lies beautiful Fortress Lake, discovered in 1893 by Dr. A.P. Coleman. It is a wild and strikingly picturesque valley, though probably not more so than many similarly situated on the Saskatchewan River. Yet the West Branch appealed to us more; there was a sense of loneliness, of freedom from all touch of human life, a purity, a bloom, which the white man's hand so quickly brushes aside. I say "white," for the red man defiles it no more than does the passing caribou or the wandering bear. His standing teepee-poles but give the touch the artist loves, while the centuries-old hunting trails are filled with soundless stories which interested eyes may easily read as they follow in the wake of the feet that have gone by and will never return.

As far as I can learn, only one white man has ever penetrated to the end of the West Branch, and this was Jean Habel, a German explorer, who visited it in the summer of 1901. He did not then recognize the superb pyramid of faultless outline which stands guard at the extreme southern limit of the valley as Mt. Columbia, and called it "Gamma." He afterwards published a short article in "Appalachia" with a fine reproduction of Mt. Columbia, but before he could do more, or his work be better known, the pen was laid aside forever; and it was with a feeling of sincere sadness that we passed his long-deserted camps, and realized so vividly the feelings which must have thrilled him as he saw the rich scenic treasures the mountains were unfolding for the first time to human eyes.

Next to being asked if we were not "afraid" in that lonely wilderness, the most common question is: "Did you go where no person had ever been before?" An Indian after all is a "person," and to find a spot where an Indian has not been in that great hunting ground, which has doubtless been hunted over from time immemorial by the plains tribes, would seem an absolute impossibility. The caribou, goat and sheep yet wander in these lonely fastnesses, and a few Indians still come to the haunts of their forefathers; but in the further valleys the teepee-poles are fallen and decayed, and thus the story of the passing of the red man is simply and sadly told. So to that question I can only reply: We found one section, and but one, where it seemed as if not even an Indian's foot had trodden. This was on the north shore of the Athabasca River after the four streams had united. The original explorer had chosen the south and more "muskeggy" ground, where we ourselves were forced to travel to avoid the arduous labor of chopping a trail. This was the only section of the eight or nine hundred miles we travelled where there was a doubt that Indians had gone; at least, it had never been a highway.

From the Athabasca we turned our attention to the sources of the Saskatchewan and Brazeau Rivers, to the "Valley of the Lakes," a branch of the North Fork of the former stream, and to the West Branch, a tributary of the Saskatchewan flowing from the Lyell group. This valley alone is worth a trip, an article to itself, and a more ready pen. It is a valley of gorges and glaciers, magnificent peaks and tumbling waterfalls, and holds a charming lake which we have named "Nashanesen."* The climax is reached at the Thompson Pass, where the traveller who has stuck to it through pretty rough "going" is at last rewarded by his first glimpse of Mt. Bryce, and from a shoulder of the mountain the vast ice-fields of Mt. Columbia.

From the West Branch we crossed by Nigel Pass to the Brazeau country lying to the north-east of the Wilcox Pass. Roughly speaking, Brazeau Lake lies in latitude 53° and longitude 117°. It is about six miles long, is wooded round its shores, and at its head stands a fine peak—Mt. Brazeau. Low mountains hem it in on all sides, and, on a calm morning, before the sun has risen or the wind has cast a ripple on its blue-green surface, the sight is one of exquisite beauty.

We no sooner reached the southern shore of the lake than a whole volume was opened for us to read. In a perfect grove among the spruces stood comparatively fresh teepee-poles, while tossed here and there, in every stage of decay, were those which had served their purpose many, many years before. An old trail was beaten deep within the forest, and from this path sprang ancient trees which held their proud boughs to the blue sky above, their lower bark scarred and gashed by hands long laid beneath the sod.

That it was and yet is a magnificent sheep country, there is little doubt. Its long distance from the now small band of Stony Indians at Morley and the nearly exhausted game country intervening, is probably a sufficient reason for the greater abundance of animal life which we saw there. We had followed a most marvellous Indian trail over the worst bed of boulders I ever met for horses to travel, had climbed on and on, lured by the old trail, until well toward 9,000 feet, when we suddenly surprised a band of sheep. They had probably never seen a human being before. On the defensive at once, they were off like a flash before our astonished gaze, along a bare rock-face and up an almost perpendicular wall covered with ice that the most fearless Swiss guide would not have dared attempt, and over which they bounded as though it were but a meadow of upland grass. Reaching the high and inaccessible crags, they paused, and for a moment gazed upon us far below; then a magnificent ram appeared to take the lead. The others disappeared, but the massive head of the leader, with its great horns, stood motionless against the grey sky, his attitude alert, his body immovable. Only, as we moved back and down the valley, we could discern that he turned to keep us in view. Such a picture! The dreary wastes of naked rock, the cold glistening glaciers all about us, the early snows in the unexposed niches, the dying alpine flowers at our feet, then, high above, clinging to the superb crags outlined against an angry sky, stood that emblem of a noble and fast-disappearing creature—the Rocky Mountain sheep.

From the Brazeau country we made our way back toward Nigel Pass, crossed Cataract Pass and descended Cataract Creek to the Kootenai Plains. Here we rested and revelled in those golden valleys, visited the Indians, and found life a very pleasant matter in that peaceful sunshine after the snows and storms among the more northern valleys.

Yet even here the late September days were stealing. They were coming with the yellowing poplars, and with the laggard dawn. We knew the winter's snows must soon sweep across the higher passes, but begged a few days' respite to visit one spot which beckoned us with its beguiling name. This was the "Valley of the Lakes." James Outram speaks of seeing it from the summit of Mt. Lyell, and says in his book (*In the Heart of the Canadian Rockies*): "It appeared as a deep enshadowed trough, jewelled with a host of little lakes." The description fascinated us, appealed to our imagination, and we were to have the pleasure of stealing the first secrets of a primeval wilderness. From the camp at the junction of the North Fork and the main Saskatchewan River, we travelled up the east bank of the North Fork for about 13 miles; here, being low water, we easily found a crossing, and followed the west shore for a mile more, when an old Indian trail led directly to the unknown valley. As far as the red man is concerned, it is many years since his moccasined foot has trodden that moss-covered way. The trail remains beaten and worn, but overgrown and impeded with huge fallen trees, and only the blaze of a white man's axe seven or eight feet above the ground showed that a hunter had gone that way in the dead of winter to test his fortune with traps and rifle.

No sooner had we left the river than we plunged into a thick growth of spruce, climbing constantly for two hours. Reaching comparatively level ground, we plodded on amidst closely grown and exasperating pines, so thick and so nearly impregnable that even our now depleted packs could not be forced through until the axe rang and woke the silence which seemed to lie like a pall on every surrounding object. So muffled and dark and still was this bit of primeval forest that no sign of life met us on the way; it seemed that with the passing of the Indian had passed the need for the little people of the wood; and yet, no doubt, bright, terror-stricken eyes were in every direction, watching the movements of the terrible and unaccountable enemy.

After long windings and turnings in the shadows, with no sign of the grass so necessary to our horses, we made our way to the banks of a tumbling torrent which seemed to come from the Lyell ice-fields. From the deathly silence of the forest, our serenade all that night was the rushing, pounding stream as it hurled itself along among the boulders of the river-bed scarce ten feet away. On each side of the very narrow valley avalanches had torn and ripped the trees from their roots in every direction, and amidst this havoc and desolation was the only feed our hungry horses could find, and very poor picking at that. As yet we had seen nothing of the lakes to which Outram had given the lovely name, the name which had lured us through those long, silent, weary hours in the deep, lonely forest.

In a rainy, misty sort of sunshine the next morning, we essayed a climb to look for the lakes. How hot it was when the sun beat down! How steep and tough the avalanche-scarred hillside! How bitter cold the wind from the ice-fields! And our reward, "the lakes like jewels," where were they? Toiling stubbornly onward to the bare cliffs above, we reached the loose unstable scree just beneath them, paused and looked eagerly to the valley below upon a chain of sloughs. Beautiful they were, too, lying in peaceful silence far below, like giant emeralds tossed there by mountain gnomes. From his height of several thousand feet above us the enthusiastic climber had beheld "lakes."

The home stretch lay over Howse and Baker Passes, the latter very beautiful but difficult to travel. It is hard, at best, to leave behind the days of freedom, the constantly shifting panorama of mountains, lakes and rivers, the balsam-laden air; to return to the beaten track, to four walls, and all the cares which know so well how to creep within them. It was a summer of almost continuous cold and storm, but with no accidents to ourselves or the horses. It was a happy sixteen weeks amidst as fine a cyclorama of changing scenery as the dear old world can offer, and there was always the sunshine of contentment and goodwill within the tent and at the camp-fire.

EDITORIAL NOTE

*Names given in Canada are subject to approval by the Geographical Board.—Editor.

SOURCE

Mary T.S. Schäffer's, "Untrodden Ways," from *Canadian Alpine Journal* 1, no. 2 (1908), 288–94.

Nodding Campion (Lychnis apetala). *Watercolour by Mary Vaux Walcott, 1905.*

(SAAM, 1970.355.617)

MARY VAUX WALCOTT

"Flowers of the Canadian Rockies" (1945)

Descriptions from the illustrated portfolios of Mary Vaux Walcott.
Plants collected and photographed by A.O. Brigden.

LYCHNIS APETALA. Nodding campion grows among the rocks and boulders of old moraines or on alpine summits. Its flowers, turned toward the ground, are inconspicuous. The tiny petals project only a little from the end of the inflated calyx. Though the species has a wide distribution, it is seldom seen by the traveler because the coloring of both leaves and flowers is similar to that of the rocks among which it grows.

Nodding campion is found in both Labrador and Greenland, and extends from Colorado and Utah northward to Alberta, British Columbia, and Alaska. It occurs also in Europe and Asia.

SILENE ACAULIS. Moss campion is one of the most attractive of the alpine plants and one frequently seen by the mountaineer climbing above timberline. Although its blooming season is short, differences in altitude and exposure in its many habitats are responsible for its blooming during a longer period than most alpine plants. It grows from a single woody root anchored deep in rocky soil, and spreads into a flat cushion often a foot or more in diameter. The bright green of the narrow leaves is beautifully contrasted with the pink, or rarely white, flowers, and the plant is always a joy to behold.

This lovely member of the Pink family is found in arctic or arctic-alpine situations, from New Hampshire to Greenland, across Canada and from the highest mountains of New Mexico to Alaska; also in Europe and Asia.

SALIX NIVALIS. When climbing in the higher altitudes of the Rocky Mountains, just above timberline, one often finds large patches of the ground covered with a low plant about an inch high, bearing spikes of tiny red flowers surrounded by small, dark green leaves. It proves to be the snow willow, one of the smallest of all the large group of willows. Later in the season the flowers are followed by tiny seeds with feathery appendages, by means of which they are carried by the wind to new locations far from the parent plants. The plant is so low that it is not torn by the winds, however violent they may become on the bleak mountain slopes. In winter, also, it is well protected by even the thinnest blanket of snow. Thus has the tiny willow become adapted to its environment.

The species ranges from Montana to Washington, and northward to Alberta and British Columbia.

Romanzoffia sitchensis was described and illustrated in the 1942–43 Journal, page 198.

SOURCE

Excerpt of Mary Vaux Walcott's "Flowers of the Canadian Rockies," from *Canadian Alpine Journal* 29 (1945), 70–71.

White Pasqueflower (Pulsatilla Occidentalis), *also known as* Anemone occidentalis. *Photograph by Mary Schäffer, c. 1907.* (WMCR V439/PS–251)

MARY T.S. SCHÄFFER

"Flora of the Saskatchewan and Athabasca River Tributaries" (1908)

ANOTHER SKETCH APPEARS in this magazine referring directly to the localities of whose florae I have been asked to write, so there is no need to duplicate a description of the ground covered.

As our stay was to be a long one, it was with dubious feelings that we asked permission to include among the necessities a plant-press and a limited supply of paper. Having collected plants from Banff to Glacier during a number of years, there were days on the earlier part of the journey when we would have been glad to get rid of the cumbersome, troublesome thing, and leave it hanging on some tree till we should return in the fall. But there came a day when a trained botanist went over the result of our perseverance, and we felt repaid for the annoyance and labor involved in gathering the unfamiliar blossoms by the wayside.

Mr. Stewardson Brown, of Philadelphia, has had them all thoroughly studied, and I herewith give a few notes, the result of his work upon them.

As far as the Wilcox Pass we found nothing particularly striking, until reaching a point at about 6000 feet we found the *Pinus flexilus*, its blue-green foliage betraying it quickly among the browner-green of the other trees. The cones, at that time a deep purple, vary from three to five inches in length. From there on we met many strangers (to us) of the plant world. The *Picea Canadensis*, not seen further south, was first noticed on the north shores of the Saskatchewan.

The *Erigeron acris* we found in August a few hundred feet below the *Pinus flexilus*, and, in the beginning of July, at 8500 feet, the *Ranunculus pygmaeus*, the tiniest butter-cup imaginable, struggling bravely to bloom in the icy winds of Wilcox Pass, and covering the ground like a golden moss wherever the winter snows had receded. Here, also, in full bloom, but [on] more exposed and barren sections of the pass, was the *Aragallus inflatus*. This was an especially interesting find as I had never seen anything more than the huge, inflated seed-pods before. The flower is a deep sky-blue, and, growing only upon higher elevations, not often seen. We gathered the beautiful crimsoning seed-vessels at the same place, the latter part of August.

From the north fork of the Saskatchewan to the headwaters of the Athabasca the *Primula mistassinica* and the *Primula borealis* grew by the river banks, frequently in beds together; they were as often found apart.

In the Su Wapta flats was growing the *Pilosella Richardsonii*, as also the *Arabis lyrata occidentalis*. The former plant, varying in general characteristics, but withal the same, made our entire journey to Fortress Lake bright, its clusters of white blossoms garnishing the sandy river-bars.

On the Wilcox Pass grew the *Viola cognata*, and in the Fortress Lake region, at about 7000 feet, the *Viola Langsdorfii*. This violet is an especially beautiful, rich, luscious-looking flower, with strong, rank foliage.

Down in the swamps of the Su Wapta we found the *Utricularia vulgaris*, and though known generally throughout Canada, I have never come across it in the mountains further south. At the same time of year, and in the same section, but at 7000 feet, we found the purple-crimson blooms of the *Telesonix heucheriformis*. Wedged deep in the cracks of the rocks, it was impossible to get any of the specimens entire. One and two hundred feet above this point we found the strawberry (*Fragaris bracteata*): great luscious berries three-quarters to one inch long. Sweeter than many a cultivated variety, they were welcome company at a height where there was no water.

On September 9th, we climbed a bare, rocky point to look for Brazeau Lake. There was little of the floral life left, though fungi of many varieties were very numerous, even to tree-line, and we were surprised to come across the little *Erigeron lanatus* at 9000 feet. The plant was a new one to me, though Professor Macoun mentions finding it at high points further south. The rays are a deep rose-violet, and the rest of the plant covered with long white hairs. As it lay blooming in the scree close to the summit of the mountain, it had the appearance of a purple flower nestling in a bed of cotton.

By the latter part of August all the river banks were a continuous strawberry bed, a welcome addition to our limited larder, but we never saw a bush of the blueberry (*Vaccinium ovaliform*) which grows so profusely in the Selkirks. Occasionally we came across the *Vaccinium erythrococcum*, whose tiny red berries made very tiresome picking, but were very good and toothsome when once gathered.

We found very many plants familiar to us as growing near the railroad, but with limited space I have only jotted down the strangers. It will be seen by this list that they are largely the plants best known as having their habitation in the more northern mountains of the Pacific slope.

We had stolen a march into the meeting grounds of two distinct floral sections, an interesting ground for a botanist who has time in the future to go so far from the beaten way.

SOURCE
Mary T.S. Schäffer's "Flora of the Saskatchewan and Athabasca River Tributaries," from *Canadian Alpine Journal* 1, no. 2 (1908), 268–70.

Silver Rock Cress
(Smelowskia calycina).
Photograph by Mary Schäffer,
c. 1911. (WMCR V439/PS–261)

MARY T.S. SCHÄFFER

"Haunts of the Wild Flowers of the Canadian Rockies" (1911)

(Within Reach of the Canadian Pacific Railroad)

FEW ARE THOSE who climb throughout the Canadian mountains to whom the flowers of the region do not appeal. When twenty years ago there was one botanist searching hills and valleys, to-day there are fifty.

Twenty years ago there was little known of a large number of the varieties, there was no Botany published to cover the ground, to-day one may study with a fair amount of information to hand to do it intelligently.

But what the Botanies do not do is to tell the visitor to our great Rocky Mountain garden of the special haunts and the special times of blooming of these children of the hills. There is a good reason for this apparent lack of valuable information, which all true lovers of flowers recognize without comment on my part, for there are thousands who gather only to throw away, those who in gathering, ruthlessly destroy the roots, and those who are collecting, who pluck till the last rare specimen is in their vasculum. To illustrate: There was a small bed of epilobium at Glacier—whose location in a moment of weakness (ignorance really), I betrayed, and as it was about to bloom I would then be able to find out which one it was. In three or four days I went to look for my treasure only to behold the party to whom I had confided my new friend returning with every specimen of the plant in his hand.

I never got a photograph of it, I never found out what one it was, but I learned to keep the haunts of rare plants to myself. If now I break to some extent my hard learned rule and mention some of the localities which contain the rarer blossoms, I trust that those who read will respect the rights of the flowers and not slaughter them.

And now the stranger to the Rockies goes forth for the first time to study the plant-life. Banff is his first stopping-point, and a very good one it is, as spring comes first there. He has read that the *gentiana affinis* is to be found in that locality in August. In faith he goes forth to get it, and most naturally turns to the beautiful Bow Valley. He returns laden with flowers, of course but not with the more or less rare gentian, which loves not the sunny Bow, but the cool shades of the Spray valley. It is a little late, but he might also be so fortunate as to find a few isolated specimens of the *primula maccalliana* and *anemone parviflora* which grow there in profusion in June and early July.

He may do as I have seen others before, search every place but the right one for the *cytherea bulbosa* (calypso) and not find it. This fairest of all the Canadian mountain flowers grows in rankest profusion on Sulphur mountain in Banff, its rosy blossoms showing above the thick mosses at the base of the mountain in early June, and as the season advances, slowly creeping toward tree-line. It is not found around Lake Louise or Glacier but plentiful at Field again. The *moneces albiflora* travels in the wake of the calypso; and the *orchis rotundifolia* another beautiful and rose-colored orchid is found in the same sections of the country as the two previously named plants growing in the river marshes.

Still another interesting plant around Banff in the early spring is the *corallorhiza*. Its greenish white blossoms are most insignificant, but gather it by the roots, wash them gently and the result pays for the trouble. It is very plentiful back of the C.P.R. hotel and through the pine forests. The gorgeous scarlet *lilium montanum* has its haunts of plenty, yet seldom more than isolated specimens are found. In the Bow River valley beneath the rugged cliffs of Tunnel mountain, the ground is dotted with flaming red by the end of June. At Field on the Ottertail road, armloads of the lily may be plucked in a few moments at certain points.

At Banff, on what is locally called the "Cave and Basin" road, may be found the *cypripedium passerinum* (white lady-slipper) in great plenty, while at Emerald Lake, near Field, the *cypripedium parviflorum* blossoms at the same time on the new-made ground at the head of the lake.

Before we leave Banff, I might mention one special point of interest which is for the botanist who is lucky to get into that country in the early spring. It is a small alpine meadow several hundred feet above the main valley, and is in plain sight from the Banff station, on the hills to the north. Here the sun on the warm slopes brings forth the growth earlier than at any other nearby point. The *myosotis alpestris* (forget-me-not) the *delphinium menziesii* (alpine larkspur), are always to be found there, and it is the only place I have ever seen the *lithophragma parviflora* growing. It was above this meadow that I found the rather rare plant *smelowskia calycina*, and but one specimen of that.

Leaving Banff, the student of flowers finds quite a different group of plants in the hills surrounding Lake Louise. It is at this point that he who goes early enough may find the Lyell's larch in bloom. It was a sight well worth the hard trudge which I had through the soft snow one sunny morning in June, when at last I stood surrounded by the *larix lyallii*. Everywhere lay snow almost two feet deep, the delicate pale green leaves were just unfolding in the hot sun, the sweet odor from the crimson cones filled the air, coaxing thousands of butterflies and bees forth, yet at the lake a thousand feet below there was no such herald of spring.

In the swamp near the hotel the *trollius albiflorus* was showing its snowy blossoms, the *oxyoccus* buds were swelling, the leaves of the *limnorchus fragrans* were three or four inches above the ground, and the tiny rose buds of the *kalmia microphylla* could be found if one looked sharp enough, but no insects hovered round, spring for the moment was on the mountain-top. But so quickly do the seasons sweep across the land, that in three days more we found a favorite spot, (lovingly called "our garden") aglow with plant life. This open spot, at the upper end of the lake, is so unfortunate as to be placed within eye-sight of all who pass toward the glacier, and as many countless hundreds pass in the course of the summer, the once prolific "garden" is sadly depleted. It is yet worth a visit from the botanist. It is, however, the slopes beneath the cliffs of Mount Fairview to which he should turn his attention, for it is there that most of that numerous family of the Rockies, the saxifrages, are to be found. We had found a few starved specimens of the *saxifraga cernua* in spots, here they were fine, and pretty much every other recorded saxifrage was there also.

Only one more plant specially associated with Louise will I mention—that is the *arnica louisiana*. I have covered much ground in my search for the flowers of that country, and it is at Louise alone I have ever come across it. So rare is it that I leave it[s] habitat to the searcher to find. Twelve square yards will cover all the home I know it to possess. The flower is a pale lemon yellow, on a short nodding stem, with blue-green leaves, and no sooner did I carry in the first specimens than it was pronounced undescribed variety.

If the hunter of flowers has time for a trip to the Pipestone Pass about thirty miles north of Laggan, he will find himself well repaid, it being a trip he can make to advantage during the months of July and August.

But as we would still take a peep at the flora of Glacier, which is essentially different from that of the eastern slope, no more time or space can be devoted to side-trips. Here the *erythronium grandiflorum* (snow-lily) runs riot over the warm hill-slopes the moment the snow leaves the ground, the *claytonia lanceolata*, the yellow violets and the bees and butterflies making a carnival of welcome for this favorite of the Selkirks. Soon the ground of the forest is covered with the millions of cl[ay]tonia and creeping raspberry blossoms in the swamp ground, the caltha and trollius spring forth, the flower season of the Selkirks is short, and everything is busy. One day in the height of the flower season I took a ride to the Cougar valley, about seven miles from Glacier. I went to see the caves, at that time just discovered, and found I had discovered more than caves. I had found a valley of rare plants and on that day added many new ones to my list. The best place to begin the search is well toward the caves themselves on the open slopes beneath the rock cliffs. There for the first time I found the *phacelia heterophylla*, the *phacelia sericea* and the *pentstemon pseudohumilis*, and throughout the forests generally the *chimaphila umbellata*.

Easy of access, the Cougar valley is a wonderful botanizing district. So I could go on indefinitely, naming little pockets in the hills where some special treasure is hidden; but once started on this interesting study, the hunter needs no more help. These notes are for the stranger, who once within the gates, is a stranger no longer.

SOURCE

Mary T.S. Schäffer's "Haunts of the Wild Flowers of the Canadian Rockies (Within Reach of the Canadian Pacific Railroad)," *Canadian Alpine Journal* 3 (1911), 131–35.

JULIA W. HENSHAW

"The Mountain Wildflowers of Western Canada" (1907)

THERE IS A REGION in Western Canada where the most exquisite wild-flowers in the whole world bloom above the clouds; not singly or in groups, but in beds and banks these blossoms of every hue, and size, and form flourish with a rich luxuriance in the alpine meadows of the Rocky and Selkirk ranges, that recalls those tropical gardens only to be found on the irrigated fringe of the desert. Yet how much more ethereal in texture and coloring are these hardy alpine plants, growing at an altitude of from 3000 to 9000 feet above the level of the sea, than their fellow-flowers which grace the sultry lands of the Orient.

In the Western mountain ranges lies the real Garden of Nature in Canada. It is a wild garden, and wild are its surroundings, a beautiful wilderness of wilding bloom, fragrant with the breadth of Heliotropes and Violets, and glorified by the sheen of scarlet Indian Paint-brushes, yellow Arnicas, and purple Phacelias.

Among the mountains there are plants peculiar to each particular locality, though there are also hundreds of species which abound equally in all the various districts. At Banff, in the Rockies, the wildflowers are within the reach of all; for there they grace the low-lying meadows in every direction, are found in the thick forests, and out upon the dry stony slopes of the hillsides. At this spot, it is quite unnecessary to climb in search of them, as is more or less the case at Lake Louise and Glacier, for they seem to cover the whole locality with a richly colored profusion, which rivals the flower-beds in cultivated gardens.

The Banff Hotel stands on the cliff, high above the confluence of the Spray and the Bow rivers; steep banks broken by large rocky prominences sweep down from its wide verandas to the boiling torrents below, and here in sheltered nooks and crannies grow the curiously-branched Coral-roots (*Corallorhiza innata*), while the tendrils of the white and purple Vetches trail over the stones, and the Wild Clematis (*Clematis Columbiana*) winds its leaf-stalks around the branches of adjacent bushes. Lower down you will find huge clumps of the Service-berry (*Amelanchier alnifolia*), an attractive shrub bearing many clusters of snow-white blossoms amid its pale green foliage, and farther on the Fireweeds flare and flash like torches burning in the long grass.

Along the banks of the Bow river stretch flat meadows where conifers grow sparsely, and the pungent scent of pine and balsam fills the air with subtle sweetness. The ground is covered with dry moss and a tangle of short green growths, above which tower tasselled rushes. Here flourish the exquisite white blossoms of the One-flowered Wintergreen (*Moneses uniflora*), which has been so aptly named the "Single Delight," its waxen-petalled cups bent downwards close to the soil, and its delicate fragrance floating forth on the July breeze.

The roads which thread the forests and lead to those hot sulphur springs which gush forth out of the mountain-sides in copious streams, are fringed by the small plant-like shrubs of the Birch-leaved Spiraea (*Spiraea lucida*), crowned in August by big clusters of creamy blossoms faintly tinged with pink, which smell extremely sweet, and are particularly attractive to the eye of the traveller. Just where the road ends and the trail, which leads to the crest of Sulphur mountain surmounted by the Government Observatory, begins, you will find vast beds of the White Dryas (*Dryas octopetala*) growing in dry soil and exposed to the full glare of the sun, its silver-backed foliage carpeting the earth, and each large white corolla holding up a heart of gold.

Then, should you leave the open road and seek to follow the narrow trail as it winds upward towards the eternal snows, what a wealth of bloom you will encounter on every side. Great orange lilies flaming out from a bank of ferns, the yellow-flecked magenta Calypso (*Calypso borealis*) growing in its solitary beauty from a single bulb with a single leaf at the base of its slender stem, Columbines, Garlics, Monks-hoods, Anemones—there is no end to the floral treasures that spring to life at every step. Or should a happy inspiration seize you to visit the Cave and Basin, where one of the hot sulphur springs has been utilized to supply the magnificent swimming baths, and an ancient geyser, now extinct, has hollowed out a marvelous cave of eccentric formation, you will be rewarded by the sight of quite a different set of plants; for there the warm overflow of the water gushing down the hillside, nourishes wonderful clumps of bright blue Lobelia, huge azure Gentians, Asters, Sunflowers, purple Mints, Butterworts, and sweetest and most fascinating of all, the large showy spikes of the Ladies' Tresses (*Spiranthes Romanzoffiana*), and the pale pink clusters of the Fly-spotted Orchis (*Orchis rotundifolia*).

Banff is by no means the only locality in the Rocky mountains where flowers abound. In the vicinity of Lake Louise the Western Anemone (*Anemone occidentalis*), with its white translucent cups, veined and tinged with purple, covers the higher slopes of the hills, following up the retreating line of the melting snows, in springtime and, later on, decorating the mountains with its fine feathery seed-heads. Here, too, the Wild Heliotrope (*Valeriana sitchensis*) grows in profusion, the pink Swamp Laurel (*Kalmia glauca*) and the White Mountain Rhododendron; Heaths and Heathers, red, rose, and white, carpet the earth beneath the Lyalls Larches, and are among the last vegetation seen at "tree-line"; the Globe Flower (*Trollius laxus*), a great white bloom with a heart of gold, pushes its way up through the icy coverlet of winter, and the Romanzoffia, with its petals of pure velvet, nestles in the crevices of the rocks at an elevation of 8000 feet.

Field is the place where you will find the large Yellow Lady's Slipper (*Cypripedium pubescens*) in all its rare perfection. On a long moraine which stretches up from Emerald lake to the foot of the Yoho valley, these huge orchids grow in thick clumps in the month of July. They are weird, uncanny flowers with big yellow pouches and long spiral petals, and very strange does it seem to find there, flourishing on alpine heights, those plants that we are accustomed to associate with South African jungles and tropical surroundings.

As if in contradistinction to the exotic growth of these giant Orchids, you will also find at Feld [sic] the hardy Ox-eye Daisy (*Chrysanthemum Leucanthemum*), the white Canada Violet, the Ragworts, the Honeysuckles, the Cow Parsnips, and the Harebells, rioting all over the meadows, and clothing the earth with a coat of many colors.

At Glacier the Yellow Adders Tongue (*Erythronium giganteum*) is, perhaps, the most attractive plant to travellers. I have seen these pale yellow blossoms, amid their pallid green leaves, glimmer at dusk with a lambent light beneath the shining star-sown fields of heaven, and at dawn have seen the whole mountain-side break into bloom with exquisite odorous flowers, as if a mantle had been flung about the shoulders of the slopes, while at each step one had perforce to crush them under foot, so closely clustered did they grow among their smooth, spear-like shoots.

To the true lover of nature there is no greater pleasure than to stand where the snow-crowned mountains tower up to heaven, where the thin blue tint of the sky is stretched out over stony bastions, rising above the tall green conifers, and the alpine streams, ice-born in the heart of the sparkling glaciers, form a silvery network enmeshing myriads of bright-hued blossoms which bud and blow at the bidding of the summer sun. Such is the Garden of Nature where the mountain wildflowers of Canada grow

"'Twixt the green and the azure sphere."

When you leave the Châlet Hotel at Lake Louise to follow the trail which leads into the Valley of the Ten Peaks, you begin the long slow ascent that ends on the shoulder of Mt. Temple, from whence you obtain an exquisite view of Moraine lake. Here you enter the wonderful flower-fields of the valley, where blossoms of every hue sweep in great waves of color from "tree-line" down into the depths, 3000 feet below. Here the Indian Paint-brushes (*Castilleia septentrionalis*) and Painted-cups (*Castilleia miniata*) are to be found in all their glory, scarlet, red, pink, white, yellow and orange they abound on every hand. Mingled with them grow golden-silvery Hairy Hawkweeds (*Hieracium Scouleri*), Harebells (*Campanula rotundifolia*), Phacelias (*Phacelia sericea*), cherry-tipped Eriogonums (*Eriogonum umbellatum*), blue-eyed Speedwells (*Veronica alpina*) and a dozen different species of Vetch, Saxifrage and Rock-cress.

An alpine meadow is a spot of supreme beauty, where the Wild Clematis (*Clematis Columbiana*) and Macoun's Gentians (*Gentiana Macounii*) are blue as the sky overhead, while the Yellow Columbines (*Aquilegia flavescens*) toss their heads in the passing breeze and a thousand flowers spangle the grass, their star-like faces upturned to meet the smile of the sun. These alpine gardens, held close in the curved arms of the hills, or set like jewels on the bare breast of the stone bastions, are one of the great marvels wrought by Nature in the recesses of the Western mountains, the contrast between the beauty of the blossoms and their barren surroundings being as vivid as it is enchanting.

The Bunch-berry (*Cornus Canadensis*) is a dweller in the dense forests, where its white cruciform flowers and scarlet fruits are familiar to all travellers. So also is the Queen-cup (*Clintonia uniflora*), so named by me in English in 1903, the name being now adopted in the Canadian nomenclature of plants; for queen it certainly is of all the lovely flower-cups which grow in the mountain valleys, its pure white petals forming a chalice fit for the First Lady in our land, and its large pale green leaves constituting a fitting background for so ethereal a bloom.

On the dry sunny flats at an elevation of from 4000 to 5000 feet above the level of the sea, the Giant Sunflowers (*Helianthus giganteus*), Great-flowered Gaillardias (*Gaillardia aristata*), full-fringed Golden-rods (*Solidago Canadensis, S. decumbens*) and Heart-leaf Arnicas (*Arnica cordifolia*) flaunt their gay golden petals; tall and handsome plants they are and very attractive. Close beside them grows the frail little Wild Flax (*Linum Lewisii*), which droops as soon as it is gathered and withers at a touch, the humble Narrow-leaved Puccoon (*Lithospermum angustifolium*), the Yellow Rattle (*Rhinanthus Crists-galli*), Tall Lungwort (*Mertensia paniculata*) and Loco-weed (*Oxytropis Lamberti*), bushes covered with softly-blushing Prickly Roses (*Rosa acicularis*), flanked by flocks of Pink Everlastings (*Antennaria parvifolia var. rosea*) and warm-scented Clovers (*Trifolium pratense*), realms of rose where the calm of green things growing tempers the lure of the coral and carmine, and the grasses are gossiping as the migrant hosts of the Dandelions march on through Summer's wide-set door, with all their golden banners unfurled to the southern wind.

Close beside the alpine lakes upon whose bosoms float flat lily-pads, and along the margin of those streams where wet-loving water-weeds wind their tendrils about the drooping, dripping willow wands and Blue-eyed Grasses (*Sisyrinchium angustifolium*) twinkle like azure stars in the green firmament of the moss, the pale globular blossoms of the Small Wintergreen (*Pyrola Minor*) hang in pearls upon each juicy stalk and myriads of Red Monkey-flowers (*Mimulus Lewisii*) glimmer like lamps in the gloom of the thickets.

Very early in the Spring the Pasque Flowers (*Anemone Nuttalliana*) appear in the land, their purple cups with silvery linings opening wide long before the fringed fern-like foliage develops about the thick downy stems. Very high up on some tiny plateau held in a hollow amongst the hills, some play-ground of the sun, where a patch of verdure is laid in the earth's brown lap, dew-drenched at dusk, ripened to sapphire by the sun at noon, wind-wrinkled by the gales that blow crisply off the glaciers, these large leaf-whorled Pasque Flowers spread in purpling waves across the waste, and turn the plateau into a paradise of flowers from whose violet rim runs the warm wine of loveliness.

To the traveller the wildflowers of the Rocky and Selkirk mountains are a wonderful revelation of the prodigality and color-painting of Nature in these alpine regions; while to the botanist they are a constant source of interest and delight. There is no more beautiful, rich or varied alpine flora in the world than that of the British Empire, and it is the proud boast of Canada that within her Western borders grow the choicest specimens of many mountain wildflowers.

EDITORIAL NOTE

The foregoing article by Julia W. Henshaw, author of "Mountain Wild Flowers of Canada," published by William Briggs, of Toronto (price $2.00), was originally written for the "Standard" of Montreal. It is now republished by permission of that paper, with amplifications, for the information of our members.

No visitor to the Canadian Rockies should come without Mrs. Henshaw's book. Written in a most delightful and artistic manner, it furnishes a text that, while appealing to the layman in the simplicity of its language, does not neglect the scientific aspect of the subject. It is designed with the purpose of enabling the traveller to identify the various species seen and it fulfils its mission well.

SOURCE

Julia W. Henshaw's "The Mountain Wildflowers of Western Canada," from *Canadian Alpine Journal* 1, no. 1 (1907), 130–137.

Mount Temple, Larches *(oil on canvas, 27.7 x 35.2 cm) by Catharine Robb Whyte, c. 1940.*
(WMCR WyC.01.412)

CATHARINE ROBB WHYTE

"Dearest Mother" (1930–1933)

Excerpts

Lake O'Hara Bungalow Camp
Hector, B.C.
Monday, September 1, 1930

Dearest Mother,

Here we are all settled for two weeks here in the mountains of painting.
We got off to a good start today and each painted one sketch this morning
& another in the afternoon at Lake Oesa or at least up that way. I went
way up with a Miss. Phillips but Pete stopped on the way to sketch & I left
the girl up there for a while & sketched quite near Pete. It's quite a climb
up there but you are right in the mountains & it really is lovely. You
follow a brook up to the Lake & pass several water falls & four lovely little
turquoise or green lakes on the way, just tiny ones.

There are only six guests here tonight. Mr. MacDonald an artist from
Toronto who comes every year in September, a red haired man & great
fun. Then a Mr. Merriman who went to the Museum School several years

ago. Miss. Philips and a Miss Kucrottan from Massachusetts. We have an awfully nice cabin right down on the shore looking right across the lake. It's a lovely view & such a nice cabin & it's such fun being off by yourself like that. We have a stove & it is easy to warm the place up in a very few minutes.

We left Banff yesterday & everything was covered with snow for it really snowed hard all Saturday afternoon & evening & the ground was covered & the mountains were so pretty. Mr. White came up with us to Wapta, the lady running the Wapta Camp let us put the car in one of the garages while we are here. We had lunch there & a delicious one too and then packed our things on a pack horse & started in. We walked the eight miles thinking it would be warmer than riding but found it was almost too hot.

Saturday night we went up to the Banff Springs to ask about getting a garage space & the result was we stayed until about two o'clock. Mr. Davenport asked if we wanted to see some pictures of Honolulu after the concert. So we stayed for that & then Bessie James (the sister of Frances James who sings in the hotels all summer & very beautifully too), arrived & we saw her as we came in & as she said to come up to their suite we went up. She is the Canadian Pacific press representative in San Francisco for all that part of the country. She is the person who conducts people like Ramsey MacDonald through & she's awfully attractive. She had lots of friends with her & we had a lively time. Its rather fun doing things like that.

Well it's about time to go to bed, the electric lights aren't on & it makes one sleepier having lamps.

I'll write as often as I can anyway. Oh, by the way direct the Banff part of your letters very legibly for there is a BAULF in Alberta & one of your letters went there first—& when I said to describe the presents I meant some like the pyrex dishes. I had no idea what kind they were or how many. I've thanked everyone though.

Loads of love to you & Cousin Harriet & Aunt Jane if they are still there.

More love
Catharine

Monday, August 11, 1930

Dearest Mother,

We just got back from Yoho valley and are waiting for Jimmy Simpson to come back to find out about going to Bow Lakes. Your letters were here & they always are great to get. I'm sure I get them all. The one from Glenwood was left in someone's pocket I think but as long as you got it at last never mind.

Pete & I had such a good time these last three days. We took the Borden and Sheldon boy part way with us and reached Castle Mt. Camp in time for lunch. Mrs. Carr gave us a lovely cabin, each one has a fire place in it and they are so attractive. The big room is so nice too & as everyone says people go there first because of Mrs. Carr. She is such a lovely person, young & so nice to everyone. Pete painted a nice sketch & then after dinner Mrs. Carr looked at Pete's sketches & then two awfully nice English chaps who had been around the world looked at them too & they did seem to enjoy them. The nicest part of these camps is that you meet such very delightful and well travelled people. We left there the next morning & stopped for lunch at Kicking Horse Tea House and saw Miss Grant. She is the friend of Allan Cameron who was so friendly to Pete in Hong Kong. He's the head of the C— there on some days. The people out here are all so interesting and as Pete says they love the mountains so that they get every job they can to be here. Then we went to Yoho. Pearl Moore Col. Moore's wife runs it and she was a Brewster. She is just as nice as she can be & great fun. Mrs. Dunbar from Boston was there & we had such fun talking with her. She usually goes to Michigan in the summer & is going there from here. She is one of the nicest people you ever knew. Then there was a Mrs. Charles (?) Woolcott [sic] there who is now about 70 but who came out here 30 years ago when all the mountains were being first climbed & was the first woman up Mt. Stephen & also was the first to discover various glaciers etc. It's all rather exciting listening to them talk.

We were at Yoho two nights & Sunday afternoon took Pearl Moore & Mrs. Dunbar & Col. Moorse [sic] sister Mrs. Raymond of Bermuda to Lake Louise. Pete saw lots of his old friends & it was fun for they all seemed so glad to see him from the policeman outside, the bell boys, various girls in the offices to the manager.

Then after having some orangeade we went back to Yoho. We've been in Canada a week & the Concord wine Mr. Rungeus brought out to drink our health with is all the drinking we have had.

It's been very warm all the time & no one can understand it. I'm glad we are here though for at least we need two blankets every night. It gets cold. We have had fires at Yoho.

It's hard to answer your questions for you haven't asked many except the one about Pete saying how I do finely. I don't know what he meant, nothing much I guess. Everything is going well. Oh I told you last letter the cost of the trip. I believe camping out off season in Banff it costs between 140–150 dollars. Of course round trip is different but then we couldn't have done that anyway. So you see we did well spending 3 weeks in the bargain and a smaller car might cost less. The further west the cheaper the hotels. In Great Falls the room with bath for both was 4.50. We were so dirty we needed baths in places.

Your letters take about 4 days not long really. What a shame about Danny Keyes but it's lucky he got the trip.

Jean's letter was great & I love to hear from anyone and everyone.

We are going now to see Mrs. Dunbar off on the train.

Loads of love,
Catharine & Pete.

Stoney Indian Reservation
Morley, Alberta
October 17, 1930

Dearest Mother,

...Today we walked home with Mrs. Two Young Men. She's pretty old & is still a great hunter. The women always go with the men & do most of the work. Making camp & packing & skinning the animals. She's a wonderful old Indian & great fun. They are all ready to laugh. I wish you could have seen her son's house. The daughter in law was doing bead work and a papoose or little baby sitting in a pile of clothes on the floor. Everything was in the one room. Stove in the center and their things hit or miss everywhere even a sewing machine and pianola. It would be hard to describe. We hope to finish the two portraits tomorrow & then have a young & old man coming Sunday & after we finish them we will probably go back for all our canvas will be gone & anyway six days of painting all day will be enough....

Loads of love & I should think we would be home for Thanksgiving.

Catharine

Dave White & Sons Limited
General Merchants
Phones 50 & 68
P.O. Box D
Banff, Alberta
Monday, Aug. 21, 1933

Dear Mother,

...We went to see Mrs. Jonie, the old lady we painted that first year, and were quite over come for she gave Pete a beautiful beaded coat she had made herself and gave me a pair of gloves. We didn't know what to do, for really a coat is such a big present, so yesterday we got Jackie & went down & brought her back in the car & let her pick out some dress material & needles & thread and a cooking thing and she seemed to love it and was so pleased....

Must go,

Loads of love
Catharine

Yoho Valley Bungalow Camp
Near Field, B.C.
Saturday, August 23, 1930

Dearest Mother,

I'm awfully sorry not to have written you more from here but it seems almost impossible to find time or a place and in fact now I'm sitting in the dining room with a victrola going & plenty of interruptions. You see three days ago—Wednesday the camp was so full we offered to sleep anywhere & so gave up our tent, packed up as best we could & moved to Mrs. Moore's cabin. She had a friend, Mrs. Fulsher spending that night with her so Mrs. Fulcher & I slept on the two cots in the Moore's living room & Pete slept on a sofa down here in the main living room but the last two nights we have both slept at the Moore's. Their whole cabin is about the size of the living room in Concord & they have two tiny bed-rooms & the living room & there are five of us in there, but it's great fun. However there isn't the same chance to write.

Last night we were sitting in the living room round the fire & a girl walked in who seemed awfully familiar. Pete recognized her & placed her right off. Harriet Gilbert's friend who was at the Larrette [?] Music school, a Miss Fenn, & she was so surprised to see us. It is funny how you run into people that way.

Thursday Pete & I each did two sketches which weren't bad. In fact the two I did were the best I have done so far. Then yesterday Pete & I walked to Summit Lake which takes about an hour and a half and the first half hour is up a very steep hill. We saw a coyote on the way up but he ran off. Edmay [?] and Aunt Julia rode up on horseback and brought our lunch to us. Then we painted all afternoon. The lake is the loveliest turquoise color, really you never saw such colors as these lakes are & constantly changing shades. We got home just in time for supper. In the evenings we usually help the girls wash the glass & silver for the chinamen wash the rest &

then sit around & talk for one girl must be on duty at the desk which is in the dining room. Tabby one of the guides usually tells stories if he is here and he does have a lot of them. He ran away as a boy of 11 and went off to sea, has been on sailing vessels & all round the globe. Then he guided round here & further north & went all through the war & was badly gassed & wounded but he is amusing & such yarns as he can spin. Its lots of fun.

Two letters come from you today and the ones of Aunt Jane, Aunt Eleanor etc. What an awful time the Agg[—] must have had. Do send us some of my pictures won't you for it seems to me there are some people I would like to send them to.

There was no duty on the trunk. Jean's letter was great & told so much of all that is going on. I hope you have a grand time in York Beach— I should think it would be awfully nice there.

There doesn't seem to be a great deal to write for we paint most of the time & talk the rest. I'm terribly sleepy & and shall have to go to bed. We hope to get a cabin in a day or two & I'll have more chance to write then.

We are having a great time & I love it more every day, one certainly gets attached to the mountains.

Loads of love & tell Russ I'll write him soon when I feel like tearing off a better letter.

More love,
Catharine

Royal York Hotel

Toronto

Tuesday, February 24, 1931

Dearest Mother,

It is now seven thirty and we have only an hour and half before the train leaves for Banff. We have had rather a full day and are waiting now on the chance of seeing Frances James who is a great friend of Pete's, sings at the Banff Springs Hotel in summer & here in the winter.

We had a good trip though it was a bit warm on the train and found it was a perfect day here. Warm & no snow on the ground. We had breakfast here at the Royal York and then went over to the Toronto College of Art to see Mr. McDonald. He was great to us, showed us all around the art school & took us through the gallery and then to Eaton's new store where we had lunch in a very remarkable modern dining room. That is the decoration was very modern, & circular room with very effective indirect lighting and a great deal of silver & black & pale grey or white and some interesting murals. From there we went to an exhibition also in Eatons & then to Mr. MacDonald's studio where we saw most of his work past & present. He sent us upstairs to see Lauren [sic] Harris who is a well known Canadian artist rather modern as he changes things from the literal to the opposite in order to give you the feeling of the place which he does succeed in doing. It was very interesting seeing what he did with places we are familiar with in the mountains and then he showed us others of Jasper Park, but most interesting of all were his sketches made on a trip last summer when he went on the government supply boat which takes provisions to the various out posts in the north, Greenland and north of Baffen [sic] land to within 500 miles of the North Pole. He was terribly nice to us, and showed us a lot of things. Then we went into another studio to see the work of a Russian girl [probably Paraskeva Clark], so you see we were kept pretty busy. After a 20 minute walk we met Mrs. MacDonald and all four of us had supper together. She told us of a trip she made to Concord two years ago. They having named their son Thoreau because he was such a favorite of theirs I guess. We have just left them and came on down here on the quietest street car you ever heard & so well run too.

Jean must have told you how she saw us off. We got to Boston by three and as soon as we met Peter we all had a cup of tea together. Then Jean saw us on the train and even waited to wave us a good bye. I'm glad Aunt Frankie and Dorothy can be in Concord for a week for it will be great fun for you. I hated to miss the best part of the visit.

I will write as often as possible....

Loads of love always and our love to all.

Catharine

SOURCES

Excerpts of Catharine Robb Whyte's letters to her mother, Ethel Robb, "Dearest Mother," written 1930,1931, and 1933. WMCR M36/84, WMCR M36/85, and WMCR M36/91.

The Indian Madonna. *Photograph attributed to Mary Schäffer, 1907.* (WMCR V527/PS–51)

She Who Colors Slides. *Photograph by Mollie Adams, 1908.* (WMCR V527/PS–1)

Above: Maligne Lake. *Photograph by Mary Schäffer, 1908. Published as* Lake Elizabeth *in Mrs. Humphrey Ward's* Lady Merton, Colonist, *1910.*
(WMCR V527/PS–69)

Left: Mount Athabasca *(from Wilcox Pass). Photograph by Mary T.S. Schäffer, c. 1907.*
(WMCR V527/PS–58)

Mary Vaux with ice axe at the Illecillewaet Glacier, 1899. (Vaux Family Fonds, WMCR V653/NG–596)

Seracs, Illecillewaet Glacier. *Photograph by Mary M. Vaux, 1901. (WMCR V653/PS–58)*

Takakkaw Falls from Below, 1901. *(Vaux Family Fonds, WMCR V653/NG–855)*

Carpet Pink (Silene acaulis). *Watercolour by Mary Vaux Walcott, 1905.*

(SAAM, 1970.355.104, sheet: 35.5 x 17.8 cm. Gift of the artist)

Nodding Campion (Lychnis apetala). *Watercolour by Mary Vaux Walcott, 1905.*

(SAAM, 1970.355.617)

Prairie Crocus, Pasque-Flower, or Wind-Flower (Anemone patens), *also known as* Anemone des prairies. *Photograph by Mary M. Vaux.*
(WMCR V653/PS–164)

Silver Rock Cress (Smelowskia calycina). *Photograph by Mary Schäffer,* c. 1911. *(WMCR V439/PS–261)*

Mount Temple, Larches *(oil on canvas, 27.7 x 35.2 cm) by Catharine Robb Whyte, c. 1940.* (WMCR WyC.01.412)

Mount Assiniboine. *Photograph by Catharine and Peter Whyte, c. 1935. (WMCR V683 l.c.1.b.88)*

FOUR

At Civilization's
Limits

Exploring Women

There are few women who do not know their privileges and how to use them,

yet there are times when the horizon seems restricted, and we seemed to have

reached that horizon, and the limit of all endurance,—to sit with folded hands

and listen calmly to the stories of the hills we so longed to see, the hills which

had lured and beckoned us for years before this long list of men had ever set foot

in the country. Our cups splashed over. Then we looked into each other's eyes

and said: "Why not? We can starve as well as they; the muskeg will be no softer

for us than for them; the ground will be no harder to sleep upon; the waters no

deeper to swim, nor the bath colder if we fall in,"—so—we planned a trip.

—MARY T.S. SCHÄFFER
Old Indian Trails, 1911

WITH THAT, Mary Townsend Sharples Schäffer (1861–1939) and Mollie Adams set out with pack horses, two guides, and plenty of food and warm clothing to explore the Rocky Mountains north of the CPR line in the summers of 1907 and 1908. Of the many women who visited the Rocky Mountains of Canada, Mary Schäffer, along with Catharine Whyte and Mary Vaux, left the greatest imprint on posterity's perceptions of the Rocky Mountains and its culture. While Vaux was a stalwart summer visitor, both Schäffer and Whyte became long-term residents of Banff, Schäffer from 1912 until her death in 1939, and Whyte from 1930 until her death in 1979. Schäffer settled in a newly constructed house in Banff, called Tarry-a-While, located across the road from the graveyard. "I also nearly died when I saw that cemetery," she claimed in a letter to Humphrey Toms in 1933. Her claim is staked in a portrait in which she is seated on a low chair by the hearth (both of which are extant in Tarry-a-While today, along with the mirror above the mantle), in dramatic contrast to the numerous

Mary Schäffer at Tarry-a-While, c. 1920. (WMCR NA66–527)

snapshots of Schäffer on the trail and in camp. Prior to 1912, however, Schäffer's popular articles and lantern slide lectures of her travels into the mountain interior, followed by her book *Old Indian Trails*, established the Rocky Mountains as something far more, and far different, than a tourist destination to be sampled from the comforts of the CPR's trains and hotels. The Rocky Mountains were wilderness; to venture into them was to find peace and healing (Warren, 24 June 1936). It was not an empty wilderness, however, but one inhabited and travelled by Aboriginal women and men, as the trails of her book title testify. Schäffer initiated pack-horse journeys into the mountain backcountry with other women companions as early as 1904 (the year in which she began to publish her Rocky Mountain travel accounts). Over the next five years, she and her preferred

Mary Schäffer climbing with Billy Warren. (WMCR V439/P–6)

wilderness travel companion from 1906 to 1908, Mollie Adams, became experienced and respected trail riders with stories to tell and pictures to show. While it was Schäffer who garnered most fame because of her articles, lectures, and books, she always paid tribute to Adams's companionship, credited the guides for the success of her journeys, and attributed instruction and knowledge of the areas in which she travelled to Stoney-Nakoda acquaintances—who in 1906 named her Yahe-Weha, meaning Mountain Woman, according to Schäffer. Her travels and growing fame in turn engaged readers' imaginations and, as was shown in the second section on literary travellers, Mary Schäffer was mentioned often, by other women writers who met her, as something other and different from the usual travelling, literary lady and inspiration for the young, immigrant woman.

Schäffer met Mollie Adams in 1906 on an ill-fated mountain camping trip with three other mountain women acquaintances, all experienced climbers: Henrietta Tuzo (a founding member of the Alpine Club of Canada), Dorothea Sharpe (of Brooklyn, Massachusetts and a 1907 graduating member of the Canadian Alpine Club), and Zephine Humphrey (a Vermont author originally from Philadelphia). Among the five women guided by Billy Warren on a pack trip to the North Saskatchewan River, only Adams, it seems, shared Schäffer's spirit of adventure and desire to experience the challenges of camp life (Warren quoted in Beck 2001, 182). Schäffer's seriousness of purpose in exploring the Rocky Mountains, as well as her experience and maturity, may have been responsible for the difference in attitudes among the group members and the subsequent parting of ways. As kindred travelling spirits, Schäffer and Adams journeyed together in the mountains for three summers before Adams died in late 1908 while travelling with Schäffer in Japan. In a letter written years later, Schäffer wrote:

> The winter after we re-located the lake my dear friend Mollie Adams and I were in Japan, Hokkaid, Formosa and a snip of China. She caught cold coming back to Japan and I left her sleeping in Kobi on the beautiful heights overlooking the Pacific, pneumonia from exposure on the deck.
>
> For something to do, I wrote the little book which cannot fail to show we had unearthed that beauty spot. I dedicated it to Mollie, the finest pal any woman could ever have had. (Warren, 21 September c. 1933)

There is much to learn yet of the life of Mollie Adams. A geologist from Boston, she was teaching at Columbia College in New York during the years in which she travelled the Rockies with Schäffer. Adams's diary, from which excerpts follow, served as a reference and memoir for Schäffer's own work.

Old Indian Trails includes eighty black-and-white photographs, many made by Schäffer but also by Adams as well as guide Sid Unwin, known as "K" in Schäffer's story, who first glimpsed and photographed Maligne Lake from the eponymous Mount Unwin. Billy Warren, later Schäffer's husband, was the chief guide on their travels, and Schäffer credits him with the success of her Rocky Mountain travels. Whether this attribution was one of socially-appropriate feminine modesty meant to garner readers' approval, a gesture of gratitude, acknowledgement of a genuine debt to her guide, or a testimonial meant to assist his future guiding prospects, the ambiguity of its purpose in her book cautions those of us reading *Old Indian Trails* a century later. We are reminded that the conventions of writing and reading travel literature in the early part of the twentieth century were complex, layered with social expectations of gender roles, meanings of travel, ideas of wilderness, and narrative strategies that included fact and humour to educate and entertain readers. Indeed, one can learn to take caution with making any literal or purely factual reading of travel literature by comparing the reproduction in *Old Indian Trails* of a sketch attributed to Sampson Beaver showing the whereabouts of the mythical Chaba Imbe (meaning Beaver Lake to the Stoneys but named Maligne Lake by Schäffer's contemporaries) with a different one reproduced in Schäffer's 1909 article about locating and exploring Maligne Lake published in the *Bulletin of the Geographical Society of Philadelphia*, but also cited as Beaver's map. Reading Schäffer's polished published stories of her travels—and she published more than one account of her quest for Maligne Lake—against the diary entries of Adams and Caroline Sharpless reveals both the flavour of the initial response and in-the-moment engagement of the women during their travels (as well the sense of the daily duty of recording one's life) and the greater impact of the tale well-told for others to enjoy as the published narrative retains a tighter grip on the reader's attention by building the sense of tension and uncertainty experienced before the fact.

In 1980, the Whyte Museum issued a new edition of Mary Schäffer's popular *Old Indian Trails*, the story of her summer travels with Mollie

Adams, originally published in 1911 by Putnam's of New York. A major cultural contribution to the province of Alberta's seventy-fifth anniversary celebrations, *A Hunter of Peace*, as the new expanded edition was titled, was hailed by the Anniversary Commissioner, R.W. Dowling, as "a lasting tribute to our forefathers"—inadvertently revealing the continuing presumption of a history in which women were absent. Nevertheless, Schäffer's story very rightly caught the imagination of a new generation of readers and has remained in print since. Since being recast in 1980 as a "hunter of peace" exploring wilderness as a personal quest, subsequent writers have reclaimed Schäffer as "no ordinary woman" but a spirited, independent adventurer who stepped off the beaten track. Some have rediscovered her as a photographer at least sympathetic, if not empathetic, to Aboriginal people. Of late, she has been lamented as complicit with colonial ideas of racial superiority and scorned as a mere tourist blind to her culpability as civilization's vanguard in the wilderness.[1] Each of these perspectives—whether complimentary or critical—are couched within turn of the twenty-first century anxieties about gender, race, the environment, and the writing of history.

Such perspectives and arguments are also based for the most part on a reading of the 1980 edition that differs dramatically from the original. Directed at historically and demographically different audiences, the redesigned edition includes an introduction by E.J. Hart and utilizes photographs, including many in colour, that differ from those chosen by Schäffer for her original book. These features combine to effect a different sense of the story of two exploring women. In 1911, publishing technology did not allow for mass reproduction of colour images, and so Schäffer's book was illustrated with black-and-white prints. On her travels, she and her companions had photographed with monochromatic glass-plate lantern slides that she later hand-coloured and used to present public talks about her travels in Philadelphia and Banff. The 1980 edition, then, is an eclectic mix of both travel narrative genres. As a result, the reproductions of Schäffer's coloured slides are a useful contribution to the dissemination of knowledge about her photographic practices.

The advantage of the focus on the Schäffer collection in the archives of the Whyte Museum is that, while Schäffer was still part of the living memory of senior Banffites in 1980 (she died in 1939), she has not subsequently disappeared into the archives to await recovery; instead, successive generations of locals and visitors know of her life, travels, and contributions to Rocky Mountain life, history, and culture. While Schäffer's legacy has sparked interest in other Rocky Mountain women's lives, much of that history and its diversity is overshadowed by this now canonical presence that is redeployed every time a new publication or exhibition of her work appears. More worrisome is that Schäffer's original contributions, as well as the complexity and colour of the era in which she made her most important contributions (c.1900–1912), are at risk of burial by mythologies that are emerging from a veritable cottage industry of Schäffer magazine and newspaper articles, books, notecards, postcards, and even visitor accommodation in the bed and breakfast now operated by the Whyte Museum in Schäffer's Banff home. Schäffer is now known in both popular and academic literature as an extraordinary woman. When reading her unpublished letters and viewing her photographs in the archives, however, she, like Catharine Whyte, Mary Vaux, and the other women who have made up half of mountain history and culture, seem more like ordinary women who experienced an extraordinary geography and rose to its challenges and provocations.

Schäffer presented herself publicly in her published writing as an experienced tourist and budding trail rider: a middle-aged woman, already familiar with the well-travelled regions alongside CPR stops in the mountains, who, seeking peace after the death of both parents and first husband in less than a year, emerged as a seasoned explorer, respected by those she met on her journeys with Mollie Adams and guides Billy Warren, Sid Unwin, and others. The change in tone in the reprint is effected by Hart's biographical introduction that presents Schäffer as a somewhat odd character, quite in contrast to the wit and grit of Schäffer's own work and life that emerges in her original edition. Most telling is Hart's emphasis on the age disparity between Schäffer and her husbands, the first, doctor and amateur botanist Charles Schäffer, being twenty years her senior, the second, mountain guide Billy Warren, twenty years her junior. Hart writes that Schäffer's "skills in both art and photography ultimately led Dr. Schäffer to appreciate his younger wife in a new way, strengthening their marriage" (Hart 1980, 6) and speculates that "While the details [of her second marriage] are not known, it seems likely it was a match of mutual admiration and convenience" (12) as later on Billy Warren was busy with "other matters. The other matters included several lady friends whom Mary certainly knew about but never made an issue of, understanding the needs of her much younger husband on this score" (14), both comments implying that physical attraction could not possibly have been part of the equation.

These assessments say more about one man's alarm at Schäffer's socially unconventional marital liaisons (let alone his need to exonerate Warren for philandering on the heroine) than their significance, if any, to Schäffer's work and legacy. Mountain artist and filmmaker Wendy Wacko scorns Hart's views—"I don't believe that for a moment. What do you think they were doing out there in the woods all that time?" (Wacko 2000, 28). Her reading on the matter is as radical as Hart's was conventional (but equally speculative), revelling in the possibilities of a sexually adventurous personality:

> I always thought that Mary Schaffer and her regular travelling companion Mollie Adams were in love—I'm sure they were lesbians. We know they were very, very close—effectively soulmates—and they both had a crush on their guide Billy Warren. It was the ultimate love triangle. (Wacko 2000, 28)

Reviews of Schäffer's *Old Indian Trails* were numerous, widespread, and unanimously approving. The example from the Portland, Oregon *Telegram* of 15 August 1911 is an especially noteworthy sample. While it casts the author as "dauntless traveler" and writer of distinctive achievement—

"Mrs. Schaffer is an intrepid explorer who has a heart for any hardship that she encounters in the glorious cause of exciting adventure"—and quotes generously from the book to summarize the tale, this particular review is distinguished for the large reproduction of the photograph of the Beaver Family.

In 1911, the Geological Survey of Canada invited Schäffer to return to Maligne Lake on their behalf to survey it. Although she had no experience as a surveyor, the publicity attendant on engaging Schäffer for this work mitigated such a shortcoming:

Not long after our discovery of the lake, I had been telling of its wonders to Mr. Dowling of the Canadian Government Survey. He said, "why not go in there with instruments and measure it?"

"*Me* measure a lake? Why I couldn't measure a pond, much less a great lake like that one!"

"O yes you can, it's very easy; I will lend you the instruments, and you will find it a most interesting thing to do." I thought to myself at the time, what next?

"The way opened, the day came which brought the instruments and all details for the work, instructions so easy that the most stupid could not fail to pluck up courage to at least attempt it; and that was how we came to have so many days on the shore of the lake. Anyone who has ever picked up a set of tools with hands and head totally untrained for the work can imagine the trepidation that stepped into H.M.S. *Chaba* with me the day on which I fixed the log at the stern for the first time, as I took my first reading through the sight of the compass and felt that a doubting and grinning sister, who had been brought up on surveying, looked on from behind. (Schäffer quoted in Stearns 1993, 146)

Unlike her first journey to Maligne in 1908, Schäffer approached from the east in 1911, travelling by train through Strathcona, Alberta (on the south bank of the North Saskatchewan River across from Edmonton) to the end of the line at Hinton and then by pack horse. She was accompanied on this journey by her sister-in-law, Caroline Sharpless (unlike most of her family, Schäffer chose to spell their surname with a single s), her nine-year-old nephew Paul, four guides, a cook, and a crew of trail cutters. As her diary reveals in an excerpt that follows, Sharpless carried to Schäffer one of the first copies of *Old Indian Trails*. Caroline Sharpless lived in New York City and was married to Schäffer's younger brother Frederick (b.1866), a metallurgist and mining engineer. Her son Paul had been ill the previous winter with whooping cough, and Schäffer, convinced of the health benefits of travel in the mountains, invited him to join her on the return to Maligne Lake. Sharpless also joined the survey party. An experienced climber and camper, she was an ideal companion for Schäffer in the absence of Mollie Adams.

Like many women of her time, Sharpless kept an engaging diary of her travels, the sites visited, and the people met, from which Schäffer borrowed when writing her story of their trip. On 29 May 1911, Sharpless left by train for Montreal from Grand Central Station after attending a Quaker meeting. There she collected passes on the Grand Trunk Pacific Railway for travel to the end of the line at Hinton, Alberta. Hers was a tale of adventure in keeping with modern times: her trunk was lost between Montreal and Edmonton where she and Paul met up with Schäffer. Sharpless proved an intrepid traveller, however, as she and Schäffer cobbled together sufficient clothing to allow them to get on their way to Hinton. On board the train once again on June 7th, she writes, "We were personally conducted through the train full of rough looking men by the brakemen and were much stared at, dressed in short skirts, buckskin coats and slouch hats."

Schäffer's fame and claim to the region of Maligne Lake was not without its detractors, however. That same summer, Arthur Wheeler, a Dominion Surveyor and co-founder of the Alpine Club of Canada, led an Alpine Club expedition to Jasper Park and visited Maligne Lake. In his account of the journey, published in the *Canadian Alpine Journal* in 1912, Wheeler expressed his opinion on Schäffer's stake in Maligne Lake:

> The lake lies at an altitude of 5,525 feet. The key-note of the eastern margin is a high central peak (altitude 10,091 ft.) of grey limestone capped with snow, rising 4,566 feet above the water surface. From all points of view it stands alone, and suggest the name of "Mt. Lone Spur." I had so named it, but find that another name has been given by Mrs. Charles Schaffer that has been adopted by the Geographic Board of Canada. Mrs. Schaffer has spent many summers in the Canadian Rockies, first coming to them with her husband, the late Dr. Charles Schaffer of Philadelphia, a charming personality, an intense lover of Nature and a good botanist, altogether a man whom it was a delight to meet. So frequently has Mrs. Schaffer visited the Canadian Rockies, that she is altogether Canadian in her love for them, and has done much as an original explorer to bring their attractions to public notice through her writings and lectures. She first visited and brought to notice this beautiful lake, which had previously been known only to the Indian and the hunter. She has, therefore, undoubtedly the right to name its features. I could wish, however, that personal names had not been so prominent, for the surrounding peaks have many striking characteristic features that seem naturally to supply the names. (Wheeler 1912, 77)

Careful to acknowledge Mary Schäffer's credentials, Wheeler's preference for a descriptive rather than honorific naming of the peaks conformed more with Aboriginal practice than American, Canadian, and British exploration and mapping traditions. The legacy of Schäffer's naming, however, is the strongest and most visible claim by women to have shaped the history—and historical memory—of human experience in the Rocky Mountains.

In the late twentieth century, Schäffer's life and experiences in the Rocky Mountains again captured the imagination of many, women and

Mollie Adams, Mary Schäffer, Billy Warren, and Joe Barker in camp. (WMCR V439/PS–1)

men alike, from climbers to photographers, academics to playwrights. Two of the latter, Elsie Park Gowan and Sharon Stearns, took up the Schäffer story. Gowan not only included it as part of her dramatic reenactment of the history of Alberta written to mark the fiftieth anniversary of the province of Alberta in 1955, reprinted in part in the first section on Métis and Aboriginal women, she also wrote one of the earliest historical biography articles on Schäffer, "A Quaker in Buckskin," in 1957. Stearns used it as the source of a play called *Hunter of Peace* (1993) that takes considerable creative license with the biography of its inspiring heroine, much as Mary Ward had done eight decades earlier in *Lady Merton, Colonist*. A documentary or dramatic film of Schäffer's story has yet to be produced, although it has been imagined by Wendy Wacko who, like Stearns and other late twentieth century readers of *Old Indian Trails* and Adams's diary, is intrigued by a reading between the lines for what went unwritten and unspoken about the relationships among the women explorers and men guides who spent many summers together in the Rocky Mountain wilderness. Mary Schäffer produced a large, varied, and rich body of work that historians and biographers concerned with matters as varied as environmentalism, colonial treatment of Aboriginal people, women's writing and women's histories, landscape photography, industrialization of the wilderness, and other varied themes will continue to examine for some time.

NOTES

1. See, for example, the works of Janice Sanford Beck, *No Ordinary Woman: the Story of Mary Schäffer Warren* (Calgary: Rocky Mountain Books, 2001); Lucy R. Lippard, "Doubletake: The Diary of a Relationship With an Image," *Partial Recall*, ed. Lucy R. Lippard (New York: New Press, 1992): 13–45; I.S. MacLaren, "Cultured Wilderness in Jasper National Park," *Journal of Canadian Studies* 34, no. 3 (1999): 2–54; and Cyndi Smith, *Off the Beaten Track: Women Adventurers and Mountaineers in Western Canada* (Canmore: Coyote Books, 1989).

EDITOR'S NOTE

The title of this section, "At Civilization's Limits," is taken from Mary T.S. Schäffer's *Old Indian Trails* (New York: G.P. Putnam's Sons, 1911/London: The Knickerbocker Press, 1911), 3. See quotation on page 296.

Nibs and His Mistress

Old Indian Trails

Incidents of Camp and Trail Life, Covering Two
Years' Exploration through the Rocky
Mountains of Canada

By

Mary T. S. Schäffer

Author of, in Collaboration with Stewardson Brown,
"Alpine Flora of the Canadian Rockies," etc.

*With 100 Illustrations from Photographs by the Author
and by Mary W. Adams, and a Map*

Toronto: William Briggs
New York: G. P. Putnam's Sons
1911

Title page and "Nibs and His Mistress." From Mary T.S. Schäffer's Old Indian Trails, *1911.*

MARY T.S. SCHÄFFER

"Why and Wherefore" (1911)

from Old Indian Trails

DURING THE TWO SUMMERS of the herein described little journeys among the Canadian Rocky Mountains, there had never been a thought that the daily happenings of our ordinary camp-life would ever be heard of beyond the diary, the family, the few partial friends.

However, when the cold breath of the mountain-tops blew down upon us, and warned us that the early winters were not far away, that the camping days were almost done for the year, when we reluctantly turned our backs upon the sweet mountain air, the camp-fire, the freedom, discarded the much loved buckskins and hob-nailed shoes for the trappings dictated by the *Delineator*, we emerged into the world—the better known world—sure of the envy of all listeners.

Did they listen? No, scarce one. With all the pigments we might use, the numbers were few who "enthused." Those who needed "enthusing," they with aches and pains, with sorrows and troubles, listened the least, or looked upon our mountain world as but a place of privation and petty annoyances.

For them I have written the following pages, tried to bring to them the fresh air and sunshine, the snowy mountains, the softly flowing rivers,— the healers for every ill. Will they close their eyes and shake their heads? Not all, I trust.

To you who are weary both in body and soul, I write the message: "Go! I hand you the key to one of the fairest of all God's many gardens. Go! Peace and health are there, and happiness for him who will search."

SOURCE

Mary T.S. Schäffer's preface, "Why and Wherefore," from *Old Indian Trails: Incidents of Camp and Trail Life, Covering Two Years' Exploration through the Rocky Mountains of Canada* (New York: G.P. Putnam's Sons, 1911/The Knickerbocker Press, 1911), v–vi.

MARY T.S. SCHÄFFER

"An Explanation" (1911)

from Old Indian Trails

TWENTY YEARS AGO, ninety-nine per cent of the tourists to the section of the Rockies of Canada mentioned in these pages, flitted across the country as bees across a flower-garden, and were gone.

There were comparatively few of them, and but a small modicum of enthusiasm distributed among them. Banff contained a hostelry which swallowed all who came and left few visible (so small was the number); Lake Louise boasted no hotel at all,—we slept in tents in '93, and from our door looked out upon that magnificent scene with chattering teeth and shivering bodies, and vowed never again to camp in the Canadian Rockies; Field, with her splendid drives and trails and Yoho Valley to-day, was an insignificant divisional point and eating station; Glacier, a tiny picturesque chalet cuddled close to the railroad track as though to shield her from the dark forests behind her, was full to the brim if so many as a dozen stopped off to view the one sight of those days,—the Great Glacier. At that time no one dreamed of the fascinating caves only seven miles away, hidden and unknown in an even more fascinating valley.

However, over an infinitesimally few those mountains had thrown a glamour and a spell so persistent and so strong, that with the first spring days, no matter where they be, warm breezes brought the call,—"Come back, come back to the blue hills of the Rockies!"

And we went; went year by year; watched the little chalets grow, watched the pushing of the trails into new points of interest, watched with veiled and envious eyes our secret haunts laid bare to all who came. And they did come, fast and furious! Steam heat and hot and cold water had done their work. The little tents on the shores of Lake Louise, with their balsam-bough beds and an atmosphere reeking with health and strength to those weary with the city's life, were banished, and only found again by the determined few who had heard of the recently discovered Moraine Lake, Lakes O'Hara and McArthur, and Ptarmigan and Yoho Valleys. Point by point we fled to them all, each one of them a stronghold at civilisation's limits, each one of them a kindergarten of the at-first-despised camping life. In them we learned the secret of comfort, content, and peace on very little of the world's material goods, learned to value at its true worth the great un-lonely silence of the wilderness, and to revel in the emancipation from frills, furbelows, and small follies.

But the tide swept on. With jealous eyes we watched the silence slipping back, the tin cans and empty fruit-jars strew our sacred soil, the mark of the axe grow more obtrusive, even the trails cleared of the *débris* so hard to master, yet so precious from the fact it must be mastered to succeed.

Where next? Driven from our Eden, where should our tents rise again? We were growing lost and lonesome in the great tide which was sweeping across our playground, and we longed for wider views and new untrammelled ways. With willing ears we listened to the tales brought in by the hunters and trappers, those men of this land who are the true pioneers of the country in spite of the fact that they have written nothing and are but little known. With hearts not entirely on pelts, they had seen and now told us of valleys of great beauty, of high unknown peaks, of little-known rivers, of un-named lakes, lying to the north and north-west of the country we knew so well,—a fairyland, yet a land girt about with hardships, a land whose highway was a difficult trail or no trail at all. We fretted for the strength of man, for the way was long and hard, and only the tried and stalwart might venture where cold and heat, starvation and privation stalked ever at the explorer's heels. In meek despair we bowed our heads to the inevitable, to the cutting knowledge of the superiority of the endurance of man and the years slipped by.

From the States came Allen and Wilcox, (men of course), gathered their outfits together and left us sitting on the railroad track following them with hungry eyes as they plunged into the distant hills; to listen just as hungrily to the camp-fire tales on their return, of all the wonders of the more northern Rockies; came Stuttfield, Collie, Woolley, Outram (names so well known in the alpine world to-day), to tell again to our eager-listening ears of the vast, glorious, unexplored country beyond; came Fay, Thompson, and Coleman,—all men!

There are few women who do not know their privileges and how to use them, yet there are times when the horizon seems restricted, and we seemed to have reached that horizon, and the limit of all endurance,— to sit with folded hand and listen calmly to the stories of the hills we so longed to see, the hills which had lured and beckoned us for years before this long list of men had ever set foot in the country. Our cups splashed over. Then we looked into each other's eyes and said: "Why not? We can starve as well as they; the muskeg will be no softer for us than for them; the ground will be no harder to sleep upon; the waters no deeper to swim, nor the bath colder if we fall in,"—so—we planned a trip.

But instead of railing at our predecessors, we were to learn we had much for which to thank them. Reading the scanty literature which dealt with their various expeditions, we had absorbed one huge fundamental fact almost unconsciously, viz.,—that though this was a land of game,— of goat, sheep, bear, deer and caribou, one might pass through the country for days yet see no signs of wild life. Fish there are in plenty, yet for weeks, when the summer sun melts everything meltable, and the rivers are clouded with silt from the glaciers, they will not rise to the most tempting bait, and the grouse disappear as though by magic.

Throughout the limited literature ran this simple ever-present fact,— a beautiful, but inhospitable land, and the cause of many an unfinished or abandoned expedition, and a hasty retreat to the land of bread-and-butter.

Thanking our informants for their unconscious hint, we laid our plans both long and deep. Our initial experience of one night's camp on the shores of Lake Louise, when we had felt frozen to the bone, and had at the time promised ourselves never to do such a trick again, had been augmented by a flight of three days to Yoho Valley when it wasn't Yoho Valley, only a lovely unknown bit of country, another chilly experience at Moraine Lake, a pause, then a week in the Ptarmigan Valley, and later a sortie of five weeks in the Saskatchewan country. In these trips we had gathered a few solid facts; surely with them we were more or less prepared for a whole summer in the country of which so little was known.

In spite of the protests of anxious relatives and friends, our plans were laid for a four-months' trip during the summer of 1907, and a vow made not to return till driven back by the snows.

The guide-in-chief was our most important factor. To whom should we more naturally turn than to him who had watched over us in the days of our camp swaddling-clothes, who had calculated the amount of our first camp-fare, given us our first lessons in camp comforts, and in fact our very first lessons in sitting astride a horse and learning to jump a log without being shot over the head of our steed?

Three years' acquaintance had taught us his value, and as he did not turn us down, but kindly spurred us on in our undertaking, and cheerfully assumed the leadership, he made us feel we had worn a considerable amount of the tenderfoot from our compositions. Having always kept a strict account of the amount of food he had packed over the trails for us on our shorter expeditions, it became a mere matter of arithmetic for a longer one. If so many pounds of bacon lasted us seven weeks, how many pounds of bacon would last sixteen weeks?—and so through the entire gamut of the food supply,—flour, baking-powder, cocoa, coffee, tea, sugar, dried fruits, evaporated potatoes, beans, rice, etc., with a week's extra rations thrown in for emergency.

On him fell the entire responsibility of choosing and buying the best outfit of horses, saddlery, blankets, the hundred and one things needed and so apt to be forgotten, for in this land to which we were going there were no shops, only nice little opportunities for breaking and losing our few precious possessions.

It was his care also to choose the second guide to accompany us, not so easy a matter as it looks. This fourth member of our party must know how to cook a bannock that would not send one to bad dreams after a hard day's travel, to fry a piece of bacon exactly right, to boil the rice, and make bean soup, all at the camp-fire; it sounds simple, but try it. He must be equally skilful in adjusting the packs that there be no sore backs, he must have a fund of patience such as Job was never forced to call upon, and a stock of good nature that would stand any strain. The man, the horses, and the food, our Chief found them all, and here to him I give the credit of our success, claiming only for ourselves the cleverness of knowing a good thing when we saw it.

It *is* an "inhospitable land"; they who first tore the secrets from those hills have recorded it so; by their experiences we profited; the wise head at the helm steadied the ship and all was well.

And so in the east, the early spring days went by at a snail's pace, with a constant discussion as to the best air-bed, the proper tents and their size, the most enduring shoe, etc., with trials and tests of condensed foods, ending mostly in trials.

There are a few of these foods which are well worth having, and there are some of them, which we were profoundly thankful we had tried before carting across the continent. For instance, beware of the dried cabbage; no fresh air in existence will ever blow off sufficient of the odour to let it get safely to the mouth. "Granulose" was a strongly recommended article to save carrying so much of that heavy and perishable, yet almost necessary, substance, sugar. The label on the neat small bottles read: "One half oz. granulose equal to one ton of sugar, price $1.00." Who would dream of passing such a bargain? Too good to be true, yet we did believe and were soon the proud possessors of "one ton" of condensed sweetness, as also of a stock of dried milk and dried eggs. Truth compels me to state that each of the three has its limitations, and to this day I wonder if that dried milk had ever seen a cow, or if any hen would acknowledge the motherhood of those dried eggs. To the inventor or discoverer of "granulose" I should like to whisper that I thought he had got slightly mixed in his arithmetic; if he had said his dollar's worth of "granulose" was only equal to thirty pounds of sugar he would have been nearer correct and we would not have had to eat so many puddings and cakes without sweetening.

The section of country which had so long been our dream, lies in the Canadian Rocky Mountain Range, directly north of that portion which is penetrated by the Canadian Pacific Railway. It is bounded by latitudes 51°, 31' and 52° 30'; and longitudes of 116° to 118°. Our chief aim was to penetrate to the head waters of the Saskatchewan and Athabaska rivers. To be quite truthful, it was but an aim, an excuse, for our real object was to delve into the heart of an untouched land, to tread where no human foot had trod before, to turn the unthumbed pages of an unread book, and to learn daily those secrets which dear Mother Nature is so willing to tell to those who seek. So the "Saskatchewan and Athabaska sources" were a little pat answer which we kept on hand for the invariable question, "Goodness! what ever takes you two women into that wild, unknown region?" It seemed strange at first to think we must announce some settled destination, that the very fact of its being a wilderness was not enough; but we could not be blind to the fact that nine-tenths of our loving relatives and friends thought us crazy, and the other tenth listened patiently as I ruminated aloud: "There is no voice, however famed, that can attune itself to the lonely corners of the heart, as the sigh of the wind through the pines when tired eyes are closing after a day on the trail. There is no chorus sweeter than the little birds in the early northern dawn; and what picture can stir every artistic nerve more than to gaze from some deep green valley to stony crags far above, and see a band of mountain-sheep, in rigid statuesque pose, watching every move of the unknown enemy below? Why must so many cling to the life of our greatest cities, declaring there only may the heart-hunger, the artistic longings, the love of the beautiful be satisfied, and thus train themselves to believe there is nothing beyond the little horizon they have built for themselves? Why must they settle so absolutely upon the fact, that the lover of the hills and the wilderness drops the dainty ways and habits with the conventional garments and becomes something of coarser mould? Can the free air sully, can the birds teach us words we should not hear, can it be possible to see in such a summer's outing, one sight as painful as the daily ones of poverty, degradation, and depravity of a great city?"

I was so strongly impressed with this very idea one day, as it came unwittingly from a dear friend who had no idea she was "letting the cat out of the bag," that I cannot resist speaking of it. She had taken the keenest interest in all our wanderings, had listened by the hour (yes, quite true) if we would but get upon our hobby, and showed a sincere pride in introducing us as her friends "the explorers" (the true explorer had better skip this part); broad-minded and sympathetic, even her thoughts were more or less tinged with the conventional colouring. Here is her introduction: "My friend, the little explorer, who lives among the Rocky Mountains and the Indians for months at a time, far, far in the wilderness. You would not expect it, would you? She does not look like it, does she? She ought to look some other way, should she not?" And then her listeners all bowed and smiled, and noted the cut of my garments, and said it really was wonderful. And I could have said: "Not half so wonderful as that you do not know the joys of moccasins after ordinary shoes, that there is a place where hat-pins are not the mode, and the lingerie waist a dream; that there are vast stretches where the air is so pure, body and soul are purified by it, the sights so restful that the weariest heart finds repose." Is it possible in such environments, for the character to coarsen, and the little womanlinesses to be laid aside? No, believe me, there are some secrets you will never learn, there are some joys you will never feel, there are heart thrills you can never experience, till, with your horse you leave the world, your recognised world, and plunge into the vast unknown. And all the thanks you will give us will be: "Why did you not tell us to go before? why have you been so tame with your descriptions? We never guessed what we should find." Alas! it takes what I have not, a skilled pen. Perhaps the subject is too great and the picture too vast for one small steel pen and one human brain to depict,—at least it is a satisfaction to think that fault is not my own.

SOURCE

Mary T.S. Schäffer's first chapter, "An Explanation," from *Old Indian Trails: Incidents of Camp and Trail Life, Covering Two Years' Exploration through the Rocky Mountains of Canada* (New York: G.P. Putnam's Sons, 1911/ The Knickerbocker Press, 1911), 1–16.

"Old Indian Trails of the Canadian Rockies" (1911)

Old Indian Trails. Incidents of Camp and Trail Life, covering Two Years. Exploration Through the Rocky Mountains of Canada. By Mary T. S. Schaffer. Price, $2 net. Published by G. P. Putnam's Sons, New York.

MRS. SCHAFFER is an intrepid explorer who has a heart for any hardship that she encounters in the glorious cause of exciting adventure. The widow of the late Dr. Charles Schaffer, the noted botanist, she accompanied and assisted her husband in collecting rare botanical specimens during 17 Summer trips through the Canadian Rockies. It is not remarkable, in the circumstances, that she writes of these Northern scenes with perfect familiarity.

But the dangers and discomforts she and her woman companion encountered do make a remarkable story. Women with less grit would have turned back before the journey was half under way; or, in the event of sticking it out, would have become sorry burdens to the male members of the party. Mrs. Schaffer and her friend were game to the end and bore their share of work and deprivation with beautiful fortitude and even downright good nature.

Being an enthusiast, the author is possessed of the missionary spirit. In vain by word of mouth has she tried to induce others to follow her example; all seem to look on her mountain world as "a place of privation and petty annoyance." Her book is written with the intent to make converts, and she earnestly invokes her readers:

"Go! I hand you the key to one of the fairest of all God's many gardens. Go! Peace and health are there, and happiness for him who will search."

Two expeditions, undertaken in 1907 and 1908, are described in this book. The objective point of the first was the Canadian Rocky Mountain range, directly north of that portion penetrated by the Canadian Pacific railway. Ostensibly the aim of the trips was to discover for themselves the head waters of the Saskatchewan and Athabaska Rivers. It is admitted such was but an excuse to satisfy the curious. "Our real object," Mrs. Schaffer confesses "was to delve into the heart of an untouched land, to tread where no human foot had trod before, to turn the unthumbed pages of an unread book, and to learn daily those secrets which dear Mother Nature is so willing to tell those who seek."

Experience taught this traveler never to put her trust in mountain streams. They are always painfully cold and always dangerous. Her advice is, even if your horse loses his footing, get out of your saddle but "cling to his mane, tail, or anything you can get hold of but don't let go of him altogether. He may get out, you never will alone."

In a search for the sources of the Athabaska the party followed a trail that took it to the base of Mount Columbia. It was but a casual experience that found the explorers climbing a peak 9000 feet high. To stand in the midst of Collie's and Stuttfield's mountains, such a peak is ascended.

If the mountain heights afford magnificent views most spectacular in character the quieter scenes are none the less attractive. The "golden plains" of the Saskatchewan, it is declared, "there is no describing." It is said that "to appreciate them one must breathe deep into the lungs, must let the soft winds caress the face, and allow the eye to absorb the blue of the surrounding hills and the gold of the grasses beneath the feet. To us, who had been storm-swept, chilled and baked by turns in the outlying valleys, it was simply heaven."

An amusing anecdote is told which would certainly shock Ernest Thompson Seton, who, in a recent book, came out with a "Nature" yarn to the effect that Indians did not require or allow their squaws to perform the laborious work of the camp or trail. Mrs. Schaffer has a different version of the noble redman's idea of gallantry. Silas was a Stoney Indian, well known to the author, who had met him on previous trips. She asked him:

"Silas, do you really let your squaw saddle and pack your horses?"

"Sure."

"And let her fix the tepee-poles and put up the tepee?"

"Yes."

"And get the wood and cook and tan the skins?"

"Yes, sure."

"Now, Silas," I said impressively, "you should be like the white men, you should do the work for your squaw. We do not put up our tepees or pack horses or cut wood, our men do it." Taking his pipe from his mouth and inspecting me from head to foot leisurely, he said, "You lazy."

The farthest north point reached in the first expedition was Mount Lyell. Retracing their steps, the party arrived at Field, B.C. At that point they struck the highway, and on it "a carriage with people in it." Travel-stained and torn, with their buckskin coats frayed and worn, all looking more like Indians than white men and women, they learned with something like dismay that the smartly dressed man and woman in the carriage were Rudyard Kipling and his wife.

The second expedition included a visit to Mount Robson, the highest peak in behind a hill, cold, icy, clean-cut in a sky unclouded and intensest blue. The mountains rising far and near were but worthy of the name of hills, leaving Robson a noble, massive vision to the pilgrims who had come so far to see her. "We gazed, and our hearts grew hot within us as on every side we saw black tree trunks strewn, ghastly reminders of careless, indifferent campers of other days."

A camp scene where the party pitched tents on the banks of a mountain lake is vividly pictured:

"Our fire, built on the very edge of the glass-like lake, was reflected in the black depths yawning beyond us; the wind died down; over the water came the faint sound of the stranger's horse-bells; then the weird laugh of a loon pierced the darkness with a taunting ridiculing sound as though calling 'Ha-ha! Left alone, left alone!' and in its wake came the cry of a coyote, which was answered by two or three others on the distant shore. The loon laughed again derisively, the firelight danced cheerily on the walls of our tent, and a few stars peeped down through the black boughs of the spruces above our heads, leaving us to feel but an infinitesimal part of the great whole."

After years of following trails over the rockiest roads a woman ever attempted, and succeeded in that attempt, this dauntless traveler voices her joy in the sport in the following eulogistic manner:

"There is no voice, however famed, that can attune itself to the lonely corners of the heart, as the sigh of the wind through the pines when tired eyes are closing after a day on the trail. There is no chorus sweeter than the little birds in the early Northern dawn; and what picture can stir every artistic nerve more than to gaze from some deep, green valley to stony crags far above, and see a band of mountain sheep, in rigid, statuesque pose, watching every move of the unknown enemy below?"

The really rough life, this author believes, is to be found in the cities. She asks, "Why must it be settled so absolutely that the lover of the hills and the wilderness drops the dainty ways and habits with the conventional garments and becomes something of coarser mould? Can the free air sully, can the birds teach us words we should not hear, can it be possible to see in such a Summer's outing one sight as painful as the daily ones of poverty, degradation and depravity of a great city?"

The book has been handsomely prepared, and the numerous illustrations from photographs by the author are rarely beautiful.

SOURCE

Excerpt of "Old Indian Trails of the Canadian Rockies," a review from *Portland Telegram*, Oregon (5 August 1911).

First sight of Maligne Lake from Mount Unwin. *Photograph by Sid Unwin, 1908.*

MOLLIE ADAMS

"Laggan to Maligne Lake and Tête Jaune Cache and Return" (1908)

Excerpts

June 8, 1908.
Monday.

HAVING SPENT THE NIGHT in great discomfort at L. Louise Chalet, the place not being officially open and in an awful mess, we started joyfully for the comforts of camp....

1st Maligne Camp.
Tuesday, July 7.

Rain in the night. Bar. down a little. Cloudy morning. A good deal of bright sunshine and a few showers during the day. Moved down the valley 7 or 8 miles, 3 1/2 hrs. drive, and camped at 5859 ft. among thick spruce trees just around the bend in the creek, where we had expected to find the end of the range of mts., and be able to see whether the lake lay behind it or not. A second range appeared however, going on down. After lunch U started out climbing to find the lake or bust, and with compass, aneroid, maps, camera and field glasses, so that nothing should escape him. He left camp about 3 P.M. and returned at 10.45, having, as he said "kept hopping" all the time. He climbed about 2500 ft. to the top of the ridge north of camp, dropped down 2000 ft., then up again on what seemed to be a shoulder of Mt.___ to 8750 ft. –saw the lake! Went down right to it, 5600 ft., and around and home again over the lower wooded shoulders. So it is discovered at last. Sampson shortened up the distances on his map, but it is pretty good all the same. We are probably six miles from the lake now, and the creek we are on flows into it about 6 miles from the lower end. U. could not see the upper end of the lake from where he was, but said the part he could see looked about 18 miles long.

M. and I out for the usual stroll this time through willow brush and very scrubby woods, and mosquitoes. The green bug nets were out in force in the evening, M. ate supper with her gloves on too. M. crawled into bed at 9.30, but the rest of us sat around a smudge and waited till the wanderer came.

Eureka Camp.
Wednesday, July 8.

The first sound this morning was W. shouting "All aboard for the lake!" He got on his fourteen foot smile when he found that all was well and we were on the right road, and he and U. have a chance of looking respectable again. They announced a few days ago that they would not shave till we found the lake—and have not. We were off at 9.30 and in about 3 hrs. were at the lake, but on the wrong side of the creek we have been travelling down for the last three days—no feed or good camp ground there, and the stream too deep to ford. So as it did not seem worthwhile to get everything wet, W. and U. went off prospecting and we waited there a long time. Found a place where beavers had been very busy in days gone by (the Stony Indians call the lake Chaba Imne, which means Beaver Lake). Finally U. came back and said they had found a ford about half a mile back, so right about face and back on our tracks. We did not come by the trail most of the way, it was probably the other side of the creek, and that last half mile, having been soft in spots, to say the least, when we first went over it, was well chewed up by the time 21 horses had plunged through it twice. We nearly lost a bag of flour; it fetched loose somehow from old Gingerbread's pack, and dropped to the ground just as he jumped up the bank out of the creek. If it had dropped when he jumped in, that would have been the last of it. The shore of the lake is not favorable for camp sites here. We settled ourselves on a little knoll with fine grassy meadows around it, and what looked like a thin fringe of trees between the meadow and the lake. But M. and I thought we would just go through to the shore after lunch, and found the lake was at least half a mile away, and the woods most amazing ones to walk in. So both gave it up. We are in doubt as to whether we can see Mt. Brazean [sic] or not. There is a high double peaked snowy mt. with a very large glacier, somewhat farther to the n.e. than Mt. Poragean should be, and there is the one U. climbed to the shoulder of, and thought was Mt. Brazean. But it seems to be too far down the lake on the s.w. side.

Chaba Camp.
Thursday, July 9.

The three boys spent the day building the raft, up to their knees or deeper in cold water. They had quite a time finding enough dead trees, had to bring some quite a distance, towing them along the shore. H.M.S. "Chaba" was finished about 6 P.M. and ready for the voyage tomorrow.

Chaba Camp.

Friday, July 10.

We had all the horses with us at breakfast, as W. gave them salt to make it more attractive to them to stay here while we are away. Two tents, beds and grub went with us and we reached the lake and had the cargo aboard by 10.30. M. and I were ignominiously picked up and dumped on too, as H.M.S. "Chaba" drew too much water to be brought quite up to shore, or even near enough for a long jump. W. took the horses back to put them with the others—Bugler, Nibs and two pack horses—and we started on the voyage, to pick him up at the mouth of the river, where he would come by a short cut not practicable for horses. They had hewed out two long oars about 12 ft. long, and one sat on the edge of the forward deck, and one aft, to row, with a wooden pin stuck up to pull against for a rowlock. The decks were about 2 1/2 ft. wide and stuck out over the sides a little so they were about 7 ft. long. The bottom logs were about 2 inches under water when all of us and the impedimenta were stowed away on board. At 11.30 W. came and we were really off. They tried making a bee line down the middle of the lake for a distant point. A head wind came up, however, and it was soon evident that H.M.S. "Chaba" would have to hug the shore if she was to make any progress. It took nearly an hour to worry her in, and then we coasted along till we reached the point about 2 P.M. Landed and ate lunch. Cameras busy during the carrying act. On again. We passed point after point, thinking each one would give us a look up the length of the lake. Finally came to the one where U. had come down to the lake on his long walk, then saw miles of water still ahead of us, and a fine range of mts. opening out. Propelling that raft was no child's play. As there were three of them to do it, each one got a rest by frequent changings off, but they were still pretty tired all the same. At about 5 P.M. we could see what looked like the end of the lake, although we had not yet come to anything which seemed like the narrow place about three quarters of the way up the lake which Sampson told us about so particularly. At 6.30 W. said "hold, enough," and we made for a point on the n.e. shore near where a stream came into the lake from the valley leading to the double peaked snowy mountain we could see from Chaba Camp. It proved to be a very pleasant camp ground, and we were soon settled and devouring supper. It was fine and sunny all the morning; cloudy afternoon,—mares' tails, mackerel scales, pink sunset, and all bad signs, but barometer high—giving the lake 5550 ft.

Unwin Camp.
Saturday, July 11.

The double, snowy mt. not in sight from camp—hidden by a thin slab of a low peak. "Mt. Unwin" just opposite across the lake (U. was on a shoulder of it July 7) also double peaked and snowy, and a fine glacier coming low down toward the lake. There was considerable doubt as how to conduct the campaign today—whether to move camp or not, and what mt. M. wanted to climb to get a look at the Brazean ice field and try to locate Mt. Brazean with regard to this lake. It was finally decided that the end of the lake not being far off, we might as well just take lunch with us and row up there, and then the climbers could attack whatever seemed the handiest. So we got off at 8.30. After about an hour we were about to round the last point and cast anchor at the foot of the long valley we could see leading up into the mts., when behold beyond the point jutting out from the n.e. shore was another from the s. w. shore, and beyond that the lake opened out again miles long and still more beautiful than before. So on we went. It was very pleasant for those of us who were not doing the hard work,—another fine day and more mts. showing up all the time. After a little more than 4 hrs. of rowing we reached a point where we actually did see the end of the lake, and it was very satisfactory, as such. The last mile lies in a valley running east and west between "Mt. Warren" to the south and "The Thumb" to the north, at the head a creek from a s.e. to a n.w. valley from east of the cliffs of Mt. Warren. At the west of Mt. Warren another creek from a very large snow field (Brazean?), a mountain some miles away. Mt. Warren was in sight from the time we first embarked yesterday, but we had no idea the lake ran up that far. It has the usual double peaked summit. Of course there was no use of anyone thinking of climbing at that time of day as it would take till 6 or 7 P.M. just to get back to camp. If we could only have stayed a week there it would have been greatly to our pleasure and profit. We landed for lunch on an old alluvial fan formed by the stream from west of Mt. Warren, and as at Camp Unwin, which is also on river deposits, the ground was covered with flowers, especially vetches, large crimson ones and smaller pink and yellow, and very fragrant, like a sort of cross between clover and locust blossoms. The Thumb, across the lake from us, was a long line of very high cliffs from that point of view—rusty, weathering rock, probably limestone or dolomite. A waterfall bursts out through a hole at one place and falls such a distance that it is spray waving back and forth in the wind long before it touches the rocks below and gathers together in a stream. We had a favorable wind part of the way back and set a pack mantle sail, but took about the same time as going up. M. kept time and they rowed in ten minute stints. Named the narrow place "Sampson's Narrows" and the slab sided peak rising from the lake to the east of the valley leading to the very snowy mountain, "Sampson Peak." Beautiful pink, almost crimson glow on the mts. at sunset.

Camp Unwin.
Sunday, July 12.

Another fine day. Very little wind, perfect reflections almost all the time. The actual rowing time back to Chaba Camp was only 4 1/2 hours. At only one place have we seen a sign of anyone having been up the lake before, and that was about half way between Camps Chaba and Unwin on the south shore. A tree was blazed conspicuously and near by a charred log, the remains of a camp fire. It may have been a trapper, timber cruiser or prospector; Indian or white man; and probably he was there in the winter on snowshoes. We all agree that Maligne Lake is one of the finest things in the Rockies or Selkirks. The upper half is right in high mountains, the lower more open and gentle looking. It will probably be a great resort some day when the Grand Trunk is done.

SOURCE

Excerpts of Mary [Mollie] Adams's unpublished diary, "Laggan to Maligne Lake and Tête Jaune Cache and Return," 1908. WMCR M79/11.

Mary Schäffer with Paul and Caroline Sharpless, 1911.

(WMCR V527/NA—78)

CAROLINE SHARPLESS

"Trip to Jasper Park, Rocky Mountains, Canada" (1911)

Excerpts

MAY 29TH, 1911. Left home at 8.25 A.M. and after going to Loeser's to return some purchases, then up to the Grand Central Station to check my baggage, went to Yearly Meeting, arriving at eleven o'clock. Had dinner there, visited with relatives and friends, attended the afternoon session, then went to Putnam's where they gave me the two very first copies of "Indian Trails", just in from their publishing house. They could not give me a copy with the colored picture on the cover so instead of leaving the space blank they put in Sidney Unwin's picture "baking bannock." I am delighted to think I am the bearer of the first copy to the author.

I feel as though we were going on a long long long long journey. Many people are interested in our trip and we go with the good wishes of our friends for a safe journey and a pleasant time.

We are leaving over the Delaware & Hudson at 6.55 tonight and are due in Montreal at 7.15 tomorrow morning. It has been a warm day.

JUNE 11TH. SUNDAY. An early breakfast and at eight o'clock, Mary, Paul and I rode away for our next camping place, Mr. Unwin to follow as soon as the pack train was ready to start. A gorgeous morning and beautiful scenery. We soon began to climb and then got down on the flats again. We rode until ten o'clock and then rested for about an hour when Mr. Unwin rode up. Then on again until 12 when we stopped beside a stream, made tea and had a bite to eat. Then on again till we reached Swift's place where we again stopped and visited the Squaw man and his family. Old Swift came in here 17 years ago expecting the railroad someday to come in. It is now here and runs right through one of his log cabins. After a half hour we again rode away until we came to the site of Henry House, another old trading post of the Northwest Trading Company. Here was a clearing on the banks of the Athabaska with only the remains of some chimneys where once had stood the houses. After a short rest we again rode on till we came to Mile 111 where we stopped to wait till the pack train came up. In half an hour they came, hungry, tired and dirty. They told us in the morning we were to go 12 miles but our 12 miles had proven to be 22. Mary was very tired and burned scarlet by the sun as she had ridden without a hat and how dirty we were as the road had been very dusty. Mr. Unwin and Mr. Otto went out to hunt a site to camp and soon rode up to us. We again mounted our horses and after crossing some fords and trailing through the bush we came to the river's edge where we were to camp. It didn't take long to take the packs and saddles off the tired horses. Mr. Unwin had tea made and a lunch spread in about ten minutes. We wouldn't listen to them getting dinner later on for it was then six o'clock and tepee and tent poles were to be cut, tents pitched and everything put in order for the night and every moment it looked as though it would rain. After a refreshing bath we were all glad to go to bed. We were camped right on the bank of the Athabaska river, which was nothing but sand and a miserable camping place it was, but was the best we could get. About nine o'clock Mr. Unwin brought in some hot cocoa and cake and then we went to sleep. We had ridden 22 miles and had been in the saddle six hours. Saw a snake to-day. I mention this because they are very rare.

JUNE 16TH. FRIDAY. Otto reported that he returned at 12 o'clock. Had to wait for the butcher till 7 P.M. At 8 the beef was running in the field but it was killed and Otto returned at midnight bringing the heart, liver and tongue. He spent a long time trying to learn something of my lost baggage. Could not phone Hinton and could get no answer from Edmonton. So discouraging! We packed up and were off at 10, keeping just ahead of the pack train. Began to climb soon after leaving camp. From 4900 feet we climbed for three hours to our next camp at 6400 ft. Not an interesting trail but the panorama opened to us was very beautiful. Saw a partridge which Mary shot at but failed to hit. Also saw a few ducks. Reached camp at one and it looked as though it would rain every moment. Horses were hurriedly unsaddled and our tepee put up. Unwin soon had lunch ready. After lunch Mary, Paul, and I began to climb a mountain right back of our camp. We climbed an hour and a half to an altitude of 8000 feet. Unwin joined us when we were near the top. He had climbed it in half an hour. We crossed over snow and in a gully near the top the snow must have been over 20 feet deep. Such a view as we had! We saw from this point 60 or 70 mountain peaks covered with snow and ice, 32 lakes and two rivers—the Athabaska and the Whirlpool—and three steams coming down the canyon. We photographed and then descended in 1/2 of an hour. Mary's knees hurt her but it was the soles of my feet as I was compelled to climb in such light shoes. Paul climbs well. Quite different than when we were in Colorado four years ago, when he couldn't seem to climb at all in that high altitude. Camp looked pretty good to us and we were inside of our tepee in no time with a nice fire going, for it is cool here in "Windy Camp", rightly named by the trail cutters as the wind blows right up the canyon. A lovely supper of fresh bannock, bacon and fried liver (the best liver I ever ate), boiled potatoes, macaroni and cheese, fresh doughnuts and cocoa. Good!

and we were hungry. Paul was very helpful in our climbing up the mountain and coming down also. Mr. Unwin helped us both down. We prepared for a cold night and as a consequence we were both hot as it wasn't cold. A few mosquitoes in the tepee in the A.M. bothered us. Paul pulled out a tooth.

JUNE 23RD, FRI. A beautiful A.M., cold and ice on the pails. Men report a heavy white frost. The surveying party (Mary, Mr. Unwin and Paul) got off at eight o'clock, with Paul as steersman. I scrubbed my skirt, had a bath, washed all my clothes and mended, read and wrote some. Went over to the other camp to talk to Bill, the cook and learned a few things from him. Otto had supper ready at 7 but the party didn't get back till 8.30. Such a good supper as we had! Corn soup, roast duck, potatoes, bacon and currant pie. Otto came to grief with his pie crust but Classon came along just in the nick of time, took the dough and fixed it up and made the pie, which was then taken over to Bill to bake in his stove. The pie turned out good and was much appreciated, as was also the duck as we had told the surveyors there would be no duck when they got home. The party had come to grief soon after starting by losing the log but they went on just the same to see what the lake looked like. They got to the other side of the Narrows and suppose they went 10 or 12 miles altogether. All were tired. Mary and Paul went to bed as soon as supper was over. About 6 o'clock Classon saw five or six goats on the mountain and it caused quite a little excitement for the men had made up their minds that there were none here. Try as hard as I could, I couldn't see the goat. The men tried every way to make me see them but my eyes are not trained to seeing goat. We thought we had a sick horse across the river and watched him for several hours but could not get to him until the boat returned. Before that time he got up and ate some. After supper Otto went over but found him all right.

JUNE 24TH. SAT. A rainy night and cool and damp this A.M. with no signs of clearing. The trail cutters expected to get off early this A.M. but did not get off till one o'clock as it was wet and they waited until it should clear up a bit. It seemed quite lonely after they went. After lunch Mary, Paul and I, with Unwin, rowed down the lake, got off to look at some Indian tepee poles, then rowed on into some little coves. Into the last one we rowed right into ducks but of course hadn't our rifle with us. Otto had such a nice supper ready upon our return, to which we did full justice. He set out bobs tonight to make sure there were no fish in the lake.

AUG. 2ND, WED. Up early and at 7.30 were off on our last horseback ride to the station at "65," Wheeler driving the packhorses with our duffle bags and blankets, Otto walking. We couldn't learn what time our train left but were told that it would come along any time from five till noon or later. We reached "65" at 8.20 and at 9.30 the train, consisting of eight [or] ten freight cars, two passenger coaches and a caboose came along and Otto put our belongings in the express car and we sat on them till the brakeman told us we could go in the caboose. We crept along slowly over the crooked road bed, every once in a while asking the men in charge if they thought we would reach Edson in time to catch the train for Edmonton. They thought we would unless the unexpected happened. About 11.30 we ate our cold lunch and then watched preparations for the railroader's dinner. Just as the brakeman had taken off his collar and necktie and washed his hands there was a grind, a sudden stop and off went the brakeman and conductor to put a car on the track which had slid off. We went out, watched the operation, took some photos, then when the car was about on again, boarded the train, started, then a grind, another stop and we were off the track again. We didn't go out this time but sat down to wait until we should start. By this time Foley's mail clerk had been pressed into service and cooked the railroaders a nice dinner of ham and eggs and tea, when done we started again and the train crew came in, washed up, sat down, took the first mouthful when there was a grind, stop and we were off the track again. By this time we had given up reaching Edson in time to catch the train for Edmonton and I settled myself down for a nap after we had had four cars off the track and had passed all the bad places of quicksand and muskeg. When it got to be five o'clock we were ready for a hot meal. Mary asked if we could buy some eggs and they asked if any of us could cook. We assured them we had the finest cook in the country and they made a fire for us, opened their cupboards and refrigerator and the best the car could afford was ours and we enjoyed our supper. Meantime we had been joined by two French nuns who proved to be very pleasant, and later on another woman came in the caboose who looked most respectable. Otto remembered that he had stopped at their "stopping place" six months ago and that her place was very dirty and the meals very poor.

We finally reached Edson at eight o'clock (about six hours late) and after looking after our luggage walked up to the Grand Pacific Hotel which had been recommended to us by Mr. Morris as the best the town afforded. They took us in and gave us the best they had which was a room with two beds in it (both having been slept in without changing the sheets), one chair and one home made table for the toilet set. Board [partitions] through which you could look into the next room, also into the room below.

AUG. 3, THURS. We slept in our clothes and were very thankful to find the beds were not inhabited. Had a comfortable night, fairly good break-fast, and then walked the streets and sat in the station until 3.45 when we were only too glad to take our train for Edmonton. As the train from "65" had not yet gotten in we had the car pretty much to ourselves. All the foreign element were herded into the front cars so that passengers in our car were very respectable. We found our same wonderful brakeman and "newsy", both glad to see us and anxious to know what kind of a time we had had. About 5.30 we went into supper and had beefsteak, tomato salad, tea and coffee and it was good. Served up in the end of a colonist car, the same as when we came. A man who lived up North somewhere ate supper with us and told us of his experiences and his knowledge of

Herschel Island. Soon after we returned to our car a large camping party got on at Wabanum [sic] Lake and thought they owned the car. Their noise was soon stopped by the brakeman coming through asking if there was a doctor on the train. Found none, then soon again he came, asking the same question, and giving us the impression that the situation was desperate. Then the women were appealed to and three of us got up and went into the car ahead where we found a poor woman about to become a mother, holding a child of twenty months asleep in her arms. The car had been cleared out and she was all alone. The eldest of us (the mother of five children) took the baby and returned to our car and Mrs. McKibbon and I remained to do what we could for the poor woman. The brakeman telegraphed on ahead to Stony Plain for a doctor. We thought we would never get there but we did and the Dr. got on. In not more than ten minutes the baby was born. The brakeman announced the fact to the passengers who were anxiously awaiting news and then the newsboy started a collection and got $40.00 for the poor mother. It was very welcome for she had only $3.00 in her pocket. Then people began to suggest names, one of them being "the Muskeg Kid." Mary suggested "Carol" after me; another suggested Atcheson as the child was born there, and another Alexis, claiming the child was born there. I wrapped the baby up and put it in the top of a telescope bag belonging to the mother and showed it off to the many who came to ask if they might see it (him), not out of curiosity but because they were interested. The train men were all so kind and were on the jump to do what they could for us to help the poor woman.

We finally reached Edmonton, an ambulance was waiting to take her to the hospital. She was strapped to a stretcher, the train uncoupled and she put in the ambulance while I took the infant to the ambulance and gave to the doctor to carry. The woman's name was Mrs. Smith who came from Entwistle. A poor woman but respectable and very clean, very bright, and a good woman for the country in which she lived, her husband being a homesteader. We went to Mrs. Otto's house and after a cup of tea were glad to go to bed, but I was too tired and excited to go right to sleep.

AUG. 5, SAT. Slept late; all hands being tired and after breakfast, which was at 10, Mary, Paul, Otto and I went over town, called on Mr. Douglass and found only his son there. Did some errands and upon returning to the house found Mr. Warren there. We had a great deal to talk about and kept it up the rest of the day. After supper we went over town. Paul and Otto had their hair cut and looked much better, then we went to a moving picture show and then had ice cream and then home. I had indigestion and went right to bed, as did Paul.

AUG. 6, SUN. Up late. Mr. Warren came and we visited till two o'clock when we went with Mr. Warren over to Strathcona to see him off for Banff. We then returned, got Mrs. Otto and went to the City Park where we heard the band and watched the people. The park had a band stand and some swings but no doubt in another year will look like a park. Returned home, had supper and were then greatly entertained by Mrs. Otto telling us of the Orkney Islands, Shetland Island and the Faro Islands, she coming from the Orkney Islands.

AUG. 7TH, MON. A late breakfast and a rainy morning but we were busy washing our soiled and smoky clothing, which took all morning. Went over town after lunch and met the other "trained nurse" who had been with me when the baby was born on the train. She had been to the hospital to see the mother and baby. After supper we went over town again and went to a moving picture show and had ice cream. In the afternoon, just as we were leaving the house Mrs. Young, Mrs. Hardisty and Mrs. Wood came to call. Three sisters and daughters of the first missionary to come up here. Mrs. Hardisty had lived 25 years here in the old fort, Mrs. Wood had lived at Athabasca Landing at a Hudson Bay Co.'s Post for twenty-five years and Mrs. Young had gone to Lesser Slave Lake when a bride of 17. All had lived among the Indians and had seen frontier life and yet not one of them would say she had had a hard life. They were so entertaining. Called on Mrs. Morris at the hotel.

AUG. 8TH. TUESDAY Up late, helped around. After dinner Mary and I walked over to the hospital to see my baby and the mother. Found both doing well and so glad to see us. The mother so grateful. We looked at the other babies and did a good deal of talking, then returned home. Mrs. Morris, Mrs. Wood, Mrs. Hardisty, Mrs. Young and her daughter came for tea and spent the afternoon, and we enjoyed them so much. After supper we went over to Mrs. Young's house where the three sisters told us more of their mother's and father's experiences.

AUG. 9, WED. Up earlier this A.M. and I ironed a good part of the A.M., then went over town with Mary. In the afternoon went on a river excursion with Mrs. Hardisty, Mrs. Wood and Miss Young, the Mrs. Otto and Paul. Boat crowded. A very pretty ride up the river about 10 miles, then back. Enjoyed talking with Mrs. Wood and Mrs. Hardisty, was introduced to many nice people. After supper Paul and I went over to call on Mrs. Abbot who came up on the boat with us. Then we went over to Mrs. Young's and showed them how to play Auction Bridge. They had tea and the loveliest cake for us. Home at midnight, tired.

AUG. 10 THURS. Went over town with Mary, looked at furs, shopped and met people, then home to lunch. Had to go over town again, then came home to pack up. Went over to Mrs. Young's to say Good Bye and returned home, when Mr. and Mrs. Morris came to call.

AUG. 11, FRI. Got up at 6 and at 7 Mary left for Strathcona to take the train on the C.P.R. for Banff, Otto going with her. I finished packing and was all ready for the expressman at 8 but he didn't show up. I was very much worried, tried to telephone the Express Co. but couldn't get them. At 8.30 Otto came and I sent him out to get a rig of any kind to take my trunk to the station. He fortunately found the expressman around the corner and my trunk got off and we all ran for the car and after we got off at 1st St. we had to run several blocks to the station and got there the same time the trunk did. We had 10 minutes to check it in and get aboard. Philps of the G.T.P. was down to see me off and to hand me a telegram with my reservations to Sarnia. He has been so nice to me and I can't say too much in praise of the G.T.P. We had a pleasant ride over the prairies. Crops are fine, and everything so beautiful and green as they have had so much rain. Fine dining car service. Paul's appetite and mine both good and everything we had was so well cooked and so nicely served.

SOURCE

Excerpts of Caroline Sharpless's unpublished diary, "Trip to Jasper Park, Rocky Mountains, Canada," from 29 May 1911 to 16 August 1911. WMCR M79/12.

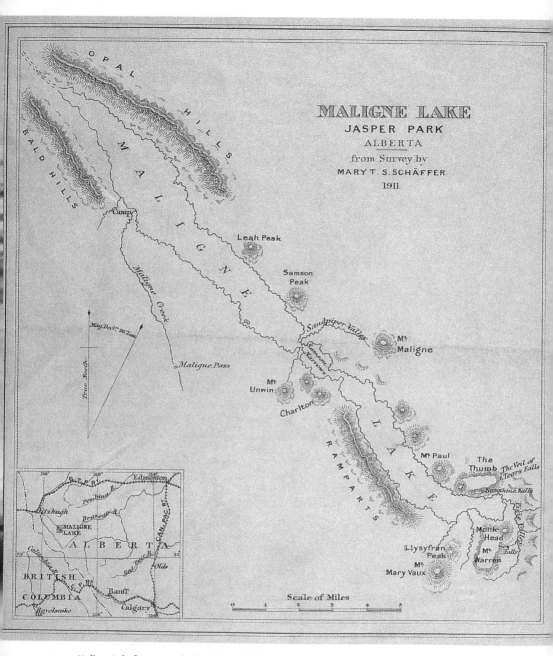

Maligne Lake from survey by Mary T.S. Schäffer, 1911. (WMCR V527/PS–69)

MARY T.S. SCHÄFFER

"A Recently Explored Lake in the Rocky Range of Canada" (1909)

IN THE SUMMER OF 1907 we heard through a hunter, of the existence of a large lake lying north or northwest of Brazeau Lake and Brazeau Mountain.[1]

When Dr. Coleman made his partial ascent of this mountain in 1898, he reached an altitude of 10,500 feet, but I presume he was following the southern or southeastern slopes, and consequently the lake did not come within his vision.

The Stoney Indians had spoken with great enthusiasm to "Jim," of a large lake (calling it Chaba Imne—Beaver Lake), and he knowing our love of penetrating to new and untried places, had passed the information to us. The early September snows of that year, however, prevented any climb at the head of the Brazeau sufficiently high to allow of a view into valleys beyond, and reluctantly the quest was abandoned for that year.

On our way back to civilized lands we halted a few days on the Saskatchewan Plains—about sixty-five miles north of Laggan—and were fortunate enough to fall in with Sampson Beaver, a Stoney, whom we promptly questioned regarding the mythical lake.

Indians have little desire to give the secrets of their hunting-grounds to the white man, but after two years' acquaintance with us, Sampson had evidently decided that the two white women were not rival sportsmen. A few tactful questions from the guides, a sharp rebuke from another member of our party, for suggesting payment for his information (when he had already had a generous supply of our scanty provender), he quickly sketched a crude map of the desired section, and gave us sundry advice on the subject in still more crude English.

On the eighth of June, 1908, with three guides, a botanist, ourselves, and twenty-two horses, we again ventured into the wilderness north of Laggan, armed with the little map, and the unknown lake a prime feature of the expedition.

Our route lay over the now familiar Bow Pass, which owing to our early start, was still heavily clad in the winter's snow, thence down Bear Creek to its junction with the Saskatchewan, and then up the east side of the North Fork of the Saskatchewan to its junction with Nigel Creek. Here we bore to the right, ascended Nigel Creek on its south side, traversed the pass of the same name, and dropped to the head waters of a branch of the Brazeau River.

Camping at an old, well-frequented Indian camp-ground two miles below the lake, our men explored some distance ahead, to see if the way was passable for horses—as Dr. Coleman is the only explorer of that section on record, he having crossed Pobokton Pass in 1892.

The trail was found very readily with Dr. Coleman's cuttings quite distinct, as well as some very old blazes, which proclaimed it a long-favored Indian highway. The lake was crossed at its mouth where the ford was but three and a half feet deep—surprisingly shallow for a body of water six miles long and a mile wide.

From there a sharp ascent was made to overcome some obstructing cliffs on the lake-shore with as sudden a drop to the lake, where we encountered a half mile of bad muskeg. Having successfully surmounted that trail, the way became well defined and led in easy gradations for some time toward the pass.

Horse-feed however was scarce throughout the entire valley, and was only obtained in moderate quantities at 6,300 feet where we camped. The ascent to the summit of Pobokton Pass from that camp proved excessively steep, and furthermore the entire pass was still clogged with heavy snow-patches into which the saddle-horses plunged and struggled as they broke a way for the sixteen laden packs following.

The descent on the other side was tedious and heavy for the animals, as the mountains on every side were discharging huge volumes of water from the melting snows.

It was at this time we should much have preferred Sampson to his rather indefinite map; and that we ever did strike the trail which eventually led us to our destination, was due rather to the dogged persistence and determination of our men, than to any very clear ideas expressed in the little sketch-map.

I suppose we trudged down that trail for at least eight miles, when we came suddenly upon a large bunch of teepee-poles standing in a grove of spruce. Here the river-trail died out, but finding fresh blazes on the hillside we followed them.

Evidently that section has been a good hunting-ground in the past, and evidently also a small party had been that way within a year or two. Hearts did not beat very high however for two or three days there; it looked too much like a lot of time and energy spent, with failure in the end.

On, on we climbed, with occasional glimpses of the river far below. At last when people and animals alike were fagged out with the long day, we came to an apology for feed in an alpine valley.

When camp had been set, three started out in three different directions to see if any point of vantage would show the mysterious lake, or if a presumable valley lying near our camp could be the one traced on Sampson's map. All returned with the dismal intelligence that the valley was a blind, and no lake to be seen from the highest point reached. We felt slightly discouraged. I might here quote from my diary: "July 4th—Last night depression reached its lowest ebb. No lake and little feed for the horses. Ther. at 30°, and such a wind blowing, that the tent, air-beds, and occupants threatened to depart into the valley below, nothing but pegging, reinforced by rocks preventing such a catastrophe. Woke at 6.30 to the call of 'hot-water,' and finally mustered courage to creep from beneath the warm blankets. The glorious 4th! I can hear the patriotic youngsters at home, I can imagine the hot sun! And here are we with the aneroid registering 7,250 feet, with great fleecy clouds rolling and rushing across the sky from the valley of the Su Wapta! and reaching our eyrie, whipping and lashing us with their millions of flakes."

That day's travel led us for six or seven miles through fatiguing burnt timber, till reaching the bed of the river once more, we again struck teepee-poles. Here the trail divided, one going on down the Pobokton, the other turning sharply into a notch of the hills. Dr. Coleman must have followed the former, the latter I have every reason to believe, no white foot had ever trod before.

The recently-cut blazes were undoubtedly Indian, the trail good, and grass plenty. In a half hour, with blankets, packs and garments soaked by a generous downpour, we halted by a musical stream and, out of compliment to the day, named valley and creek "Independence." The next day was devoted to exploring by some, and botanizing by others. In the evening when all gathered around for bacon, bannock and coffee, it was announced that there was a pass leading off from the left of Independence Valley, there was a well-marked trail leading to it, and there were teepee-poles a half mile beyond our own camp. Was it the one Sampson had sketched? Well, there was nothing to do but go and see, and we went.

Considering the altitude of the pass (7,300 feet), and the amount of snow still covering it, the heavily loaded packs got through very well, this being largely due to the four saddle-horses ahead breaking the way. The summit proved a very short one, with a tiny frozen lake—probably one hundred yards long—nestling among the snowbanks at the top. As our horses slowly stumbled and plunged through the masses of soft snow, we had little time to think of their troubles, so busy were our thoughts and eyes rushing ahead to the unknown beyond. And then suddenly there burst upon us such a valley as I never saw before in this country of valleys.

From our very feet it stretched before us in limitless miles of green, green, green. As far as the eye could see there was not one hideous scar (of which there are so many in the Rockies), from fire. Out of the snow we waded down through fields of trollius, caltha and pulsatilla, halting finally where the first spring grasses had but recently sprung.

Dr. Coleman, in his account of the attempted ascent of Mt. Brazeau, mentions beholding a wonderfully green valley from his highest point of vantage, and calls it Pobokton. From later developments, and with our knowledge of both valleys, I think he was looking into this one—the real Pobokton, owing to many old forest-fires, has few claims to beauty. The second camp in the valley was a memorable one for those who so long had been "hunting a needle in a haystack."

We were twelve miles from the new pass when we pitched our tents at the edge of a fine forest of spruce on July 7. All the morning we had passed signs of the hunter, and though we had covered the ground rapidly, every bend still opened up to us that limitless vista of green. At lunch our alpine-climber announced that "he meant to take the field-glasses and climb, and he wouldn't be back till he was assured whether that lake was within a radius of fifty miles of us or not." He kept his word. With the coming of the night, the anxious watchers could do nothing to aid him but keep a bright fire burning, and with the instinct of the hunter after plunging for two hours and a half through the black forest, he stumbled into the circle of firelight at 10.30, having walked twenty miles over the worst possible ground. He had eventually reached a point where his aneroid registered 8,750 feet, when the lake suddenly burst into view from a long valley at his feet, and he knew his hard walk was rewarded. To him had come the glory of the beautiful find, and I venture to say that all of the eager listeners wished they had been there too. The next day with light hearts we walked out upon the shores of Chaba Imne, whose opposite shores at this point were fully a mile apart and whose ends were not visible, owing as we thought at the time, to the impenetrable spruce and pine forests, which swept the water's edge.

Crossing the now somewhat formidable river which flowed through the green valley, a perfect paradise was found for the horses and busy hands turned to the construction of a raft to explore the lake. On the evening of the ninth we were informed that H.M.S. *Chaba* would sail at eight next morning for the upper end of the lake, provisioned for a three days' absence. My first experience on a raft, I felt it might be the last, but three days' life on her proved that nothing short of a water-spout could have wrecked her.

To our complete astonishment, the lake was so long that the whole three days were absorbed in rafting, not one left for climbing as we had hoped. We saw but one sign of human life along those miles of wooded shore, and that read of the passing of the hunter in the dead of winter. It was a three days' trip of as wonderful a panorama as could be imagined. Sampson had sketched "narrows" in the upper end of the lake (remember he was only a boy of fifteen when last he was there, and now a man of thirty-five); we found those narrows just where he had drawn them, and above them a towering rocky peak which we named for him. Emerging again into broader waters, we slowly paddled beneath the shadow of a snow-capped summit, when Unwin suddenly pointed to a high shoulder and said: "There is where I stood when I saw the lake first." How I envied him, and could only express my sentiments by suggesting the peak should bear his name.

To our left loomed "The Thumb," and just beyond frowned down upon the strange invaders a double mass of rock which we called Mt. Warren. Among the lower peaks directly south of the lake rose a snowy pyramid which may be Mt. Brazeau, and to the east, an unusually superb mountain of conical form which if not Brazeau, we would call "Maligne." It was a keen disappointment that no certainty could be reached, as to the definite position of these peaks, but time and lack of food proved masters of the situation and we were forced to turn our backs on all this magnificence and return to the "grub-pile."

At the upper end, glaciers swept their long tongues to the lakeshore, streams of water from hidden snow fields reached the brink, and tossed themselves hundreds of feet over vertical cliffs, little deep green coves bade us slip among them and rest, but necessity called, and reluctantly and laboriously we paddled back to our horses and pork and beans.

Camping for a few days at the lower end of the lake, where by the way is an inexhaustible camp-ground, we calculated the sheet of water to be at least twenty miles long, found that a river which came from it, fell by steep and dangerous rapids for a length of twelve miles to Medicine Lake, and from there as Maligne River on the maps, flowed into the Athabasca about eleven miles away.

The Yellowhead Pass and Mt. Robson being our next points of interest our natural route was via Medicine Lake, but after several days of exploring and cutting, it proved impracticable.

Many years ago a forest fire, probably starting on the Athabasca, swept relentlessly up the entire valley, leaving scarce a tree standing, even a half mile of the west shore of the lake at its outlet being destroyed. Time and storms have left a network of fallen timber too great for so small a force as ours to cut through and the "longest way round" proved the shorter.

On the morning of July 24, with sunlight and cloud shadows chasing each other across the rippled surface of the lake, creeping up the green mountain slopes, and dying away behind the peaks, we said farewell to one of the fairest scenes that even we who have travelled so many of these valleys, have ever seen.

The long detour to the Athabasca was made through the valley we now call "Maligne," along the river and over the pass of the same name, then down through the fallen timbers and muskegs, which make the Pobokton one of the very worst valleys for traversing.

Dr. Coleman's trail that way in 1892 had long fallen in, and though he had done enormous cutting to get through, our men had troubles of their own. Once on the shores of the Athabasca, there came a parting of the ways. Mr. Brown, the botanist, and his guide, were to return to civilization via Wilcox, Nigel, Cataract and Pipestone Passes, we to go on for a glimpse of Mt. Robson, the highest known peak in the Rocky Range, then to flit down for a look at the present Tete Jaun Cache [sic], before the Grand Trunk Pacific should annihilate the wilderness about it.

On July 29 we waved good-bye to our companions of seven weeks, weeks of pleasure and hardships, of sunshine and rain. With them they carried letters, our regrets at their going, a little longing for the news from the outside world which would soon be theirs, and a little pity that they would not finish the game with us.

Then followed days and miles of pleasant or weary travel down the right bank of the Athabasca. Undoubtedly this part of the river had formerly been much more used than the more familiar section further south. For many miles, however, the hunter's trail had died away almost to oblivion, and the most obvious signs of life were those of Dr. Coleman, the timber-cruiser and prospector.

Game trails were numerous, the ripped logs bespeaking bruin's presence, and the river sands marked by deer tracks, sheep, goat, lynx and the smaller animals. The flora changed perceptibly, as we were reaching much lower levels, and the large luscious strawberries made a delicious feast daily.

Within fifteen miles of the Miette, every sign of the trail vanished owing to the numerous fires of recent origin, so we plodded along, keeping close to the now wild, high banks of the river. There were few natural obstructions, and a horse could wander almost anywhere, so naturally we were puzzled to know where that trail had gone. But we certainly found out in due time why it was not near the river.

The banks became more and more abrupt, and we were forced to climb high, and yet higher on the mountain-sides to get around the impenetrable walls which rose sheer from the water.

On the sixth of August, as our outfit, dwindled now to fifteen horses, stood silhouetted against the deep blue sky, on a high bluff fully a thousand feet above the river, there came faintly on the breeze, the tinkle of a horse-bell. It sounds a small matter to set the heart beating with excitement, the pulses throbbing. But remember that for two months we had seen no faces but our own, heard no other voices, knew absolutely nothing of the outside world—and here was something and somebody. And as we listened, across the water came the sharp crack of a rifle. Was it Indian-hunter, prospector or surveyor? (for we were now within sight of the valley through which the Grand Trunk Pacific proposes to run its line to the coast.)

Weeks after we met the man, an Indian, who fired the rifle. Though a mile and a half away from us in air line, he had seen our outfit against the sky-line, thought it was a fellow hunter for whom he was looking and signalled. At the time, with curiosity unsated, we went on our way, to have solved for us the problem we had asked ourselves so many times in the last thirty-six hours—"Where is that trail and why is it not beside the river?" The reason why was a rock bluff whose sheerest portion was twenty feet high. To go over that bluff or retrace a weary ten miles to the true trail, was a matter for the consideration of those of us who knew the limitations of a horse as mountain-climber. We took the bluff (not without some profound misgivings however). It was a highway for deer, and goat, and sheep, but the men who had come that way had turned about, preferring to search for the Indian trail which lay miles back in the stony hills. When the solitary white man, Swift, and the few half-breed Crees, who live a few miles below this point, heard our horses had been brought that way, they frankly disbelieved it, but photographs have proven the fact, that fifteen horses, minus all but their halter-shanks to which a long rope was attached, were one by one gently coaxed ten feet down a very steep portion of the bluff, and then prevailed upon to take the final plunge over almost vertical rocks to the soft ground twenty feet below.

It was rather curious to watch the individuality of each horse as he took his leap. The more intelligent the horse, the more difficult it was to prevail upon him to make the attempt. Neither could there be any force or insistence used; for once he had to be left to his own sweet will, as an excited slip or hurried plunge might easily hurl him on the jagged rocks, from whence he would plunge with risk of a nasty injury, to the depths below.

We had frequently wondered why the Maligne River ever received the ominous name it had. Like the question of the bluffs, we soon came across a practical answer. On attempting to cross the river at its mouth (it was about seventy-five yards wide), the force of the water was so great, no man could have swum, or animal have kept its footing in it. The second in command felled a tall spruce, throwing it across as a bridge; as it touched the water, the torrent gripped the reaching boughs, and before it could come to rest, grasped and hurled it with terrific force into the Athabasca, only a few yards away. This torrent doubtless loses much of its terrors toward autumn, for a well-marked trail leads down the bank and appears again on the opposite side. At first we were puzzled how to reach that bank so near and yet so far away, but remembering McEvoy's description of an underground outlet for Medicine Lake, the men explored and found that an easy crossing could be made about one and a half miles above the mouth of the river. This made a morning's hard work clearing a passage for the horses.

When the entire outfit was taken over it, we found it, though excessively steep and choked with fallen timbers, one of the most beautiful bits of trail we had seen for several days. In places the trail clung almost to the very brink—very wild and a little startling as one gazed from the saddle into the boiling, seething depths below—while a terrific roar and rumble swept over us which drowned all attempts at conversation. No one really wished to speak, it was too splendidly wild and interesting, and was also fraught with just sufficient danger, to cause us to keep a close watch on the already well- trained feet of our steeds.

After a climb of about six hundred feet, sure enough, there was the tiny stream so small we could almost have wadded across it. Somewhere between that point and Medicine Lake it had dropped from sight, the greater volume of water to appear for the first time from the various strata of rock in the gorge just passed.

The crossing of the Athabasca by the human element of our party, was made in two dugouts lashed together, the horses being forced to swim three hundred yards in the ice-cold, rapidly-flowing river. It looked pretty dubious for the poor creatures, as with only noses and ears visible, we could hear them snorting and blowing, and laboriously fighting their way through the flood. Then as they emerged, spent and weary on the other side, and we counted fifteen tired horses slowly crawling up the bank, we all felt a just sense of relief. From now we had McEvoy's government report, which is so clear and distinct in every detail, there can be no reason for duplicating what he has already so concisely explained.

Our crossing was made three miles below the Maligne River, opposite John Moberly's place. Moberly is one of the half-breed Crees who made for himself a little home on the east side of the sunny valley of the Athabasca, after Swift (a white man who went there fourteen years ago), had demonstrated that any crops of a temperate zone could be grown there. John was away at the time of our arrival, and Mr. Swift, hearing our rifle signal, paddled us across.

He was frankly astonished at our coming, especially as we denied being either "prospectors or timber-cruisers." And we were equally surprised at his cordiality and hospitality, which took the form of liberal donations of fresh milk, eggs, and new potatoes, all the result of his own labor on a small tract of land which he had wrested inch by inch from that northern wilderness. To appreciate fully such generosity, and to know the true value of such a gift, one needs to have had two full months' training of bannock and bacon three times a days. We shall long remember Mr. Swift, who is famous for his hospitality to all who pass his door.

The trail, in spite of its having been traversed nearly two hundred years ago by coast Indians crossing the Pass to trade with the fur companies, used in later years by explorers and prospectors, then by Canadian Pacific survey outfits, and recently by those from the Grand Truck Pacific, we found in very bad condition.

No effort seemed ever to have been made to lighten the hardships of the hundreds of horses which must have passed that way in the last thirty years. Muskegs, steep, bowlder-strewn, rocky hillsides and great logs across the trail were reasons enough for the piles of bleached bones which we daily passed on our way to the Tete Jaun Cache [sic]. But overlooking the misery, what a wonderful valley of berries it was! Not only were they there in plenty, but in quantities so great that for three days we passed carpets of a small and very delicious *Vaccinium* (blue-berry) which gave the ground the appearance of being blue. There were at least five other varieties of *Vaccinium*, strawberries, luscious raspberries, a trailing red black-berry, any number of the Saskatoon bushes, and on the western slope a small wild cherry.

Our first glimpse of Mt. Robson on the afternoon of August 18 is thus recorded in the little much-worn diary: "After the last five miles had been traversed, as it seemed three or four times over, we swung around a stony corner, and suddenly on our right there appeared a snow-clad peak. Not over impressive at first, surrounded on all sides by low, rocky hills, we could scarce believe we were looking at Mt. Robson. But that it does stand out "immeasurably supreme,"[2] there is no doubt, for there is nothing in the way of a peak for miles to detract from it. Neither was there one feature of foreground to beautify it till we reached Grand Fork a couple of miles down the valley. The forests about us had all been destroyed by fire, and between us and this giant among the hills, gaunt, burnt tree-trunks rose like threatening hands. The ground was arid and stony, the day intensely hot, and not a cloud in the sky to soften the ridge of white which cut with icy lines into the hard blue sky. Our horses were foot-sore and weary from the week's trip up the Miette and down the Fraser, and all of us a little too fagged perhaps to be instantly impressed."

Viscount Milton and Dr. Cheadle, two Englishmen who passed through this section on a hunting expedition in 1863, assert that the original Tete Jaun Cache [sic] (supposed to be the cache of a yellow-headed Indian) was situated at the junction of the Grand Fork and the main river. What their authority was they do not say, nor do I know if their statement is correct, how it ever got transplanted fifteen miles further down the Fraser river.

It was with many doubts that a few days later we wended our way to the present cache, but curiosity had overcome our antipathy to a probable meeting with any stray surveyors or prospectors, and the one permanent resident of whom Mr. Swift had spoken in glowing terms.

What we found was one tiny log shack, a tent beside it, another tent a stone's throw away, four white men, and a few Indians from the village across the Fraser. The "resident" proved to be a Philadelphian, his companion originally from Boston, I think; at any rate their courtesy, cordiality and hospitality were worthy both those cities. We went dreading I know not what, we came away wondering when we would ever learn the lesson—that though nature may wrap a rough cloak about those who follow her footsteps, she purifies and refines the heart within.

We had wandered far, very far from home, certainly into the very depths of the wilderness itself, and were meeting the men who were grappling with the secrets of the country. They told us we were the first white women known to have crossed the oldest known pass in the Canadian Rockies, and one and all paid us as deep and kindly a homage as it has ever been ours to accept.

NOTES

1. See *Bulletin Geog. Society Phil.*, Vol. 6, No. 2, 1908.
2. Milton and Cheadle.

SOURCE

Mary T.S. Schäffer's "A Recently Explored Lake in the Rocky Range of Canada," from *Bulletin of the Geographical Society of Philadelphia* 7 (22 July 1909), 123–34.

SHARON STEARNS

Hunter of Peace (1993)

Prologue and Act One, Scene One

Prologue.

(Winter, 1939. Spotlight up on OLD MARY sitting in her chair at the side of the stage—at her home in Banff.)

OLD MARY: Winter's coming. This old pile of bones never fails to let me know. The final season. Brittle bones, fallen skin, misty eyes. In winter, everything contracts and I too am getting smaller, saving my breath against the cold, against the end. Soon it will be 1940 and somewhere a war is raging. I hardly notice. I'm waiting for the young people to come. They'll be here any day now. Young bodies skiing down the slopes, drinking in the chalets, bathing in the hot springs. But a few of you, the curious ones, will come to visit me, looking for some remaining vestige of Yahe-Weha, the Mountain Woman.

"How did I ever come here?" you ask. "Such a dainty lady with my urban sentiments. 1907! It must have been so primitive and wild back then!" Yes, it was wild—a country graced with Indian trails winding through untouched wilderness, unsullied by our white, conquering hands. How could you know? It's all so different now. But I look into your young faces and it all comes back to me. The past becomes the present and I am once again hurrying along just a step ahead of the great sweeping tide—the 'Hideous March of Progress' so awful to those who love the real wilderness.

(Silhouette lights up to reveal young MARY, MOLLIE, PEYTO, MRS. JULIET DE LA BEACH-NICHOL and BILLY poised somewhere on the trail in 1907.)

I explored these hills first. I savoured them when they were all secret places with no human sign but a canvas tent and a balsam bough bed. Then I was the hunter, exploring each day with all the excitement of a child let loose in a toy store. Now I am a shadow, stalking memories. Sweet, ghostly companions that are my comfort and my lament. I am all that is left of those days. Can you hear the wind? Listen to the wind sighing through the forest. It echoes through every corner of my heart, coaxing me back, back into the wild mountains with Mollie, and Peyto, and with my Chief.

(Lights fade.)

Act One, Scene One.

(Late spring, 1907. On the trail outside Banff. MARY and MOLLIE sleep in their bedrolls on a mat of balsam branches. In the absolute silence that occurs as night slowly gives way to dawn, MARY cries out in her sleep, bolting up from her bed.)

MARY: No! Not right! Must be perfectly correct! Every petal!

(MOLLIE stirs in her sleep. Silence. MARY looks around in the growing light, shivering, waking up.)

MARY: (*Whispering.*) Will you stop? I've buried you. I won't live with a ghost. You hear me? Wherever you are out there, am I your ghost to bear as well?

(*MOLLIE wakes, sits up.*)

MOLLIE: Mary? What's wrong?

MARY: Sh...sh. Nothing.

MOLLIE: Maybe it was a grizzly I heard talking in her sleep.

MARY: (*Looking around.*) I forgot where I was. (*Pause.*) I woke you. Sorry.

MOLLIE: (*Yawning.*) It's almost dawn anyway.

MARY: I was dreaming about Robert. He was yelling at me like I was a child. I was doing everything wrong. I mixed all his flower specimens up, and the plants on my lantern slides were painted all the wrong colours. He was so angry! And then I woke up and I felt him right beside me, as cross as two sticks because I came here.

MOLLIE: He's just jealous because you're here and he's not. (*Looks up.*) Listen, Robert. Your wife will do a brilliant job on your book so leave her alone, you hear? We've got enough to worry about without a ghost on our trail. Especially such a fussy one!

MARY: (*Softly.*) Dear Robert.

MOLLIE: (*Looking up.*) You'd think heaven would be enough for you!

MARY: It's an omen. His ghost. He's telling me I don't belong out here. And he's right Mollie. He's right!

MOLLIE: It's just a bad dream! Perfectly normal after all you've been through.

MARY: Every time I close my eyes I see his face.

MOLLIE: You've made the right choice Mary. Trust me—coming here is the best thing you could have done.

MARY: He always said women don't belong in the wilderness.

MOLLIE: Sounds like Peyto. But you never saw me bowing down to his rot—now that Robert's gone, it'd be plain foolery to bow to his.

MARY: I'm not you. How can I expect to find rare alpine flora in the wilds of Canada when I can't even saddle my horse properly, let alone sit on the poor thing!

MOLLIE: *(Laughs.)* It's true we're gonna have to plant some horse sense in you. I never saw a funnier sight than you trying to get your foot in the stirrup yesterday. Wearing that stupid corset. And your skimpy little boots!

(She mimics MARY'S attempts at trying to cheer her.)

MARY: I got on, didn't I?

MOLLIE: Oh yes, you certainly did. With style. A very unique style.

MARY: I should find a tamer botanical adventure. Maybe I could finish Robert's book with the material he already collected. There's over forty catalogued...

MOLLIE: *(Laughing.)* And we're barely a day's ride from Banff! Haven't even hit the wild country yet. Wait till we're lost on the trail, with only moldy biscuits and tea left for supper. You might have something to complain about then.

MARY: Oh Mollie! *(Pause.)* I feel like child who's lost her parents. Suddenly the world is awfully big and dangerous.

MOLLIE: You're afraid of yourself.

MARY: Yes.

(Pause. Dawn has now beat out the night. Morning birds sing.)

MOLLIE: Every year I come back here I think—this is it. This time I'm staying. Give up teaching, the city life, and carve a home out of the side of one of these mountains.

MARY: *(Laughs.)* Oh, you wouldn't give up teaching. You love it.

MOLLIE: I love geology, not teaching it to students who don't give a damn.

MARY: What could you do out here?

MOLLIE: We could live together. Explore these hills while they're still wild. Now that Robert's gone, you have no ties to Philadelphia. You could easily give up hat pins and the lingerie waist. You could spend your days searching for rare alpine flora while I explore every mountain range from here to the Pacific.

MARY: And none of these dreams include a certain Mr. Peyto?

MOLLIE: As a guide. Maybe.

MARY: I see...

(Smiling, getting out of her bedroll.)

MOLLIE: Petyo says the headwaters can't be found. And certainly not by a woman. I figure to prove him wrong.

MARY: So that's why you've lured me on this trip.

MOLLIE: You'll thank me in the end. You can bet on it.

MARY: *(Smiling.)* Ah yes. You can see us both in twenty years...two old ladies protecting the beauties of these hills from the 'Hideous March of Progress.'

MOLLIE: Exactly. Just look at this morning! Have you ever seen mountains so glorious? C'mon. Let's go water the horses then make ourselves a giant batch of biscuits. It's a day's ride back to Banff and I wanna stop in and surprise Peyto before dark.

MARY: I'll light the fire. You used up nearly every match last night.

MOLLIE: Good! One night in the mountains and you're a wilderness expert.

MARY: I know how to light a fire. That's one thing I can hold on to.

MOLLIE: And me. You can hold on to me.

MARY: I just felt Robert turn over in his grave.

MOLLIE: He was a good man Mary. But he never gave you a free rein.

MARY: I don't know that I ever felt the need for one.

MOLLIE: Well, you've got it now. You're as free as that eagle up there.

MARY: *(Looking up.)* What a terrifying thought.

(Lights fade.)

SOURCES

Prologue and Act One, Scene One, from *Hunter of Peace*, by Sharon Stearns (Victoria, B.C.: Scirocco Drama, 1993) 11–15.

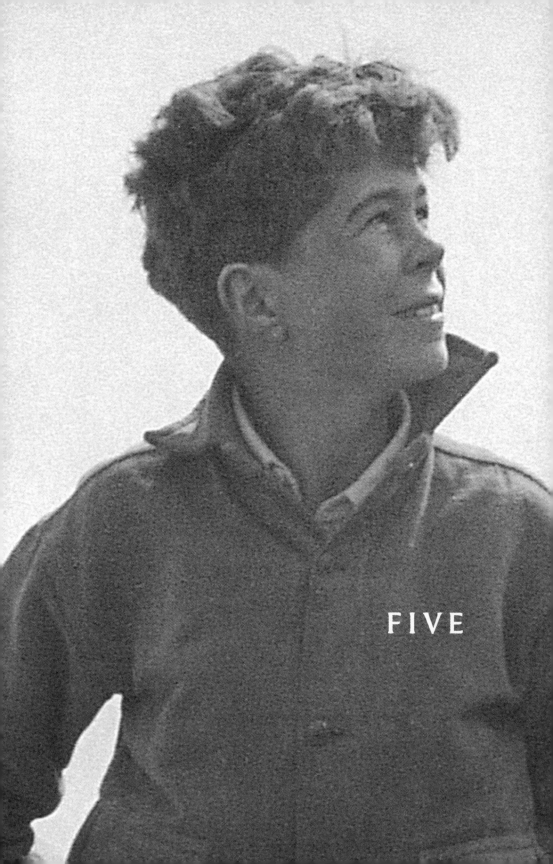

FIVE

On the Rockies Stark

Mountaineers

"IF FOR THE SAKE OF ARGUMENT the question 'Should women climb mountains?' were brought up it would be found exactly one hundred years behind the times," wrote Winnipeg physician Mary Crawford in the 1909 issue of the *Canadian Alpine Journal*. Furthermore, argued Esther Merriam in *Harper's Bazaar* in 1910,

> Women no longer require a separate record, devoted to the exploitation of feats of *women*. They compete now, we are proud to say, and compete successfully, with climbers of note, regardless of sex, in all parts of the world. As long as the unexplored mountains hold out, we may expect to see them win greater and greater fame, and sign their names to more and more "first records." (Merriam 1910, 634)

Climbing dominates the literature and romance of Rocky Mountain histories, and it is in climbing and the stories told that the divide of gender has been most prominently displayed. Crawford's concern for women's health and her belief in fresh air and exercise for women, such as mountaineering offered, and the conclusions she reached, has been recognized by David Mazel as representative of something more socially profound than possibly Crawford meant to argue:

> The view from the mountaintop embraces more than mere scenery. Seemingly far removed from the strictures of society—at liberty, in the comparative utopia of the mountain wilderness, to use their bodies towards ends of their own—women climbers apply their previously divided energies to personal fulfillment rather than the care of others. And, in a metaphor charged with political meanings, every step upward offers a tantalizing vision of a "new world" of hitherto inaccessible possibilities. (Mazel 1994, 8)

Women's climbing achievements evolved with experience. Crawford reported that the first women mountaineer was in fact carried up Mont Blanc, and that she undertook the adventure for the financial gain that such an enterprise would garner (to Crawford's disapproval). There followed the practice of a woman or two being allowed to participate with men on a climb followed by women climbers' desire for the "manless climb" or the cordée féminine (women's rope team). While Mazel has argued insightfully that the cordée féminine represents women's "mutual ambitions and mutual support" (Mazel 1994, 22) many women climbers who wrote of their experiences, such as Miriam Underhill O'Brien, explained their actions by saying simply that they could see no reason to prevent women climbing, and climbing on their own teams. Much of the trouble was that, in men's eyes, women's ascent of desirable or infamous peaks degraded their challenge for men climbers. A notorious comment made by British climber Alfred Mummery in 1895 encapsulated the sentiment: "It has frequently been noticed that all mountains appear doomed to pass through the three stages: An inaccessible peak—The most difficult ascent in the Alps—An easy day for a lady." (Mummery 1908, 186). Men's climbing feats lost their lustre when a woman made the same ascent, or worse, if a woman made it first.

In the summer of 1904, famed British climber Gertrude Benham arrived in the Canadian Rockies prepared to claim first ascent of numerous peaks that season. Among them was Mount Fay, yet to be summited. Charles Fay, a well-known American climber, had been invited to choose a peak to be named in his honour. He had chosen Peak One in the Valley of the Ten Peaks at Moraine Lake and planned to made the first ascent that same summer. Benham did so first, considerably diminishing Fay's honour and accomplishment. In contrast, Mary Schäffer celebrated Benham's achievements—and ensured their widespread publicity—in a short article about her climb of Mount Lefroy in the August 1904 issue of *Rod and Gun in Canada*. Schäffer offers a double entendre in her article's title: "Breaking the Way."

Esther Merriam of *Harper's Bazaar* was well-aware of the impact of Mummery's comments and how they had become a means of marking a climb:

It is still no easy task to climb Mt. Blanc or the Matterhorn, in spite of the scornful words of a recent writer, who speaks of the ascent of the Matterhorn as having become a "good walk for a lady." This is said just because huts and ropes have been placed on the mountain for the benefit of those climbers who are not experts. The 'lady' will still require a tremendous amount of pluck, nerve, strength, and endurance to accomplish the climb successfully. (Merriam 1910, 634)

Climber Dora Keen's own description of her ascent of the Matterhorn convinced Merriam: "This account does not impress one with the feeling that the ascent has yet become mere child's play or an achievement lacking the glorious thrill of accomplishment." (Merriam 1910, 634)

The imperialist and masculine language of mountaineering—from "conquering" mountains to ascending "virgin" peaks—has been noted by many writers in the past. And although successful climbs are dependent on the aptitude of guides, including the Swiss guides who immigrated to the Canadian Rockies during the period around the turn of the century, victory was claimed by the mountaineers who employed the guides' services. The notion of climbing as a physically and psychologically challenging endeavour whose success depended on both decisive leadership and collaborative teamwork on the rope was transparently acknowledged by women climbers from the beginning. Gertrude Benham's story of her climb of Mount Lefroy, related by Mary Schäffer, is a good example of this particular means by which women intervened in the singular claims of male mountaineers and climbing clubs.

Women were fundamental to the establishment and success of a Canadian tradition of mountaineering in the Rockies. Until the early 1900s, British and American climbing teams, all-male and mixed alike, made most ascents. Counted among these is the Vaux family's climb in 1900 when Mary Vaux became the first woman to attain the summit of Mount Stephen. In September 1905, Winnipeg journalist Elizabeth Parker (1856–1944), stirred by the power of the mountains and their salubrious effect on a person's well-being after living eighteen months in Banff, urged

Mount Stephen, 1900. *(Vaux Family Fonds, WMCR V653/NA–241)*

Canadians to establish an Alpine Club. She envisioned a club that would
promote and participate in the climbing explorations of the Canadian
mountain ranges, especially in claiming first ascents to Canadian peaks.
Surveyor Arthur Wheeler had proposed a Canadian branch of the American
Alpine Club, but Parker argued for an independent group. Her ambition
was realized in March 1906 when the first meeting of the Alpine Club of
Canada convened in Winnipeg. Seventy-nine members were attracted in
the first year, one-third of which were women. Parker served as secretary
and Wheeler as president. The *Canadian Alpine Journal* was also established
in Winnipeg and Parker contributed to its inaugural issue. (Despite these
founding facts, it was 1942 before the journal had its first woman editor,
mountaineer and teacher Margaret Fleming.)

Setting out the objectives of the Alpine Club, Parker aligned Wheeler, a surveyor and photographer, with the scientific mandate for exploration and study of mountain regions. In retrospect, her own work aligns readily with the mandates to cultivate "Art in relation to mountain scenery" as well as to educate Canadians about their mountain heritage and the conservation of mountain wilderness. Elizabeth Parker was educated as a teacher in Nova Scotia. She began a career as a literary critic a dozen years after moving with her husband and three children to Winnipeg in 1892. Her articles for the *Manitoba Free Press* appeared under the bylines of M.T. (the initials of her mother, Mary Tupper), A.L.O.W. (A Lady of Winnipeg), or The Bookman. In 1904, she moved with her three children to Banff temporarily to recover her declining health in the mountain air and hot springs. Her experiences contributed directly to the establishment of a national Alpine Club. They also expanded the scope of her writing to include articles about mountaineering in the Canadian Rockies and a book, *The Selkirk Mountains: A Guide for Mountain Climbers and Pilgrims*, co-written with Arthur Wheeler in 1912. Although Parker's state of health prevented her from climbing, she attended Alpine Club camps until 1913 when her health prohibited further trips to the Rockies. Parker's passion for the mountains was shared with her daughter, Jean, who became an accomplished mountaineer, climbing in the Rockies and Selkirks with the Alpine Club of Canada. Jean was also a member of Alpine clubs in England and Scotland.

Stories and studies of women mountaineers in Europe and the United States began to emerge in the 1970s when women's histories started to attract interest and attention during the second wave of feminism in the twentieth century. Wide-ranging histories of women climbing in Canada, or of Canadian women climbing around the world, have yet to be published, however. Their stories appear only in anthologies, such as Chic Scott's engaging *Pushing the Limits: The Story of Canadian Mountaineering* (2000), which offers a sample of the most prominent women or unusual climbs woven into a narrative infrastructure of male-driven adventure. Bruce

Fairley's anthology, *Canadian Mountaineering Stories* (1994), includes five articles by women among the sixty-three reproduced. Such ratios do not reflect the historical percentage of women climbers in Canada: one-third of the founding members of the Alpine Club of Canada in 1907 were women; in 1917, half of the membership was female, a rate that stabilized at an average of about 40 percent between the 1920s and 1940s, and many of these women published accounts of their climbs in the Club's journal (Reichwein 1994, 6; Reichwein and Fox 2004, xvii). In contrast, there are numerous mountain histories and anthologies that focus exclusively on women in Europe and the United States, the best of which include Bill Birkett and Bill Peascod's *Women Climbing* (1989), Janet Robertson's *The Magnificent Mountain Women* (1990), Rachel da Silva's *Leading Out* (1992), and David Mazel's *Mountaineering Women* (1994).

Among recent biographies of mountaineers in Canada, only two— both significant contributions—focus on climbing women: *Mountain Diaries: The Alpine Adventures of Margaret Fleming, 1929–1980* (2004), edited by PearlAnn Reichwein and Karen Fox (mountain women themselves); and Katherine Anne Bridge's *Phyllis Munday: Mountaineer* (2002). A wealth of primary materials bequeathed or collected from twentieth-century women mountaineers in Canada—diaries (such as Lillian Gest's twenty-five years of leather-bound pocket diaries full of travel notations in the Whyte Museum of the Canadian Rockies), letters exchanged with family and friends, published articles, photographs, paintings, and films—wait in the archives to be drawn on for such works. The samples included here only suggest the range of work that has been created. They have been chosen with an eye to the cultural accomplishments of the women's work that emerged from their climbing experiences as a means of conveying a sense of the spirit of women's engagements with the Canadian Rockies. Among the work contributed by women to the *Canadian Alpine Journal* are Mary Crawford's earnest call to climb and Rhoda W. Edwards's 1918 poem that, as if to prove Crawford's claim, glows with the satisfaction of accomplishing a graduating climb of a mountain at least ten thousand feet above sea level, required for

Georgia Engelhard, c. 1933.
(Lillian Gest Fonds, WMCR
V225/P10 (26))

active membership in the Alpine Club of Canada (Wheeler and Parker 1907, 169). In contrast, there is also a humorous, self-deprecating account of a graduating climb by a novice recreational climber, Ethel Johns, who caricatured the tradition and convention of mountaineering literature that described climbs and that was consulted by others to plan their own ascents.

On a more evocative note, American climber and photographer Georgia Engelhard's work encompasses the celebrity and glamour that attended her climbs in Canada (and Europe) and the publicity she garnered. Engelhard (1906–1986) enjoyed financial independence as the daughter of a well-to-do New York family. Her mother, Agnes, was a sister of well-known American photographer Alfred Stieglitz and Engelhard had a warm relationship with her uncle. She also spent some time as a child painting in the company of artist Georgia O'Keeffe who was married to Stieglitz for a time. Engelhard began climbing at age twenty, starting in the summer of

"Get a lift with a Camel," featuring Georgia Engelhard. (WMCR M200/ACooM)

1926 by accompanying her father on climbs of Mount Rainer in Washington State followed by ascents in the Lake Louise area. She returned to the Rockies and Selkirks many times and became known for both the speed with which she climbed and the number of peaks visited (including nine peaks in nine days in 1929, ranging from 3,070 to 3,493 metres, and eight climbs of Mount Victoria at 3,464 metres in 1931, seven of which were made for the biographical film *She Climbs to Conquer*). Her popular fame reached such heights that, in addition to the movie about her mountaineering, she was featured in a print ad endorsing the "energizing effects" of Camel cigarettes in 1934. Engelhard was a photographer as well as a climber, two vocations she began to combine in the 1940s. In 1943, she visited the Rockies with the objective of making a photographic portrait of Mount Assiniboine. Engelhard recounts her success in an article published in *American Photographer* and reproduced with one such portrait here.

Finally, poetry has a long standing place in mountaineering culture in the annals of the *Canadian Alpine Journal*, although over the years only a few mountain poems by women have appeared there or elsewhere. For women and men alike, poetry has served as an expressive vehicle for sharing something of the romantic nationalism and spiritual ardour evoked by the mountains. Moira O'Neill and Lynda R. Woods, writing forty-five years apart, portray the Rocky Mountains as symbols representative of Canada—whether as "The mountainous snows that take no mark,/Sun-lit and high on the Rockies stark" in O'Neill's "The North-West—Canada" of 1909 or "friendly and kind,/They bring rest to the spirit and peace to the mind" in Woods's "Canada's Mountains" of 1954. Moira O'Neill was not a mountaineer, however. Rather, Moira O'Neill was the nom-de-plume of Agnes Higginson Skrine (1864–1955) who became a famed Irish poet. Skrine had married in 1895 and joined Irish husband Walter on his ranch near High River, Alberta, which he had established in 1883. They lived there until 1900 when the first of their five children arrived and they returned permanently to Ireland. This poem appeared in O'Neill's first poetry collection, *Songs of the Glens of Antrim*, published to acclaim in 1910 in Edinburgh and London. An excerpt was first published, however, in the *Canadian Alpine Journal*.

In contrast, most who published poetry in the *Canadian Alpine Journal*, such as Lynda R. Woods and Elizebeth Ferguson, were mountaineers and members of the Alpine Club of Canada who participated in the nightly campfire gatherings of Club members during climbing season. Woods claims a certain modesty about her work appearing in the *Journal*, noting that each of her poems published in the mid-1950s was written in response to requests by other members. Ferguson's *Sonnet* of 1963 invokes the compelling pull of the mountains and the peace found there that are shared themes in many of the poems, by women and men alike, that continue to appear in the *Canadian Alpine Journal*: "Unceasingly my spirit forces me/ To climb in search of peace and quiet song."

Climbing in the Rockies and Selkirks has served to dare generations of women—some of them writers, poets, photographers, and artists— from Canada and abroad, seeking physical and psychological challenge. The history of their experiences and contributions to both early and contemporary Canadian mountaineering history and mountain culture, including first climbs and obstacles set in the way of their ambitions, remains to be explored at length. So too does the manner in which women embraced new mountaineering technologies and new opportunities for a life embracing adventure that, as Parker claimed, the "waiting, chal- lenging" mountains provided (1907).

EDITOR'S NOTE

The title of this section, "On the Rockies Stark," is taken from Moria O'Neill's "The North- West—Canada," *Canadian Alpine Journal* 2 (1909), 128. See quotation on page 401.

ELIZABETH PARKER

"The Alpine Club of Canada" (1907)

ITS APOLOGETIC is summed in the second paragraph of the circular announcing the organization of the Club.

"The objects of the Club are: (1) the promotion of scientific study and the exploration of Canadian alpine and glacial regions; (2) the cultivation of Art in relation to mountain scenery; (3) the education of Canadians to an appreciation of their mountain heritage; (4) the encouragement of the mountain craft and the opening of new regions as a national playground; (5) the preservation of the natural beauties of the mountain places and of the fauna and flora in their habitat; (6) and the interchange of ideas with other Alpine organizations."

When the Club was organized in March, 1906, it was a red-letter day to some who had long felt the reproach of Canadian apathy to Canadian mountains. For, while English and American mountaineers had, year by year, seized the summers following the advent of the railway, and had explored and climbed—here and there a man with the "magic of the words" telling the story,—an increasing few of our own people had also been climbing for love of it. Thus learning of the immensities of the alpine regions of their own land, they became jealous for their compatriots' sake. Why should not mountaineering become one of our national sports?

Not until November, 1905, did any positive movement towards organization begin. The response from all parts of the Dominion was a surprise, and ought to have been a rebuke to us who had loudly lamented Canadian indifference to a sport for which Nature had provided so vast a playground on our own immediate territory. We had awakened out of sleep, and would redeem the past by a vigorous mountaineering organization. But whatever the Alpine Club of Canada achieves of climbing, of discovery, of purely scientific work; whatever the Club may eventually become, it must never forget how great and splendid service, and affectionate withal, has been rendered to our mountains and Canadian mountaineering by the members of the Appalachian Mountain Club, the American Alpine Club, and the Alpine Club of London. They have done the work, and published the tidings in a series of publications that already make a considerable library of Rocky Mountain literature. When the Canadian Alpine Club was organized, it counted itself honored to confer honorary membership upon some representatives of these Clubs, and happy to receive others as active members. The first life-member on our list is Professor Herschel C. Parker of Columbia University, one of the boldest pioneers of them all.

What does the Alpine Club of Canada propose to do? Does it take itself too seriously? There may be learned cosmopolitan alpinists whose many years' experience of hardy holidays among the glaciers and upper snows of the mountain ranges of the world, would incline them to look with patronage, if not incipient scorn, upon an organized effort to popularize the exclusive sport. They might say that to popularize was to vulgarize. Not so. Mountaineering is too toilsome, too hard a sport, and demands qualities of mind and character quite other than vulgar. Many pastimes and sports, many vocations and avocations may become vulgarized. But it must be obvious to any who know ever so little about the glaciers and *névés* and precipices—the unimaginable visions from the upper heights; it must be obvious that, from the very nature of the sport, to popularize mountaineering is not to vulgarize nor degrade it. The mountains themselves hold the high effort and achievement in fee. The vulgar reach the mountain summits by a way against which the Alpine Club of Canada will set a face of flint. We know what way that is: the way of the monster, Mammon. By virtue of its constitution, the Alpine club is a national trust for the defence of our mountain solitudes against the intrusion of steam and electricity and all the vandalisms of this luxurious, utilitarian age; for the keeping free from the grind of commerce, the wooded passes and valleys and alplands of the wilderness. It is the people's right to have primitive access to the remote places of safest retreat from the fever and the fret of the market place and the beaten tracts of life. We are devoutly grateful, as we ought to be, that the Canadian Pacific Railway Company has shown itself wise in a national sense, by refusing to follow in the wake of the cog-railways of the Rigi and Pike's peak. Our associate member, Mr. Whyte, the Second Vice-President of the Company, than whom a shrewder man of commerce does not live in Canada, nor one with a clearer vision of the people's good, would deplore any wanton defacement of the wild natural beauty and grandeur of these now secluded fastnesses. If I had space I could give tangible proof of this.

It is the Club's business to support the picturesque and wholly enjoyable transit to the mountain-places by pack-horse and saddle, and to promote the too much neglected exercise of walking. Your true lover of Nature is also a man of the unfamiliar roads and forest trails. It would be a great thing for young Canadians if all the automobiles vanished into space and walking for pleasure became the fashion. As soon as prudence will warrant, huts will be built in remote strategic situations for the convenience of the members, and persons put in charge for the season; bivouacs will be established on the long trails at distances of a day's journey, and the Club will co-operate, where possible, with the Railway and the Government, in making new trails, giving comfortable access to all the places already known or yet to be discovered. And it is the Club's business to support all measures towards preservation for all time of the fauna and flora in their wild habitat. All members are expected to be alert to this end.

First named among the reasons for the Club's existence is the claim of science: "the promotion of scientific study and the exploration of Canadian alpine and glacial regions." This clause makes its appeal to the exclusive class already referred to, whose work is of the schools, a thing apart from, though it may and ought to include mountaineering as an ennobling, ethical and aesthetic pastime. This section has a distinct work to do; and will, we hope, include a considerable number of men of science. And though much snow may fall upon the mountains and much water run in torrents from the glaciers ere it achieves its predestined high place in alpine and glacial science, its progress towards that consummation is in safe guidance. The President will look to that. He is keen for progress, and has withal, an appalling capacity for dogged hard work—and for making other people work. The Scientific Section is not likely to languish while Mr. Wheeler is alive.

Concerning the cultivation of Art, prizes are to be given for the best photographs; and as soon a circumstances will permit, a competition in oils and water colors will be opened for active members. A reliable guide-book, too which will include instruction on the details of mountaineering, will be published for the benefit of any who come to climb in the Canadian Alps.

There is nothing quixotic about the Alpine Club of Canada: it is a sane, sober institution, organized by sane, sober men. As indicated, its mission is manifold. The education of Canadians to an appreciation of their alpine heritage, is of itself a *raison d'etre*. The Canadian Rocky Mountain system, with its unnumbered and unknown natural sanctuaries for generations yet unborn, is a national asset. In time we ought to become a nation of mountaineers, loving our mountains with the patriot's passion.

A great Canadian, who wore himself out for the love he bore to God and Canada, was wont to say that a country which could grow wheat could grow men, by which he meant a race made of the flesh-stuff and the soul-stuff that builds up nations. This is the composite human material out of which mountaineers are made. But the peril is, that men become satiated with wheat, and there follows that effeteness which is worse than the effeteness of an unbalanced culture. Among other correctives none is more effective than this of the exercise of the mountain-craft. No sport is so likely to cure a fool of his foolishness as the steady pull, with a peril or two of another sort attending, of a season's mountain climbing in one of those "thrilling regions of thick-ribbed ice" in the wild alpine playground of Canada. The ethical value of mountaineering is a subject upon which our statesmen would do well to ponder; and there is a considerable Canadian Alpine literature from which they may gather data.

Any young man of latent intellectual and moral force, who comes to close grips with the waiting, challenging mountains, and puts one summit after another beneath the soles of his feet, has gained immensely in the Spartan virtues. Moreover, he has, by climbing to these skiey stations and standing face to face with Infinitude, learned some things he may not tell, because they are unspeakable. It is given to very few, to utter such experiences. But there comes to the mountaineer of pure mind and willing spirit the sense of which Wordsworth tells, of the presence inter-fused in Nature; the presence that dwells among the sheer peaks and in the living air and the blue sky and in the mind of man; the motion and the spirit that rolls through all things. Browning sums it in his swift way: "which fools call Nature and I call God." To this climber is given a key to many an utterance of the Masters, which else remained for him unlocked. It is quite true that every climber has not, nor may not acquire the philo-sophic mind that is curious regarding the divine interpretation of Nature; but traversing the sources of the great ice-rivers and breathing the virgin air above their mute snows is conducive to that philosophic mind. And whether or no, if that high exercise and that environment fail to arouse a sense of Nature malignant and Nature benignant, his case is hopeless as one who stands among men at the making of the nation.

One word more: the standard for membership may not be lowered. That it will be raised is almost certain; just as, with the progress of education, the standards for matriculation in a new university are raised.

SOURCE

Elizabeth Parker's "The Alpine Club of Canada," from *Canadian Alpine Journal* 1, no. 1 (1907), 3–8.

MARY E. CRAWFORD

"Mountain Climbing for Women" (1909)

IF FOR THE SAKE of argument the question "Should women climb mountains?" were brought up it would be found exactly one hundred years behind the times.

In 1809 the first historical mountain ascent by a woman was made when Maria Paradis was taken to the summit of Mont Blanc by Jacques Balmat. Sad to say, her motive was not of a very high order, the excursion being made entirely for the mercenary one of personal gain. Neither can she be said to have "climbed" the mountain as she was literally "taken" by Balmat and hauled up like a sack of potatoes. "But," she said, "thanks to the curiosity of the public I have made a very nice profit out of it, and that was what I reckoned on."*

From this time on, the possibility of making ascents seems to have found favor in the eyes of the more adventurous women, until, to-day it is doubtful if any woman who has climbed over 10,000 feet could make one cent out of the erstwhile profitable public curiosity.

In 1834 a Bavarian Princess ascended the Mittaghorn, 10,328 feet. In 1838 Mlle. D'angeville ascended Mont Blanc. In 1863 Mrs. Watson was one of the party which conquered Balfrin, 12,500 feet. In 1864 Miss Lucy Walker ascended the Balmhorn, 12,176 feet. In 1868 as recorded by Whymper in his "Scrambles in the Alps," a young woman of the Val Tournanche arrived within 350 feet of the summit of the Matterhorn, the mountain being as yet unconquered. In 1870 Mrs. Brevoort stood on the summit of the Meije, 13,026 feet. And so on to the present day, when the names of Miss Peck, who so recently scaled Huascaran in the Andes, a peak over 24,000 feet high; of Mrs. Bullock Workman, who with her husband has made first ascents of the giants in the Himalayas; and of Miss Benham, with about 200 ascents to her credit, prove that women also are making history in the alpine world.

Ordinarily, the idea of mountaineering as a recreation only occurs to those who live in the vicinity of mountains or whose business takes them there, or in whose family the love of mountaineering is inherited. But now that alpine clubs exist which admit women to membership, and which, by assuming all responsibility of equipment at a reasonable rate, place the mountain summits within reach of all, there is no reason why every woman may not seriously ask herself "Why should I not spend my holiday this year in the mountains?"

There is no recreation which, in all its aspects of surrounding and exercise, will bring about a quicker rejuvenation of worn out nerves, tired brains and flabby muscles than mountaineering. It is for women one of the new things under the sun and every fresh mountain is a new delight. Ennui has no place in the vocabulary of the woman who climbs, the words which rout it are enthusiasm and exhilaration. Diseases of the imagination cannot be discovered anywhere on a mountain side, where Nature asserts herself so grandly to the consciousness and with such insistence that the "ego" with its troubles sinks out of sight.

In the actual climbing the whole attention is so absolutely concentrated on the business in hand that every worry is put to flight and nothing is of any moment beyond reaching the top of the mountain. The therapeutic value of this one feature alone is inestimable.

Take the woman whose usual occupation is a sedentary one—whose daily life is one of routine in the office, the school-room, the sick-room; and who is constantly giving out to others her nervous energy. Put her on the train and send her to the mountains. The imperfect glimpses of this peak and that gorge are small foretastes of what she is going to enjoy, for no one knows the mountains who sees them only from the car window. Now she has reached her destination and is left to exchange for the rattle of the train the music of rushing torrents, to breathe in the keen pure air which finds its way to the very last air-cell of her lungs, and to rest her tired eyes on beauties of form and color never before imagined. Every influence by which she is surrounded is alternative in its effect.

She spends a night under canvas and feels the first pangs of healthful hunger to which she has long been a stranger. And now—suitably dressed, and with feelings of excitement and wonder—she waits with her party of guides and companions the word which starts her off on her first mountain ascent. Nervous about the new experiences to come? Perhaps—for the almost invariable reply given by the woman to whom is presented the new idea of mountain climbing for herself, is—"Oh! I never could climb for I am always dizzy when at a height—I cannot look down—I should be afraid." But there are guides, men of experience, whom she has only to obey, and who will show her the right thing to do; there is the rope, tested and strong; and she has her alpenstock and her nailed boots whose efficiency against slips she has already experienced. She knows that every precaution against danger is provided and perhaps remembers Mrs. Jellyby's remark that "You may go into Holborn without precaution and be run over; you may go into Holborn with precaution and never be run over. Just so with"—the mountains, to change the quotation. Then there is the company of former novices who also had always been dizzy at heights, but who now ascend their peaks without a qualm and with confidence.

There is another factor which she has not taken into account, but which comes to her as surely as there is a cliff to climb or a torrent to pass, and that is the infallible instinct of self-preservation. She is going to know herself as never before—physically, mentally, emotionally. And so she starts out, gains confidence with every step, finds the dangers she has imagined far greater than those she encounters and arrives at last upon the summit to gaze out upon a new world. Surely not the same old earth she has seen all her life? Yes—but looked at from *on top*—a point of view which now makes upon her mind its indelible impression.

This woman returns to her round of daily duties in the workaday world—but she has only to close her eyes for a second and she is transported to her mountain top. Brain fag? Nervous exhaustion? Asthenic muscles? They have lost their dread meaning. Time cannot drag now, for to the mountaineer "the year passes quickly looking back and looking forward."

Not many books on athletic sports for women—if there are any—devote a chapter to mountain climbing; perhaps because the idea is a new one, or perhaps because it is only a short time in the year that can be given to it by the average woman, while other forms of physical exercise can be practised more continuously. Beyond presenting the idea, however, books cannot do much to teach the "knack"—it can only come by experience. Preparation for the climb can be made by following these more every-day exercises and, viewed in this light, they take on a fresh interest. The daily physical drill has an object now, and every long walk leads to the mountains. Rowing with the sliding seat has been recommended as the best exercise for training for mountaineering—but for those to whom this is out of the question the Japanese method of individual muscle training is excellent; and walking every day and in all weathers, with perhaps a pedometer to add zest, is best of all. Many women take no previous training beyond this. Mrs. Bullock Workman who, as she says of herself, is not a light weight, made ascents of over 16,000 feet in the Himalayas without any, and her highest and hardest work was accomplished in the low levels and moist atmosphere of Ceylon and Java. She recommends for those who wish to reach the higher peaks, a previous residence of a few weeks at 11,000 feet.

The ambition of the average woman, however, will not lead her beyond the more easily obtainable ascents, and she can almost disregard any fears of the effects of high altitudes. Mountain sickness does not usually attack its victims under 12,000 feet, and many attain far greater heights than this without any untoward sensations. Climbing is for the stout woman as well as the thin, and while it is the rule to lose weight during the period of making mountain expeditions, the normal equilibrium is soon gained. Stout and thin alike find themselves in much better proportion than before.

Any woman who contemplates this form of recreation, and who has any fears as to her physical ability, should be properly examined first. Should she be below the average, however, she has only to think of Switzerland—the Mecca of the invalid, among whose heights are to be found sufferers from diseases of every system of the body—circulatory—respiratory—nervous. These find in that wonderful air and beautiful environment their restoration to a large degree and, knowing that our Canadian mountains possess the same power, she can confidently expect like results.

The following data of physical characteristics and personal experience have been gathered from nine women who have made more than two ascents of over 10,000 feet. These follow their daily occupation at sea-level and in the prairie provinces, and include teachers, nurses, housekeepers, stenographers.

(a) Height ranges from 5 feet to 5 feet 9 inches.
(b) Weight ranges from 98 lb. to 140 lb.
(c) State of appetite while climbing—in all cases never falls below very good.

(d)   Ability to sleep between climbs—very good except in two cases, these being influenced by temperament.

(e)   Temperament—classification of: Energetic or Indolent, Excitable or Deliberate—while none acknowledge to indolence, every variation under the other heads is given, from highly strung and extremely excitable to very calm and deliberate. Dizziness at heights was felt in two cases on first climb but not subsequently. *All* unite in asserting the beneficial effects experienced.

The following are extracts made from general remarks in the list of questions sent out. "Mountain climbing is a splendid cure for nervousness."

"From various climbs during five summers I believe that any woman with fairly sound organs can do mountain climbing with very great benefit to body and mind. I am convinced that making a fairly dangerous climb, where every sense must be alert and cool, makes a woman more fearless in attempting difficult tasks in her ordinary life. The ideas gained of the beautiful and sublime cannot be valued."

"In my experience I have found, that when tired, there is a mental exhilaration which supplies new energy; and in time any feeling of fatigue departs so as to allow of finishing the trip with no ill effects whatever."

"I lost weight during the week of climbing, but never felt better in my life."

And so the woman goes back to her tasks revivified. For the teacher new lights have been thrown upon history, literature, geography or mathematics. The artist and writer have found a mighty inspiration. The student of natural history has fresh specimens to classify. The nurse need not rack her tired brain for material to while away the heavy hours of pain for her patient—she has a fund of thrilling and amusing anecdotes to give out of her own experiences.

There is a field of interest in the mountains to satisfy every branch of mental enquiry. And for the body? When the mountaineer's friends one and all greet her with the exclamation "How well you are looking, I never saw you looking better in your life!" she knows that she is the happy possessor of the beauty of health gained from her sojourn among the heights.

* M. Durier's "Le Mont Blanc."

SOURCE

Mary E. Crawford's "Mountain Climbing for Women," from *Canadian Alpine Journal* 2 (1909), 85–91.

MARY M. SCHÄFFER

"Breaking the Way" (1904)

CANADA HAS VISITING her mountains this summer a more or less notable climber, Miss Gertrude Benham. Miss Benham has made her name known in the Alpine world by the good work she has done the last ten years in Switzerland, and the border Alps.

Some little idea may be gained of the enormous work she has accomplished in this way, when it is realized that she has compassed peaks and passes 1000 feet and over, to the number of 132, not counting the times she has duplicated them. Hearing of the great beauty of our Canadian Alps, Miss Benham decided to come over and test them for herself. Arriving in Canada the latter part of May she has been playing a waiting game among the snowy peaks. The uncommonly heavy snow of last winter has kept her back from her work, but at last a few days of intense heat unbarred the door to the snowy fastnesses. The well known guides, Christian and Hans Kaufman, at last decided that on June 27th they might try for Mount Lefroy. The weather had been all that could be desired for days and the eager watcher, accompanied by the two Swiss guides and an American,

Mr. Frost, started for her first climb on the Canadian peaks. To quote her own words, "After an early breakfast we started from the Chalet at Lake Louise, at 4.15, to explore the beautiful peak of Lefroy, which had beckoned me for days. The morning was simply perfect. A superb rosy glow, the herald of the sun, touched the fleecy clouds, and the snows on Mt. Victoria gathered to themselves the soft pink flush. Alas for our hopes!— the walk to the glacier was the end of fine weather, and we were greeted with a snow fall. With no spot for shelter, we debated our advance, and finally decided to go on for a short distance.

Up Abbott's Pass we floundered, sinking constantly in the soft snow up to our knees, and with the cutting wind filled with icy needles, the day seemed unpropitious, to say the least. It was humiliating to return, but Mr. Frost and I finally determined to put pride in our pockets, and await a better day. At the head of the Pass we confided our conclusions to our guides, just as they were preparing to rope us.

Hans replied: "All right, but we will rope to go down." Which we did, when the guides quietly started on up the mountain. We might decide on our own pride, but we had not calculated for Christian and Hans, so laughing and rather satisfied to have our day's destiny decided for us, we plunged ahead into the teeth of the storm. After a half hour's stiff work, we suddenly heard a terrific crash, and looked to see if the mountain was coming down upon us—our leading guide had disappeared. The snow bridge on the bergscheund had given way, but fortunately the scheund was full of snow, and he was soon out again, and no damage done. The weather failed to improve, we were constantly surrounded by mists, and pelting snow, seeing only fifteen or twenty feet beyond us at any time, and only realizing we had not reached the summit, because constant views of looming rocks rose before us. Lefroy had about twenty summits that day, making it a most disheartening ascent. At last we really reached a cairn, and nothing more rose above us, save our own wind-driven, ice-covered selves. Each strand of my blown hair contained an icicle, which jingled musically as I shook my head, while the men were encased in ice, on the side exposed to the worst of the storm. It was no place for lunch, and we turned back into the mists. Our steps were obliterated and enclosed; as we were in the fleecy clouds we had a sensation of walking down into nothingness. Through Abbott's Pass and the Death Trap, the wind swept too savagely to permit a stop for lunch and we hurried on to shelter, opening our packs at six P.M., not having eaten since eight in the morning. Coming off the Glacier, a little spot of blue greeted us, and clear skies escorted us the next three miles to the Chalet. But in spite of wind, and cold, and snow and all discomforts, we thanked the guides for taking us on. Mount Victoria proved much kinder to the stranger on her slopes a few days later. Accompanied by the same good guides, starting at about the same time, we had a glorious day on that beautiful mountain. The snow this time was in fine condition, there were loose rocks, avalanches, and snow crevices to avoid, and the route is a much longer one than Lefroy, though the mountain is not so high by a few feet. The view from the top was one to linger for, and I remained as long as I dare. Nine P.M. saw me safely back at the Chalet, and the day a perfect memory to be stored away as one of the pleasantest pictures I may carry away with me from Canada."

SOURCE

Mary M. Schäffer's "Breaking the Way," from *Rod and Gun in Canada* 6, no. 3 (1904), 111–12.

ETHEL JOHNS

"A Graduating Climb" (1910)

IT WAS THE ALPINE JOURNAL THAT DID IT. Journeying peacefully along the sunny Portage Plains in the train one day a copy lay beside me belonging to a fellow traveller. It fell open at a page showing "The McTavish" scaling a giddy precipice on Crows' Nest. Further along was an article describing some climb which ended with the magic sentence—"We had been out fourteen hours." I drew a long breath, suddenly I was wearied of "the great spaces washed with sun" and remembered the Rockies as I had once glimpsed them, eighty miles away, a fairyland of rose and grey and silver. The one desirable thing in life seemed to be to climb Crows' Nest and to be out fourteen hours.

So it came to pass that one glorious August morning a very scornful porter deposited me and my possessions on the platform at Hector among a crowd of people all talking at once and engaged in dragging their own particular dunnage out of a pile almost high enough to constitute a qualifying climb. This mountain was regarded with extreme disfavor by the pack train officials, who evidently considered my modest addition to the heap as the proverbial last straw, and were openly dubious of my sworn statement that it weighed only forty pounds. I must confess that at this particular moment I never felt more lonely in my life. The air was full of shouted greetings and reminiscences in which I had no part, but presently two of the lady members came over to me and told me that a party was going to walk out to camp in a short time and were so good to me that I took heart of grace again.

While we were waiting one of my long cherished dreams came true. I saw a Swiss guide in the flesh. So many of one's dreams are spoiled in the realization; but that Guide was, as the Virginian puts it: "better than I dreamed." He wore the official badge on his coat lapel. He even sported the Tyrolean feather. His boots were as thick and full of nails as I had hoped. He carried an ice-axe, a rucksack and a coiled rope. I walked round him at a respectful distance and regarded him from every angle. He was a most satisfying person.

Presently there was a gathering of the clans and a start was made. Such a morning! All blue and silver and deep green, and not a sound but the rush of the torrent over the broken boulders. Far ahead strode the guide of my admiration followed by a select party who were going to make a "quick trip." I wished I had gone with them and not stayed with these people who trusted themselves to an irresponsible individual who didn't look like a mountaineer at all and whose slogan seemed to be "Hop along, Sister Mary, hop along." The ascent began to grow steeper. I began to feel awfully queer, as though some one were sitting on my chest. I decided this must be the result of transporting myself from seven hundred feet above sea level to six thousand and then indulging in physical exercise. It was a very disagreeable sensation. A kindly individual with a handkerchief gracefully draped over the back of his neck noticed my distress and suggested that the party halt as he was tired. I sank down on a log and made noises like a dog who has been chasing a rabbit. This was my first experience of Alpine chivalry. For some strange reason it is always the strongest member of the party who gets tired first. Just as the weaker ones are praying for death as a relief from their sufferings one of the strong ones who could go all day without stopping, suddenly discovers that he is quite exhausted, in fact, cannot go another step. This condition of affairs terminates abruptly when the weaker vessels have got their breath and are beginning to take some interest in life once more. This power of getting suddenly and unaccountably tired increases in direct proportion to the number of difficult climbs made by the individual concerned—or, in other words, the better the climber the more sympathy he has for those weaker than himself. Which after all is what one would have expected. It was at this juncture that I discovered that the irresponsible one whom everybody addressed as "P.D." was really half of the McTavish entity. It was rather a disillusion. He was not dressed as I imagined a mountaineer should be. But apparently clothes are no criterion of mountaineering. The real celebrities don't bother with frills. They often scorn artistically adjusted puttees and tie their trousers round their boot tops with a bit of string instead. They wear fearsome sweaters and shocking bad hats. So much for the modesty of true greatness.

The trail was not to be without adventure for me. After my rest I started out like a giant refreshed and presently came to a torrent bridged by a log of somewhat slender proportions. Over they all went like a flock of mountain goats. That is to say—all except me. I stopped half way. In fact I wallowed in that torrent. It was not deep but I made the most of it, and emerged therefrom looking more like a muskrat than a human being. It was not very comfortable walking in wet clothes and when at last we did reach camp I found that my outfit was left behind at Hector. There was nothing for it but to drape myself about in blankets and seek the chaste seclusion of tent number five while my clothes were sent to the cook tent to be dried.

It is useless to attempt a description of the camp at Lake O'Hara. Those who were there need no description. They have but to close their eyes to see again that mountain meadow, starred with ling, flaming with painter's brush—its rows of white tents, the shining Adonis pool and all about it the snowy hills of God.

After all my most vivid abiding memory is of the day on Huber. The side trips had helped my wind considerably and had given me some experience of scrambling, so on Thursday evening my name figured among a large number of others who were to attempt Huber on the following day. Sleep did not come easily that night and it seemed a long time before I heard the President's voice repeating the well-known formula—"It is now five o'clock, if you are not ready in an hour's time the party starts without you." On this particular morning he added a corollary that still further dashed my wavering spirits—"the rocks are slippery to-day, those going do so at their own risk." Soon we were assembled round the smouldering embers of the camp fire, and the various "ropes" answered the roll call. Ours was the last rope to start, it was the last rope to reach the summit, strange to say it was the last rope to get in at night. In fact, it was a very bad rope. Edouard Feuz said we were "the limit"—and he ought to know for we were his rope.

Mindful of good advice I planted myself next the guide as we skirted the shores of the lake. It was a glorious morning—Cathedral was reflected in the mirror of O'Hara, its summit already touched with flame. Little wisps of mist still clung about Odaray but Huber towered above us, its castellated summit dark against the morning sky. Before long we were out of the timber on to the scree, the incline grew steeper and my troubles began; I was soon gasping like a dying fish. About half way up we paused to rest. Edouard looked us over with a cynical eye and much to my disgust put me back to the middle of the rope and put another member of the party, a most plucky climber, next to him. I made a feeble protest but it was no use. "You'll get your second wind pretty soon—You can make it allright" said heartless Edouard and off we started again.

People who have never done any climbing have since asked me how I enjoyed the glorious view which unfolded before us as we went up. I have been forced to draw on my imagination for a reply to this question. As a matter of fact all I saw on the way up Huber was Edouard's boots. They pervaded the whole landscape and rose and fell with the regularity of clock work. Occasionally, *very* occasionally, these boots were near enough to be studied in detail, but more often I had to content myself with mere impressionistic glimpses of them disappearing upwards, ever upwards.

After we left the col we roped up and here we overtook the party ahead of us who had had to wait at "the rope ladder" familiar to all who graduated on Huber. Somehow or other that rock work was traversed. We had perforce to go slowly and here Edouard's prophecy came true—I got my second wind. Looking back on the climb as a whole the worst part of it was struggling through the timber and up the scree to the col. In Mr. Mantalini's immortal words, that was "one dem'd horrid grind." Finally we arrived at the snow slope immediately below the summit. Photographs of this interesting spot are most misleading. They represent it as a mild and innocuous slope, whereas it was really, according to my recollection of it and also from tales told previously by newly graduated ones, almost perpendicular. Even our accomplished end man acknowledged it was "an awkward little place." Slowly we crept out—one man moving at a time— and at last it was done. We had climbed Huber and stood on the very Peak of Things.

We spent about half an hour on the summit and then started the descent. By this time the steps on the snow slope were pretty well worn and the going was decidedly slippery. Edouard's adjurations to the "lady in the middle" became more and more peremptory. "Stick your feet in" said he, "don't walk like a chicken." The words were hardly out of his mouth before the aforesaid chicken was accidentally pulled off her feet by the gentleman ahead who took an unusually long stride and pulled the rope taut. Something had to go, so I did. At least I started, but as they say in describing big climbs: "The rope held." I should say it did. It nearly cut me in half. Fortunately my knee caught in one of the steps and I managed to hold on to my alpenstock, so before long the chastened chicken and the rest of the party were safely down on the snow-field leading to the rock work. Here Edouard decided we might try to glissade. For some reason it was not a success. Either we started too soon or we did not all start together. Something went wrong evidently, for all I can remember is trying to dodge the gentleman behind me, who being heavier naturally came down faster and insisted on using me as a toboggan. From the distance we must have resembled a baby avalanche. However, we covered considerable ground and, as it was getting late and the rock work had still to be negotiated, perhaps it was just as well we did hurry involuntarily.

Oh! that rock work—Coming up was nothing to getting down. To Edouard's disgust I made the attempt with my back to the rock instead of in the conventional manner. I knew I didn't look a bit like the picture of The McTavish on Crows' Nest, but I also knew that if I turned I should get dizzy. But turn I did in answer to Edouard's pleadings, and dizzy I got, and when finally I half slid half tumbled to the bottom of that rope ladder (ladder indeed!) I asked to be let alone to die in peace. Edouard's treatment of my sad collapse was to force upon me a little piece of hard cake and some water which he found in a crevice. These had a marvellous effect and before very long we reached camp where the evening fire was blazing gloriously and the President as usual was prowling around the outskirts on the lookout for late parties. They gave us three cheers—I never heard a sweeter sound in my life—and we gave three croaky ones for Edouard who certainly deserved them—for had he not shepherded us to the top of Huber "by the power of man"? Then some one gave me tea and more and more tea, and presently, sinful pride having rule inside I went out to the camp fire to tell fearsome tales of the day's adventures. Now for the first time I felt as though I belonged in that circle. Never, never should I be a mountaineer, the precipices of Crows' Nest were not for me, but nevertheless the climb had been made, badly, falteringly, but to the top and accordingly I was made free of the great and noble company of mountaineers.

That night as I vainly twisted and twined to ease my aching bones I lived the whole day over again. The vision from the summit of Huber unfolded itself again before me—that sea of peaks, height calling unto height and depth to depth—the Kingdoms of the Earth and the glory thereof spread out before us.

In conclusion let me not forget to record—"We had been out fifteen hours."

SOURCE

Ethel Johns's "A Graduating Climb," from *Canadian Alpine Journal* 2 (1910), 158–65.

RHODA W. EDWARDS

"Graduation" (1918)

In the morning, oh! ye climbers,
Though the dawn be cold and grey,
You must leave your beds of balsam
And with ice-axe pick your way.

You must climb above the timber,
Cross the fields of ice and snow,
Ere the avalanche be on you
Or crevasses wider grow.

Though the shale be slipping, slipping,
Though the rocks are flying fast,
Though your brow with sweat be dripping,
You will reach your goal at last.

Up the chimney, round the cornice,
Then a traverse on the ridge,
Hold the rope taut! Here's a chasm,
One by one you'll have to bridge.

Grip with knee, with toe, with finger,
There's the peak with cairn in sight.
When you've scaled it you may linger,
With a mountaineer's delight.

Then retrace your footsteps slowly
To the glacier fields below,
Where you glissade homeward swiftly,
Coasting, sliding down the snow.

Oh, the welcome that they give you,
When you reach the Camp at night,
And they lead you to the bonfire
Where you've earned a seat by right.

SOURCE

Rhoda W. Edwards's "Graduation," from *Canadian Alpine Journal* 9 (1918), 134.

Mount Assiniboine.
Photograph by
Georgia Engelhard, 1943.
(WMCR V751/PA–162)

GEORGIA ENGELHARD

"Portrait of a Giant" (1946)

MOUNTAINS HAVE PERSONALITY. Really? Why, of course, you probably never thought of that, but they have personalities and moods just as Mr. X or Miss J who come to the studio to have their portraits made. Even little peaks in small ranges have this quality: in Bear Mountain Park on the Hudson where the summits rise no more than 1300 feet, Timp, West Mountain, Catamount, all have different and individual characteristics. But let's go a bit farther afield—not too far for the average person. Let us go to the Canadian Rockies and look at 11,872 foot Mt. Assiniboine, a personality peak if I ever saw one. Whether you conquer its lofty, cloud-swept summit, whether you camp in its shadow, whether you see it dominating all around from a distance of twenty miles, you cannot fail to be impressed by its power, its grandeur. Sometimes, standing on summits fifty to seventy-five miles away, the horizon is filled with hundreds of shining, glittering peaks, but there is one and always one that we mountain climbers see first, raising its proud crest into the heavens: "Look, there is Assiniboine."

Dubbed "The Matterhorn of the Canadian Rockies" because from the north both peaks present a bold, triangular form with a sharp central ridge, Assiniboine lacks the demoniac quality of its counterpart. Both rise sheer and forbidding from whichever angle you see them, but whereas the Matterhorn combines a certain sinister quality with its strength and boldness, Assiniboine is aloof, powerful, cloud piercing, but never willfully malignant. It is honest and straightforward: on its crest lurk no demons. But, nevertheless, like all high mountains, it commands awe and respect, for it is the biggest, the most outstanding peak for miles around.

To me, there is nothing more stimulating, more interesting than to get to know such a big peak. This knowledge, personally, was gained by climbing it, by physically knowing its steep snow slopes and rocky, spine-like ridges, its sheer cliffs and corniced summit. The mountaineer, meeting the challenge of a mighty peak and conquering it, instinctively feels the personality of the great natural opponent. But I have also learned to know this mountain by living in its shadow for many days, in successive years, by seeing it in spring, in midsummer, and in autumn, in fair weather as well as in storm, by having observed it from all sides and angles, by watching its form change with the shifting light and cloud. And what more fascinating than to record such a giant personality with the camera?

The first time that I saw Assiniboine was in the early summer of 1928. Our pack train rounded a cliffy corner, and there it was, its stark 12,000 feet of crag and snow glittering against the burning blue, high altitude-sky, its noble, sweeping lines the embodiment of challenge. It was a thrilling and unforgettable sight. I have seen it, lived with it for a good many days and weeks since then, have climbed its sheer north ridge and prowled around its lower crags on many other sides, but not until the summer of 1943 did I feel qualified to make a portrait study of it. Of course, on first acquaintance I took snapshots, but to make a portrait, a true portrait, takes longer acquaintanceship, longer study of the proper angles, the proper light conditions. In 1943 I spent three weeks camped at its base, and more than ever its giant force impressed itself upon me. Day after day it towered 6000 feet above our tiny camp, day after day it stood stark and eternal, until its personality became almost oppressive. Its terrific, continuous dominance at times got on my nerves—it was so everlastingly omnipotent and omnipresent. I could not keep my eyes off it, for it has a magnetism that forces you to look at it continually, a magnificent fascination, ever changing in form and mood as the hours and clouds float by. But I had ample opportunity to take the set of pictures that I had in mind, to portray the mountain's varying physical characteristics as well as its moods, to meet its eternal challenge once more, not as a mountaineer this time, but as a photographer.

To do this portrait, I had no light but the sun. I could not, as with human portraiture, arrange a setup of source light, fill-in, and back light, but I could wait until the celestial "source light" came into the right position, I could wait until atmospheric conditions were just what I wanted. I could not ask my mountain model to "turn its head" or shift its position before my camera, but as a seasoned mountaineer I was able to scramble to many a high location, far away from base camp, from where I could get a new and unusual view of the mountain, a view which would further enhance the collection of pictures to go into the making of this portrait of a giant. And furthermore, as photographer, I could use camera, film, filters, exposure, and previous experience in this type of work to serve my ends. It took endless patience at times, it meant a lot of hiking and climbing carrying a heavy load of photographic equipment; it often meant standing for an hour or more in a biting, icy gale, but to me it was well worth while. Only if you love and understand mountains, only if you have lived with them, if you have observed them keenly and thrilled to their moods, can you make really effective pictures of them. Lacking this love and understanding you might just as well leave your camera at home and save film.

So let me tell you how some of these pictures were taken. No soft focus lens for this work; only the sharpest of the sharp, the f:4.5 Zeiss Tessar, for Assiniboine is built of brittle ice and sharp stone, and therefore the lens must cut as sharp as the mountain's narrow ridges, must yield results as crisp as the keen mountain air. I used the seven-inch lens rather than one of shorter focal length, because it gives greater perspective and depth. The camera was a 4 by 5 press type, with rising and falling front, invaluable in making mountain pictures as it enables you to avoid distortion and foreshortening caused by tilting. I used this large size in preference to the 2 1/4 by 3 1/4 model as it is easier to make croppings for enlargement from the bigger negatives. A tripod, yes, a nuisance to carry about, but it insures maximum steadiness in a windy country and also absolutely accurate composition on the groundglass. Fast pan film, slightly over red-corrected, which yields dark, dramatic skies in the clear, high air without the use of a filter, and also enabled me to use smaller apertures and faster exposures in uncertain light conditions than slower film would have. I did carry a K1 and a red filter, the latter used with infrared film for moonlight or stormy effects. I carried no exposure meter, for my eyes are so trained through years of experience in this line of work that I need no mechanical aid. Besides, the rough life in the mountains is hard on the delicate meters, which I find best to use at home. Add to the list plenty of lens tissue, a knapsack to carry the equipment, and a fairly strong pair of legs, plus patience—patience to wait for the day, the hour, the moment that will give the proper light conditions to fulfill a rich portrait of the giant peak.

To get the opening picture of it, towering above relatively high surrounding peaks, I walked sixteen miles and climbed cliffs and shale slopes to the 8500 foot summit of Citadel Peak, some fifteen miles away from my subject. Yes, I could have saved myself considerable muscular exertion by taking the shots from the pass below the peak, but they would have been marred by too much green foreground, and I wanted a view of Assiniboine from a high angle, just mountain and cloud, aloof, splendid, and impersonal. When I reached the top of Citadel, Assiniboine's crest was veiled in scudding mists, and I had quite a wait until it emerged. When it did clear, I had to shoot quickly before it became veiled again, but the sight was a magnificent one, the sky filled with great cumulus clouds, and shadows playing on the mountain, giving it plasticity and a three-dimensional quality. In these shots I deliberately cut out foreground and avoided the inclusion of human figures, as they would have detracted from the lonely grandeur of the panorama.

Later I moved in to camp at its base, and here there was scarcely a day that I did not make pictures. At first the weather was warm and cloudless, the mountain black and snow free, and framed by dark evergreens it appeared in its most benign and friendly mood. A group of trail riders camping nearby provided the necessary touch of human interest. Soon, however, bad weather pulled in, and we had thirty-six hours of terrific blizzard, the mountain completely blotted out by fog and swirling snow. The wind roared and howled, shaking the tepee in which we sheltered. Snow poured down the poles inside and drifted under the canvas. To protect the camera and plates from moisture, I put them in a heavy wooden pack box covered with a raincoat. When the storm had spent itself and the weather began to clear, I devoted an entire day to photographing the peak. To many of you, this might sound like a very dull way of passing time, but to me it was utterly engrossing. Little by little, the mists thinned, and with enormous elemental effort the sharp ridges of Assiniboine began to struggle through them, appearing for a moment, then swept out of sight again, only to pierce through more and more defiantly. I felt I was witnessing the battle between supernatural forces, between clouds and the gods of the mountain. Under these conditions, Assiniboine was menacing, temperamental, mysterious. I photographed it without a filter for a high key shot; later as it emerged, its form becoming gradually more and more definite, a yellow filter was used to intensify the dramatic effect, and finally to give a picture of it, angry, wild and turbulent, I used infrared film with a red filter, which, although giving extreme overcorrection, was nevertheless most successful in creating the desired mood.

The next few days were sunny and gorgeous, and the mountain stood at its most splendid, gay and glittering, great plumes of snow streaming from its crest against the cloud-flecked sky. Only a hint of a threat broke the golden glory of those days as we heard avalanches roaring down, the warning voice of the mountain lest some rash climber dare set foot on its cliffs. I posed two of my companions lounging before the tepee, whose triangular form made an interesting repeat pattern, the sun-drenched meadows contrasting with the majesty of the implacable peak. I waited until mid-afternoon to get this picture, as cross lighting would give more form to the mountain as well as outline the edge of the tepee poles, thus giving more drama and crispness to the picture than would the flat light of noon. And as twilight approached, I shot the same scene, this time without figures, to show Assiniboine austere in its lonely grandeur.

Next I wished a picture of the peak in its most tranquil mood, and the natural time to make this was in the early morning before clouds appeared. At the base of the mountain lies a relatively large, blue-green lake, and I thought to get a reflection picture of it at about six in the morning. But arriving at the selected spot, I found it too close to the peak to be able to include both summit and total reflection on the negative. Besides, the body of water was too extensive to be absolutely unruffled. This was a puzzler: what to do to get that picture? The day was saved by my photographic and climbing partner, Eaton Cromwell, who remembered a tiny tarn, merely a pool of melted snow water about a mile away. So, taking down the camera and tripod, we trudged through the brushy meadows to this location which proved to be the answer to our problem. By using the rising front of the camera, I was just able to include the entire mountain and reflection, which was a perfect one. Cromwell posed in the middle distance to give a note of scale and human interest, and I told him to look toward Assiniboine rather than the camera, thus leading the eye into the picture. You will note that in many of the pictures I included figures; however, I always kept them subordinate, as I wished to give the impression of the vastness of the mountain scene contrasted with the relative insignificance of man. It was nearly eight o'clock by the time that the shot was taken, and I was more than thankful that no clouds had pulled in, for dramatic as they are on most occasions, in this case their presence would have ruined the mood of the picture, would have destroyed the feeling that I wished to convey of the utter purity and clarity, the breathless tranquility of the great peak at Alpine dawn.

By now I had enough varied pictures of Assiniboine from its best known side, the north. Many years ago, while horse wrangling on the lower slopes of a nearby mountain, I had caught a glimpse of its eastern aspect. From this angle it loses its triangular shape, but to me, is even more impressive, rising like a gigantic bastion surrounded by many minor, jagged turrets. To get this view in all its immensity, we waited for several days for one when the clouds were big and fluffy in a bright blue sky and then climbed this neighboring mountain, which is nearly 10,000 feet high. It was a long, hot grind up the dull shale slopes, and the camera equipment seemed to get heavier and heavier with every step. Sweating, panting, and silently cursing, we plodded upward. Well above timberline an enormous herd of elk with their young dashed madly past us down the mountainside, but so unexpected was their appearance, and so swift their flight, that we missed an unusual picture. After four hours of climbing, hot and a trifle weary, we came out on the long, flat summit ridge. And here a fierce and icy gale from the east struck us, buffeting us around like reeds. But the view of Assiniboine *was* magnificent and breathtaking. It looked more gigantic, more like the stronghold of the gods than ever before. Its proud summit swept skyward, high above green meadows, rock towers, and snowfields to almost Himalayan proportions. We hastily set up the camera and tripod, but operating in the raging wind was neither easy nor pleasant—which belongs to the department of understatement. The usually sturdy quickset tripod shook and shuddered, lens tissue and filters were blown hither and yon, the sunshade refused to stay in position, and fine shale dust was whirled up on to the surface of the lens, which had to be cleaned before each exposure. We were shivering, and my fingers, clumsy and inept with cold, did not help toward quick picture taking. I do not think that I have ever made pictures under more annoying or uncomfortable circumstances. But years of mountaineering have taught me persistence, and I had set my heart on getting effective shots of this stunning view. We spent more than an hour on that wind-swept ridge, as the sun flirted and hid behind fast-moving cloud banks, sometimes for as long as twenty minutes, often appearing momentarily only to hide itself again before my numbed fingers could click the shutter. Some shots were made without a filter, some with a light yellow one. The K2 would have yielded less effective results, for with Super-XX film it tends to darken the sky too much. And from this side the sheer peak is mostly black rock so that with the heavier filter there would have been a lack of separation between crag and sky. It was with a feeling of relief, the photography done, that we sped down the mountainside, out of that tearing, howling wind to warm ourselves in the sheltered, flowery meadows below.

From the south, Assiniboine's aspect again changes. From here it rises like a giant sperm whale, a great black mass, overpowering all around it. On this side its cliffs are utterly sheer, overhanging, and unclimbable; its form not as pleasing as from the north and east, but its impact the greatest. To get this view we took our pack train to a region about ten miles distant. Up a narrow and precipitous trail, difficult for the heavily laden horses to negotiate, we traveled to a charming, lake-dotted park-land, from where, however, our peak was not visible. To gain sight of it, we again had to climb a mountain, but this time the day was sunny and warm, the only untoward episode being an encounter with two young grizzlies at rather too close range, and later seeing their track high up on the mountain. If I recall, we did our photography at top speed, returning to camp as fast as possible. On another occasion, when climbing a nearby difficult peak, we had a splendid view of Assiniboine from the southwest, the sky black with approaching storm. But as the air had for some time been filled with forest fire smoke, and the climb a long and technically trying one, we had left all cameras behind. Even had we had them, I doubt if we would have lingered on that summit with thunder growling ominously. Such storms are of great danger to climbers, who, equipped with steel headed ice axes and nailed boots become veritable lightning rods. So that picture will have to be taken another year under more propitious circumstances.

Even with the many pictures that I made of Assiniboine that year, I will go back again some day and make more, just as I will climb to its haughty summit once again, for its fascination and its power are compelling, its variety of form and mood never ending. Like the sea, it is always essentially the same, yet forever changing in aspect, and it lures me irresistibly. I don't think that I have ever enjoyed a photographic assignment more than this self-imposed one. For never among men or mountains have I had a more photogenic model, one which was so excellent from all angles and in all lightings, whether direct, cross, or backlighting. Furthermore, I was working with a subject inspiring to me. Many people's names and faces fade in memory with the passing of time, but this lofty peak will always remain to me an unforgettable personality. And I hope with all my heart and soul that in this series of photographs I have fulfilled my wish: to present to you a portrait of one of nature's giants.

SOURCE
Georgia Engelhard's "Portrait of a Giant," from *American Photography* 40 (November 1946), 12–15.

MOIRA O'NEILL

"The North-West—Canada" (1909)

Oh, would ye hear, and would ye hear
   Of the windy, wide North-West?
Faith! 'tis a land as green as the sea,
That rolls as far and rolls as free,
With drifts of flowers, so many there be,
   Where the cattle roam and rest.

Oh, could ye see, and could ye see
   The great gold skies so clear,
The rivers that race through the pine shade dark,
The mountainous snows that take no mark,
Sun-lit and high on the Rockies stark,
   So far they seem as near.

SOURCE

Moira O'Neill's "The North-west—Canada" from *Canadian Alpine Journal* 2 (1909), 128. A longer version is also published in *Songs of the Glens of Antrim* (London: William Blackwood & Sons, 1910), 58–59.

LYNDA R. WOODS

"Canada's Mountains" (1954)

(Tune: "The Mountains of Mourne")

O Canada's mountains are rugged and tall,
    So many there are you can't count them at all,
Their glaciers and snows touch the sky's azure blue,
    Their sheer rock cliff-sides reflect every hue,
Their magnificent summits—all corniced snow—
    Look down on the green wooded valleys below.
There's no place on earth where I'd rather be
    For Canada's mountains are heaven to me.

O Canada's mountains are friendly and kind,
    They bring rest to the spirit and peace to the mind.
The wild glacial torrents—they sweep away care,
    And all troubles and ills float away in the air.

The flower-strewn meadows with beauty ablaze
    Fill you brimful of joy and contentment for days.
There are glories afar—even over the seas—
    But Canada's mountains surpass even these.

What joy 'tis to climb in these mountains so tall,
    What fun in the summer, the winter, the fall.
To see the green trails and the heights high above
    Makes you want to soar up on the wings of a dove.
But the hard work of climbing, it purges the soul,
    As you strive ever on till you come to the goal.
All who climb to these heights or these green trails have trod
    Are closer to nature and nearer to God.

SOURCE

Lynda R. Woods's "Canada's Mountains," from *Canadian Alpine Journal* XXXVII (1954), 113, written in camp on 30 July 1953 at the request of E.R.G.

LYNDA R. WOODS

"Mountaineer and Mountains" (1957)

He, who
Has seen
The rosy blush of dawn
Hit snowy mountain top,
Has watched
That blush creep down
Along the sides,
Push back the clouds,
The fleecy, roseate clouds
Beneath whose blankets lie
The lesser peaks
In jumbled disarray
Assembled
'round the base of
Monarchs.
He, who
Has witnessed this

Has seen the hand of God
Create a day.
He, who
has seen
The Alpine Glow
Strike snow-white lofty crests
And hold them
Silhouetted high
Against the
Dimming evening sky
He, who
Has watched
That soft ethereal glow
Dissolve
Into the soul of night
Has seen the unseen
Master Hand

Turn out the light of day.
Between these mists
And shadowy veils
There lies
The day itself,
The day
Beloved of mountain folk
A day in which
To strive
For lofty, high flung goals
For crafty, skilled maneuvers
Surmounting obstacles
Well nigh impossible.
A day
To end sometimes
With exultation
"We have made it!"
Sometimes
With mingled satisfaction
"Next time may GO."
But always with assurance
That the challenge was worth-
    while
The physical exertion
Like the purging of the soul.
For this they come
These mountain folk.
They come in throngs
To Camp.
To tent
Among the spicate trees
Beside the rippling brook

Or raging torrent
To bask beneath the sun,
Beneficent and kindly,
Which lifts
Quite imperceptibly
The snowy covers of retreating
    Spring
From off the blazing handiwork
of Gardener Supreme.
The meadow
Now in beauteous perfection
And color riotous
Where yesterday was trackless-
    white.
They come
To view once more
This floral paradise
Untouched by human hands
A glorious display
Of lavish
Color nonchalance.
For this they come
Year after year
For fifty years they come
From many climes they come
And many walks of life.
And
On the Sabbath morn
Assemble in a circling dell
To sing, and pray and worship
Each in his way.
To hear the word—

Eternal like the mountains—
Fall from the lips of mortals
Mortals
Whose stay is transient
But words
Constant, true, uplifting

Inspiring like the lofty peaks
That point
Eternally toward heaven
To higher things
And peace
And God.

SOURCE

Lynda R. Woods's "Mountaineer and Mountains," from *Canadian Alpine Journal* XL (1957), 71–72, written June 1956 at the request of the club secretary.

ELIZEBETH FERGUSON

"Sonnet" (1963)

The mountain rises high and dominates
The sky and land and all the scene for miles
With lofty majesty that stimulates
My blood and pulls me near with secret wiles.
Unceasingly my spirit forces me
To climb in search of peace and quiet song
That thrills my heart and causes me to be
Secure in knowing that I there belong.
When once the summit's height is reached, then far
Below the azure waters murmur not
In mountain lakes; for each is but a star
That shines for'er too bright to be forgot.
How high must each man climb to reach the peak
Of all the dreams and hopes he cannot speak?

SOURCE

Elizebeth Ferguson's "Sonnet," from *Canadian Alpine Journal* XLVI (1963), 113.

SIX

Wild and Solitary and Beautiful

Mountain Culture/Mountain Wilderness

MARY SCHÄFFER CONCLUDED *Old Indian Trails* on a poignant note. Departing Suzette and Lewis Swift's homestead in Jasper on their journey back to Field in 1908, she writes:

> "all set," we said, "Good-bye; will see you when the first Grand Trunk Pacific train comes through," and passed on, knowing we were coming to the beginning of the end. As we crossed the Athabaska, we realised that next time we came that way our horses would not have to swim for it, all would be made easy with trains and bridges; that the hideous march of progress, so awful to those who love the real wilderness, was sweeping rapidly over the land and would wipe out all trail troubles. (Schäffer 1911, 359)

From 1886, women explored the Rocky Mountains and their reactions to the physical, intellectual, and spiritual challenges encountered there. Most arrived by train, on the leading edge of Schäffer's "hideous march of progress." Some were exhilarated by the adventure of travel by rail through spectacular geography; others sought adventure at a distance from the tracks, immersed in an environment traversed but not claimed by humans, awed by its grandeur and its fragility alike.

Attempts to capture the spirit of the quest emerged in poetry, prose, and pictures by both women and men. In 1915, W.C. McNaught called to "Alpine men and Alpine women/See the peaks above you gleaming/From their tips the sunlight streaming/Flings the challenge far" (McNaught 1915, 232). This poem takes its title, "The Challenge of the Mountains," from an advertising booklet published by the CPR in 1909, its most ambitious tourist guide to that time. Featured in colour on the cover is the dramatic image of a woman mountaineer, and with it was founded the custom of using women's images in advertising for the Rocky Mountains of Canada. Women's participation, active and passive alike—either as writers and artists or as figures on display—in the promotion of the Rocky Mountains as a tourist destination was complex and fluid. The concurrent impact of women's commercial alignment with the Rocky Mountains is equally

The Challenge of the
Mountains, 1909.
(CPRA BR.326)

complicated to access. The sample texts and images included in this section encompass and demonstrate this phenomenon.

The Woman Question at the turn of the century informed not only exploratory adventures, such as Schäffer's, but the texts and images of women who followed. *The Challenge of the Mountains* was published in the year following Schäffer and Adams's successful quest for Maligne Lake to promote the Rocky Mountain travel season. The mountaineering woman depicted on its cover is the quintessential model of the modern alpine woman of the day. She is dressed in the manner decreed by the newly founded Alpine Club of Canada as essential for a woman climber:

> Those climbing require heavily soled leather boots, well set with Hungarian nails. Knickerbockers, puttees, sweater and knockabout hat furnish the most serviceable costume.

No lady climbing, who wears skirts, will be allowed to take a place on a rope, as they are a distinct source of danger to the entire party. Knickerbockers or bloomers with puttees or gaiters and sweater will be found serviceable and safe. (Wheeler and Parker 1907, 170)

The New Woman climber, at least as portrayed on the cover of *The Challenge of the Mountains*, is nonetheless feminine and fashionable, her alpine wear flat-tering to an hourglass figure. The physical freedom implied and aided by her clothing matches that of the environment in which she stands and to which she gestures, perhaps in welcome and possibly in wonder at the challenge the mountains present. Ultimately, it is an image that mobilizes the New Woman as a metaphor for modernity and progress. Two decades earlier, the tracks and trains piercing the Rockies had epitomized that idea. In the new century and the broadening world of advertising and consumerism, however, modernity and progress in the Rocky Mountains were imagined and marketed through the shape, clothing, activity, and place of the woman depicted.

When the Canadian Pacific Railway began to nurture the tourist market so as to financially invigorate its enterprise, mountain scenery was its lure. Promotion began in May 1886, at the beginning of the first summer of intercontinental service, when paintings and photographs of the Canadian Rockies and Selkirks were exhibited at the Colonial and Indian Exhibition in London, and at the CPR's offices there. Advertising pamphlets followed, and the publicity was successful immediately. Women such as Mary Vaux and Mary Schäffer were among the earliest summer seasons' tourists in the late 1880s to visit the Rockies, arriving aboard a CPR train. The scenery did not fail to meet expectations, and demand became such that the meal stops established at sidings in sight of the Illecillewaet Glacier and further west at Mount Stephen very quickly transformed into hostelries of international repute.

The picture chosen to promote travel in 1909 is a compelling example of the impact of women—as well as the idea of "woman"—on the social geography of the Rocky Mountains. The CPR is best known in conventional Canadian history as the technological and industrial force that literally linked a new country across the vast North American continent, realizing the political promises of the fathers of Confederation and the acumen and hubris of men of great imperial imagination and financial derring-do. It is striking, therefore, that the CPR's popular success was marketed to tourists—specifically women tourists—by means of women's images.

Banff, Jasper, and Waterton national parks in the Rockies, along with Yoho and Glacier national parks in the Selkirks, were established with the mandate to preserve large areas of mountain wilderness in which there was no evidence of sustained human presence, at least by European standards. Rooted in a social interest in the environment, conservation, and humanity's place in nature that began to emerge among Euro-North Americans in the 1850s, the national parks movement claimed the heritage of wilderness as part of the national identity of the newly constituted Canada. Wilderness parks, in the contemporary lexicon, were promoted as sites for the education and improvement of Canadians to encourage good health and well-being through outdoor activity and an engagement with nature. In turn, visitors commonly took up promotional terminology and called the parks their "playgrounds," a term that unsettled Lucy Lippard when she first read Mary Schäffer's story. (See her article in the first section on Métis and Aboriginal women.) Climbing and hiking were the cardinal examples of how the founding philosophy of the national parks intersected with their purpose and potential. Simultaneously, in the late nineteenth and early twentieth centuries, industry and private enterprise had a place in the parks. These ranged from the CPR's spectacular presence in the railway and hotels to coal mining in the Pocahontas area on the northeastern edge of Jasper National Park and in Bankhead at the foot of Cascade Mountain in Banff National Park (a mine opened originally to supply CPR fuel needs). In the historical imagination of Canadians, therefore, the Rocky Mountain parks are as much a site of human culture as nonhuman wilderness.

Women's creative work in the Rocky Mountains contributed to the popularity of the national parks and the growth of tourism, with its attendant enterprises, in concert with the CPR's marketing of the region prior to the First World War. In the 1920s and 1930s, the relationship shifted, becoming a predominantly commercial interaction. Irene Todd's account of Jasper, published in *Saturday Night* in 1924, is an enthusiastic, if inadvertent, account of the area as exactly what Schäffer had predicted and more, especially in the form of the Canadian National Railway's Jasper Park Lodge.

The Dominion government's Department of the Interior undertook its own promotional efforts, employing women's skills, in the early 1920s. The secretary to the National Parks Commissioner, Mabel Williams, made perhaps the most significant contribution by women in this capacity, writing a number of books that set the tone for the ways in which tourists, whether Canadian or foreign, were invited to understand and engage with Parks' wilderness following the First World War. Williams presents as hand-in-hand seemingly contradictory ideas of human engagement with the wilderness—conquering of formidable peaks, confronting extremes of physical challenge—and human control of it, whether in development of transportation lines through the mountains, first railways and then highways, or the building of creature comforts such as CPR and CNR resorts. Ultimately, those responsible for the mountain parks crafted a widely received idea of them as regions of sustained, if apparently transitory, human habitation and use.

Williams solidified the concept in her 1924 introduction to the Canadian Rockies, *Through the Heart of the Rockies and Selkirks*:

> Mountain ranges that combine sublimity and beauty in equal measure are few in number. Among these for centuries the Alps have stood pre-eminent. In the last half century, however, a new mountain region, The Canadian Rockies, equalling the Alps in mingled beauty and grandeur yet with a marked individuality and character

of its own has been opened to the world. It is a little less than forty years since the Canadian Pacific Railway unlocked the long closed door to the Canadian mountains. Already their fame has spread to all parts of the world and each year sees an increasing stream of travel from every country under the sun coming to admire the wonders of these glorious ranges. Yet, there is no danger of the Rockies becoming overcrowded. Their extent is so tremendous that they may well serve as the playground of almost unlimited numbers. A great part of them has not yet been really explored. Each year new trails are being opened up, new beauties discovered. One of the chief charms of the Rockies is that their territory is and will be for many years to come still a virgin land. One may travel through the heart of it in luxurious Pullmans and find accommodation comparable to the best on the continent, yet half an hour's walk from the railway Nature is still as wild and solitary and beautiful as she was before the white man came. (Williams 1924, 1)

Just three years later, the Parks were claiming some autonomy from the CPR, promoting easier access for tourists along highways that opened the Parks to automobile traffic—and marking the start of the demise of the train as the central force and benefactor of tourism in the region. In the excerpt from Williams's work that follows, the ways in which development was being promoted and celebrated for improving the opportunity for interaction of nature and humans is very clear.

In the 1920s, as state and commercial promotion of the parks expanded, women of international renown continued to bring lustre to Rocky Mountain culture and stoke its tourist allure. A shift took place, however, in the type of woman that was admired and aligned with the Rockies in the prosperous years that followed the First World War. In 1916, for example, the mountain embracing the Angel Glacier in Jasper National Park had been named in remembrance of British nurse Edith Cavell, who died by a German firing squad in 1915 for allegedly aiding Allied soldiers

Anna May Wong on the set of "The Alaskan" at Castle Mountain, Banff, 1924. (WMCR NA66–1670)

in hiding during the occupation of Belgium. An account of the memorial service held at Mount Cavell marking the tenth anniversary of her death was published, along with a photograph of the site, in the women's section of the *Canadian National Railways Magazine*. In contrast to the sobriety of the Cavell memorial, women of Hollywood set a new tone in public relations, casting a celebrity glow on landscape attractions marketed by the CPR and Department of the Interior to the aspiring tourist. In the summer of 1924, for example, both Mary Astor and Anna May Wong spent time filming in Banff National Park, mixing cinematic glamour with wilderness exoticism.

It was in the CPR's promotional graphics of the late 1920s and early 1930s that a conjoining of women, wilderness, and culture for the purposes of human pleasure and enticement to travel to the Rockies was most

Mary Astor skijoring at Lake Louise during filming of "The Silent Partner" with Banff residents looking on, 1924. (WMCR NA66–1665)

evident. The CPR no longer looked to adventurous New Women travellers, explorers, and climbers to publicize the Rocky Mountain region through their own photographs and stories. Although a new generation of women such as Georgia Engelhard and Catharine Whyte, as well as the many women members of the Canadian Alpine Club, the Trail Riders Club, and the Skyline Hikers Club continued to climb, ride, and hike in the Rockies, camping along the way, the CPR promotional graphics of the 1930s enticed the potential tourist with images of the active woman's antithesis: glamorous women of means delighting in the luxuries afforded by CPR resorts.

Much has changed since the New Woman mountaineer claimed the cover of *The Challenge of the Mountains*. The women are portrayed as young,

Chateau Lake Louise.
Illustration by A.C. Leighton,
c. 1937. (CPRA A.6358)

slim, tall, and sophisticated, a popular female figure style that emerged in North American advertising in the 1920s. Known as the "Fisher Body girl," this female figure type was introduced in advertisements for Fisher car bodies. Illustrations of modern-looking women rather than the vehicles made by Fisher (Marchand 1985, 179) were featured. A vintage (some might say old-fashioned) automobile graphic appeared as a silhouette in the company's logo that accompanied the ad. Likewise, CPR promotional graphics feature women dressed in fashionable sportswear. They appear to be modern young women enjoying leisure activities in an exotic locale. Both the car body figure and those of the women serve entirely decorative purposes.

Another significant change from the New Woman mountaineer graphic two decades earlier is placement of the figures in the landscape: a moun-

Banff Springs Hotel.
Illustration by R.H. Palenske,
1929. (CPRA A.635)

tain range remained as backdrop, but the women have been moved from
the mountain tops to the confines of the hotels and the recreation facilities—swimming pools, golf courses, and lounges—on their grounds.
The 1929 cover of a brochure promoting the Banff Springs Hotel is the
most literal rendering of this theme, positioning in counterpoint two
women gazing out on the mountain range across the Bow River through
the arched frame of the hotel, one dressed for riding, the other for reading,
leather boot contrasted to high heel. Such coupling of sportiveness and
elegance was the hallmark of CPR promotion during the 1930s, rendered
again, for example, on a brochure for the Chateau Lake Louise the following
year. Unlike the earlier image, where the climber stands dynamically in
the mountain range, arriving there under her own prowess, these women
are confined to the hotel. Rather than portrayed in the saddle or on the

summit, these figures are static, sitting or standing in repose, and gazing out at the famed—and framed—mountain landscapes. Always invoked is a lively mix of adventure and glamour, physical activity and physical comfort, sublime landscape and luxurious accommodation. The former—adventure and activity in the landscape—are implied only; the latter—glamour, comfort, and accommodation—are rendered visibly. Throughout, women are but chic observers of the environment beyond, rather than the active, athletic participants of a generation earlier. This particular composition proved to be popular and recurs a number of times in the 1930s in various graphics promoting other mountain resorts.

For the potential tourist viewing these images, the women are as visually enticing as the mountain environment in which they pose. For the male viewer, the women appear as much a feature of the landscape available for the tourist's pleasure as the hotel accommodation or mountain ranges on display. The matter is more complex for the women viewer. She is the consumer courted by the images and identification with (or desire to be) the elegant, youthful, modern women pictured is encouraged. The challenge of the mountains that was issued in 1909 has given way by 1929 to consumption of the mountains with no more effort than a glance from the comforts of a hotel. While no doubt appealing to many women, for others like Engelhard and Whyte, these images resonate with the restricted horizons that Schäffer and Adams found themselves facing twenty-five years earlier.

In *Living Up to the Ads: Gender Fictions of the 1920s*, Simone Weil Davis verifies that the consumer was "conceived primarily as female" (Davis 2000, 2) and print advertisements were crafted with the intention of appealing particularly to women. That men might derive pleasure from the images of women, and become persuaded to purchase the product promoted, was of secondary concern to an industry that focused on women as its principal target. As for the figures in the images, Davis writes, "the female advertising model...functions as a metaphor, her own commodified but canny presence representing and augmenting the appeal of the commodity with which she poses...[and] uses her charm to bolster the allure of something

RESORTS IN THE ROCKIES

CANADIAN PACIFIC

Resorts in the Canadian Rockies, *c. 1930. (CPRA A.636)*

else..." (Davis 2000, 3) in this case, the Rocky Mountain playgrounds and their CPR recreational amenities.

Herein lies one of the complexities of the relationship of women to the environment portrayed: dressed in sportswear that implies an active lifestyle, they stand or sit in a leisured pose gazing at the scenery. *Resorts in the Canadian Rockies* is an especially good example of this contradictory composition. A modern "Fisher Body" woman, dressed in elegant riding wear, is seated in an abstracted mountain environment. Rather than independently exploring the landscape, she is supported and guided, and perhaps protected, by a classic male RCMP officer in full dress uniform. The Mountie appears as an additional feature of the Rocky Mountain landscape to lure the potential female tourist. The woman viewer, however, like the figure who is excluded by a frame from the vista, is directed to consuming the landscape by means of her gaze alone, aided by a knowledgeable male authority.

Marilyn Monroe at Becker's Cabins, Jasper. Photograph by Anne Pedersen, 1954. (WMCR NA66–1670)

The pinnacle of the pitching of women and nature, mountain culture and mountain wilderness, together in imagery was attained in 1954 with the arrival of Marilyn Monroe in the Rocky Mountains. The *New York Times* reviewer was blunt on this point: "The mountainous scenery is spectacular, but so, in her own way, is Miss Monroe. The patron's preference, if any, probably will depend upon which he's interested in" (Crowther 1954, 13). *A River of No Return* casts the daring romantic hero portrayed by Robert Mitchum against spectacular and threatening mountain geography and charges him with the safety of Monroe—or at least her character. The plot and characters in *A River of No Return* fly in the face of women's history and experiences (and those of Aboriginals) in the Rockies, but the movie enticed viewers with powerful and provocative ideas about femininity and women's natural place under the protection of men in the decade

Canada for Holidays.
Illustration by Tom Purvis,
1937. (CPRA A.6539)

following the Second World War. These were ideas well-understood by Monroe herself, it appears, as a snapshot made by Anne Pedersen, a young chambermaid at Becker's Cabins in Jasper where Monroe lodged while filming, shows. Taking a cue from the script, Monroe played the defense-less female in real life as well. Protesting director Otto Preminger's legendary mistreatment of her on the set, Monroe strategically acquired an ankle injury that put her on crutches, garnered her sympathy, and slowed filming.

• • •

IN CONCLUSION, a 1937 CPR graphic promoting "Canada for the Holidays" is an extraordinary condensation of ideas about women, culture, and the mountains that had emerged over the decades following women's initial forays and interactions in the late 1880s. A young, Euro-North American woman is portrayed seated on a grassy knoll against a mountain backdrop and dressed in minimal summer outdoor leisure wear. Her appeal is heightened by adornment with archetypal masculine Aboriginal accoutrements of feathered headdress and peace pipe. With a look of pleasure on her face, her gaze seeks that of the viewer. The golden sky, water, and outline of her limbs emanates a warmth that is almost palpable. The layers of allusion to an exotic, inviting sexuality plays upon a colonial legacy of gendered and racial ideas and relations. It is a politically and commercially provocative image that speaks to the elision of actual women—Aboriginal, Métis, and white, young and old, active and idle—in the historical record in favour of an imaginary amalgam to symbolize culture and wilderness in the Rocky Mountains of Canada.

EDITOR'S NOTE

The title of this section, "Wild and Solitary and Beautiful" is taken from M.B. Williams's *Through the Heart of the Rockies and Selkirks*, second edition (Ottawa: F.A. Acland, 1924), 4. See quotation on page 419.

IRENE TODD

"Jasper National Park" (1924)

Canada's Vast New Mountain Playground

"I am homesick for the Mountains
My heroic Mother hills,
And the longing that is on it
No solace ever stills.

I would climb to brooding summits
With their old untarnished dreams,
Cool my heart in forest shadows,
To the lull of falling streams."

SURELY BLISS CARMAN, our own Canadian poet was thinking of those majestic mountains and beauteous valleys in Jasper National Park when he wrote the foregoing lines. Perhaps in dreams he could hear the song of the swift-flowing Athabasca and the whispering of the poplars and pines. Perhaps he drifted again on Lac Beauvert and gazed down into its

429

translucent green depths. Or did he long to stand again on Mt. Tekarra with the world apparently at his feet, yet with a hundred mountain pinnacles, domes and towers rising on every hand, to greet the sky and lure him still onward and upward? Who knows.

Certain, it is that no one who has ever visited that vast mountain playground, known as Jasper National Park, but longs to return to it. Those mountains in the Northern Canadian Rockies, once you have holidayed in them, seem to cast a spell upon you from which you can never quite rid yourself; their attractions are so numerous; their grandeur is on such a stupendous scale. Memories of thrilling climbs, of wondrous rides over the winding mountain trails, pleasant evenings around the blazing fire in Jasper Lodge, fishing and dreaming by gleaming lakes, glorious sunsets and mystic nights haunt you forever, but seemingly with more insistence after the long cold winter when spring comes round again and you feel the need of rest and recreation. But, if you have never been to Jasper, what a rare treat lies in store for you, what a wonderful holiday awaits you!

Jasper National Park, which was set apart by the Dominion Government in 1907, as a sanctuary for wild life and a great National mountain playground for man, is the largest National Park in the world. It lies entirely in the Province of Alberta, extending westward, to the British Columbia boundary and comprising 4,400 square miles of some of the most magnificent virgin mountain scenery in the world, all in its pristine beauty, unspoiled and unmarred by man, having been completely off the beaten track until 1914, when the steel rails of the transcontinental line of Canadian National Railways pierced the Yellowhead Pass. This is the historic pass discovered by the dauntless explorer and fur-trader David Thompson when making his way overland to the Pacific in 1811 and which twice every year after, for over half a century, resounded with the passing of brigades of fur-traders, on their way between the Western Department and Jasper House, Rocky Mountain House and other posts in the Northern Rockies. So that, while to the tourist and the sportsman it is a new playground, it is at the same time historic, and hallowed ground for it its valleys and its passes have been trodden by many an explorer, fur-trader, missionary and adventurer, and long before the coming of the white man, who knows what bitter Indian wars waged within its confines.

Its primal appeal, however, is and always will be its natural grandeur. Within its precincts are broad flowering valleys through which mighty rivers go singing. There are sublime snow-clad mountains, a number of which have never been named and hundreds of which tower between 7,000 and 10,000 feet in altitude, while Mount Edith Cavell, the highest and most outstanding mountain in the park rises to an altitude of 11,033 feet. It stands as a monumental shrine to that brave English nurse whose name it bears. There are glaciers, both small and great, forever chiselling and filing the granite cliffs; wild mountain torrents, leaping through gorges and tumbling in white foaming cataracts; snowfields and clear sparkling lakes that gleam like liquid jewels amid the dark green pines and poplars that flank the mountain sides.

One particularly outstanding feature of this mountain kingdom, is the ample breadth of its valleys which give you an opportunity of seeing the great mountain cathedrals and palaces in all their perfection of outline and glory of coloring unspoiled by crowding and with the added enchantment of distance, for mountains when seen at too close range seem to lose some of their glamor, to hem you in and almost fill you with fear. But this is never felt at Jasper.

Visitors in this wild romantic mountain country may live the life of the veriest vagabond and experience all the thrills of the real explorer and adventurer, without any of his inconveniences, for while the park is for the most part just as Nature planned it, hundreds of trails wind through its valleys and around the base of the mountains. There are also a number of good motor roads in the park, while on the shore of Lac Beauvert, that lies like a great emerald in the broad valley of the Athabasca River, three miles from Jasper station, stands a rustic Alpine Chalet known as Jasper Park Lodge, where the best of accommodation is obtainable. Nothing could be more attractive than this hostelry in the mountains, consisting of a large main lodge and a number of various sized cabins, all built of logs and with their rustic architecture blending in so completely with their rugged natural surroundings that they seem to be part of the scenery.

The Main Lodge, entirely new, contains a large lounge with huge stone fireplace, dining-room, ball-room, billiard room, barber shop and twelve bedrooms, with all modern conveniences, while a spacious verandah surrounds lounge and dining-rooms, commanding a superb view of Lac Beauvert and its guardian mountains. But the cabins, here and there among the trees will perhaps interest you most, for no matter what size or type of party you would like to bring, there's a cabin to suit. For the bridal party there's a tiny cabin "just big enough for two" containing a bed-sitting room, dressing room, sleeping porch and bathroom. Then there are two-suite cabins, four-roomed cabins and twelve-roomed cabins. All electric-lighted with modern conveniences throughout, running water in each room, baths, etc.

Guides and ponies may be procured at the Lodge and dozens of enchanting trips made over the winding mountain trails to various outstanding peaks, canyons or cataracts. The swift-flowing mountain streams abound in Dolly Varden and Rainbow trout and while no game may be taken in the park, guides will conduct parties to the big game country just beyond its confines, where big horn mountain sheep, mountain goat, bear, moose, caribou and deer abound. Adventurous spirits who enjoy "roughing it," find real sport in going off with a pack train on a trip lasting several days, to the Tonquin Valley, the Amethyst Lakes or Mt. Edith Cavell. Those who do not care to engage in quite so strenuous a journey, may make the trip on horseback to Signal Mountain, Whistlers Mountain or Caledonia Lake and return in one day, while those who are stopping over in the park for a few days only, appreciate the motor trips to Maligne Canyon and Pyramid Lake. The various peaks as they rise in all their glory, seem to be constantly challenging you to a climb and there are dozens close to the Lodge that may be negotiated by the inexperienced climber.

When weary of riding, climbing and hiking you may recline in a canoe and drift and dream on Lac Beauvert, you may enjoy a swim in the cool limpid waters of some Alpine tarn or pack a lunch basket and go off to the shore of some little lake or stream and fish for a half a day. There is a good tennis court at the Lodge, and dancing is indulged in almost every evening, but, whatever you do, wherever you look are the sublime, awe-inspiring mountains, luring, inspiring and keeping guard, while the voice of many waters is ever to be heard.

SOURCE

Irene Todd's "Jasper National Park: Canada's Vast New Mountain Playground," from the Woman's Section of *Saturday Night* 39, no. 26 (17 May 1924), 25.

M.B. WILLIAMS

The Kicking Horse Trail (1927)

Excerpts

"Cleaving the mountain barriers,
Opening the long closed gates."

THERE ARE PEOPLE who really profess to believe that this is an unimaginative age. They refer regretfully to our mechanical civilization, as if today men had ceased to see visions and to dream dreams. Yet, in reality, was there ever an age in which the imagination had been so daring and so victorious! Dreams that our fathers counted for madness, how they have taken shape before our eyes! Architectural and engineering achievements that to them would have seemed unthinkable, inventions that have given man a command over space and time as wonderful as the powers bestowed by the genii of the fairytale—they are so rapidly becoming the realities of commonplace for us that we are in danger of losing the sense of their romance. Not the least wonderful among these, "the horseless carriage" itself, fantastic chimera for so many centuries of wildly imaginative minds. A mere mechanical contrivance, it is true, but already what gifts of new power and enjoyment has it not brought to man? Out of the machine, truly, there has come, if not a god, at least a genius of untold capabilities. Already, in two short decades, have we not seen it practically revolutionize our way of life, sweeping away with one gesture, the old measures of time and distance, and for the first time since he exchanged his nomadic existence for the warm security of the fireside, enabling man to escape from the narrow boundaries of his local parish and to enter upon a wider, more joyous, more adventurous life.

For the new genius had but to speak and what was once far has become near, what was impossible, easy. At its command the world over, east, west, north, and south, thousands of miles of roads have unrolled like magic carpets. Engineering difficulties regarded as insuperable have been surmounted, and into regions long considered impassable a way has been found.

With this new contrivance have come too, new developments in man himself. Through it he is finding his way back to new health and vigour, to a new companionship with the sun and the wind and the sky, to a new love of the beauty of the Earth. At the gates of all her loveliest regions he is asking for entrance and one by one they are opening to let him in. Distance is no longer a barrier, for a man has but to step into a motor car and he has fastened wings to his ankles like Mercury himself. The continent has become his playground, his holiday possibilities reach to the uttermost ends of the land.

Among the long-closed regions of wonder and romance into which a way has at last been found are the Canadian Rockies. Each year the door opens a little farther, until now a good part of the most beautiful sections of these glorious ranges is within the motorist's reach. The opening this year of the new highway, "The Kicking Horse Trail," marks the fulfilment of one more daring engineering conception, the building of a transmontane highway through the heart of the Central Rockies, across the difficult regions traversed by the Canadian Pacific railway.

The history of the motorist's entry into the Rockies has been progressive. In 1914 the completion of the Calgary-Banff road opened the way to

Banff in the Rocky Mountains Park, admitting him to the great ante-chamber of the mountains. The Banff-Windermere Highway, completed in 1923, extended his opportunities. It carried him across the main divide, through Kootenay National Park, to the Columbia valley, and, by linking up with existing roads, provided a direct through route from both the east and the west. The extension from Castle to Lake Louise gave him the opportunity to see this exquisite lake—the pearl of the Rockies—which is everywhere regarded as one of the great landscape masterpieces of the world.

Now, as has been said, with the completion of The Kicking Horse Trail, a new door opens. The whole beautiful region from Lake Louise west to the Columbia valley—pre-historic trench between the Rockies and the older ranges to the west—is at last accessible. Following the same route as the first transcontinental railway, he may cross the famous Kicking Horse pass to Yoho Park, visit the magnificent Yoho valley, see lovely Emerald lake, and then go on by the great Kicking Horse valley, to the western confines of Yoho Park and there cap his spectacular journey with the eleven-mile traverse of the thrilling Kicking Horse gorge.

The Road to Acardy.

O those mountains, their infinite movement
Still moving with you.
For ever some new head and breast of them
Comes into view.
*   —Browning.*

A CHARMING ENGLISH WRITER recently complained that it seemed to him there was a serious gap in most descriptions of Paradise. Nothing was said about a site for the Lake of Geneva. Those who have come to know and love the highways of the Canadian Rockies might put forward a plea for still one more addition—a mountain road, winding up hill and down valley among glorious snow-crowned peaks. For in the Canadian

Rockies the road not only leads to beauty but has become part of beauty itself. Laid out by experienced engineers, it has sought, not the shortest distance between two points, but the giving of the greatest pleasure that may be.

Taken in its entirety the new mountain circle has a variety that is at once a surprise and a delight, a sort of balance in its different sections, that gives one something of the pleasure of an artistic composition. Indeed, if one were to let the fancy play a little, the road is not unlike a piece of music itself. Taken, if you will, from Calgary, there is the long approach across the plains as prelude, with the beautiful theme of the snowpeaks hovering exquisitely and growing clearer with each mile. The road slips through the mountain gateway and of a sudden, like the strong chords of the full movement, the great peaks are all about. Like music, too, are the endless variations and surprises the delicate embroideries of the main theme. Like music the tremendous crescendoes of those glorious up-sweeping climbs to the heights, the long diminuendoes of the downward glide, followed, lest the senses should grow weary, by the smooth andantes, the quiet stretches of level road through the forest or along the valley floor.

And indeed, to travel one of these splendid highways from end to end is to realize that the new Genius has not only lightened man's labours, and extended his power over space and time, but that it has brought him a fresh world of experience not unlike that of art itself. The swift rhythmic flight of the car over the long rhythmic curves of the road, the constant dipping and rising, the great sweeping descents to the valley—like the cutting of bird's wing through the air—the magnificent spiral climbs to the heights, what are these but a new poetry of motion? An earlier generation loved the quiet contemplation of a beautiful landscape, the absorption of one particular scene. But this age is set to a swifter tempo which creates its own pleasures, less static but no less ecstatic. And, certainly, to move with the swiftness and rhythm of a bird's flight, now close to the valley, now high above it, against a changing background of unimaginable splendour that weaves a new pattern of beauty with every mile, with the sun and the wind as companions and the blue sky overhead, is to know a new ecstasy of movement, to feel half delivered from our animal bondage to the solid earth.

Moving from beauty to beauty, along paths carved by ancient glaciers, through the valleys of the Bow and the Kickinghorse, the new highway goes. Towering upwards, on either hand, rise the great peaks, a countless succession, yet each distinct in individuality, hewn into every massive architectural form, making a splendid natural Avenue of Temples, through which road, rivers and railway take their processional way for over two hundred miles. And everywhere, what enchanting light and colour, a many-coloured kalaedescope changing from mile to mile! The green plumes of the pine trees feathering the lower slopes, the silvery grey limestones splashed and banded with old reds, delicate pinks, yellows and purplish maroons, the crystal veil of a waterfall swaying from far heights, the dazzling gleam of a snow peak or the glitter of green ice where a glacier clutches at some steep face of rock; the intense blue of the sky, stretched like a sheet of thin silk behind the peaks, the slow white clouds, moving in little puffs up the slopes or winding and unwinding their airy scarves about the serene foreheads of the peaks, the changing patterns woven by their purple shadows and the deep shadow of peak on peak—the whole marvellous, dissolving diorama that unrolls for two hundred miles from the eastern gateway of the main Rockies to their western portal, seems almost to belong to another world.

Within the national parks, along these beautiful highways, where nothing that is vulgar or ugly is allowed to meet the eye, one catches a glimpse, too, of the world which the new Genius is encouraging us to make. It is not enough now that the road should carry us somewhere. It has become an end in itself. A man is no longer satisfied with mere movement. He is beginning to desire—he will probably soon come to demand—everywhere the beautiful and harmonious environment as the background for the Road. What this will ultimately mean, what changes it will work in our whole civilization, it is impossible to say. For the Road Beautiful means the Village Beautiful, the Town Beautiful, and in the end the Nation Beautiful as well. Some hint of a possible new reverence for the landscape, for the wild life that enriches it, for wild flowers and shrubs and trees, for the carefully preserved vista, that may one day become universal, the traveller may catch in the national parks. Once caught, he will realize that it satisfies a hunger, deep and unsuspected, for a life beautiful and harmonious in all its parts such as was dreamed of by the Greeks of old.

He who travels through this glorious region can hardly fail to return with treasure. If he be a Canadian he will bring home a new love of his country, a new pride in her superb mountains and her great national parks. If he be a stranger within Canada's gates he will realize how truly all who have the power to see and enjoy are co-owners of beauty wherever it be found. He will perceive that such gifts are the possessions in a sense of the whole world and that all should feel an interest, even a responsibility in their preservation. And everyone, whether native or visitor, will almost surely return with new health and vigour, the stimulus that comes from even a few hours or days of heightened living, catching, perhaps, the meaning of those penetrating words of W.H. Davies, the English poet, who reminded us recently that time was not the true measure of life, and that it is not the number of breaths we draw that matters so much as the number of times we draw breath in wonder and awe at this beautiful world.

SOURCE

Excerpts of M.B. Williams's introduction from *The Kicking Horse Trail: Scenic Highway From Lake Louise, Alberta to Golden, British Columbia* (Ottawa: Department of the Interior, 1927), 5–9 and 33–40.

"Honor Memory of Edith Cavell" (1926)

*Guests at Jasper Park Lodge Join with the Residents of Village
in Memorial Service to Heroic Nurse for Whom Mount Cavell Is Named*

*"They shall not die, as others die;
Early in the morning and at the
    going down of the sun,
We shall remember them."*

ELEVEN YEARS AGO, on August 5th, the imagination and sympathy of
the civilized world was stirred by the arrest in Belgium by the Germans of
a British Nursing Sister, Edith Cavell. Two months later, on October 12th,
men and women stood aghast at the news of her execution by a firing
squad; her crime devotion to a duty to which she had consecrated her life,
the alleviation of suffering among mankind. The charges against her were
that she had given succor to wounded and sick officers and men of the
allied forces who had escaped the notice of the invading forces and taken

refuge among friendly people in the occupied territory. The evidence upon which her execution was ordered was provided by her own testimony; evidence which she gave without fear or restraint, conscious of what the consequences might be in the hands of biased judges and an unscrupulous court-martial jury, but given because she knew—as the whole world will always believe—that her course of action had been right, that the things she had done were those which any nurse, worthy of the name and understanding the bond she had given when she accepted her cap and apron, would perform under similar circumstances.

For that, they murdered her.

But the world does not always forget those who serve mankind. It is to the everlasting credit of the people of Canada that they supported the proposal to give the name Edith Cavell, to one of the most majestic mountain peaks in the world, a peak that is snow capped all through the year and which dominated the whole of the Athabaska Valley of Jasper National Park, raising its lofty head in stately grandeur far above its sister mountains for miles about. Here it was on Sunday afternoon, August 1st of this year, that almost four hundred people met in reverent mood to pay their individual tribute to the memory of a womanly heart and an heroic soul. It would be difficult to conceive a setting more beautiful or more harmonious than that which graced the service, which was conducted by Rev. H.A. Edwards, chaplain of Jasper National Park and Rev. Canon R.M. Swan of St. Michael's Church, Edmonton.

Behind the congregation, assembled on the rising glacial moraine, rose the white turban of Edith Cavell, a crown of purity and chastity, gleaming like silver in the summer sun. Lower down, on the breast of the mountain, the great ice wings of the Glacier of the Angels hung like a benediction above the gathering. To the right rose the sombre wall of Mount Sorrow and behind it the snow capped peak of Throne Mountain looked down from its lofty eminence. Down in the valley, upholstered in green, the pure jade waters of The Lake of Forgiveness lay still and tranquil as though symbolic of the soul of the heroine who went to her death with calm, untroubled heart, eleven years ago, in the great cause of humanity. In and about the moraine thousands of flowers flung their gay colors almost to the foot of the snow from where issued a milky stream which foamed through the rocks until it was lost in the depths of the valley.

A simplicity as natural and as beautiful as that which animated the life of Edith Cavell herself, marked the course of the service. There was nothing in it that spoke of bitterness; no note of regret; only the ennobling and uplifting thought of a life well spent and a death heroically met; of a life that was dedicated to the service of suffering and of a death that spelled immortality.

The service was opened with the singing of "Rock of Ages," the orchestra of Jasper Park Lodge and the gowned choir of the chaplain's church leading the congregation. Then followed the reading of the beautiful Twenty-Third Psalm and a prayer. Next came the address of Mr. Edwards into which no note of heroics crept, but the keynote of which was the purity of service consecrated to God and to humanity. The closing hymn was the one sung by Edith Cavell and her chaplain a few minutes before she faced her firing squad, "Abide With Me."

Immediately following this hymn the congregation remained standing while the bugler blew "The Last Post," that haunting, plaintive call of the British Army which ends with an unfinished note. As the clear notes of the bugle rang out to be echoed by the mountain walls, the flag which had stood at full mast during the service dipped slowly in salute, to complete a picture no one present will ever forget.

The last note of the bugle melted slowly into the air, the echo softly returned and the chaplain raised his arms in the Benediction. As he stood there silhouetted against the snow, the congregation below him with bowed and reverent heads, a passing cloud moved slowly away from the sun to allow a stream of brilliant light to steal across the face of the great glacier overhead. It was as though Edith Cavell had heard and smiled.

SOURCE

"Honor Memory of Edith Cavell: Guests at Jasper Park Lodge Join with the Residents of Village in Memorial Service to Heroic Nurse for Whom Mount Cavell Is Named," from the Woman's Section of *Canadian National Railways Magazine* (September 1926), 21 and 42.

BOSLEY CROWTHER

"Marilyn Monroe vs. Scenery at Roxy" (1954)

IT IS A TOSS-UP whether the scenery or the adornment of Marilyn Monroe is the feature of greater attraction in "River of No Return," the Twentieth Century-Fox outdoor drama that showed up yesterday on the Roxy's wide screen. The mountainous scenery is spectacular, but so, in her own way, is Miss Monroe. The patron's preference, if any, probably will depend upon which he's interested in.

Certainly, Scriptwriter Frank Fenton has done the best he could to arrange for a fairly equal balance of nature and Miss Monroe. He has bluntly confronted Robert Mitchum, as a hardy fellow of the North-west frontier, with a menacing situation compounded of generous portions of the two. Not only does Mr. Mitchum have to spend several days guiding a flimsy log raft down a raging mountain stream, relentlessly stalked by Indians who make it perilous for him to come ashore, but he also has to ward off temptation in the shape—and we mean shape!—of Miss Monroe. The fact that he makes his destination without fouling on either is the show.

And that should not be too lightly taken. For Director Otto Preminger has thrown all the grandeur and menace of these features upon the eye-filling CinemaScope screen. A sickening succession of rapids, churned into boiling foam, presents a display of nature's violence that cannot help but ping the patron's nerves. The raft tumbling through these rapids is quite a sight to see. And layouts of Rocky Mountain landscapes are handsome in color, too.

· · ·

BUT MR. MITCHUM'S and the audience's attention is directed to Miss Monroe through frequent and liberal posing of her in full and significant views. At the outset, she shows in spangled costumes, playing a guitar in a saloon and singing appropriate ballads that can easily be left where they lie. But for rafting on the river, she is garbed in a sort of dude rancher's duds, which cling rather closely to her figure when she is liberally soaked in spray.

Indeed, to make sure that the resistance of Mr. Mitchum is clearly understood, Mr. Preminger poses one situation that is the test of Hercules. He soaks Miss Monroe so completely that she must clothe herself in a blanket, nothing more, and then he has Mr. M. massage her to avoid her taking a chill.

The magnitude of the dramatic dilemma is indicated by this sort of thing.

Along for the ride on the log raft is a lad named Tommy Rettig, who plays Mr. Mitchum's son. On one occasion, he becomes an unsuspecting chaperone. And the role of a trouble-making gambler is played by Dory Calhoun. He is fully dispatched as a hindrance to the fulfillment of love at the end.

SOURCE

Bosley Crowther's "Marilyn Monroe Vs. Scenery at Roxy," from *New York Times* (1 May 1954), 13.

Mary Schäffer climbing with Billy Warren. (WMCR V439/P–6)

Above: Mollie Adams, Mary Schäffer, Billy Warren, and Joe Barker in camp.
(WMCR V439/PS–1)

Right: Mary Schäffer and Mollie Adams scrambling.
(WMCR V439/PS–4)

Left: Mount Assiniboine.
Photograph by Georgia
Engelhard, 1943.
(WMCR V751/PA–162)

Below: Mount Edith Cavell and
Angel Glacier, Jasper National
Park, 1928. (JYMA PA7–191)

The Challenge of the Mountains, 1909. *(CPRA BR.326)*

Beautiful Lake Louise. *Illustration by Kenneth Shoesmith, c. 1930. (CPRA A.6190)*

Chateau Lake Louise. *Illustration by A.C. Leighton, c. 1937.* (*CPRA A.6358*)

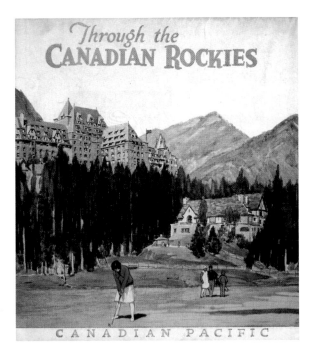

Through the Canadian
Rockies, *c. 1931. (CPRA BR.92)*

Resorts in the Canadian
Rockies, *c. 1930.*
(CPRA A.636)

Canada for Holidays. *Illustration by Tom Purvis, 1937. (CPRA A.6539)*

Selected Bibliography

* *Indicates an excerpt included in* This Wild Spirit

Introduction

Bendell, Beverley, ed. *The Canadian Alpine Journal Cumulative Subject and Author Index Volume 1, 1907 to Volume 70, 1987*. Banff: The Alpine Club of Canada, 1988.

Schäffer, Mary T.S. *Old Indian Trails: Incidents of Camp and Trail Life, Covering Two Years Exploration through the Rocky Mountains of Canada*. New York: G.P. Putnam's Sons, 1911 / London: The Knickerbocker Press, 1911.

Seton-Thompson, Grace Gallatin. *A Woman Tenderfoot*. New York: Doubleday, Page & Co., 1900.

Vaux, Mary M. "Letter to Dr. Charles Walcott," 11 March 1912. SIA record unit 7004, box 5, folder 2, image 2005–26214–16.

Ward, Mrs. Humphry [Mary Augusta]. *Lady Merton, Colonist*. Toronto: Musson Book Co., 1910.

Warren, Mary Schäffer. "Letter to Humphrey Toms," 26 November 1937. WMCR M429.

———. "Tepee Life in the Northern Hills (1924)." In *No Ordinary Woman: The Story of Mary Schäffer Warren*, Janice Sanford Beck, 170–91. Calgary: Rocky Mountain Books, 2001.

1. Taking a Deep Interest

*Adams, Mary [Mollie]. "Laggan to Maligne Lake and Tête Jaune Cache and Return." Unpublished diary, 1908. WMCR M79/11.

Albers, Patricia C., and William R. James. "Illusion and Illumination: Visual Images of American Indian Women in the West." In *The Women's West*, eds. Susan Armitage and Elizabeth Jameson, 35–50. Norman: University of Oklahoma, 1987.

———."Travel Photography: A Methodological Approach." *Annals of Tourism Research* 15, no. 1 (1988): 134–58.

Coleman, A.P. *The Canadian Rockies: New and Old Trails.* London: T.F. Unwin, 1911.

Davidov, Judith Fryer. *Women's Camera Work: Self/Body/Other in American Visual Culture.* Durham, N.C.: Duke University Press, 1998.

Emberly, Julia V. *Thresholds of Difference: Feminist Critique, Native Women's Writings, Postcolonial Theory.* Toronto: University of Toronto Press, 1993.

Fleming, Paula Richardson, and Judith Luskey. *The Shadow Catchers: Images of the American Indian.* London: Lawrence King, 1993.

———. *The North American Indians in Early Photographs.* Oxford: Phaidon, 1988.

*Gowan, Elsie Park. "The Jasper Story." Unpublished manuscript, 1955. UAA 87–123.

———. "Jasper's First Lady." *Heritage* 5, no. 4 (July/August 1977): 19–20.

Green, Rayna. "Native American Women." *Signs* 6, no. 2 (1980): 248–67.

*Lippard, Lucy R., ed. "Doubletake: The Diary of a Relationship With an Image." In *Partial Recall: Photographs of Native North Americans*, 13–45. New York: New Press, 1992.

MacLaren, I.S. "Cultured Wilderness in Jasper National Park." *Journal of Canadian Studies* 34, no. 3 (1999): 2–54.

*Munro, Janet. "Hosts of Mountain Oasis." *Canadian National Railways Magazine* (1929): 24–26.

Owens, Louis. "Their Shadows Before Them: Photographing Indians." In *Trading Gazes: Euro-American Women Photographers and Native North Americans*, eds. Susan Bernardin, Melody Gaulich, Lisa MacFarlane, and Nicole Tonkovich, 186–92, 219. New Jersey: Rutgers University Press, 2003.

Rahder, Bobbi. "Gendered Stylistic Differences Between Photographers of Native Americans at the Turn of the Century." *Journal of the West* 35, no. 1 (1996): 86–95.

Schäffer, Mary T.S. *Old Indian Trails: Incidents of Camp and Trail Life, Covering Two Years' Exploration through the Rocky Mountains of Canada.* New York: G.P. Putnam's Sons, 1911 / London: The Knickerbocker Press, 1911.

Stevenson, Winona. "Colonialism and First Nations Women in Canada." In *Scratching the Surface: Canada Anti-Racist Feminist Thought*, 49–80. Toronto: Women's Press, 1999.

Strobel, Margaret. "Gender and Race in the Nineteenth- and Twentieth-Century British Empire." In *Becoming Visible: Women in European History*, 2nd ed., eds. Renate Bridenthal, Claudia Koonz, and Susan Stuard, 375–96. Boston: Houghton Mifflin, 1987.

Taylor, Colin F., and Hugh Dempsey. *With Eagle Tail: Arnold Lupson and 30 years among the Sarcee, Blackfoot and Stoney Indians on the North American Plains.* Toronto: Key Porter Books, 1999.

Wall, Wendy. "Gender and the 'Citizen Indian.'" In *Writing the Range*, eds. Elizabeth Jameson and Susan Armitage, 202–29. Norman: University of Oklahoma Press, 1997.

2. Being a Woman, I Wanted to Tell About Them

Adams, W.H. Davenport. *Celebrated Women Travellers of the Nineteenth Century.* London: Swan Sonnenschein & Co., 1906.

Bird, Isabella L. *A Lady's Life in the Rocky Mountains (1879).* Introduction by Pat Barr. London: Virago Press, 1991.

Birkett, Dea. *Spinsters Abroad: Victorian Women Explorers.* Oxford: Basil Blackwell, 1990.

Buck, George H. *From Summit to Sea: An Illustrated History of Railroads in British Columbia and Alberta.* Calgary: Fifth House, 1997.

Chaudhuri, Nupur, and Margaret Strobel, eds. *Western Women and Imperialism: Complicity and Resistance.* Bloomington: Indiana University Press, 1992.

Commire, Anne, ed. *Women in World History: A Biographical Encyclopedia.* Waterford, Conn.: Yorkin Publications, 1999.

* The Countess of Aberdeen[Ishbel Gordon Marchioness of Aberdeen and Temair]. *Through Canada With a Kodak (1893).* Introduction by Marjory Harper. Toronto: University of Toronto Press, 1994.

*Cran, Mrs. George [Marion Dudley]. *A Woman in Canada.* London: John Milne, 1910.

*Duncan, Sara Jeannette. *A Social Departure: How Orthodocia and I Went Round the World by Ourselves.* 3rd ed. London: Chatto & Windus, 1893.

Foster, Shirley. *Across New Worlds: Nineteenth-Century Women Travellers and Their Writings.* New York: Harvester Wheatsheaf, 1990.

Hall, Derek, and Vivian Kinnaird. "A Note on Women Travellers." In *Tourism: A Gender Analysis*, eds. Derek Hall and Vivian Kinnaird, 188–209. Toronto: Wiley, 1994.

Heaps, Denise A. "Genre and Gender in Sara Jeannette Duncan's Travel Satire, *A Social Departure: How Orthodocia and I Went Round the World by Ourselves.*" *Essays in Canadian Writing* 74 (2001): 73–94.

Huenemann, Karyn. "Art and Photography: Sara Jeannette Duncan's Response to Kipling." *Victorian Review* 21, no. 1 (1995): 17–35.

Kipling, Rudyard. *Letters of Travel (1892–1913).* London: Macmillan & Co., 1920.

Lawrence, Karen R. *Penelope Voyages: Women and Travel in the British Literary Tradition*. Ithica: Cornell University Press, 1994.

*Macdonald, Agnes. "By Car and by Cowcatcher." *Murray's Magazine* (1887): 215–35, 296–315.

———. "An Unconventional Holiday." *Ladies' Home Journal* VIII, no. 9 and 10 (1891): 1–2.

Magill, Frank N., ed. *Cyclopedia of World Authors*. Pasadena, Calif.: Salem Press, 1997.

Mills, Sara. *Discourses of Difference: An Analysis of Women's Travel Writing and Colonialism*. London: Routledge, 1991.

Robertson, Janet. *The Magnificent Mountain Women: Adventures in the Colorado Rockies*. Lincoln: University of Nebraska Press, 1990.

Schäffer, Mary T.S. *Old Indian Trails: Incidents of Camp and Trail Life, Covering Two Years Exploration through the Rocky Mountains of Canada*. New York: G.P. Putnam's Sons, 1911 / London: The Knickerbocker Press, 1911.

———. "Untrodden Paths in the Canadian Rockies." Brochure. Minneapolis, Minn.: Soo Line, n.d.

*Seton-Thompson, Grace Gallatin. *A Woman Tenderfoot*. New York: Doubleday, 1900 / Page, 1900.

Spragge, Mrs. Arthur. *From Ontario to the Pacific by the C.P.R.* Toronto: C.B. Robinson, 1887.

*———. "Our Wild Westland." *Dominion Illustrated* (21 September 1889): 183.

Squires, Shelagh J. "In the Steps of 'Genteel Ladies': Women Tourists in the Canadian Rockies, 1885–1939." *Canadian Geographer* 39 (1995): 2–15.

Story, Norah. *The Oxford Companion to Canadian History and Literature*. Toronto: Oxford University Press, 1967.

Sutton-Ramspeck, Beth. "Shot Out of the Canon: Mary Ward and the Claims of Conflicting Feminisms." In *Victorian Women Writers and the Woman Question*, ed. Nicola Diane Thompson, 204–22. Cambridge: Cambridge University Press, 1999.

Thomas, Clara. *Our Nature, Our Voices: A Guidebook to English-Canadian Literature*. Toronto: New Press, 1972.

Thompson, Nicola Diane. "Responding to the Woman Questions: Rereading Noncanonical Victorian Women Novelists." In *Victorian Women Writers and the Woman Question*, ed. Nicola Diane Thompson, 1–23. Cambridge: Cambridge University Press, 1999.

Wallace, W. Stewart. *The Dictionary of Canadian Biography*. 2nd ed. Toronto: Macmillan, 1945.

Ward, Mrs. Humphry [Mary Augusta]. *Canadian Born*. London: Smith, Elder & Co., 1910.

*———. *Lady Merton, Colonist*. Toronto: Musson Book Co., 1910.

Warren, Mary Schäffer. "Letter to Humphrey Toms," 24 June 1936. WMCR M429.

———. "Tepee Life in the Northern Hills (1924)." In *No Ordinary Woman: The Story of Mary Schäffer Warren*, Janice Sanford Beck, 170–91. Calgary: Rocky Mountain Books, 2001.

Who Was Who among English and European Authors, 1931–1949. Detroit: Gale Research Co., 1978.

3. Free Among the Everlasting Hills

Brown, Stewardson. *Alpine Flora of the Canadian Rocky Mountains (Illustrated With Water-Colour Drawings and Photographs by Mrs. Charles Schäffer)*. New York: G.P. Putnam's Sons, 1907 / London: The Knickerbocker Press, 1907.

Cavell, Edward. *Legacy in Ice: The Vaux Family and the Canadian Alps*. Banff: Peter and Catharine Whyte Foundation, 1983.

Cavell, Edward, and Jon Whyte. *Mountain Glory: The Art of Peter and Catharine Whyte*. Banff: Whyte Museum of the Canadian Rockies, 1988.

Ferguson, Colin. "The Evolution of the Ice Axe." *Mountain* 3, no. 2 (Summer 2000): 20–25.

*Glacier House Scrapbook. Unpublished, 1897–1910. WMCR M352.

Henshaw, Julia W. *Mountain Wild Flowers of America*. Boston: Ginn & Co., 1906.

*———. "The Mountain Wildflowers of Western Canada." *Canadian Alpine Journal* 1, no. 1 (1907): 130–37.

Laut, Agnes C. *Enchanted Trails of Glacier Park*. New York: Robert M. McBride & Co., 1926.

Putnam, William Lowell. *The Great Glacier and Its House*. New York: American Alpine Club, 1982.

Reichwein, PearlAnn. "Guardians of the Rockies." *The Beaver* 74, no. 4 (1994), 4–13.

* Schäffer, Mary T.S. "Flora of the Saskatchewan and Athabasca River Tributaries." *Canadian Alpine Journal* 1, no. 2 (1908): 268–70.

* ———. "Haunts of the Wild Flowers of the Canadian Rockies (Within Reach of the Canadian Pacific Railroad)." *Canadian Alpine Journal* 3 (1911): 131–35.

*———. "A Maiden Voyage on the 'New' Lake." In *Old Indian Trails: Incidents of Camp and Trail Life, Covering Two Years' Exploration through the Rocky Mountains of Canada*, 254–56. New York: G.P. Putnam's Sons, 1911 / London: The Knickerbocker Press, 1911.

*———. "Untrodden Ways." *Canadian Alpine Journal* 1, no. 2 (1908): 288–94.

Spears, Betty. "Mary, Mary, Quite Contrary: Why Do Women Play?" *Canadian Journal of the History of Sport* 18, no. 1 (1987): 67–75.

Taft, William Howard. "Great Britain's Bread Upon the Waters: Canada and Her Other Daughters." *National Geographic* 29 (1916): 217–72.

*Vaux, Mary M. "Camping in the Canadian Rockies." *Canadian Alpine Journal* 1, no. 1 (1908): 67–71.

* ———. Letters to Dr. Charles Walcott, 1912. SIA record unit 7004, box 5, folder 2 images 2005–26214–16, 2005–26210–13, 2005–26217–18.

———. "Observations on Glaciers." *Canadian Alpine Journal* 5–6 (1913–1915): 59–61.

*Walcott, Mary Vaux. "Flowers of the Canadian Rockies." *Canadian Alpine Journal* 29 (1945): 70–71.

———. *The Glaciers of the Canadian Rockies and Selkirks*. 3rd ed. Byrn Mawr, Pennsylvania: In conjunction with the CPR, 1922.

————. *North American Wild Flowers*. Washington, D.C.: Smithsonian Institution, 1925.

Ward, Mrs. Humphry [Mary Augusta]. *Lady Merton, Colonist*. Toronto: Musson Book Co., 1910.

*Warren, Mary Schäffer. "Our Dear Mrs. Young," 20 December 1934. WMCR M429.

*Whyte, Catharine Robb. "Letters to Mother," Ethel Robb, unpublished, 1930, 1931, and
1933. WMCR M36/84, WMCR M36/85, and WMCR M36/91.

4. At Civilization's Limits

*Adams, Mary [Mollie]. "Laggan to Maligne Lake and Tête Jaune Cache and Return."
Unpublished diary, 1908. WMCR M79/11.

Beck, Janice Sanford. *No Ordinary Woman: The Story of Mary Schäffer Warren*. Calgary: Rocky
Mountain Books, 2001.

Benham, D.J. "Jasper Park in the Rockies: Canada's New National Playground." *Toronto
Globe*, 10 January 1910.

Converse, Helen. "'Old Indian Trails....'" *Cincinnati Ohio Tribune*, 2 July 1911.

Dafoe, John. "Jasper's Colorful Early History Told in Town's Annual Pageant." *Edmonton
Journal*, 17 July 1958, sec. 3, 23.

Gainer, Brenda. "The Human History of Jasper National Park." MS #441 Research Paper for
the Canadian Parks Service, 1981. JYMA 84.161.6.

Gowan, Elsie Park. "A Quaker in Buckskin." *Alberta Historical Review* 5, no. 3 (1957): 1–6, 24–28.

Hart, E.J., ed. *A Hunter of Peace: Mary T.S. Schäffer's Old Indian Trails of the Canadian Rockies*. Banff:
Whyte Museum of the Canadian Rockies, 1980.

"Jasper Park: The Mountain Park on the Line of the Grand Trunk Pacific Railway." *Canadian
Life and Resources* (1910).

Kipling, Rudyard. *Letters of Travel (1892–1913)*. London: Macmillan & Co., 1920.

Lippard, Lucy R. ed. "Doubletake: The Diary of a Relationship With an Image." In *Partial
Recall: Photographs of Native North Americans*, 13–45. New York: New Press, 1992.

MacFarlane, Lisa. "Mary Schäffer's 'Comprehending Equal Eyes.'" In *Trading Gazes: Euro-
American Women Photographers and Native North Americans, 1880–1940*, eds. Susan Bernardin,
Melody Gaulich, Lisa MacFarlane, and Nicole Tonkovich, 108–49. New Jersey: Rutgers
University Press, 2003.

MacLaren, I.S. "Cultured Wilderness in Jasper National Park." *Journal of Canadian Studies* 34,
no. 3 (1999): 2–54.

*"Old Indian Trails of the Canadian Rockies." Review. *Portland Telegram* (Oregon), 5 August
1911.

Schäffer, Mary T.S. "The Finding of Lake Maligne." *Canadian Alpine Journal* IV (1912): 92–97.

————. "Hunting a Lost Lake." *Travel* (1911): 321–23, 364.

*————. *Old Indian Trails: Incidents of Camp and Trail Life, Covering Two Years' Exploration through the Rocky Mountains of Canada*. New York: G.P. Putnam's Sons, 1911 / London: The Knickerbocker Press, 1911.

*————. "A Recently Explored Lake in the Rocky Range of Canada." *Bulletin of the Geographical Society of Philadelphia* (22 July 1909): 123–34.

Schäffer, Mrs. Charles. "The Valleys of the Saskatchewan With Horse and Camera." *Bulletin of the Geographical Society of Philadelphia* (April 1907): 108–14.

*Sharpless, Caroline. "Trip to Jasper Park, Rocky Mountains, Canada." Unpublished diary, 29 May–16 August 1911. WMCR M79/12.

Smith, Cyndi. *Off the Beaten Track: Women Adventurers and Mountaineers in Western Canada*. Canmore: Coyote Books, 1989.

*Stearns, Sharon. *Hunter of Peace*. Victoria, B.C.: Scirocco Drama, 1993.

Stirling, Claire. "Life Carries on at Mary Schäffer Warren's Historic Home." *Crag and Canyon*, 7 June 1995, sec. Bow Valley This Week, 1, 5.

Sullivan, Zohreh T. *Narratives of Empire: The Fictions of Rudyard Kipling*. Cambridge: Cambridge University Press, 1993.

[Wacko, Wendy]. "Homegrown Mountain Movie Maker." *Mountain* 3 (Fall 2000): 28.

Ward, Mrs. Humphry [Mary Augusta]. *Lady Merton, Colonist*. Toronto: Musson Book Co., 1910.

Warren, Mary S. "In the Heart of the Canadian Rockies Part I." Unpublished lantern slide lecture, n.d. WMCR M79/10C.

————. "In the Heart of the Canadian Rockies With Horse and Camera Part II." Unpublished lantern slide lecture, n.d. WMCR M79/10C.

Warren, Mary Schäffer. Letter to Humphrey Toms, 13 December 1933. WMCR M429.

————. Letter to Humphrey Toms, 24 June 1936. WMCR M429.

————. Letter to Miss Nickell, 21 September n.y. WMCR M429.

————. "Tepee Life in the Northern Hills (1924)." In *No Ordinary Woman: The Story of Mary Schäffer Warren*, Janice Sanford Beck, 170–91. Calgary: Rocky Mountain Books, 2001.

Wheeler, Arthur O. "The Alpine Club of Canada's Expedition to Jasper Park, Yellowhead Pass and Mount Robson Region, 1911." *Canadian Alpine Journal* 4 (1912): 59–83.

5. On the Rockies Stark

Birkett, Bill, and Bill Peascod. *Women Climbing: 200 Years of Achievement*. Seattle: The Mountaineers, 1990.

Bridge, Kathryn Anne. *Phyllis Munday: Mountaineer*. Montreal: XYZ Publications, 2002.

The Challenge of the Mountains. Booklet. Montreal: CPR, 1909.

*Crawford, Mary E. "Mountain Climbing for Women." *Canadian Alpine Journal* 2 (1910): 85–91.

*Edwards, Rhoda W. "Graduation." *Canadian Alpine Journal* 9 (1918): 134.

Ellis, Rueben. *Vertical Margins: Mountaineering and the Landscapes of Neoimperialism*. Madison: University of Wisconsin Press, 2001.

Engelhard, Georgia. "Lake Louise Days: A Letter From Georgia Engelhard Cromwell." In *Lake Louise: A Diamond in the Wilderness*, Jon Whyte, 43–46. Banff: Altitude Publishing, 1982.

*———. "Portrait of a Giant." *American Photography* 40 (1946): 12–15.

Fairley, Bruce, ed. *Canadian Mountaineering Anthology: Stories from 100 Years at the Edge*. Edmonton: Lone Pine Publishing, 1994.

*Ferguson, Elizebeth. "Sonnet." *Canadian Alpine Journal* XLVI (1963): 113.

Gest, Lillian. "Color Photography in the Mountains—A Symposium: Summer Movies in Color." *Canadian Alpine Journal* XXVI (1938): 105–7.

———. "Hike With Caroline Hinman and Marguerite Schnellbacher to Maligne Lake and Jasper. " Unpublished diary, 1925. Lillian Gest Fonds, WMCR M67.

*Johns, Ethel. "A Graduating Climb." *Canadian Alpine Journal* 2 (1910): 158–65.

Machar, Agnes Maule. *Lays of the 'True North,' and Other Canadian Poems*. Toronto: The Copp, Clark Co., Limited, 1899.

Marty, Sid. *Men for the Mountains*. Toronto: McClelland & Stewart, 2000.

Mazel, David, ed., with an Introduction. *Mountaineering Women: Stories by Early Climbers*. Texas: Texas A & M University Press, 1994.

McNaught, W.C. "The Challenge of the Mountains." *Canadian Alpine Journal* 6 (1915): 232.

Merriam, Esther. "Women Mountain-Climbers." *Harper's Bazaar* 44 (November 1910): 634.

Mummery, A.F. *My Climbs in the Alps and Caucasus*. London: T.F. Unwin, 1895; reprinted London: Thomas Nelson & Sons, 1908.

*O'Neill, Moira. "The North-West—Canada." *Canadian Alpine Journal* 2 (1909): 128.

———. "The North-West—Canada." In *Songs of the Glens of Antrim*, 58–59. Edinburgh: William Blackwood & Sons, 1910.

*Parker, Elizabeth. "The Alpine Club of Canada." *Canadian Alpine Journal* 1, no. 1 (1907): 3–8.

Reichwein, PearlAnn. "Guardians of the Rockies." *The Beaver* 74, no. 4 (1994), 4–13.

Reichwein, PearlAnn, and Karen Fox. "Margaret Fleming and the Alpine Club of Canada: A Woman's Place in Mountain Leisure and Literature, 1932–1952." *Journal of Canadian Studies* 36, no. 3 (2001): 35–60.

———, eds. *Mountain Diaries: The Alpine Adventures of Margaret Fleming 1929–1980*. Calgary: Historical Society of Alberta, 2004.

Reid, Christine L. "Canning Sunshine in the Canadian Rockies." *Canadian Alpine Journal* XXVI (1939): 62–69.

Robertson, Janet. *The Magnificent Mountain Women: Adventures in the Colorado Rockies*. Lincoln: University of Nebraska Press, 1990.

*Schäffer, Mary M. "Breaking the Way." *Rod and Gun in Canada* 6, no. 3 (1904): 111–12.

Scott, Chic. *Pushing the Limits: The Story of Canadian Mountaineering*. Calgary: Rocky Mountain Books, 2000.

da Silva, Rachel, ed. *Leading Out: Women Climbers Reaching for the Top*. Seattle: Seal Press, 1992.

Sutter, Cora. "Lady Climbers in the Tonquin and Mount Robson Region." *Canadian Alpine Journal* XXIX, no. 1 (1945): 65–69.

Wheeler, Arthur, and Elizabeth Parker. "Report, Yoho Camp." *Canadian Alpine Journal* 1 (1907): 169–70.

———. *The Selkirk Mountains: A Guide for Mountain Climbers and Pilgrims*. Winnipeg: Stovel Co., 1912.

Williams, Cicely. *Women on the Rope: The Feminine Share in Mountain Adventure*. London: George Allen & Unwin, 1973.

*Woods, Lynda R. "Canada's Mountains." *Canadian Alpine Journal* XXXVII (1954): 113.

*———. "Mountaineer and Mountains." *Canadian Alpine Journal* XL (1957): 71–72.

6. Wild and Solitary and Beautiful

Benham, D.J. "Jasper Park in the Rockies: Canada's New National Playground." *Toronto Globe*, 10 January 1910.

The Challenge of the Mountains. Booklet. Montreal: C.P.R., 1909.

Choko, Marc H., and David L. Jones. *Canadian Pacific Posters 1883–1963*. 4th ed. Montreal: SIAP, 1999.

*Crowther, Bosley. "Marilyn Monroe Vs. Scenery at Roxy." *New York Times*, 1 May 1954, 13.

Davis, Simone Weil. *Living Up to the Ads: Gender Fictions of the 1920s*. Durham: Duke University Press, 2000.

Hadley, Margery Tanner. "Photography, Tourism and the CPR: Western Canada, 1884–1914." In *Essays on the Historical Geography of the Canadian West*, eds. L.A. Rosenvall and S.M. Evans, 48–69. Calgary: University of Calgary, 1987.

Hart, E.J. *The Selling of Canada: The CPR and the Beginnings of Canadian Tourism*. Banff: Altitude Publishing, 1983.

*"Honor Memory of Edith Cavell." *Canadian National Railways Magazine* (1926): Woman's Section, 21, 42.

Hustak, Bill. "The Banff/Marilyn Monroe Connection." *Banff Life* Autumn (1985): 16–18.

Lippard, Lucy R., ed. "Doubletake: The Diary of a Relationship with an Image." In *Partial Recall: Photographs of Native North Americans*, 13–45. New York: New Press, 1992.

MacBeth, R.G. *The Romance of the Canadian Pacific Railway*. Toronto: Ryerson Press, 1924.

Marchand, Roland. *Advertising the American Dream: Making Way for Modernity, 1920–1940*. Berkeley: University of California Press, 1985.

McNaught, W.C. "The Challenge of the Mountains." *Canadian Alpine Journal* 6 (1915): 232.

Patton, Brian. "Hollywood in the Rockies." *Banff Life* Autumn (1985): 19–27.

River of No Return. Twentieth Century-Fox, 1954.

Schäffer, Mary T.S. "Attractions in the Canadian Rockies." *Crag and Canyon*, 4 September 1911, 6.

——. *Old Indian Trails: Incidents of Camp and Trail Life, Covering Two Years Exploration through the Rocky Mountains of Canada*. New York: G.P. Putnam's Sons, 1911 / London: The Knickerbocker Press, 1911.

Schwartz, Joan. "Lofty Images: Government Photography and the Canadian Rockies." *The Archivist* 14, no. 2 (1987): 6–7.

*Todd, Irene. "Jasper National Park: Canada's Vast New Mountain Playground." *Saturday Night* 39, no. 26 (17 May 1924): Woman's Section, 25.

Warren, Mary S. "The Byways of Banff." *Canadian Alpine Journal* 10 (1919): 78–91.

Wheeler, Arthur, and Elizabeth Parker. "Report, Yoho Camp." *Canadian Alpine Journal* 1 (1907): 169–70.

Williams, M.B. *Jasper National Park: A Descriptive Guide*. Hamilton: H.R. Larson Publishing Co., 1949.

*——. *The Kicking Horse Trail Scenic Highway From Lake Louise Alberta to Golden, British Columbia*. Ottawa: Department of the Interior, 1927.

——. *Through the Heart of the Rockies and Selkirks*. 2nd ed. Ottawa: F.A. Acland, 1924.

Winters, Shelley. *Shelley*. New York: William Morrow & Co., 1980.

Permissions

The University of Alberta Press gratefully acknowledges permissions granted by the following authors and publishers:

Pages 21–28: Janet Munro's "Hosts of Mountain Oasis," from *Canadian National Railways Magazine* (1929), 24–26. Used by permission of CN.

Pages 41–58: Act two of Elsie Park Gowan's "The Jasper Story," unpublished, 1955. UAA 87–123. Used by permission of Gary Gowan.

Pages 61–74: Copyright © 1993 "Double Take" from *Partial Recall: Photographs of Native North Americans* by Lucy Lippard. Reprinted by permission of The New Press. www.thenewpress.com

Pages 203–9: Mary M. Vaux's letter to Dr. Charles D. Walcott, unpublished, 19 February 1912. SIA record unit 7004, box 5, folder 2, image 2005–26214–16. Used by permission of the Smithsonian Institution Archives.

Pages 210–18: Mary M. Vaux's letter to Dr. Charles D. Walcott, unpublished, 11 March 1912. SIA record unit 7004, box 5, folder 2, image 2005–26210–13. Used by permission of the Smithsonian Institution Archives.

Pages 219–24: Mary M. Vaux's letter to Dr. Charles D. Walcott, unpublished, 1 April 1912. SIA record unit 7004, box 5, folder 2, image 2005–26217–18. Used by permission of the Smithsonian Institution Archives.

Pages 257–61 and 263–64: Catharine Robb Whyte's "Dearest Mother," letters to her mother Ethel Robb, unpublished, 11, 17, 23 August 1930; 1 September 1930; 19, 20 October 1930. WMCR M36/84. Used by permission of the Whyte Museum of the Canadian Rockies.

Page 262: Excerpt of Catharine Robb Whyte's "Dearest Mother," letter to her mother Ethel Robb, unpublished, 21 August 1933. WMCR M36/91. Used by permission of the Whyte Museum of the Canadian Rockies.

Pages 265–66: Catharine Robb Whyte's "Dearest Mother," letter to her mother Ethel Robb, unpublished, 24 February 1931. WMCR M36/85. Used by permission of the Whyte Museum of the Canadian Rockies.

Pages 317–26: Excerpts of Caroline Sharpless's "Trip to Jasper Park, Rocky Mountains, Canada," unpublished, 29 May 1911 to 16 August 1911. WMCR M79/12. Used by permission of the Whyte Museum of the Canadian Rockies.

Pages 343–47: Prologue and act one, scene one of Sharon Stearns's *Hunter of Peace* (Victoria, B.C.: Scirocco Drama, 1993), 11–15. Used by permission of the author.

Pages 367–73: Mary E. Crawford's "Mountain Climbing for Women," *Canadian Alpine Journal* 2 (1909), 85–91. Used by permission of the Alpine Club of Canada.

Pages 391–99: Georgia Engelhard's "Portrait of a Giant," *American Photography* 40 (November 1946), 12–15. Used by permission of the Copyright Board of Canada.

Pages 403–4: Lynda R. Woods's "Canada's Mountains," *Canadian Alpine Journal* XXXVII (1954), 113. Used by permission of the Alpine Club of Canada.

Pages 405–7: Lynda R. Woods's "Mountaineer and Mountains," *Canadian Alpine Journal* XL (1957), 71–72. Used by permission of the Alpine Club of Canada.

Page 409: Elizebeth Ferguson's "Sonnet," *Canadian Alpine Journal* XLVI (1963), 113. Used by permission of the Alpine Club of Canada.

Pages 429–33: Irene Todd's "Jasper National Park: Canada's Vast New Mountain Playground" *Saturday Night* 39, no. 26 (17 May 1924), Woman's Section, 25. Used by permission of the Copyright Board of Canada.

Pages 441–43: "Honor Memory of Edith Cavell: Guests at Jasper Park Lodge Join with the Residents of Village in Memorial Service to Heroic Nurse for Whom Mount Cavell Is Named" *Canadian National Railways Magazine* (September 1926), Woman's Section, 21–22. Used by permission of CN.

Pages 445–46: Bosley Crowther's "Marilyn Monroe Vs. Scenery at Roxy," *New York Times* (1 May 1954), 13. Copyright © 2006 by The New York Times Co. Reprinted with permission.

Index

Page numbers in bold refer to illustrations, paintings, and photographs.

Abbott Peak 189

Abraham, Silas 17, 69, 305

Adams, Mollie (Mary) xxi, xxv, 8–11, **9**, 17, 71–72, 278, 280–85, 287, 289, **289**, 415, 424, **448**; as appears in excerpts 25, 93, 146, 344–47; "Laggan to Maligne Lake and Tête Jaune Cache and Return" 31–39, 309–15; photographs by **30**, **268**

Alpine Club of Canada xxv, 173, 281, 287, 353–56, 361–64, 415, 421

"The Alpine Club of Canada" 361–66

Alpine Flora of the Canadian Rocky Mountains 71, 145, 170

American Alpine Club 353, 362

Appalachian Club 145, 362

Astor, Mary 420, **421**

"at civilisation's limits" 296

Banff xxvii, 11, 22, 45, 61, 64, 69, 85, 99, 105, 110, 283; residents living in 352, 354, **421**, 437

Banff Hot Springs 106, 108

Banff Indian Days 13, 69

Banff National Park 108, 164, 170, 176, 417, 420; as appears in excerpts 112–13, 133–34, 239, 244–45, 252, 260, 324–25, 344, 346–47

Banff Springs Hotel 105, 107, 109, 162, 250, 258, 265, 423, **423**

Barker, Joe **289**, **448**

Beaver Family 12, **12**, 15–17, **60**, 61–66, 68–69, 73, 286

Beaver, Frances Louise 12, **12**, 14, **60**, 69, 73

Beaver Lake (Chaba Imne). *See* Maligne Lake

Beaver, Leah xviii, 12, **12,** 14, 17, **60,** 70, 73

Beaver, Sampson 12, **12,** 17, **60,** 61, 63, 68, 70–71, 73, 146, 148, 282, 312, 329–30; map by 310, 330–32, 334

Becker's Cabins **426,** 427

"being a woman, I wanted to tell about them" xxiii, 117

Benham, Gertrude 351–52, 368, 375

Bird, Isabella 82–83

Bohren, Christian 185, 187

"Breaking the Way" 375–77

Brewster, Angelique 5, 7

"By Car and by Cowcatcher" 97–103

Calgary 98–100, 143–44, 438

Cameron, Ellen Elizabeth 89. *See also* Spragge, Mrs. Arthur

"Camping in the Canadian Rockies" 195–98

camps **9, 142, 152, 269, 289, 316, 448;** at Castle Mountain 259; at Maligne Lake 309; Caledonia Camp 36; Chaba Camp 311–14; Eureka Camp 310; Moberly Camp 32, 34, 339; Ten Mile Camp 44; Unwin Camp 313–14; Wapta Camp 258; Windy Camp 319; Yoho Valley Camp 263

"Canada's Mountains" 358, 403–4

Canadian Alpine Journal xxv, 145, 164, 173, 288, 350, 353, 355, 358–59, 379

Canadian Born. See Lady Merton, Colonist

Canadian National Railway Line 23, 89, 430

Canadian National Railways Magazine 5, 28, 420, 441, 444. *See also* "Honor Memory of Edith Cavell" and "Hosts of Mountain Oasis"

Canadian Pacific Railway (CPR) xviii, xxi, xxiii–xxiv, xxvi, **79,** 80, 88–89, 92, 113, 163–65, 170, 278, 363, 416, 419–21; as appears in excerpts 22, 45, 49, 92, 113, 173, 304, 325; hotels 162, 180, 192, 245, 417–19; promotional materials 167, 190, 414, **415,** 420–25, **423, 425, 427, 450–54;** stops **79,** 284, 300, 436–37

Canmore 98–99

Cavell, Edith 419, 441–43. *See also* mounts: Mount Edith Cavell

Chaba Imne (Beaver Lake). *See* Maligne Lake

Chalifour, Suzette. *See* Swift, Suzette Chalifoux

Challenge of the Mountains 414–16, **415, 450**

Chief Walking Buffalo (George McLean) xxvii, 13, 25

clothing 82–83, 85–87, 93–94, **116,** 415–17; *A Woman Tenderfoot* 118–21, 128–29

Colin's Range 24, 27

Countess of Aberdeen 88; *Through Canada with a Kodak* 88, 111–15

cowcatcher **81,** 100–103, 136–38

Cran, Mrs. George (Marion) 88, 93; *A Woman in Canada* 89, **142,** 143–50

Crawford, Mary E. 350–51, 355; "Mountain Climbing for Women" 367–73

creeks: Bath Creek 102; Bear Creek 330; Cataract Creek 231; Independence Creek 332; Mistaya Creek 227; Nigel Creek 330

Crowther, Bosley: "Marilyn Monroe vs. Scenery at Roxy" 445–46

Curtis, Edward 64, 67

"Dearest Mother" 257–66

Department of the Interior (Canadian) 3, 5, 418, 420

Dominion Government of Canada 89, 108–9, 418, 430

"Doubletake: The Diary of a Relationship with an Image" 61–74

Drummond, Henry 88

Duncan, Sara Jeannette 80, 88, 90–92; *A Social Departure* 80, **81,** 88, 133–41

Durham, Julian 171. *See also* Henshaw, Julia W.

Edmonton 143–44, 287, 319, 321–23

Edson 321–22

Edwards, Rhoda W. 355; "Graduation" 387–88

Engelhard, Georgia xxi, **348–49,** 356, **356–57**, 358, 421, 424; photographs by **390**, **449;** "Portrait of a Giant" 391–99

Ferguson, Elizebeth 358; "Sonnet" 358, 409

Feuz Jr., Eduard 188–89, 382–84

Field, British Columbia 93, 135, 148, 153, 163, 170, 192, 244–45, 252, 263, 295, 305, 414

Fisher Body Girl 422, 425

Fleming, Margaret 353, 355

"Flora of the Saskatchewan and Athabasca River Tributaries" 239–41

flowers: anemone **169**, 244, 251, 254–55, **273;** arnica 246, 249, 254; caltha 247, 333; campanula 252–53; castilleia 249, 253; clematis 250, 253; corallorhiza 244, 250; cypripedium 245, 252; erigeron 240–41; erythronium 246, 252; gentiana 244, 251, 253; kalmia 246, 251; larix 245, 252, 256; lychnis **234**, 235, **272;** moneces 244, 250; orchis 244, 251; phacelia 247, 253; primula 240, 244; pulsatilla **238, 242,** 333; romanzoffia 236, 252; saxifraga 246, 253; silene 235, **272;** smelowskia **242,** 245; trollius 245, 247, 252, 333; vaccinium 241, 340; vetch 250, 253; viola 240; yellow violets 246, 249

"Flowers of the Canadian Rockies" 235–36

Fortress Lake **228**, 240

"free among the everlasting hills" 168, 198

Gest, Lillian xxi, 355

Gibson, Mary 162–64, 185

Gilpin, Laura 15, 67

Glacier House xviii, 80, 90, 162–64, 166, 170, 180–81, 184, 187, 189, 192, 250, 295

"Glacier House Scrapbook" 162–64, 179–90

Glacier National Park 163–64, 169, 172–73, 190, 239, 243–44, 246–47, 252, 417

glaciers: Angel Glacier (Glacier of the Angels) 28, 419, 442, **449**; Balfour Glacier 219; Bow Glacier 219; Illecillewaet (Great) Glacier xviii, 85, 90, 130, 138–40, 162–66, **166**, 185, **270**, 295, 416; Lily Glacier 186; Victoria Glacier 196, 204; Yoho Glacier 219

Gordon, Ishbel (Marchioness of Aberdeen and Temair). *See* Countess of Aberdeen

Government of Canada 44, 99, 108, 112, 364

Gowan, Elsie Park 2, **40**, 289; "The Jasper
Story" 41–58
"A Graduating Climb" 379–85
"Graduation" 387–88
Grafton, Garth 90. *See also* Duncan, Sara
Jeannette
Grand Trunk Pacific Railway 37, 42, 45, 51,
157–58, 287, 315, 336–37, 339, 414

Hardisty, Mrs. 324–25
"Haunts of the Wild Flowers of the
Canadian Rockies" 243–47
Hector Station 196, 379, 381
Henderson, Julia Wilmotte 171. *See also*
Henshaw, Julia W.
Henry House 22, 31, 50, 318
Henshaw, Julia W. xxi, 170–73, **171**; "The
Mountain Wild Flowers of Western
Canada" 249–55
Himalayan Mountains 368, 371, 397
Hinton 287, 319
H.M.S. Chaba 286, 311–12, 334
"Honor Memory of Edith Cavell" 441–44
"Hosts of Mountain Oasis" 5, 21–28
Hudson's Bay Company 13, 21–23, 27, 324
Hunter of Peace 289, 343–47

Ice-fields: Brazeau ice-field 313; Lyell ice-
field 232
Indian Madonna **16**, **267**

Jasper xx–xxi, 2, 5, **7**, 8, 11, **20**, 21–22, 24,
26, 53
Jasper House 22–23, 27, 430
Jasper National Park 42, 44, 53–55, 71,
265, 287, 417, 419, 429–30, 442, **449**
Jasper Park Lodge 22, 25, 418, 430–31, 443

"The Jasper Story" **40**, 41–58; cast of characters 41
Jasper-Yellowhead Museum and Archives
5, 11
Johns, Ethel 356; "A Graduating Climb"
379–85

Käsebier, Gertrude 15, 67
Kaufman, Christian 375–76
Kaufman, Hans 375–76
Kicking Horse Trail 436–37
The Kicking Horse Trail 435–40
Kipling, Rudyard 73, 86–87, 146, 305
Kodak snapshot camera xxvi, 168, 197
Kootenay Plains 11–12, 17, 69, 73, 148, 154,
231
Kootney, Mary McLean 13, **13**

Lac Beauvert 429, 431–33
Lady Aberdeen. *See* Countess of Aberdeen
Lady MacDonald. *See* MacDonald, Agnes
(Lady MacDonald)
Lady Merton, Colonist xxi, 92, **152**, 153–58,
269, 289
Laggan Station 100–102, 154, 227, 246,
329–30
"Laggan to Maligne Lake and Tête Jaune
Cache and Return" 31–39, 309–15
Lake Elizabeth. *See* Maligne Lake
Lake Louise 72, 154–55, 196, 244–46,
250–51, 260, 295–96, 298, 357, **421–22,**
452; Chateau Hotel at 253, 309,
376–77, 423
lakes: Amethyst Lakes 432; Bow Lake 219,
259; Cold Lake xxviii; Devil's Lake 108,
110; Emerald Lake 147, 245, 252, 437;
Jasper Lake 42; Lake Brazeau 230, 241,

329; Lake Caledonia 432; Lake George 157; Lake McArthur 195–96, 296; Lake Nashanesen 230; Lake Oesa 196, 257; Lake of Forgiveness 442; Lake of Geneva 437; Lake O'Hara **84**, 195–96, 257, 296, 381–82; Lake Peyto 193; Lake Sherbrook 219; Lake Summit 263; Lesser Slave Lake 5, 324; Marion Lake 162, 184, 189; Medicine Lake 335, 338; Moraine Lake 195, 253, 298, 357; Pyramid Lake 432; Spray Lake **10**. See also Lake Louise, Fortress Lake, and Maligne Lake

Larches, Mount Temple. See Mount Temple, Larches

Leanchoil, British Columbia 145, 148

"Letters to Dr. Walcott" from Mary M. Vaux 203–24

letters to Ethel Robb from Catharine Robb Whyte. See "Dearest Mother"

letter to Humphrey Toms from Mary Schäffer Warren. See "Our Dear Mrs. Young"

Lippard, Lucy R. 15–17, 61, 75, 417; "Doubletake: The Diary of a Relationship with an Image" 15, 61–74, 290n1

MacDonald, Agnes (Lady MacDonald) **79**, 80, 82, 88, 136; "By Car and by Cowcatcher" 97–103

MacDonald, Sir John A. **79**, 80

"A Maiden Voyage on the 'New' Lake." See Old Indian Trails

Maligne Lake xxi, xxv, 11, 17, 31, 39, 47, 71, 92, 146, 282, 287–88, 315, 415; as Chaba Imne (Beaver Lake) 282, 311,

329, 333; as Lake Elizabeth 93, 153, 157, **269**; camp at **142**, 309; Mount Mary Vaux at head of 176, **200**; photograph of **152**, **269**, **308**; surveying of 286, **328**

"Marilyn Monroe vs. Scenery at Roxy" 445–46

Matterhorn 352, 368, 392

McGibbon, Helen 163, 185

McLean, George. See Chief Walking Buffalo (George McLean)

The McTavish 379, 381, 384

Merton, Lady Elizabeth 154–58

Mile 111, 318

Mitchum, Robert 426, 445–46

Moberly, John 36, 39, 339

Moberly, Walter 22, 32

Mollison, Annie 163, 180–81

Mollison, Jean 163, 180–81

Monroe, Marilyn **426**, 426–27, 445–46; River of No Return 426, 445–46

Mont Blanc 250, 252, 367–68

Morley Reserve xxviii, 11, 230, 261

Morris, Mrs. 324–25

"Mountain Climbing for Women" 367–73

"Mountaineer and Mountains" 405–7

mountains: Cascade Mountain 98–99, 108, 185, 188, 417; Castle Mountain 99, 259, **420**, 437; Great White Mountain 56; Lookout Mountain 179; Palisade Mountain 5, 42, 50; Pyramid Mountain 22, 24, 27; Signal Mountain 432; Sulphur Mountain 108–9, 244, 251; Throne Mountain 442; Tunnel Mountain 113, 245; Whistlers Mountain 432

"The Mountain Wild Flowers of Western
Canada" 249–55

Mountain Woman (Yahe-Weha). *See*
Schäffer, Mary T.S. (Warren)

Mount Assiniboine **274**, 358, **390**, 391–95,
397–99, **449**; called "Matterhorn of
the Canadian Rockies" 392

Mount Cascade. *See* mountains: Cascade
Mountain

mounts: Mount Abbott 181, 185–87, 189;
Mount Afton 185–87, 189; Mount
Athabasca **226, 269**; Mount
Avalanche 181, 187–89; Mount Bonney
185–87, 189; Mount Brazeau 230, 311,
313, 329, 333–34; Mount Cathedral
196, 382; Mount Columbia 35, 229–30,
304; Mount Edith Cavell 27–28, 420,
431–32, 442, **449;** Mount Huber 196,
382–84; Mount Lefroy 196, 351–52,
375–76; Mount Lyell 231, 305; Mount
Mary Vaux 176, **200**, 202; Mount
Oderay 196, 382; Mount Robson 36,
47, 147, 305–6, 335, 340; Mount
Stephen xxi, 99, 145, 148, 166, 181,
196, 219, 259, 352, **353**, 416; Mount Sir
Donald 35, 110, 141, 181–83, 186, 189;
Mount Temple 253; Mount Unwin
282, **308,** 313; Mount Victoria 196, 357,
376–77; Mount Warren 313–14, 334.
See also Mount Assiniboine

Mount Temple, Larches **256, 274**

Munro, Janet: "Hosts of Mountain Oasis"
5, 21–28

New Woman: climber 416; mountaineer
421

Norris, Albert. *See* Swift, Albert

North Fork 230–31, 330

"The North-West–Canada" 358, 401–2

Old Indian Trails xxi, xxix, 8, 14, 16–18, 25,
87, 200, **200,** 278–79, 282–83, 287, 289;
"A Maiden Voyage on the 'New' Lake"
201–2; "An Explanation 295–302;
excerpt from 278, 414; map xvi;
reviews of 285; title page of **292;** "Why
and Wherefore" 293–94

"Old Indian Trails of the Canadian
Rockies" 303–7

O'Neill, Moira 358, 401; "The North-
West–Canada" 358, 401–2; *Songs of the
Glens of Antrim* 358

"on the Rockies stark" xxv, 401

"Our Dear Mrs. Young" 191–93

"Our Wild Westland" 105–10

Orthodocia 134–41

Otto, Mr. 318–21, 324–25

Otto, Mrs. 323–25

Outram, James 231–32, 296

Parker, Elizabeth xxv, 352, 354, 359; "The
Alpine Club of Canada" 361–66

Partial Recall. See "Doubletake: The Diary of
a Relationship with an Image"

passes: Abbott's Pass 196, 376–77;
Asulkan Pass 181; Athabasca Pass 36;
Baker Pass 233; Bow Pass 193, 195,
330; Burgess Pass 149; Cataract Pass
231, 336; Crows' Nest Pass 379, 384;
Howse Pass 233; Kicking Horse Pass
22, 110, 154, 163, 437; Nigel Pass
230–31, 336; Pipestone Pass 195, 246,
336; Pobokton Pass 330–33; Roger's
Pass xviii, 163; Thompson Pass 230;

Wilcox Pass 145, **226,** 230, 240, 336;

Yellowhead Pass 22, 35, 37, 42, 56, 145, 335, 430

peaks: Abbott Peak 189; Eagle Peak 180, 184; Ross Peak 187; Sampson Peak 314; Twin Peaks 106, 108; Wiwaxy Peaks 196

Phillips, Curly (Curley) 2, 24

Portland Telegram. See "Old Indian Trails of the Canadian Rockies"

"Portrait of a Giant" 391–99

Preminger, Otto 427, 446

Princess White Shield. *See* Whyte, Catharine Robb

"A Recently Explored Lake in the Rocky Range of Canada" 329–41

River of No Return 426, 445–46

rivers: Athabasca (Athabaska) River 24, 39, 42, 145, 227, 229, 240, 300, 304, 318–19, 335–36, 338–39, 414, 429, 431; Bow River 99, 107–8, 113, 250, 423; Brazeau River 229, 330; Fraser River 340–41; Maligne River 25, 335, 338–39; Miette River 145, 336, 340; North Saskatchewan River 281, 287; Saskatchewan River 69, 147, 227–29, 231, 240, 300, 304–5, 330; Spray River 108, 250; West Branch River 228–30; Whirlpool River 36, 227, 319

Robb, Catharine. *See* Whyte, Catharine Robb

Roche Miette 27, 36, 56

"The Rocky Mountains." *See Through Canada with a Kodak*

"The Rocky Mountains and British Columbia." *See A Woman in Canada*

Saturday Night Magazine xxv, 418, 433

Schäffer, Dr. Charles 71, 170, 285, 288, 303–4

Schäffer, Mary T.S. (Warren) xxi, xxv, xxix, 3, 8, 10–12, 14–18, 71–73, 86–88, 93, 162–63, 170, 175–76, 289, 351–52, 414, 416–18, 424; as appears in excerpts 25, 61–69, 145, 183, 303–5, 318–22, 324–25, 343–44; *Alpine Flora of the Canadian Rocky Mountains* 71, 145, 170; and *Lady Merton, Colonist* xxi, 92, 153; and stake in Maligne Lake 288, 415; as Yahe-Weha (Mountain Woman) 14, 70, 280, 343; "Breaking the Way" 375–77; "Flora of the Saskatchewan and Athabasca River Tributaries" 239–41; "Haunts of the Wild Flowers of the Canadian Rockies" 243–47; husbands of 285; in Banff (Tarry-a-While) 71, 278, **279,** 284, 343; "Our Dear Mrs. Young" 191–93; photographs of **9,** 11, **171, 279–80, 289, 316, 447, 448;** "A Recently Explored Lake in the Rocky Range of Canada" 329–41; anger at Julia Henshaw, 172–73; "Untrodden Ways" 227–33; visual works by **7, 12, 16, 60,** 61–62, 83, **142, 152, 200, 226, 228, 238, 242, 267, 269, 273,** 328. *See also Old Indian Trails*

Schäffer, Mrs. Charles. *See* Schäffer, Mary T.S. (Warren)

Selkirk Mountains xviii, xxviii, 9, 85, 162–64, 170, 354, 357, 359, 417; as appears in excerpts 111, 130, 137, 188, 241, 246–47, 249, 255, 315

Seton-Thompson, Ernest ("Nimrod") 84, 117, 127–28, 130–32, 305

Seton-Thompson, Grace Gallatin xxi, 78–79, 83–84, 94; *A Woman Tenderfoot* xxi, 78, 83, **116,** 117–132

Sharpless, Caroline xxv, 282, 287, **316;** "Trip to Jasper Park, Rocky Mountains, Canada" 317–26

Sharpless, Paul 287, **316**, 318–21, 324–26

She Who Colors Slides 11, **30,** **268**

Skrine, Agnes Higginson 358. *See also* O'Neill, Moira

A Social Departure 80, **81,** 88, 133–41

Songs of the Glens of Antrim. See "The North-West–Canada"

"Sonnet" 358, 409

Soo Pacific Line 83, 106. *See also* Canadian Pacific Railway (CPR)

Spragge, Mrs. Arthur 89; "Our Wild Westland" 105–10

Stearns, Sharon 289; *Hunter of Peace* 289, 343–47

Stieglitz, Alfred 167, 356

Stoney-Nakoda xviii, xxii, xxvii, 11, 13, 16–17, 280. *See also* Wesley Band

Stoneys 61, 65, 68–70, 146, 174, 230, 282, 305, 311, 329

Strathcona 286, 324–25

Swift children **7;** Albert 5; Dean 5, 26, 36; Ida 5, 26, 35; James 5; Jimmy 7; Lottie 5, 26, 35

Swift homestead 11, **20,** 25, 32, 34, 36, 38–39, 318, 414

Swift, Lewis 5, 7, **20,** 21–25, 28, 33–37, 39, **40,** 337, 339, 341

Swift, Suzette Chalifoux xviii, xxi, **2–3,** 5, 7–11, **7,** 14, 17, **20,** 21, 23, 26–28, 35, 38,

40; Certificate 284 North West Half-Breed Commission **6**; Certificate 521 North West Half-Breed Commission **6**; certificate of claim (declaration) 3, **4**; Letter of Cessation as Treaty Indian/Edmonton Straggler **4**, 5

Takakkaw Falls **167, 194, 271**

"taking a deep interest" xxii, 1, 8

Tarry-a-While 278, **279**

Tête Jeune Cache 36–37, 39, 49, 52, 145, 336, 340

"this wild spirit" xviii–xxix, xxv–xxvi, xxviii–xxix

Through Canada with a Kodak 88, 111–15

The Thumb 313–14, 334

Todd, Irene 418; "Jasper National Park" 429–33

Toms, Humphrey xxi, 191–93, 278

"Trip to Jasper Park, Rocky Mountains, Canada" 317–26

Twoyoungmen, Mrs. 175, 261

"Untrodden Ways" 227–33

Unwin, Sid ("K") 71, 282, 284, **308,** 317–21, 334

valleys: Athabasca (Athabaska) Valley 442; Bow River Valley 11, 105–6, 110, 145, 154, 227, 244–45, 439; Columbia Valley 437; Cougar Valley 247; Independence Valley 332; Jasper Valley 2, 24, 28, 53–55, 57; Kicking Horse Valley 437, 439; Maligne Valley 335; Paradise Valley 195; Ptarmigan Valley 296, 298; Spray Valley 106–7, 244; Su Wapta Valley 332; Valley of

Ten Peaks 253, 351; Valley of the Lakes 229, 321; Yoho Valley 219, 252, 259, 295–96, 298, 437

Vaux family 164–65, 168, 170, 174–75, 352

Vaux, George Jr. **10,** 164, 220

Vaux, Mary J. 9–10, **10,** 83, **84**

Vaux, Mary M. (Walcott) xvii–xviii, xxi, xxix, 9, 162, 164, **165–66,** 166–67, 169–70, 173, 175–76, 259, **270,** 278, 284, 352, 416; "Camping in the Canadian Rockies" 195–98; "Flowers of the Canadian Rockies" 235–36; "Letters to Dr. Walcott" 203–25; *North American Wildflowers* 168; visual works by **169, 171, 234, 270, 272–73**

Vaux, William **84,** 164

Walcott, Dr. Charles xvii, 170, 203–24

Walcott, Mrs. Charles. *See* Vaux, Mary M. (Walcott)

Ward, Mrs. Humphry (Mary) xxi, 91–94, 289; *Canadian Born* 92; *Lady Merton, Colonist* 92, **152,** 153–58, **269,** 289

Warren, Billy 71, **280,** 281–82, 284–85, **289,** 324, 344, **447–48**

Warren, Mary Schäffer. *See* Schäffer, Mary T.S. (Warren)

Wesley Band 11, 70. *See also* Stoney-Nakoda

"Why and Wherefore." *See Old Indian Trails*

Whyte, Catharine Robb xxi, xxvii–xxix, 174–76, **174,** 278, 284, 421, 424; as Princess White Shield 13, **13**; "Dearest Mother" 257–66; visual works by 176, **256, 274**

Whyte Museum of the Canadian Rockies xxvii–xxviii, 9, 17, 39, 64, 69, 164, 282, 284, 355

Whyte, Peter xxvii, 174, **174,** 257, 259–60, 262–63, 265, **274**

"wild and solitary and beautiful" 419

Williams, M.B. (Mabel) 418–19; *The Kicking Horse Trail* 435–40

A Woman in Canada 89, **142,** 143–50

Woman Question xxiv, 78, 83, 86, 91, 94, 415

A Woman Tenderfoot xxi, 78, 83, **116,** 117–32

Wong, Anna May 420, **420**

Woods, Lynda R. 358; "Canada's Mountains" 358, 403–4; "Mountaineer and Mountains" 405–7

Workman, Mrs. Bullock 368, 370

Yahe-Weha (Mountain Woman). *See* Schäffer, Mary T.S. (Warren)

Yoho National Park 164, 260, 417, 437

Young, Mrs. Julia 163, 182, 185, 191–93, 204, 324–25